Spiritualities of

Front cover image: Lucy Raverat, *Flying the Kite*.
Lucy Rawlinson, who paints under her maiden name, is a dear old friend. A person with a profound spiritual sensibility, *Flying the Kite* captures the magic of expressive freedom; of harmony. Viewing Ingleborough from the farmhouse where she and her family used to live, not far from our own family home, the painting captures the 'presence' of nature as well. I'm sure Lucy would appreciate the words of the Lonsdale hermit – 'To all blessed with true insight, he ['the mere man of craggy limestone'] is nothing less than a real personality, a creature with a soul'. In the spirit of Lucy, a hermit who has rejected the clamour of life distorted by the lures of the capitalistic mainstream:

> I often seek his quiet company and take advantage of his noble patience. How can I estimate in words or numbers the calm that he has breathed down upon me from his ancient heights when the stirring voices of the far away multitudes have broken through to my seclusion and tempted me from my loneliness into the thick of human conflict? Or how can I describe the benediction of contentment he has bestowed upon me when thoughts of foolish ambition and of the plaudits of crowds have risen to make me restless? He is a being full of speechfulness, full of experience, full of romance, full of history... a living influence. (H. M. White, 1904, *Old Ingleborough*. Ingleton: J. Brookes, pp. 6–7)

RELIGION AND SPIRITUALITY IN THE MODERN WORLD

Series Editors: Paul Heelas, Linda Woodhead, *University of Lancaster*

Editorial Advisor: David Martin, *Emeritus Professor of the London School of Economics*

Founding Editors: John Clayton, *University of Boston*, and Ninian Smart, *formerly of University of California – Santa Barbara*

The *Religion and Spirituality in the Modern World* series makes accessible to a wide audience some of the most important work in the study of religion and spirituality today. The series invites leading scholars to present clear and non-technical contributions to contemporary thinking about religion and spirituality in the modern world. Although the series is geared primarily to the needs of university and college students, the volumes in the *Religion and Spirituality in the Modern World* series will prove invaluable to readers with some background in Religious Studies who wish to keep up with contemporary thinking about religion, theology and spirituality in the modern world, as well as to the general reader who is seeking to learn more about the transformations of religion and spirituality in our time.

Published

Don Cupitt	*Mysticism After Modernity*
Paul Heelas, with the assistance of David Martin and Paul Morris	*Religion, Modernity and Postmodernity*
Linda Woodhead and Paul Heelas	*Religion in Modern Times*
David Martin	*Pentecostalism: The World Their Parish*
Steve Bruce	*God is Dead*
David Smith	*Hinduism and Modernity*
Peter Berger	*Questions of Faith*
Paul Heelas, Linda Woodhead, Benjamin Seel, Bronislaw Szerszynski and Karin Tusting	*The Spiritual Revolution*
Bronislaw Szerszynski	*Nature, Technology and the Sacred*
Paul Heelas	*Spiritualities of Life*

Forthcoming

Simon Coleman	*The Gospel of Health and Wealth*

Spiritualities of Life

New Age Romanticism and Consumptive Capitalism

Paul Heelas

Blackwell
Publishing

© 2008 by Paul Heelas

BLACKWELL PUBLISHING
350 Main Street, Malden, MA 02148–5020, USA
9600 Garsington Road, Oxford OX4 2DQ, UK

The right of Paul Heelas to be identified as the author of this work has been asserted in accordance with the UK Copyright, Designs, and Patents Act 1988.

All rights reserved. No part of this publication may be reproduced, stored in a retrieval system, or transmitted, in any form or by any means, electronic, mechanical, photocopying, recording or otherwise, except as permitted by the UK Copyright, Designs, and Patents Act 1988, without the prior permission of the publisher.

Designations used by companies to distinguish their products are often claimed as trademarks. All brand names and product names used in this book are trade names, service marks, trademarks, or registered trademarks of their respective owners. The publisher is not associated with any product or vendor mentioned in this book.

This publication is designed to provide accurate and authoritative information in regard to the subject matter covered. It is sold on the understanding that the publisher is not engaged in rendering professional services. If professional advice or other expert assistance is required, the services of a competent professional should be sought.

First published 2008 by Blackwell Publishing Ltd

1   2008

Library of Congress Cataloging-in-Publication Data

Heelas, Paul.
  Spiritualities of life : New age romanticism and consumptive capitalism / Paul Heelas.
    p. cm.—(Religion and spirituality in the modern world)
  Includes bibliographical references and index.
    ISBN 978-1-4051-3937-3 (hardcover : alk. paper)—ISBN 978-1-4051-3938-0 (pbk. : alk. paper) 1. Spirituality—Western countries—History. 2. Western countries—Religious life and customs. I. Title.

  BL695.H44 2008
  204.09′03—dc22
                                                            2007046638

A catalogue record for this title is available from the British Library.

Set in 10/11.5pt Galliard
by SPi Publisher Services, Pondicherry, India
Printed and bound in Singapore
by C.O.S. Printers Pte Ltd

The publisher's policy is to use permanent paper from mills that operate a sustainable forestry policy, and which has been manufactured from pulp processed using acid-free and elementary chlorine-free practices. Furthermore, the publisher ensures that the text paper and cover board used have met acceptable environmental accreditation standards.

For further information on
Blackwell Publishing, visit our website at
www.blackwellpublishing.com

*In memory of my teachers, E. E. Evans-Pritchard,
Rodney Needham and Ninian Smart,
and my old friends, Malcolm Crick and Ursula Lister*

Contents

Preface		ix
Introduction		1
Part I	Portraying Spiritualities of Life	23
1	From the Romantics: The Repertoire	25
2	Wellbeing Spirituality Today	60
Part II	The 'Consuming Growth' Debate	79
3	The Debate	81
4	The Language of Consumption and Consumeristic Aspects of Mind-Body-Spiritualities of Life	97
5	The Sacred and the Profane: Spiritual Direction or Consumer Preference?	113
6	The Matter of Personal Significance: Profaned Superficiality?	137
7	Work: Consumptive or Productive?	151
Part III	To Work Beyond the Consuming Self	165
8	A 'Fag Ending' of the Sacred or Fit for the Future?	167
9	Inside Out	195
Epilogue: Birthright Spirituality Beyond the West		222

Appendix: Evidence Indicative of Inner Life 'Beliefs'	233
Notes	236
References	255
Name Index	276
Subject Index: Some Main Themes and Arguments	283

Preface

I was extremely fortunate to have been born in 1946. This has meant that I have witnessed, and in measure experienced, the unfolding of spiritualities of life from the time I came of age during that great 'inner era' known as the sixties. My awareness of what has come to be called the 'New Age' dawned whilst I was studying at Oxford. I was more a participant than an observer. Since moving to the Yorkshire Dales, I have also been fortunate to live so close to the homeland of the English Romantics, the Lake District. Students who I taught at Lancaster University during the later 1970s and the 1980s helped keep me abreast of developments: the way in which Bhagwan Shree Rajneesh's movement sustained the 'sixties' after the decline of the counter-culture in the West (Thompson and Heelas, 1986), and the seminar spirituality which flourished at this time, thereby contributing to my research on 'alternative spiritualities' during the period. From 1997, I have been much preoccupied with what has come to be called the 'Kendal Project' – a project which has helped take me into the realm of wellbeing spirituality. During the last decade or so, I have also been studying spiritualities of life overseas – first Dacca, then Kampala, currently Islamabad and environs. All settings where 'wellbeing' is frequently a *much* more fundamental issue than in most western settings.

During this long period of looking at the New Age, I have had three experiences which will be with me until the day I die. In the spirit of Aldous Huxley, a trip to remoter realms whilst listening to the Pink Floyd during an open air festival; 'participant' observation of a 100 or so hour long Exegesis seminar; and a sudden realization concerning the significance of the term 'life' whilst waiting at Schiphol airport. Academically useful experiences – but not as useful as having had the fortune to live through the 'working out' of what Charles Taylor (1991) calls the 'massive subjective turn of modern culture' (p. 26): a turn which is very much bound up with the growth of subjective wellbeing culture, including wellbeing spirituality.

This book completes a trilogy with Blackwell Publishing on the topic of alternative spiritualities. The first volume, *The New Age Movement*, was published in 1996. Much of it dwelt on seminar spirituality, studied during the 1980s. The second volume, co-authored with Linda Woodhead, *The Spiritual Revolution*, was published in 2005. It contains a fair amount on the wellbeing spirituality which has become increasingly popular since the early 1990s. Neither of these two volumes was of an especially 'evaluative' nature; and neither paid much attention to the matter of consumption. Attending to these matters, *Spiritualities of Life* is significantly different from what has gone before. Furthermore, account has had to be taken of the consideration that the key word has ever more become 'life', in measure supplanting 'self'. I have also felt that it is now time to spread my wings, to turn more controversial.

Consumption, it is often said, dominates life. Subjective wellbeing culture – in the form of shopping to satisfy desire – is widely held to be a primary, perhaps *the* primary, exemplification of consumer culture. My interest in consumption derives from the consideration that New Age spiritualities of life have come to make their mark within various realms of the culture of subjective wellbeing. Accordingly, much of what follows is a critical assessment, written through the lens of consumption.

During the heyday of the Lancaster University Centre for the Study of Cultural Values, the early 1990s were devoted to the interdisciplinary study of aspects of consumer society and selfhood. Edited by Russell Keat, Nigel Whiteley and Nicholas Abercrombie, *The Authority of the Consumer* (1994) was perhaps the most significant outcome. The volume explores an apparently radical shift of authority, away from the provider or producer, towards the recipient or consumer. Judging the value and meaning of the activities involved in this shift, judging the character of the social relations at stake, the volume contributes to the debate between those who decry the commercialization, populism and loss of integrity associated with the apparent shift of authority, and those who commend the shift on the grounds of its anti-elitism, empowerment and democratization. Stimulated by the intellectual creativity of the Centre for the Study of Cultural Values, I tried my hand at writing an essay – 'The Limits of Consumption and the Postmodern "Religion" of the New Age' – which appeared in *The Authority of the Consumer*. The buzz of the time, however, was rather overwhelming. As a consequence, the essay left me with a series of questions: questions which have been nagging me ever since; questions which are now tackled to the best of my ability.

Profound thanks are due to the inspiration of the 'core' team of the Centre during the early 1990s, Nicholas Abercrombie, Russell Keat, Scott Lash, Celia Lury, Paul Morris, John Urry and Nigel Whiteley. More recently, I owe a great deal to conversations and correspondence with Colin Campbell – whose writings on consumer culture and spirituality are surely of the highest order. Steve Bruce – the Gordon Brown of the social scientific assembly north of the Border – has been as invaluable as ever, his no-nonsense arguments providing the perfect foil to what I hope are equally effective counter-arguments. My wife, Mia Haglund Heelas, has been even more invaluable. Having experienced holistic activities, she emphatically outdoes Steve Bruce on the forthrightness front: simply consumeristic, ineffectual, money-making 'nonsense', as she recently concluded after staying in that hotbed of holistic activities, Bangkok. Discussion with the National Cancer Research Institute's Psychosocial Oncology Spirituality Subgroup has proved exceptionally helpful, as have detailed comments provided by one of the readers of the manuscript of the present volume and the first-rate copy-editor, Jack Messenger. I also greatly appreciate insights provided by my daughter, Elissa Standen, friends and colleagues Dick Houtman, Gordon Lynch, Stefania Palmisano, Elizabeth Walton and Scott Taylor, and – as ever – my students, some of whom are referred to in what follows. A great debt is owed to Steve and Zeba Rasmussen, guides *par excellence* in Pakistan. At Lancaster University, I must acknowledge my gratitude to colleagues and personal friends Gavin Hyman and Deborah Sawyer for having helped keep me sane during a most difficult time at work, a time when I also benefitted from close friends Bobby and Besty Ben, and GP Bill Hall. Born in the sacred city of Kanchipuram, our 12-year-old son, Sebastian Heelas, has been of great significance: not only by being so patient whilst I have worked away in Islamabad, but also for being such an enthusiastic student of culture, stimulating my concern for inner-life universalism and freedom, and for telling me more about the slogans of wellbeing culture.

> What a piece of work is a man! How noble in reason! how infinite in faculty! in form, in moving, how express and admirable! in action how like an angel! in apprehension how like a god! the beauty of the world! the paragon of animals! And yet, to me, what is this quintessence of dust? man delights not me; no, nor women neither... (*Hamlet*, Act II, Sc. II)
>
> ✤
>
> It is in reverence for life that knowledge passes over into experience... My life bears its meaning in itself. And this meaning is found in living out the highest and most worthy idea which my will-to-live can furnish... the idea of reverence for life. Henceforth I attribute real value to my own life and to all the will-to-live which surrounds me; I cling to an activist way of life and I create real values. (Albert Schweitzer, 1966, p. 261)

> Like the ocean is your god-self;
> It remains for ever undefiled.
> And like the ether it lifts but the winged.
> Even the sun is your god-self;
> It knows not the ways of the mole nor seeks it
> the holes of the serpent.
> But your god-self dwells not alone in your being...
> He who defines his conduct by ethics
> imprisons his song-bird in a cage.
> (Kahlil Gibran, 1976, pp. 46, 90)

❧

> ...an...explosion in cultural consciousness – the fusion of people not with one another, but with material. Modernism has done much to unseat the humanist tradition ... The demise of romanticism ... (Kenneth J. Gergen, 2000, pp. xix, 227)

❧

> He who knows only his own side of the case knows little of that. (John Stuart Mill, *On Liberty*, 1859)

Introduction

Of all conceivable forms of enlightenment the worst is what... people call the Inner Light. Of all horrible religions the most horrible is the worship of the god within... That Jones shall worship the god within him turns out ultimately to mean that Jones shall worship Jones... The mere pursuit of health always leads to something unhealthy. (G. K. Chesterton, 1909, pp. 136, 138)

I believe that art therapy saved my life by giving me the opportunity to get in touch with my authentic self. This part of me is now allowed to have a life. The part that existed before was a highly developed false self... [Art therapy] was a process of gathering – my grief, my desolate childhood, my feminine qualities, divinity. They were brought to my centre, later I mixed with a pulse of light and leaps of joy. (Julie, with breast cancer, cited by Connell, 2001, p. 105)

... a spiritual stew. (Christopher Lasch, 1987, p. 80)

All life is sacred, interdependent and growing to fulfil its potential.
Love, Support and Protect all beings.
Connect. Grow. Serve. (William Bloom, www.williambloom.com)

There's only one corner of the universe you can be certain of improving and that's your own self. (Aldous Huxley, *Time Must Have a Stop*, 1944)

Surprisingly, a recent survey finds that 37 per cent of the British sample agree with the statement, 'I believe that God is something within each person, rather than something out there'. Whatever might be made of this – and some will express disbelief – the finding serves to direct attention to inner forms of the sacred. More specifically, it serves to direct attention to looking at *spirituality* within *life*. Not the life of a transcendent theistic God, but the life embedded within the here and now. A life, it is said, which can only make a 'true' difference when it is experienced by the self. And a life which is very much to do with the free expression, and thus development, of what it is to be 'truly' human. Such is the subject matter of this volume. So to the big question of the volume: what, if any, are the capacities of New Age spiritualities of life to make a positive difference to individual, social or cultural life?

The significance of this question derives from the nature of modernity. In the contemporary west, powerful forces are at work. Life is becoming ever more regulated by legal, quasi-legal or economically justified procedures, rules, systems. David Boyle (2000) writes of 'the tyranny of numbers'. As has frequently been argued, the sacrifices to be paid for the positivistic rule of reason are considerable. The freedom of the expressive self to live 'out' its own life by exercising experimentation is stifled. The affect/ive is disempowered. Quality of life suffers by virtue of the stresses generated by the culture of targets. The instrumentalization of relationships for the sake of economic utility threatens the integrity and possibilities of personal relationships, not least 'being trusting'. Spontaneity – well! It might well seem that life is becoming more and more akin to the antlike life of Dubai, that most capitalistic of places, with money, security, comfort, wellbeing galore for the better off, but with a deep, *boring* vacuity when it comes to self-expression, creativity, that great Romantic theme of learning through 'bitter' experience. From atop a skyscraper in Dubai, the flow of gleaming Mercedes revolving around the gleaming malls really does look like a series of columns, manifesting those perquisites for control – barren purity, officiated mundanity and self-mendacity.

Human flourishing is at stake. And I have to admit that as a libertarian humanist, with a liberal Quaker background, I look with horror at the ways in which life is becoming ever more restricted. *The expressive self undergoing the suffocating squeeze*. The ability of modernity to 'kill the spirit', as Kieran Flanagan (2007, p. 1) puts it. What makes things worse is that the value of expressivistic-cum-humanistic values is increased in the face of opposition. The possibility of becoming institutionalized aside, one never values freedom so much as when one is in prison. Analogously, one never values 'human' aspects of life – time to ponder, the opportunity to *be* oneself, the possibility of living as a free spirit – so much as when one feels oneself *under* the systems of capitalistic or quasi-capitalistic modernity; the experiences of engulfment, of invasion; the sense of the doors clanking shut to exclude 'life'. What provides hope, though, is that by enhancing the value of the values it excludes, capitalism fuels its own opposition. Furthermore, without capitalism or similar 'spanners in the works', values like freedom and equality would presumably lose their significance: now on the grounds that to be free and equal all the time means that freedom and equality cease to matter. (A reason, incidentally, why the utopian is 'no where'.)

Emphasizing autonomous expressivity, emphasizing the 'unbounded self' (Wexler, 2000, p. 2), New Age spiritualities of life appear to be opposed to the restrictive, the regulatory, those impositions of external sources of authority which are served by formal rules and regulations. So to the political dimension of this volume. Quite simply, are New Age spiritualities of life up to the task of responding to the 'iron cages' so widespread within mainstream society and culture, with their strongly positivistic, that is measurable and 'narrow', criteria of what it is be a 'successful' human? Do we find significant responses to what Guy Debord (1995, p. 26) calls 'the world of the spectacle', 'the world of the commodity ruling over all lived experience'? Do we find a form of the sacrality of the 'bare life' able to resist the sociocultural inscriptions explored in Giorgio Agamben's *Homo Sacer* (1998)? In the spirit of Richard Sennett (2008), do we find 'crafts of life', cultivating human flourishing, 'making' it happen, in the face of mainstream forces as they move ever closer to the deeply pessimistic appraisal of modernity provided by Weber in the closing pages of *The Protestant Ethic and the Spirit of Capitalism* (1985)? Do we find a *counter-balance* to the fact that life is ever more threatened by the ever-increasing ability of capitalist, quasi-capitalist and other organizations (including state education) to implement the idea that a (variously) specialized, boxed or *bounded* self is the prerequisite for renumerative progress?

A great deal hangs on the extent to which New Age spiritualities of life are privatized or consumerized. The common assumption among academics is that the internalized authority which is such a pronounced feature of New Age understanding is used to consume. Here we find 'the self for itself'. Here we find intake for the sake of what it *brings* to what lies within. Here we find those 'living a life turned in on itself where people ignore the consequences of their actions', as the Bishop of London, Richard Chartres, puts it in a succinct formulation (Leake, 2006, p. 1). Here we find people intent on capturing their dreams by way of commodities.

If autonomy is exercised to consume in a self-absorbing *fashion*, the response to positivistic iron-cage tendencies is going to be minimal, if not non-existent. If Zygmunt Bauman is right with the theme of his book, *Consuming Life* (2007), life is used up, engorged, for the sake of capitalistic consumer culture. New Age spiritualities of life are an integral tool of capitalism. If all those who treat New Age spiritualities of life as a form of *junk* capitalism – providing tacky forms of 'interior decoration', handling the suffocating squeeze by contributing to the great engorgement – are right, their 'revolutionary' capacity is obviously zilch.

Alternatively, the argument is that 'life' is 'consumed' and 'consuming'. From this perspective, inner-life spirituality is drawn upon, that is 'consumed' in the sense of 'used' and put to work, to cultivate what it is to *be* alive. To explore what it is to live beyond the narrow horizons of that utilitarian individualism which focuses the self on the quantifiable externals of life. And at least for some, inner-life spirituality takes one over (that is, is 'consuming'). Rather than the emphasis lying with the 'good life' of materialistic utilitarianism, the emphasis lies with the 'good life' of expressivistic humanism.

Reflections on Shirley MacLaine: Possibilities

'It all starts with self', writes Shirley MacLaine (1988, p. 5). With this proclamation in mind, we can ask questions of the kind:

- To what *extent* do the fruits of the New Age spiritualities of life *stay* locked within the self alone, remaining in and of the self itself?
- To the extent that these spiritualities stay within the self itself, what kind of self is at stake?
- Is this a privatized self devoting itself to its 'intray' to develop 'exceptional interiors', with New Age spiritualities of life largely – if not entirely – serving to encourage the self-indulgence of narcissistically or sybaritically pleasuring the self? Or is this a self devoted to the interior spiritual quest?
- Is the 'starting point' relational rather than atomistic? Epistemologically solipsistic or learning through others? Or both?
- To what extent do New Age spiritualities of life take a relational, *engaged* form, participants working from their 'grassroots', ignoring the private-public distinction to contribute to the world about them?
- If contributions to the world are in evidence, are iron-cage tendencies addressed head on? Are contributions found in connection with ways of life – perhaps through downsizing or early retirement – which circumvent the 'bounding' of the capitalistic mainstream?
- Most fundamentally, are New Age spiritualities of life best thought of as a component of the enlightenment trajectory of modernity in capitalistic mode, or the romantic, expressivist strand? Or, with logical options in mind, both?

Questions of this variety direct our attention to the greatest of the issues raised by inner-life spirituality.[1] For if New Age spiritualities of life simply encourage what many regard to be the primary 'sin' of capitalism, namely consumptive self-interest, we have an increasingly popular form of the sacred, one which is increasingly rivalling the sway of Christianity in western settings and which could well be doing more harm than good. On the other hand, if the 'spirituality' of spiritualities of life lives up to its promise, not least addressing the deleterious consequences of consumer-producer capitalism, it provides an avenue for 'true' human flourishing.

Do we side with Chesterton and Lasch or with Julie, Bloom and Huxley? To scorn or to praise – or some combination of both evaluations?

Introducing Inner-Life Spirituality

Spiritualities of life today, on which I focus, typically take a holistic, life-affirming form. Whether it be yoga in Chennai or yoga in San Francisco, aikido in Islamabad or aikido in Birkenhead, one will encounter the theme that what matters is delving within oneself to experience the primary source of the sacred, namely that which emanates from the 'meta-empirical' depths of life in the here-and-now (Hanegraaff, 1999, p. 152; see also Robertson, 1972, p. 47, on the 'superempirical'). And it is also highly likely that one will encounter the theme that experiential contact with inner-life spirituality enables it to 'flow' through other aspects of one's being to integrate, 'harmonize' or 'balance' oneself; to draw one's mind, body and spirit into a whole by way of the sacralization of the body-cum-subjective life; to find self-fulfilment by way of the craft of life; to enable 'natural' spirituality to 'fill' the unique life rather than letting it 'drain away' by using up life for the sake of the consumptive.

With the possible exception of a few countries like Somalia (although indigenous healers there could very well be working with inner-life forces), holistic activities are now found across the nations of the globe. In western settings, mind-body-spirituality *activities*, in the hands of *spiritual practitioners* – which is what is concentrated on in this volume – have grown fairly rapidly, especially during and since the counter-cultural sixties. In some western countries, inner-life 'beliefs' have almost certainly become more popular than beliefs in the theistic personal God of traditional Christianity.

A Beneficial Development

Needless to say, many participants and believers are delighted with what is underway. As an experiential spirituality, nothing less than the transformation of the quality of personal, subjective life lies to hand. As an expressive spirituality, rather than ending with the self itself, inner-spirituality is held to (greatly) enhance the quality of personal relationships, one's creativity and self-responsibility whilst being with others. And as a humanistic, egalitarian spirituality, rather than a secular form of humanism, concern is expressed for human wellbeing in *all* its aspects. The inner-life is held to contribute to what Martha Nussbaum (1997) calls 'the cultivation of humanity' – the liberation of 'the mind from the bondage of habit and custom, producing people who can function with sensitivity and alertness as citizens of the whole world'; people who 'recognize the worth of human life wherever it occurs' (pp. 8–9). The jobs are clear; for participants, so is the efficacy of the work.

No wonder that considerable numbers of the medical profession in various western countries have been attracted by what inner-life spirituality is seen to offer when caring and quality of life matters are to hand. No wonder that

CAM (Complementary and Alternative Medicine), where mind-body-*spirituality* is often in evidence, has become so popular. No wonder that inner-life spirituality is proving increasingly attractive to primary school teachers in the UK and elsewhere, with the child-centred approach emphasizing the 'whole' of the individual pupil. No wonder that inner-life spirituality is proving increasingly attractive to secondary school teachers in the UK, the importance it attaches to the shared spiritual life of all humans serving as a way of addressing multiculturalism. No wonder that inner-life spirituality is a growing presence within the domain of paid employment, among other things being taken to contribute to the self-work ethic. No wonder that this kind of spirituality has been deemed worthy of government support in the UK and elsewhere, President Musharraf of Pakistan, for instance, lending his official backing, as Patron-in-chief, to an inner-life orientated Sufi organization, the National Council of Sufism, primarily designed to combat the exclusivistic with the inclusivistic.

Whether it be the personal life of subjective experience, the personal life of the 'familiar' world of daily activities, or the cultivation of humanity, it seems as though holistic spirituality has a great deal to offer.[2] We might well want to conclude that if it continues to become more popular, it will provide a worthy successor to Christianity in western settings; and, in the longer term, to exclusivistic, iron-cage forms of Islam (for example) in countries like Pakistan. Indeed, among other reasons, the ability of spiritualities of life to handle both the unique and the universal could mean that it will provide a *more* worthy successor: quite probably the best hope for the future of the sacred in a world where the cry 'Only Connect' is likely to become more and more urgent – not least to combat the divisive Truths of numerous forms of religious tradition.

A Deleterious Development

Turning to the other side of the coin, New Age spiritualities of life have long been subject to criticism. Think of Chesterton. Providing a very brief history of the main tools which have been used to beat New Age spiritualities during the last few decades, forty years ago talk was of the acid-riddled hippies of the counter-culture, twenty-five years ago of the brainwashed participants of fascistic enlightenment seminars; today, talk is of the consumption of mind-body-spirit dross. Of all the controversies surrounding contemporary inner-life spiritualities, by far and away the most significant within the academy and beyond revolves around the criticism that the great majority (or virtually all) of provisions and activities serve as consumer products. The refrain is that the key product of the New Age is experience. 'Spiritual' experiences, if that is what they can be called, are taken to be consumed, used, for the sake of enhancing hedonistic experiences – broadly on a par with a pampering session at a mind-body spa, or reading pulp fiction.

Putting it vividly, only the self can consume – by and for itself. One cannot consume for others. When individuals consume, they, and they alone, absorb or use what is on offer, the experiences belonging to their private, interior, life. Especially when people consume for the sake of their own pleasure rather than out of necessity, 'the pursuit of happiness' only too readily results in 'the *dead end* of a narcissistic preoccupation with the self' (Lasch, 1980, p. xv; my emphasis). The joys, wonders, experiences of one's own essence – that is, one's own 'spirituality' – might themselves be consumed. In answer to one of the questions raised earlier – namely, to what extent do New Age spiritualities of life stay locked into the self, itself? – the short answer is that this is where they remain. And in answer to another question – to the extent that these spiritualities stay with the self itself, what kind of self is at stake? – the answer is equally obvious. We are in the land of the self-indulgent self; the self consumed by worldly provisions. We are in the land of those rational-choice and post-modernist theorists who, in Stephen Hunt's (2002, p. 42) summary, see spirituality as 'partak[ing] of the consumer ethic'. We are in the land of the 'I am what I am – and I want more from the material world'. We are in the land of Burger King's 'Get the Urge, Get to Burger King'; of the 'Have it Your Way'.

Whatever value or usefulness New Age spiritualities of life might possess – as a way forward, perhaps as a force for good in the longer-term future – is ravaged, dissipated by consumption. Worse, we shall see, it can be argued that these spiritualities contribute to the very thing that they proclaim, in egalitarian mode, to be combating: elitist, show-off, indulgent, excessive capitalism, the wealthier affirming their difference from the less well-off; exploiting their position in life to fuel experiences of deprivation. Except for successful capitalists, spiritualities of life do much more harm than good.

Comparison

The beneficial and deleterious ways in which holistic spiritualities of life are understood and appraised are poles apart. On the one hand, we find a person-centred, expressivistic, humanistic, universalistic spirituality. We find a spirituality praised by participants for the ways in which it stimulates the flourishing of what it is to be human; a spirituality credited with the power to heal 'dis-ease', to enhance wellbeing or 'wellness'; a spirituality which professionals seek to introduce or encourage within the mainstream realms of education, health and the capitalist workplace (etc.); a spirituality deemed worthy of governmental support; a spirituality which provides a 'politics' of values to bring about a better world in which to live.

On the other hand, we find capitalist-driven gratification of desire, the pleasuring of the self, self-indulgence, if not sheer greed. Rather than contributing to the quality of life for increasing numbers of people, the growth of New Age spiritualities makes things worse. Increasingly, purveyors dress their products and services with spirituality to make 'The Promise'. Their aim is to stimulate demand by titillating hopes and desires. Playing on the 'consumer emotions' of the individual – of the '*I'll* only be happy when *I* have experienced this...' variety – the end result is Lasch's dead end. Prompted by provisions and services to dwell on the state of play and requirements of their pleasure zone, the more that individuals take in (or are taken in *by*) what is on offer, the more privatized or selfish they become, perhaps to the extent of treating even 'close' relationships in the mode of instrumental self-gratification. Consequently, the less likely they are to contribute to the wellbeing of those around them during their daily lives, let alone to engage in 'direct' political action more generally.

Introducing the Argument

What is to be made of this clash of understanding and evaluation? What is to be made of the argument that consumerism is alive and well, if not rampant, within the sphere of inner-life spirituality? To the degree that the language of consumption is rejected by participants, do the 'implied' meanings of these spiritualities, their nature, form or function, nevertheless justify the application of the language? It would be rash in the extreme to reject the claim that the growth of New Age spiritualities of life *can* contribute to self-indulgence and other forms of consumption. It would also be rash to reject the claim that the purveyors of 'spiritually' significant products or services 'sell out' in the context of consumer culture, with some having 'sold out' to it. However, there are good grounds for concluding that attempts to 'reduce' spiritualities of life more or less *in toto* – which is what some critics do – is to neglect the irreducible.

Recent years have seen the publication of a number of volumes, articles and Ph.D. theses written in the spirit of Christopher Lasch. That is to say, the emphasis lies with the 'nothing (much) more than hedonistic consumption' point of view. It is time for a response: one which is not driven by purist ideas of what counts as true, that is world-rejecting, spirituality; one which does not derive from particular versions of what counts as political activism (those to the left arguing that the turn within deflects from 'real', that is secular, activism); and, for that matter, one which is not driven by the doctrines, fear or envy of the Christian establishment (see Ward, 2006). To counter the sledgehammer approach of so much of what has become the 'reduction' to consumption orthodoxy of many critics, as well as to generate debate, I attempt to dislodge some familiar arguments. It is time to rectify the balance against the polemical, rhetorical and – it has to be said – the frequently ill-informed.[3]

In *The Politics of Experience* (1967), R. D. Laing writes:

> Our behaviour is a function of our experience. We act according to the way we see things... If our experience is destroyed, we have lost our own selves. (p. 2)

In *The Art of Happiness* (1998) the Dalai Lama speaks the language of highly egalitarian, humanistic, expressive, 'loving kindness' spirituality, arguing for what he calls '*basic spirituality*': 'the basic human qualities of goodness, kindness, compassion, caring' (p. 258; his emphasis). As the Dalai Lama continues,

> as long as we are human beings, as long as we are members of the human family, *all* of us really need these basic human values. Without these, human existence remains very hard, very dry. As a result, none of us can be a happy person, our whole family will suffer, society will be more troubled. So, it becomes clear that cultivating these kinds of basic spiritual values becomes crucial. (p. 258; his emphasis)

Drawing on Laing and the Dalai Lama, it is virtually a truism that the ways in which people experience, understand and value themselves, those around them and those further abroad, has huge significance for how they act in the world. And as anthropologists, for example, have demonstrated, to have new experiences, to acquire new understandings, to change values during the ritual process – exemplified by *rites de passage* – frequently has profound significance for life.[4] Leaving exploration of the 'changes' which *might* occur during the 'ritual process' of participation in holistic, mind-body spirituality until later in this book, the important point for now is that the values of the Dalai Lama's 'basic spirituality' (and of course his list is not exhaustive) are widely abroad within spiritualities of life. For introductory purposes, it suffices to say that participation *can* serve to make a *difference* to the ways people live 'out' their lives.

My main intention is to argue the case for 'spiritual' significance or reality, arguing in turn that the growth of New Age spiritualities of life is by no means entirely 'eaten up' by the bodies-cum-psychologies of consumers. That instead, 'ethical demands' are frequently experienced as emanating from within. Adopting a term from Isaiah Berlin's *Against the Current* (2001) – an analysis of those precursors of contemporary spiritualities of life, the Romantics – I argue as forcefully as possible that holistic, face-to-face activities (in particular) can facilitate a 'current' of meaningful experiences. These flow through the lives of participants to infuse their outlook on life and their values. Flowing through those who have, in measure, moved *beyond* the allures of consumer culture; those who are cultivating basic spirituality rather than merely using their activities to gratify their consumptive emotions; those who aim to 'Grow into Life' (an apt expression!), as a psychodrama group which has met in Lancaster calls itself; those who seek 'to bring the daily activities of our lives into a more health-promoting way', as a leaflet circulated by a Kendal practitioner of the Alexander Technique and Reflexology puts it; those who seek what 'The Headless Way' has to offer, according to a promotional flyer – 'See Who you really are. Our self-concept affects our behaviour, so an expanded sense of self has important implications for our lives.'

A Personal Bias?

To engage with the 'reduction' to consumption thesis by drawing attention to its defects, and to do this by referring to the 'spiritual' significance or reality of holistic activities, could easily be taken to mean that I am defending spiritualities of life.[5] It can then be inferred that my defence is due to the fact that I am committed to what they have to offer. It can thus be concluded that I am biased in favour of these spiritualities. And indeed Steve Bruce (2006, p. 42) writes that I am one of those who is 'sympathetic to New Age spirituality'.

In one sense, Bruce understates his case. As will become perfectly apparent, I am deeply committed to the beneficial *efficacy* of inclusivistic (albeit tension-laden) humanistic values – the same values which are sacralized by so many New Age spiritualities of life. In another sense, though, Bruce's observation has to be qualified. I am equally committed to basing as many interpretations and judgements as possible, most especially those to do with beneficial efficacy, on publicly accessible evidence. Given the absence of publicly available empirical evidence for inner-life spirituality itself, I am certainly not committed to the unscholarly exercise of couching inquiry in terms of the presumed ontological-cum-experiential truth of what lies deep within. As reported by participants, the 'spiritual' significance of holistic activities is, of course, another matter. For it is then an aspect of ethnographic reality.

Furthermore, on the point of evidence and efficacy, it should be born in mind that it is not as though I am making things easy for myself. For some time now, I have argued that the provisions and activities of holistic spiritualities of life in measure belong to subjective wellbeing culture.[6] Writes David Cohen (2000) in an article on a course at the University of Alberta which attends to Oprah Winfrey, *The Oprah Magazine* 'maintains that one can and *should feel better about oneself* – "This magazine is about helping you *become more of who you are*," says Winfrey's introductory note' (my emphases). With the emphasis on quality experiences for the (relatively) well-to-do, subjective wellbeing culture in its purchasing, high-street mode is often seen as epitomizing the self-indulgent aspect of consumer culture; a bourgeois bastardization of that great theme of the *fin-de-siècle* Decadents, critical fascination with insatiability and the quest for sensual gratification at all costs. To argue, as I do in this volume, that holistic, mind-body-spirituality activities *also* have much to do with a subjectivized rendering of the ethic of humanity – which in effect is what the Dalai Lama is referring to – flies in the face of what readily come to mind when one thinks of quality of life purchasing culture: luxuries for the spoilt.

More Controversies

Hopefully, this volume is controversial. Given that it intersects with several debates within various quarters of the academy, it should be.

Thinking of the (ill-named) sociology of *religion* (for spirituality should now be included), the sometimes heated debate is between those who emphasize the market, self-interest and preferences and those who emphasize the continuing significance of the 'Durkheimian' sacred as an authoritative order. Including New Age spirituality under the rubric of religion, Stephen Hunt (2002) writes, 'if there is any one theme which unites sociologists in the area today then it is the matter of choice and consumption in the field of religion' (p. 210). True, not all the sociologists he has in mind are united in the importance they ascribe to self-indulgent consumption. However, his generalization stands – which means that I have to argue against the consensus: among other strategies, by adopting a modified Durkheimian approach.

A related point of controversy concerns the growing tendency for secularization theorists to explain away the growth of New Age spiritualities of life by arguing that activities (and beliefs?) have much more to do with the ends of individualistic, secular or psychological consumption than with anything over and above that which is 'taken in' to satisfy preferences.

Within that important field of cultural studies, namely the investigation of the consumer, consumer culture and consumption, the debate between those who envisage the consumer as a passive, decentred, saturated, more-or-less conformist, opiated victim of the formations and stratagems of capitalism, and those who emphasize the libertarian, emancipatory role of consumer activities and autonomous self-expression, is as hotly contested as ever. The debate between those who are negative – sometimes exceedingly so – about what consumer culture has to offer, and those who emphasize creative, 'meaning-making' aspects, cannot be ignored in what follows. Even when mind-body-spirituality activities or provisions are consumeristic, they could be enabling more than the passive consumption of 'mere' pleasure.

Controversy is fuelled by virtue of the fact that the topic of consumption more or less inevitably raises issues to do with elitism. For Graham Ward (2006), 'rather than functioning as an integrating factor in the life of a society', religion – especially what he calls 'spiritualism' – is well on the way to becoming 'self-help as self-grooming', providing forms of 'custom-made eclecticism that proffer a pop transcendence and pamper to the need for "good vibrations"' (p. 185). Ward might be partially correct. Before making assessments of this variety, however, it is worth taking a close look at the evidence. It is only too easy to make disparaging judgements of New Age provisions or services, dismissing them as consumer garbage. (I wonder what Ward would have to say about *Enhancing Your Mind Body Spirit* magazine, each £2.99 issue complete with 'Course Equipment' such as an amethyst crystal, advertised on TV in Britain over the last few years during the Christmas period?) Indeed, it could well be argued that there is a long tradition, going back to Weber (for example) with his category of the *virtuosi*, which parallels the kind of cultural elitism exemplified, more generally, by the likes of Nancy Mitford. My own 'bias' is to value respect – not just as a value, but because of the importance of ethnographic accuracy.

It might be easy to poke fun at the £2.99 pack. It might be easy to ridicule the adaptation of the 'Tao' as in 'With Tao Tile Imports it's not merely about seeing – it's about experiencing our range'. It might be tempting to dismiss 'Aromatherapist Glenda Taylor, founder of Cariad essential oils' when she tells journalist Jacqui Ripley (2002) that the oil 'sooths frayed emotions, calms nerves and lifts the spirits' (p. 311). It might be easy to laugh at the '6,000 square ft Roman Spa, complete with marble columns and floors, offering all kinds of herbal baths and therapy' (*CTS Magazine*, 1991, p. 3) which has been built in Norway. It is equally easy to note that, 'These days, you can get hold of green-tea bags infused with ancient wisdom and £80 tracksuit bottoms with the Buddha writ large in self embroidery' (Ives, 2007). It might be very easy indeed to ridicule Tony Blair for drinking from a personalized 'name' mug which begins, 'Anthony, your refined inner voice drives your thoughts and deeds'. But let us first look closely at what the £2.99 pack, for instance, contains: whether 'eastern' themes have been recontextualized to incorporate *significant* values; whether there is spiritually informed advice about how to become a better person, both for one's own sake and for the sake of others. Let us also first hear what purchasers have to say. Their judgements ('Oh, I realized it was complete junk and chucked it' or 'eye opening') can then inform academic assessments. Despite the postmodern sensibility – the value attached to 'little things', the importance of 'valuing the other', the egalitarian ethos – the (supposedly) refined tastes of the scholar only too readily (I shall argue) translate into summary devaluation: especially when ignorance of anything other than surface *appearances* is involved. The inspirational, the auratic, need not be limited to Wagner. Basically, I'm anti-elitist, my adherence to cultural democracy entailing equal adherence to ethnographic contextualization – and vice versa.

Probably, there is also a degree of disrespectful elitism – together with self-interested protectionism – at work among those (often high-ranking) medical professionals like Nobel prizewinner for medicine Sir James Black who dismiss CAM as ineffectual tosh. The counter-argument is that CAM provisions and activities, including the spiritually informed, are best seen as a major aspect of subjective wellbeing culture, the popularity of CAM helping demonstrate its success in enhancing the quality of life.

On his deathbed, blind and unable to speak, Aldous Huxley made a written request to his wife, Laura Huxley, for an intramuscular injection of 100 mg of LSD. He died peacefully a few hours after the injection. A form of escapism, akin to the role played by soma which he had so sharply criticized in *Brave New World*? A CAM-like intake to 'ease' his 'final journey' and render it 'a more conscious experience', as Susan Blackmore (2006) would have it? An ecstatic experience, with the expectation of providing experiential ratification of his understanding of *The Tibetan Book of the*

Dead? Or simply a final act of consumption, with hedonistic under- or overtones? Although the 'simply' hedonistic is (highly) unlikely, I doubt that we will ever know. But in the contemporary world, we are at least in the position to explore the significance of consumption, as intake, at first hand: to do our best to put our prejudices aside to explore what is taking place before reporting – or judging – whether it is edifying or demeaning; a force for the better or for the worse.

Other points of controversy are raised as we proceed. One, though, deserves immediate note. It concerns the ethic of humanity, an ethic which revolves around the values ascribed to the 'golden triangle' of life, equality and freedom, an ethic which is dominant in western cultures, and an ethic which is central to spiritualities of life. The ethic is also highly controversial. It has been subjected to what can only be described as savage criticism, proclamations of the 'death of the human' or of 'humanity' itself serving to reject its very foundations. Sacralized within spiritualities of life, to argue that the growth of these spiritualities can contribute to personal and multicultural relationality therefore entails defending the ethic. Fortunately, help is to hand – provided, for example, by Martha Nussbaum and Amartya Sen (1993), Nussbaum (1997, 2000, 2007), Sen (2005, 2006) and Sarbani Sen (2007).

A Brief Guide to this Book

The first chapter provides an overview of contemporary mind-body spirituality, introducing the reader to main characteristics and how this form of spirituality differs from others. To ground the contemporary, as well as to illustrate basic themes and their variations, it includes a fair amount of historical contextualization. Evidence of recent growth is looked at in the second chapter, attention being paid to the nature of wellbeing spirituality today, including how it appears in various sociocultural settings in the West.

Focusing on activities, the central section of the volume concentrates on the 'consuming growth' debate. The most important argument employed by secularization theorists to handle the growth of New Age spiritualities of life is to interpret them as engulfed by the psychologies of consumption, including secular consumer culture. What is growing is consumed, used (up), to the extent that significantly spiritual growth (especially values experienced as spiritually informed) is unimportant, or virtually absent. Having gone further into the contours of the debate in the third chapter, the fourth serves to introduce the reader to the language of consumption. At the same time, I draw attention to how the key senses of this language have been, or can be, applied to tease out consumeristic aspects of New Age spiritualities of life. Notwithstanding the presence of consumeristic aspects, however, the remaining chapters of the central section provide a battery of arguments designed to reveal the limitations of the 'reduction' to consumption approach, especially when the approach takes the form of *in toto*, or virtually *in toto*, blanket coverage. The arguments take into consideration the fact that the commodities and holistic mind-body-spirituality activities of broadly conceived subjective wellbeing culture are more likely to be consumeristic in some contexts (upmarket stores, for instance) than others (terminal life-care in many hospices).

In the concluding section, attention is turned to what inner-life activity can contribute to a 'politics' of the 'good life'; to a politics which explores avenues, ways of life, which are not reducible to the 'spiritual' consumption of consumer capitalism; to a politics which might not have much to do with Timothy Leary's *The Politics of Ecstasy* (1970) of the counter-cultural sixties, but which nevertheless shares with it an expressivistic, humanistic, value-laden alternative, response to, if not stand against, the 'high road' of capitalism, specifically in the mode of 'excessive' consumption.[7] A *Politics Beyond Excess*. The argument is that spiritualities of life, today, inform a more subtle, whilst more effective, 'counter-culture' – better, 'counter-current' – than that of 35 or so years ago; ways of living which are 'normal', familiar, everyday, yet able to make a difference. Having discussed this in connection with western settings, the Epilogue introduces an international perspective. It raises the question as to whether the growth of inner-life spirituality in countries like Pakistan or India can serve as a 'counter' to the excesses of individualistic, self-centred, discriminatory consumer capitalism. It raises the matter of how spiritualities of life can function 'in their own right' – that is significantly beyond consumption – to play a crucial, universalistic or inclusivistic role in combating divisive, dangerous exclusivism. To combat those Truth-driven 'us-them' mentalities which, in Marxist vein, owe a great deal to capitalism, not least inequalities generated by the lust for consumption among wealthy elites.

To what extent has inner-life spirituality resisted sliding into self-absorbed consumption? Readers looking for a comprehensive and determinate assessment of the extent to which New Age spiritualities of life are bound up with the dynamics and values of consumption – or not – will be disappointed. Apart from the fact that the research agenda stretches well into the future, I argue that it is highly unlikely that any particular activity or provision is *either* an act of consumption *or* not. My answer to the question 'When is an act of consumption?' is that acts (or indeed natural 'events' like fires, triggered by spontaneous combustion, consuming forests) are *never* simply a matter of consumption. Aldous Huxley might have consumed LSD; but given his life, it would be foolhardy to limit attention to the ingestion itself.

In Short

At a time when the incidence of Christian practice (gauged by church attendance) and belief (gauged by 'personal God' survey data) is collapsing in many European countries, as well as elsewhere, the question is whether the incontestable growth of holistic, mind-body spirituality activities (publications, etc.) is primarily to do with the engorgement of capitalism or the development of a valuable, perhaps invaluable, ultimate resource. Rather than activities collapsing into the secularities of self-centred emotions and feelings to dissipate the *significance* and *distinctiveness* of growth, are we witnessing the flowering of the 'practically spiritual'? A flowering of that Romantic trajectory of modernity which is provided by spiritual practitioners whose practices bring spirituality to life, inspiring participants to live a life of good practice? A flowering which is only *sometimes* 'practically spiritual' in the sense of being 'not quite' the 'real thing'?

Two Provisos

With 200,000-plus separate mind-body-spirituality activities run by spiritual practitioners taking place in Great Britain today, with the figure for the world going into the millions, it is inevitable that the present volume is of a somewhat tentative nature. Although I have been studying and researching New Age spiritualities of life for some 35 years (longer, if one includes sixties experiences), it is simply impossible to keep up with all that has developed. And though it is wonderful learn from colleagues in a number of countries, they, too, are faced with the challenge of keeping abreast with what is appearing or developing. There is certainly a wealth of things to research, a wealth which is increasing virtually everywhere. We researchers hardly have time to draw our breath. In the field of readership studies, for instance, very little is known about the role of texts written out of the 'sacred' (inspirational? helping place 'issues' in perspective? titillation? 'authoritative'?). We do not even know, for example, the approximate percentage of New Agers who are pacifists, who opposed the invasion of Iraq. With so many gaps in the evidence, I have sometimes felt that I have been ploughing a rather uncertain furrow. My consolation is that the more insecure, less certain passages of the volume will nevertheless set something of a research agenda: of value to those non-committed academics who are intent on exploring whether the 'balance' can be rectified by seeing what New Age spiritualities of life have to offer – rather than simply indulging in criticism.

Some of the content of this book is certainly rather less well informed than would be the case if there were more researchers in the field: not just in Britain, but more importantly in countries like Pakistan. I am *reasonably* confident, however, that the rather 'utopian' (as some might see it) account of New Age spiritualities of life is just that – reasonable. Inevitably, the portrayal, the generalizations made in what follows, are open to the criticism, 'But *x* is not like this' or '*y* differs in the following ways ...'. I just pray that I am reasonably accurate – that is, accurate enough to encourage the search for greater accuracy. I am fully aware – indeed, hoping – that what follows will be criticized, especially on the basis of better ethnographic evidence. There are too many provisos of the 'it is highly likely...' kind for my taste. On the other hand, the relative paucity of relevant information cuts both ways. Just as I sometimes flounder for evidence, so – presumably – do those who advocate the 'reduction' to consumption interpretation. Hopefully, it is easier to undermine the generalizations of the 'deleterious' camp than vice versa.

Although contemporary aspects of capitalism play an important role in this book, the topic of spirituality and commodified production for the market is not dwelt on to the extent that it deserves. To do justice to this enormous topic, involving the diverse ways in which inner-life spirituality is put to work within the context of economic productivity, would require another volume.

Starting with the Self to 'Big Designs'

One of the characters of Ian McEwan's *Black Dogs* reflects:

> Everyone has to take responsibility for his own life and attempt to improve it, spiritually in the first instance... Without a revolution of the inner life, however slow, all our big designs are worthless. The work we have to do is within ourselves if we are ever going to be at peace – the good that flows from it will shape our societies in an unprogrammed, unforeseen way, under the control of no single group or set of people or set of ideas.

The emotionally dead aside, we all know the difference that activities (from sleep to tennis) can make to subjective life; we all know the difference that subjectivities can make to our daily lives – our routine tasks, our work, our relationships; generally speaking, we appreciate the value of empathy, of understanding others; generally speaking, we enjoy having a sense of purpose or hope and the driving force which goes with looking to the future; we all value the cultivation of companionship, of love, of learning about ourselves with others, of coming to terms with problems; to some degree or another we all appreciate the ways in which self-expression can contribute to the lives of others – reciprocally, what our own lives owe to others; a great many of us seek to become more fully human – not by filling life up with material commodities or trivia, but by affirming and 'extending' life with and 'through' other people in 'postmaterialist' vein.[8] On common-sense grounds alone, finding ways of being calmer, or more focused, can make a great contribution to the art of life. Maybe this does not have to do with 'a *revolution* of the inner life'. But this is the kind of subjective-life territory where inner-life spiritualities get to work. Improving life for oneself, and therefore for others. The nurse who has problems at work; who joins a tai chi group; who returns to work to contribute more 'life' to the ward.

In his *Anthropology from a Pragmatic Point of View* (1978), Kant wrote:

> The cynic's purism and the hermit's mortification of the flesh, without *social good-living*, are distorted interpretations of virtue and do not make virtue attractive; rather, being forsaken by the Graces, they can *make no claim on humanity.* (p. 191; my emphases)

In not dissimilar vein, Julian Huxley, in his *Religion Without Revelation* (1941), argues, 'any religion which stresses the need for propitiating an external Power will be diverted away from the more essential task of *using* and organizing the spirituality forces that lie within each individual' (p. vii; my emphasis). Without for one moment wishing to imply that Kant and Huxley belong to the camp of spiritualities of life (although scientistic Huxley sometimes veers perilously close), the thrust of mind-body spirituality is very much towards practical application; their spiritual realities are very much to do with 'social good-living'. At least from the perspective of the great majority of spiritual practitioners, and many of their participants, it is all about spiritually suffused, expressivistic, humanistic, wellbeing 'flow'.

In *The New Age Movement* (1996a) I wrote, 'The New Age is "of" the self in that it facilitates celebration of what it is to be and to become; and is "for" the self in that by differing from much of the mainstream, it is positioned to handle identity problems generated by conventional forms of life' (pp. 173–4). Developments since the 1980s, when most of the research for *The New Age Movement* was carried out, mean that I am no longer so happy with the terms 'celebration' and 'identity problems'. Developments also mean that I now greatly prefer the formulation 'a spirituality "of" and "for" what it is to live out of life'. Fundamentally, we are looking at a spirituality 'of' and 'for' *being* truly human: 'of' because it is experienced and understood to emanate from the depths of subjective life, if not life itself; 'for' because of its practicality – its (apparent) ability to make a positive difference to subjective life and the life around us: as well as elsewhere.

The point (or criticism) is often made that one of the most significant differences between New Age spiritualities of life and many forms of traditional religion is that the former don't make much of a difference – when, as we know only too well, the latter can readily implement or support 'big designs'. Whether taken individually or collectively, New Age spiritualities of life, it is argued, are too superficial, too insubstantial, too vague, too inward looking, too selfish, and – of course – too consumerized, too much 'of' and 'for' the pleasures or luxuries of secular consumption, to be other than inconsequential, ineffectual. Casual and largely irrelevant to important matters, they lack 'impact'.

However, if participant testimonies, the spiritual meaningful realities of their activities, the literature they read, the work they do (for example) is anything to go by, spiritualities of life *are* able to make a *real* difference. As experienced and valued, 'spiritual power' or 'force' (as Comte called it in quasi-secular mode) *works*. Such is my central argument. The greatest challenge, though, is arguing the case when so much difference is of a qualitative nature. As anyone who has read Robert Pirsig's *Zen and the Art of Motorcycle Maintenance* might well appreciate, 'quality' is a tricky matter – certainly not one readily tackled quantitatively. Quality, though is not invisible.

But what of humanity? It is frequently claimed that 'the aim' of the New Age is to 'change oneself rather than change the world' (the point is made here by Nadia Garnoussi, 2005, p. 197). Even if sceptics grant that inner-life spirituality can serve to inform the life of the self together with a politics of ethics, with values-cum-experiences serving as a (relatively) gentle current within more personal, familiar, localized settings, it might well be objected that spiritualities of life, today, show little of the political clout of, say, the counter-cultural sixties. As a universalistic spirituality of humanity, one would expect to see New Agers regularly protesting outside the American Embassy (etc.), to protest against the situation in Iraq – as counter-culturalists did against the war in Vietnam. One might expect to see more effort being put into working from the self, and the 'local' or familiar where the self spends much of life, to the far away.[9] Or is this unfair? The matter is returned to later – including the significance of inner-life humanism as a force of (and for) good, able to work wonders. So too is the consideration that there is sound evidence that as nations become increasingly wealthy, democratic, ethic of humanity values tend to become increasingly significant, as do expressivist values, as does inclusivistic, humanistic spirituality: or is this last a mask for the possessive, consuming individualism of the wealthy in countries like Pakistan or India? Not so much commodity worship, but the 'worship' of their own experiences?

More harm than good or more good than harm? That is the question. Given the decline of traditional religion in western settings (and the damage it can do elsewhere), given the growth of the inner-life spirituality 'replacement', the stakes are high. A genuine attempt to incorporate more spiritual values and practices within the mainstream in order to 'transform' it, or mumbo-jumbo – Christopher Lasch's (1987) 'spiritual stew', 'lacking any intrinsic value'? Who is right – Chesterton or Julie? Or are both somehow making valid points? Is it in order that humanistic spirituality is being developed within the mainstream of institutions in England, with 'nursing spirituality' being developed, with the government agency Ofsted inspecting spiritual development in schools? In short, what, if any, is the significance beyond consumption – especially in the world 'beyond' the self, where the inner-life could have a critical role to play in contributing to the harmonization of the cultures of the globe?

Policy Implications

When I tell my wife about the exciting data (most especially the percentage who 'believe' in the God within) from her home country, Sweden, the response is a shrug. And as County Director of the INGO Plan Pakistan, it certainly appears that she has more important statistics to consider. However, the growth of inner-life beliefs and activities seems to have a great deal to offer the sociocultural realm – in the west and most especially elsewhere. Among many other considerations, humanistic, perennialized spirituality provides a middle way between the dangers of multiculturalism informed by exclusivistic, life-as-a-True-believer forms of theism and the various values of the 'merely' secular domain. Emphasizing the shared whilst embracing diversity and the unique, humanistic inner-life spirituality can enter into the educational system without much fear of offence – especially if proper attention is paid to inner-life aspects of Sufism and Hinduism, for example. In hospitals and hospices, all but the most die-hard of atheists and the most conservative of the religious are likely to appreciate what inner-life carers or therapists have to offer. Which is why the policy of the UK Department of Education and Skills, and that of Health, is to encourage inner-life practices (teaching and healthcare); which is why the government-supported, best-established and largest system of private education in Pakistan is grounded in the work of that influential inner-life educationalist, Montessori. The SLS Montessori & School, with its "Seek the Light & Spread it" manifesto – facing a traditional Islamic school in Islamabad, a school belonging to the AIMS Education System, whose manifesto is 'Learning with Faith'.

At least in the present context, it is not my job to provide suggestions for policy makers, let alone offer concrete proposals. It is my job, though, to explore what inner-life spirituality has to offer. The sacralization of subjectivity: a kind of 'cult' for the self-absorbed and absorbing, a route to self-fulfilment and happiness, a way of propagating or vitalizing the ethic of humanity to find a way within the multi-religious...? Are government agencies getting it right, or will social significance always remain minimal? And recalling the quotation from Shakespeare which appears in the preface to this volume, even if social impact is insignificant, do we so to speak find a way of cheering Hamlet?

Conceptualizing New Age Spiritualities of Life

To contextualize the volume, and to alert the reader to complementary reading, I provide a brief list of some of the most relevant ways in which 'alternative spiritualities' have been conceptualized by contemporary academics. In alphabetical order, Michael Brown (1997), North American culture; Steve Bruce (2002), secularity; Colin Campbell (2007), eastern themes; Jeremy Carrette and Richard King (2005), capitalism; Andre Droogers (2007), Kim Knibbe (2007) and Peter Versteeg (2007), Christian spirituality; Wouter Hanegraaff (1998), western esotericism; Paul Heelas, life; James Herrick (2003), enlightenment liberal Christianity; Dick Houtman and Peter Mascini (2002), individualization; Joel Kovel (1999), liberation; Gordon Lynch (2007), progressive pan(en)theism; Christopher Partridge (2004, 2005), occulture; Wade Clark Roof (1999), baby boomers; Leigh Schmidt (2006), leftist American religious liberalism; Robert Solomon (2002), emotional engagement; David Tacey (2004), spirituality; Charles Taylor (2002), the subjective turn, 'a secular age' (2007); Mark C. Taylor (1992), art; Steven Tipton (1982), ethicality Philip Tovey, John Chatwin and Alex Broom (2007) and Jennifer Barraclough (2001), CAM; Robert Wuthnow (1998), spiritual trends. Bar 'life' (perhaps!), I agree and disagree with much of this literature. To my regret, I did not read an additional key publication, Philip Wexler's *Mystical Society. An Emerging Social Vision* (2000), until completing what follows. His volume is brimming with ideas to do with the meaning of the new spirituality for daily life and education (and social theory), and will be invaluable for the book which I am currently writing: *Expressive Life* (2008a).

On the grounds that it is always useful to locate publications within the extant literature, the most relevant of the above is Jeremy Carrette and Richard King's spirited $elling Spirituality. The Silent Takeover of Religion (2005). Spiritualities are taken to fall along a spectrum running from 'revolutionary or anti-capitalist spiritualities' to 'business-ethics/reformist spiritualities' (providing ethical guidance within capitalism) to 'individualistic/consumeristic spiritualities', then to 'capitalist spiritualities' (providing means to wealth creation) (pp. 17–21). There is a great deal to be said for this spectrum (Heelas, 1996a). There is even more to be said for Carrette and King's politics: their argument that 'engaged spiritualities' have a very considerable amount of work to do in western (and other) contexts to challenge or resist neoliberal consumer and corporate capitalism (see, for example, pp. 169–82). However, there is considerably less to be said for their claims of the kind, 'Privatized spirituality emerges... as the new *cultural prozac* bringing transitory feelings of ecstatic happiness and thoughts of self-affirmation, but never addressing sufficiently the underlying problem of social isolation and injustice' (p. 77; their emphasis). Maybe not 'sufficiently' (for what would sufficiently be?). But among other things I shall be arguing that 'cultural prozac' is not the be-all and end-all of 'privatized spirituality', not least yoga.

Contextualizing on a broader scale, a significant amount has been written on the relationship between humanistic, expressivistic and subjective wellbeing values/experiences on the one hand, and the market economy/capitalism on the other. The 'good society' debate is flourishing. Together with publications referred to in what follows (and much else besides), Robert Lane's *The Loss of Happiness in Market Democracies* (2000) is well worthy of consideration. So is Amitai Etzioni's *The New Golden Rule. The Community and Morality in a Democratic Society* (1998), a volume of particular note in that it explores the values required for social interactions of a kind which combine with the exercise of autonomy.

Narrowing down the contextualization, it is probably fair to say that James Beckford is one of the few 'critical edge' academics to have drawn attention to what holistic activities can *contribute* to the quality-cum-ethicality of life. He is also one of the first academics in Britain to have identified and emphasized the theme of the holistic (Beckford, 1984; Hedges and Beckford, 2000).

Immanent frames and the vitality of the contemporary study of spiritualities of life

Steven Tipton's *Getting Saved from the Sixties* (1982) remains the touchstone against which all subsequent studies of 'the immanence' of alternative spiritualities have to be gauged – despite the fact that Wade Clark Roof and Robert Wuthnow have also made invaluable contributions. However, it very much looks as though a research era is now emerging which will add up to at least an approximation of the great days of Durkheim, Simmel and Weber; which will be much more in the spirit of the 'immanence-life' themes of Simmel rather than the emphasis on transcendent theism of Durkheim and Weber.

Thus a major theme of Mark C. Taylor's *After God* (2007) is encapsulated in the lines, 'After God – art; after art – life' (p. 345), life being understood holistically in the here-and-now. Minimally, the theme 'to be is to be connected' (p. 313) is to reject stronger, 'wholly other' forms of transcendence. Similarly emphasizing the increasing salience of 'the immanent' in the culture and academy, Robert Bellah's *summa*, *Religion in Human Evolution: From the Paleolithic to the Axial Age*, is nearing completion. Then there is Charles Taylor's magisterial publication, *A Secular Age* (2007). In accord with the Latin *in manere*, 'to remain within', but without monism or anything akin to it, the primary sense of 'the immanent frame' refers to the secular; that which 'constitutes a "natural" order, to be contrasted to a "supernatural one," an "immanent" world, over against a possible "transcendent" one' (p. 542; and see p. 594). Taylor also argues, though, that for a variety of reasons some tend to deal with the restrictions of the immanent by seeking the transcendent. Accordingly, there are 'a number of middle positions, which have drawn from both sides' (p. 595). Arguably, though, Taylor rather downplays another form of immanence – that 'God within' which is pretty much all that is left as Christianity (in particular) detraditionalizes; what is left of the immanent which was once closely bound up with, 'descended from', the transcendent (Heelas and Houtman, forthcoming). Equally arguably, Taylor also rather downplays 'Holy Spirit' forms of transcendent theism, especially those forms where the indwelling Holy Spirit becomes relatively divorced from its traditionalized setting to become quite strongly 'immanentized'. Then there is 'dual source' spirituality, anchored in both the transcendent and the inherently 'within' (Heelas, forthcoming). Furthermore, I'm pretty certain that Taylor underestimates the 'functional' significance of another aspect of the 'immanent frame'. Directing criticism at myself, the argument is that spiritual 'immanence' of the inner-life variety does relatively little to cater for the aspiration of going 'beyond ordinary human flourishing' (p. 510). Whatever the truth of this – and I shall be arguing to the contrary – the overall virtue of the Taylor, Bellah, Mark Taylor triumvirate is the attention being paid to 'immanent (and life-inherent) frames': the kind of attention which is called for by significant religio-cultural developments. The immanent frame has come into focus. Whether it be the secular aspect, Taylor's 'middle way', the immanence of 'post-Christian' loss of transcendent theism, the immanence of some forms of Holy Spirit religion, the (partial) immanence of the 'dual source', or the 'immanence' of ('birthright') spiritualities of life, numerical (etc.) significance is very considerable. Studying these frames and – of course – their interplays, we are in for an exciting time! With the foci they provide, the frames are great to think with.

In Britain, what might be thought of as the postwar wave of sociologists of religion – most noticeably Eileen Barker, James Beckford, Grace Davie, David Martin, Bernice Martin and Bryan Wilson – have largely applied their well-honed expertise to the sociology of *religion* (including new religious movements). Together with myself (if I may be permitted to say so), Steve Bruce, Colin Campbell, Don Cupitt – whose *Taking Leave of God* (2001, orig. 1980), and subsequent volumes, have done much to illuminate *life*-freedoms (pp. xiv–xviii) – and, more recently, Gordon Lynch, are, I suppose, rather exceptional in devoting considerable attention, over the years, to matters New Age. The 'immanent' has come into focus on this side of the Atlantic, too. Unfortunately, there is something of a generation gap between those scholars, like Campbell, who have been studying what he calls the monistic, and younger (post-doctorate, etc.) researchers. But perhaps this is not such a worry. If Suha Taji-Farouki's ground-breaking *Beshara and Ibn 'Arabi: A Movement of Sufi Spirituality in the Modern World* (2007) is anything to go by, the future of the study of 'the immanent' by scholars in Britain looks most promising.

Part I

Portraying Spiritualities of Life

Chapter 1

From the Romantics: The Repertoire

The ground-concept is life. (M. H. Abrams, 1973, p. 431)

… *the spirit of life.* (Wordsworth, Preface to the 1798 edition of the Lyrical Ballads)

Life in the spirit of love. (Hilma af Klint)

… *a way of living life itself.* (Georg Simmel, 1997, p. 21)

Grow into Life. (Flyer for a Kendal psychodrama group)

The New Age movements represent several very different dynamics, but they thread together to communicate the same message: there is an invisible and inner dimension to all life – cellular, human and cosmic. The most exciting work in the world is to explore this inner reality. (William Bloom, 1991, p. xvi)

The Core Repertoire

The expression 'spiritualities of life' refers to all those 'teachings' and practices which locate spirituality within the depths of life. Spirituality is identified with life-itself, the agency which sustains life; spirituality is found within the depths of subjective-life, our most valued experiences of what it is to be alive. In all its forms, spiritualities *of* life can be contrasted with those varieties of spirituality which operate from beyond whatever life in this world has to offer, thereby serving as spiritualities *for* life.

Bearing in mind the confusion that currently reigns over the meaning of the term 'spirituality', let alone attempting to distinguish between different forms of spirituality, the aim of this historically informed chapter is to arrive at a clear idea as possible of the expression 'spiritualities of life', and to show how it differs from other forms of spirituality or spirituality-cum-religion. This paves the way for addressing the matter of consumption. When appropriate, points made now are reactivated and developed later in the volume.

Thinking of the meaning of the expression 'holistic spiritualities of life', my own 'realization' of the key term, 'life', remains vividly etched in my mind. For a number of years leading up to 1998 I had been content with the expression 'Self-spirituality', even 'New Age'. Early in 1998, however, I was waiting for a flight at Schiphol airport, reading Martin Goodman's *In Search of the Divine Mother. The Mystery of Mother Meera* (1998) – a volume about Goodman's encounter with a 'mystic' from Tamil Nardu, resident in southern Germany. Arriving at page 216, I read of 'the forces of life'; of the 'current of life'. On the same page, I came to the passage which runs,

> Slowly, against my resistance, I was brought back into connection with what I call the divine but what is really the essence of living. Slowly, I was brought to see that what is so is so. There is one force that connects all life, that is all life. (Goodman, 1998, p. 216)

These lines triggered a eureka moment. 'Life' is *the* term, not 'Self-spirituality', with its connotations of the self-obsessed. 'Life' is what lies at the heart of the so-called 'New Age movement'; the 'life' of so-called 'alternative spiritualities' is what provides the crucial link with the greatest, the most fundamental of all our cultural values – life-itself and the fulfilled experiential life. Reflecting upon the eureka moment as I flew back to Manchester, I became more and more convinced of what had in fact long been staring me in the face – that the term was perfect for the job. I thought of all the New Age publications with the term in their titles, for example Count Hermann Keyserling's *The Art of Life* (1937); I thought of the massage outlet I had just walked past at Schiphol, namely 'Back to Life'; I recalled what I had read of the Romantics, not least Wordsworth's 'the spirit of life'; I appreciated the significance of what I had quoted in *The New Age Movement* (1996a), namely William Bloom's 'All life – all existence – is the manifestation of Spirit, of the Unknowable, of that supreme consciousness known by many different names in many different cultures' (p. 225). By the time I arrived home, I had come to the conclusion that the key to making sense of a very great deal of the 'alternative' sphere lay with the simple equation *life = spirituality = life = spirituality*, *when* this conjunction is taken to *be* at the heart of what it is to live *in* the here and now. My vocabulary changed: from 'Self-spirituality' to 'inner-life spirituality', 'spiritualities of life' or (for the sake of publishers), '*New Age* spiritualities of life', for example. (Given terminological controversies, this last must be emphasized.)

Seeking to test this realization, I first turned back to the Romantics – in particular M. H. Abrams' classic, *Natural Supernaturalism* (1973). Having drawn attention to 'the high Romantic words', namely 'life, love, liberty, hope, and joy', Abrams continues:

> The ground-concept is life. Life is itself the highest good, the residence and measure of other goods, and the generator of the controlling categories of Romantic thought... Life is the premise and paradigm for what is most innovative and distinctive in Romantic thinkers. Hence their vitalism: the celebration of that which lives, moves, and evolves by an internal energy, over whatever is lifeless, inert, and unchanging. (1973, p. 431)

Alongside other Romantics, Hegel's 'Only the living, that which is spirit, sets its own self in motion and develops' is then referred to by Abrams (p. 432).

I then turned to the nineteenth-century, predominantly Germanic, popular romanticisms of healing, health, nature and education; the counter-cultural 1960s (which bear many resemblances to the applied romanticisms of the nineteenth century); the seminar spirituality of the 1970s and 1980s (of which est is the most famous); and the beliefs and activities found today: the wellbeing spirituality of the purchasing culture of high street shops, spirituality in business, spirituality in education, spirituality in CAM, spirituality in mainstream healthcare, and so on.

Notwithstanding the fact that the language of 'life' – of inner-life spirituality or spiritualities of life – has rarely been given prominence in the academic literature on the history of 'alternative spiritualities' and their contemporary manifestations, I became convinced that the 'life' epiphany at the airport was justified. For whatever the differences between the ways in which 'alternative' spirituality has been manifested during and since the Romantic Movement, the enduring refrain is that spirituality lies at the heart of life *in* the here-and-now. For participants, spirituality *is* life-itself, the 'life-force' or 'energy' which flows through all human life (and much else besides), which sustains life, and which, when experienced, brings all of life 'alive'. For participants, spirituality *is* the truth of subjective-life, the truth of expressivity, love, harmony, vibrant health, agency; the essential truths *of* what it is to *be* alive. And granted the importance of holism, especially today, spirituality ultimately *belongs to* – more accurately, *should be enabled to flow through* – the mind-body nexus. Hence the (current) appropriateness of the term 'mind-body-spirituality' or 'holistic spiritualities of life'.[1]

Spiritualities of life can readily be distinguished from spiritualities associated with the God of transcendent theism. Quoting from *Webster's New International Dictionary of the English Language*, Charles Hartshorne's (1987) characterization of 'transcend' runs, 'The term is used of "the relation of God to the universe of physical things and finite spirits, as being... in essential nature, prior to it, exalted above it, and having real being apart from it"' (p. 16). As for theism, Robert Wuthnow's (1976) characterization of a theistic worldview is one which involves 'an understanding of life that identifies God as the agent who governs life. God is assumed to have a purpose for each person's life' (pp. 3–4). Accordingly, transcendent theism involves a God who is essentially located beyond this world, acting upon this world and the life within it. The spiritualities of transcendent theism are spiritualities *for* life. The spirituality of experiencing the Godhead itself, typical of more God-focused paths (including the path of many mystics), serves *to* transform life; the spirituality of the Holy Spirit, most pronounced in more charismatic or Pentecostal paths, is a spirituality which emanates from the transcendent realm *to* inform life in this world; the spirituality of obeying the will of God, typical of more conservative religions of the text, serves *to* direct life in this world.

The contrast, then, is between spiritualities *for* life and spiritualities *of* life. Fundamentally, the God of transcendent theism is not *of* the world of the here-and-now. ('My kingdom is not of this world': John 18: 36.) Remove the God of transcendent theism, and Christianity – as it is widely understood – collapses. As Caryl Matrisciana (1985) puts it, 'Without Him there is no spirituality' (p. 184). Remove the God of transcendent theism, and spiritualities of life continue much as, if not entirely as, before. Quite simply, when spirituality emanates from the depths of life within the here-and-now, with the inner realm of life serving as *the* source of significance and authority, the realm of transcendent theism does not enter into the monistic ontology.[2]

Going further into the contrast, the God of transcendent theism is revealed, put into operation, in this world by way of tradition-informed or tradition-rendered religion and spirituality. As *the* source of truth and authority, God is put into practice by renderings of the sacred which transpose *the* source into human affairs. Religion-cum-spirituality is thus of a *life-as* nature. For the adherent, what matters is obeying *the* source. To strive to live one's life as a good Christian is to strive to conform to what has been laid down from on High. And it is this *conformity* – ultimately to the 'life' of the God of transcendent theism – which generates a crucial disjuncture with inner-life spirituality.

Leaving to one side for the moment holistic versions of inner-life spirituality where the whole is more than the sum of the parts, with the whole thereby functioning with transcendent, totalized supra-self authority, inner-life spiritualities are very much bound up with the theme of transforming the quality of the *unique* life of the person. When spirituality *is* experienced as one's true, essential self, when spirituality *is* experienced as flowing through other aspects of one's life, it can but only serve to cater for one's distinctive, *singular* life. Clearly, uniqueness – and the freedom which is required to develop and express one's uniqueness – is attacked if one has to conform to an order which is not of one's making. In short, life as conformism prevents inner-life spirituality from doing its job, the reverse side of the coin being that inner-life uniqueness throws various spanners into the operation of transcendent theism.

Durkheim (1971) found it necessary to distinguish his 'social' definition of religion as 'a unified system of beliefs and practices relative to sacred things' from another form of 'religion' (as he called it), one 'which would consist entirely in internal and subjective states, and which would be constructed freely by each of us' (p. 47). The *ruach* ('spirit') of the Old Testament *gives* life and animation rather than being the same as this-worldly life-itself. Jesus' 'I am' pronouncements, most famously '*I* am *the* way, *the* truth and *the* life' (my emphases), are far removed from Romantic Georg Simmel's (1997) insistence that '*We* are life in its immediacy' (p. 24; emphasis provided). The spirituality of 'God's Way Is the Way' certainly need not be the same as the spirituality of 'My Way'. 'Surrendering' to the authority and power of the Holy Spirit clearly differs from the egalitarianism found between selves who are at heart equally spiritual. 'Aspiring to Higher things' is different from 'getting in tune with what lies within'. The expressions 'Let the spirit take you' or 'May be spirit be with you' mean one thing when the theistically grounded Holy Spirit is at issue, another when the spirit is 'your' spirit and the 'relationship' is utterly egalitarian. Spirit possession from 'on High' is not the same as from within or from another 'level' source. Being directed or instructed by a transcendent spiritual being (which might have been 'transposed' from life in this world) is one thing; interacting with spiritual beings in much the same way as interacting with (human) spiritual practitioners is another.

Faith and belief are not the same as experience and veridical or 'inner' knowledge. Faith in the texts of traditions is very different from treating the past by way of the present to liberate the future. The formulation 'For the best psychiatrist in town, talk to god. He knows you better than anyone' (New Year card from India) means one thing for those who are 'talking' to a theistic God, another to those who are having an internal conversation within themselves. 'Life' dependent on the sacrality of another is not the same as 'life' which is ours and ours alone. Chesterton's (1909) 'Insisting that God is inside man, man is always inside himself. By insisting that God transcends man, man has transcended himself' (p. 248) is clearly very different from the rhetorical line of a Zen poem, 'If you do not get it from yourself, where will you go for it?' Being true to 'oneself' by being faithful and obeying (or 'having') the will of God is very different from what Charles Taylor (1991) calls the 'ethic of authenticity', an ethic where 'Being true to myself means being true to my own originality...something only I can articulate and discover' (p. 29). Finding *the* Truth of the transcendent *for* oneself is not the same as finding *what* is true *about* oneself. With Truth differing between the different *formalized* traditions of transcendent theism, Truth (including the Truth of life) is *exclusivistic*; with Truth *experienced* by way of the spirituality at the heart of all (human) life, Truth is *inclusivistic*. In a nutshell, the hierarchical dualism of the spiritualities of transcendent theism contrasts with the egalitarian, monistic holism of spiritualities of the unique life; the sanctity of life deriving from the God of Catholicism contrasts with the sanctity of life *per se*; finding life within life, the self-life, the living life, contrasts with finding the true life through what often amounts to the scripted life of scripture. With Abrams' 'Life is itself the highest good, the residence and measure of other goods' in mind, when 'goods' do not measure up to what life has to offer, the Romantic route goes within. Denying that life within this world 'is itself the highest good', the Christian route is to apply the 'measure' of the requirements of tradition to go beyond human life as such. And above all – authority over life is very different from authority within life.

The heart of the matter

The heart of the matter lies with a spiritually informed fusion of expressivism (owing a great deal to Romanticism) and the ethic of humanity (owing a great deal to the Enlightenment and Romanticism). In the scholarly literature, these two ethicalities are almost always discussed in relative isolation from one another. On the one hand, discussion is of expressivist values and assumptions: the 'true' or 'authentic' self; the importance of breaking through disfigured aspects of selfhood to experience one's truth; the value of self-expression and creativity. On the other hand, discussion is of humanistic values: the 'ultimate' value ascribed to the value of humanity *per se*; the 'ultimate' value ascribed to life-itself; egalitarianism, respecting the other, and freedom. Furthermore, on the one hand the 'language' of expressivism is – well – expressive: the arts, poetry, music, the emotionally charged, the language, sentiments and sensibilities of the heart, the expressive ethicality of inner-wisdom. And it is perfectly true that one can readily 'be' expressivistic without paying much attention to humanistic values, by heeding the voice while being self-absorbed, greedy or selfish, for example. On the other hand, one can readily be humanistic without being expressivistic – by heeding legalistic renderings of the ethic for fear of being caught, for example, or by heeding the injunctions of liberal Christianity because of one's faith in what has been laid down by God. In addition, formulations of the ethic of humanity provided by national constitutions or international charters (etc.) relatively rarely incorporate subjectivities by according happiness (say) the status of a human right. (Increasingly, though, the 'rights' of subjectivities are entering the picture.)

Typically, the 'teachings' of spiritualities of life fuse the two by avoiding the individualism often associated with expressivism and the legalistic formalism often associated with the ethic of humanity. Hence their *expressivist humanism* or *humanistic expressivism*. Value clashes can occur between the values found *within* the expressive ethic and *within* the ethic of humanity (for instance, between freedom and equality), but the fusion as a whole is perfectly smooth. The 'freedom' component of the ethic of humanity fuses with self-expressive freedom. The 'egalitarian' component of the ethic of humanity fuses with the theme of spiritual unity, and thus equality. Egalitarian respect for the other permits self-expression. Most fundamentally, the idea of the 'true' self fuses with monistic humanity itself – which is where spirituality is found by participants: the depths of the subjective life (as emphasized by expressivists) and the universal life-itself (emphasized by humanists). The voice of ethical authority is *experienced* as coming from within: one can readily argue that this voice (or 'conscience', to mention a much more widely used term) derives from the internalization of formalistic renderings of the ethic of humanity (as taught at school, for example), but it is experienced as 'natural' – as expressive rather than as a socioculturally laid down 'ought'. The ethic of humanity is so to speak 'expressivized'. (One consequence of the fusion, it will be noted, is that humanism is recast away from that old enemy of religion and spirituality – the secular humanism of atheists.)

Near the beginning of this chapter, I offered an equation, *life = spirituality = life = spirituality*. Taken alone, it is of course too simplistic. Theistic, *life* of God-on-High believers could agree. Adding 'holistic' to the equation does not do the trick, for theistic believers could very well hold that the Holy Spirit serves to unify or harmonize the self. Adding the term 'nontheistic', in the sense of moving beyond transcendent theism, and used by Talcott Parsons (among others) in his discussion of the spirituality of the counter-culture (1978, p. 313), is a help. Perhaps even more fundamentally, though, the defining marks of inner-life spirituality – as the term is used in this volume – are 'the equal', 'the unique' and 'the interior'. This is a spirituality which serves the life of the unique person – which means it has to belong to the person, or flow from others on an *egalitarian* basis: rather than exercising superior authority from without to disrupt or take away from the unique. Putting it somewhat differently, the way to cultivate the unique life is considered to be for people to experience their 'own' spirituality – albeit an aspect of the universal – flowing through the intricacies of their own lives to 'transform' *them* – not by belonging to a 'whole' organized 'from the top', hierarchically. (And see Taylor, 1989, p. 376.)

Be yourself only better, as perfect as possible: when the strong tendency, in inner-life circles, is for the search for the 'better' to occur within the activities which emphasize expressivist-cum-human values. 'The essence of what you want *will* arrive', writes Gill Edwards (1993, p. 79) of her practice. What you want, though, is unlikely to be just any 'old' thing. It is much more likely to be informed by key 'inner' values or experiences. The equation is thus *I am what I truly am + I aim to become 'better' + in the way I 'know' to be good*: the search for the fulfilment of life taking place *in the context of expressivistic humanism, all understood spiritually*. 'Fuzzy'?

An *a priori* definition carving out what I want to carve out? Maybe there is *some* truth in this – but the characterization *is* much more significantly informed by what is clearly going on in the culture. To use jargon, the characterization is etic (conceptual) and emic (empirical).

In his analysis of the ethics of wellbeing, Richard Kraut (2007) argues that human beings flourish 'by developing properly and fully, that is, by growing, maturing, making full use of the potentialities, capacities, and faculties... they *naturally* have at an early stage of their existence' (p. 131; my emphasis). 'The elements in the life of the soul' (p. 137), to which he also refers, provide the basis for the good life, in both senses of the word (morally and psychologically). A Rousseauian-akin account, which conceives human nature in a way which elevates virtues like honesty, justice, respect, fulfilment and commensurate pleasures, whilst devaluing the pursuit of things like riches, fame and domination and the pleasures they bring. New Age spiritualities of life, we shall see, are often not far removed from this vision of wellbeing.

Keywords

Going deeper into what spiritualities of life are all about, keywords – signalling recurrent, prominent themes – are now briefly introduced. The illustrative material is drawn from a range of sources going back to the late eighteenth century, with particular attention being paid to the contemporary context.

To emphasize the obvious fact that 'spiritualities of life' are all about what it is to *be alive*, countless examples could be provided of the ways that the deceptively simple word 'life' is used in 'alternative' spirituality circles. 'Trust in the process of life', writes 'practising metaphysician' Gill Edwards in her book *Stepping into Magic. A New Approach to Everyday Life* (1993, p. 79). Robin Oxley (2001), also working in the Lake District, says, 'Your life is strewn with reminders and messages from you inner self that can be understood when you start to listen' (p. 13). 'Spirit-soul-matter are a Trinity synthesized by Life, which pervades them all', says a recent edition of the Alice Bailey-inspired *World Goodwill Newsletter*. To further set the tone, we can think of book titles – Larry Rosenberg's *Living in the Light of Death. On the Art of Being Truly Alive* (2000); the volume published by the Dalai Lama and Howard Cutler (1998), *The Art of Happiness. A Handbook for Living*; Don Cupitt's *The New Religion of Life in Everyday Speech* (1999). Most graphically, perhaps, we can think of Pierre in Tolstoy's *War and Peace* – 'Life is everything. Life is God... To love life is to love God'; or Wordsworth's 'spirit of life'. As for academics, Martin Ramstedt (2002) puts it aptly: 'the realization of life-affirming values'; 'life-affirming experiences of sacredness' (pp. 2, 4).

But what does 'life' mean? In general terms, two dimensions are found. In the spirit of D. H. Lawrence or Virginia Woolf (and many others of their time), one aspect has to do with *life-itself*. For the secularist, '*Life*... is the something which a man or any other organism loses at death' (C. S. Lewis, 1967, p. 269). Enriching this raw 'something', there is what Madeleine Bunting (2000) describes as the 'vital animating essence' (p. 22) – again, constitutive of life itself. Taking a step further, this is explicitly identified with spirituality. Belonging to our very nature, this is not something to be acquired through worship, or by being born again. It *is* the heart of life, the 'vital energy', 'universal energy', 'life-force', chi, ki, prana, yin and yang, the force of kundalini (Krishna, 1997), typically, the intangible 'inner spirituality' with which we are born (hence the expression I have coined, 'birthright spirituality'). The language of energy, of a force which *flows*, is widely abroad in the realms of spiritualities of life, as when Goodman (1998) refers to Mother Meera facilitating 'the free flow to the full force of life' (p. 37); E. P. Thompson (1997) notes that Coleridge 'postulat[ed] a God who was in some sense identifiable with "Nature's vast ever-acting Energy' (p. 138); 'The primary IMAGINATION I hold to be the living Power...the infinite I AM', as Coleridge wrote (cited by Taylor, 1989, p. 379).

Turning to the second dimension, 'life' has to do with *subjective-life*. Broadly speaking, the term 'subjective-life' refers to anything which enters into the realm of conscious experience: from unprovoked memories to only-to-be-expected bodily sensations; from internal conversations or the life of the mind, to raw passions or the life of the emotions; from judgements made on the basis of objective knowledge to judgements made on the basis of the promptings of conscience. Narrowing our focus, Wade Clark Roof (1999a) observes that 'spirituality' has come to be associated with 'yearnings for a reconstructed interior life' (p. 35). Flowing from the heart of life, spirituality is expressed as love, tranquillity, the wisdom of the 'inner voice', health, wellbeing, creativity, a sense of holistic integration; a plenitude of being. 'Occultist' Count Hilma af Klint (1862–1944) attached the words 'Life in the Spirit of Love' to her painting 'Rose' (wording which surely provides one of the best of renderings of subjective-life spirituality); Liza Fodor, who looks after a meditation centre in the Yorkshire Dales, says 'Love is God, God is Love'. Flowing from the core experiences of life, spirituality also comes to bear on negative subjectivities – depression, low self-esteem, isolation, for example. Rather than sacralizing these subjectivities *per se*, they are thereby 'transformed' or 'experienced in a new light'. Human nature is *perfect* in and of itself; so are the subjectivities it can interfuse. The contrast with Hobbesian or Freudian views of what lies within is stark. (See John Passmore's *The Perfectibility of Man* (1970) for a general discussion.)

The life-itself dimension only comes to matter when it enters into consciousness. To be a spiritual being, by nature, whilst not experiencing this spirituality, is of little value. Hence the importance attached to *activities* or *practices*. Ranging from yoga (relatively longstanding in western settings) to spiritual aromatherapy, these enable participants to make contact with, and thus *experience*, the spirituality of life-itself – thereby making a difference to their *subjective-lives*. In the graphic words of the founder of the School of Wisdom in Darmstadt (1920), Count Keyserling (1880–1946), 'In Life, as in music, the lived subjective element stands foremost...– a melody that is not played does not exist, nor a life that is not lived by a subject... Essentially, Spirit *is* personal and subjective' (1937, pp. 43–4). Practices: to experience spirituality and to put spirituality into practice. Practices: not taken to 'construct' the 'truth' of what we are through 'laid-down' performance (as the likes of Foucault would have it), but experienced as *revealing* the truths of life to *create* life-with-a-difference (as the Romantics would have it).

With activities enabling participants to experience spirituality flowing through their lives – for many, through all lives in nature – spiritualities of life are *holistic*. Albeit in various ways, once experienced inner-life spirituality is *always* held to enter into other aspects of what it is to be in the world – a consideration which serves to distinguish this form of spirituality from dualistic Gnosticism. Schiller's 'transmutative force', he 'felt', heals the 'rift between the world and the spirit' (cited by Hinderer and Dahlstrom, 1998, p. x). Turning to holism and personal life, the widely used expression of contemporary culture, 'mind-body-spirit', serves to indicate the importance attached to bringing together the various dimensions of personal life. To draw on interviews which took place during the Kendal Project,[3] yoga teacher Gill Green says, 'What I'm aiming for really is a union between body, mind and spirit; to make people feel more integrated'; kinesiologist Jan Ford Batey talks of 'dealing with emotional, mental, physical and spiritual aspects of the whole being'; astrologer Helen Williams says, 'If you've got a sense of all the bits of you and how they can be integrated together, you can actually move through and grow'; yoga practitioner Celia Hunter-Wetenhall talks of the importance of 'weaving in the spiritual element, the relationship between the mind and the body and the spirit'; and Eliza Forder, who runs a meditation centre, seeks 'to feel at one'. To give another example, this time from an editorial, 'Spirituality Defined', for the magazine *Women in Action* (1996), 'spirituality *is* the integration of our being'. Thinking back over the last two hundred or so years, dualistic themes ('lower' v. 'higher' self, for example) have often been in greater prominence – although as we shall see shortly, this does not mean that the theme of union has not also been prominent.

The holistic thrust of subjective-life spirituality is intimately bound up with the importance widely attached to healing. Whether it be among CAM spiritual practitioners (providing homeopathy or reflexology, for example), or nurses and counsellors who have adopted the mind-body-spirituality approach, an important goal is to enable people to deal with their suffering. 'Dis-ease', to use contemporary parlance, is to be 'out of balance'. It is to be the victim of those stresses, strains, bad habits, 'blocks', and negative emotions generated by the rush or isolation of life in the mainstream of society. The outcome of living without spirituality, dis-ease is tackled by cultivating the spiritual dimension of life; by tapping into the personal vitality and energy which lies deep within. As a Kendal homeopath says, 'I pick the right remedies'; 'the homeopath is only the instrument'; the healing comes from 'you'.

Over the last two hundred or so years, spiritualities of life have sometimes focused on healing, in the sense of curing, physical complaints – complaints due to 'externals' disrupting life-itself. Today, the term 'healing' is most frequently used in connection with 'ill-being'. That is to say, it is used in connection with dealing with those 'issues' or complaints which prevent people from experiencing all that their *subjective wellbeing* is capable of achieving. Above all, the holistic milieu of Kendal and environs – where around

100 spiritual practitioners provided mind-body-spirit activities during the autumn of 2001 – is a subjective wellbeing zone. With questionnaire respondents reporting above-national average satisfaction with their health, participants are engaging with activities which generally focus on improving the *quality* of their 'health'. A reiki practitioner, for example, offers an activity which 'energizes, relaxes, and promotes a feeling of wellbeing'. And it is not without significance that one of the best-known figures in the holistic world today, Deepak Chopra, has established The Chopra Centre for Well Being.

Together with healing and wellbeing, another widely encountered theme in subjective-life spirituality circles involves *love*. Love is 'the characteristic *par excellence* of the spiritual person', as Clive Beck puts it (1986, p. 150). One might recall Klint's arresting 'Life in the Spirit of Love'. Countless more illustrations could be provided of the way in which love is valued as a spiritually suffused experience of the good life, including what the austere Talcott Parsons (1978) wrote of the counter-culture of the sixties: 'The most salient feature ... is the emergence of a movement that resembles early Christianity in its emphasis on the theme of love' (p. 313). More recently, John and Eliza Forder (Eliza's meditation centre is in Dent, not far from Kendal) cite a Yorkshire life-mystic, Richard Rolle (1290–1349): 'Love is indeed a transforming force, diffusive and binding' (Fodor and Fodor, 1995, p. 51).

Closely bound up with love, spiritualities of life generally incorporate *humanistic values* – values that are experienced as 'natural', flowing from the inner life. In not dissimilar vein to Rousseau, Tennessee folk singer Nanci Griffith (2001) says, 'I'm into everything that's about *the goodness of humanity*, spiritually' (my emphasis). Thinking of the Kendal Project, we found that a considerable number of those active in the realm of spiritualities of life equate spirituality with 'being a decent and caring person'. To give another example, David Bell, the Chief Inspector of Schools of England and Wales, has humanistic values in mind when he notes that 'spirituality has come into its own as encapsulating those very qualities that make us human' (cited by Smithers, 2004). Going back in time, Schiller might have been more theistically inclined than many of his peers, but his 'theism' was undoubtedly considerably more egalitarian than hierarchical: 'The destiny of man is to be God's peer' (Hinderer and Dahlstrom, 1998, p. x). From Schiller's 'Ode to Joy', that paean to an expressivist, quasi-theistic rendering of the ethic of humanity, and gloriously put to music by Beethoven:

> Joy, bright spark of divinity,
> Daughter of Elysium,
> Fire-inspired we tread
> Thy sanctuary.
> Thy magic power reunites
> All that custom has divided,
> All men become brothers
> Under the sway of thy gentle wings.

And Wordsworth emphatically announced his commitment to (counter-cultural) *egalitarianism* when he wrote, 'I am of that odious class of men called democrats' (cited by Thompson, 1997, p. 75).

'Loving', 'caring', 'being decent', 'respecting others', 'being compassionate, forgiving and sensitive', 'being companionable', or, to use a rather old-fashioned expression, 'showing fraternity': terms like these show the extent to which spiritualities of life involve *affective, expressive relationality*. William James (1960) famously wrote of 'the feelings, acts, and experiences of *individual* men in their *solitude*, so far as they apprehend themselves to stand in relation to whatever they may consider the divine' (p. 50; my emphases). This obscures the fact that during the last two hundred or so years a great deal has revolved around relational activities. The popular image of the Romantic as a 'wandering exile' does not do justice to the fact that the Romantics were too relational, too intent on the unitary quest, too informed by experiences of the unitary within for this characterization *per se*. One can think of all those Romantics with their deep, 'holistic' friendships; for instance, Coleridge, Southey and de Quincey spending time with the Wordsworths at their cottage in the Lakes. And affective relationality was frequently experienced with nature. One can think of Byron's

> I live not in myself, but I become
> Portion of that around me; and to me
> High mountains are a feeling.

or Wordsworth's

> To every natural form, rock, fruit and flower
> Even the loose stones that cover the highway,
> I give a moral life; I saw them feel,
> Or linked them to some feeling

More recently, one can think of the spiritual communes of the sixties. Then there is Star Wars and 'The force linking everybody'. Today, one can think of the relationality, the close encounters found within mind-body-spirit circles (Heelas and Woodhead, 2005, pp. 98–107). As our 2000–2 research in Kendal shows, a great many of those participating in holistic activities attach very great significance to the importance of working with others – in small groups or on a one-to-one basis – in order to 'grow' by way of relational experiences (what Leder (1990) calls 'co-feelings'; what is perhaps better described as 'feeling with'). Among other factors, people participate because they have 'issues' in their lives – issues which they cannot deal with by themselves or during their everyday life with spouses, relatives or friends; people participate because they appreciate that they need to work with others in order to progress. Furthermore, spiritualities of life are often found in *person-centred* – and thus relational – contexts within the mainstream of society: for example, child-centred classrooms in primary schools; patient-centred nursing (most especially in hospices); and client-centred spas or health and fitness centres.

The value attached to experiencing or developing relationships is grounded in a closely linked characteristic of spiritualities of life – the *unitary* nature of inner-life spirituality. The spirituality or life force which flows through all that lives is essentially the same. It is Coleridge's 'benevolent world-spirit' (Thompson, 1997, p. 137). Wordsworthian life-itself *is* life-itself, wherever it is found. As Taylor (1989) says of contemporary expressivism, 'A cosmic dimension intrudes to the extent that we see the source not just as nature in us but as linked with the larger current of life or being, as most of the great writers did in the Romantic period' (p. 377) – to which it can be added that for many the 'source' is explicitly sacred and utterly egalitarian. Then there is Edward Carpenter, coining the expression 'cosmic consciousness'. Going further back to Wordsworth himself,

> O'er the wide earth, on mountain and on plain
> Dwells in the affects and the soul of man
> A Godhead, like the universal PAN;
> But more exalted.

To provide a key finding from the Kendal Project, 82.4 per cent of respondents to the questionnaire distributed to those participating in holistic, mind-body-spirituality activities say that 'some sort of spirit or life force pervades all that lives'. 'Others', especially 'other' people, are valued as 'manifestations' of the spiritual whole. In contradistinction to Joseph de Maistre's famous observation – 'I have seen in my time Frenchmen, Italians and Russians. I have known, thanks to Montesquieu, that one may be a Persian, but as for *Man*, I declare that I have never met him in my life; if he exists it is without my knowledge' (cited by Leach, 1982, p. 56) – Tennyson wrote, 'I am part of all that I have met' ('Ulysses'). And today one encounters expressions like 'There are no strangers in the New Age'. Going a little back in time, when seminar spirituality was much more popular than it is today, Steven Tipton (1983) writes of est:

> *est* professes a[n]...ethic of compassionate service based on the monistic identification of each individual with every other by reference to the universal 'being' they all share. 'Transformation of Self as humanity' will make the world work. (pp. 280–1)

And no doubt inspired by the counter-culture of the 1960s and its immediate descendents, Marilyn Ferguson (1982) says,

> All souls are one. Each is a spark from the original soul, and this soul is inherent in all souls...You are joined to a great Self...And because that Self is inclusive, you are joined to all others. (p. 418)

At heart we are all the same. At the same time spiritualities of life emphasize the value of the *unique*. Rousseau, that pivotal figure of the cultural history of the turn to subjective-life, begins his *Confessions* (completed 1765; first published 1781) with the lines,

> I have resolved on an enterprise which has no precedent, and which, once complete, will have no imitator. My purpose is to display to my kind a portrait in every way true to nature, and the man I shall portray will be myself.
>
> Simply myself. I know my own heart and understand my fellow man. But I am unlike any one I have ever met; I will even venture to say that I am like no one in the whole world. I may be no better, but at least I am different. (1954, p. 17)

Having lived a life which no one else has experienced, one's subjective-life is unique. The more experiences one has, not least those through relationships, the more unique one becomes. Embedded within the person, spirituality caters for this often 'ego' uniqueness. The spirituality 'itself' might be universal. But since it 'flows' through the specific life-experiences of each person, it comes to be experienced as one's 'own' spirituality; a spirituality of singularity. As Taylor (1989) makes the point, 'We are all called to live up to our originality... If nature is an intrinsic source, then each of us has to follow what is within; and this may be without precedent' (p. 376). Turning to the present, and a couple of interviews carried out during the Kendal Project, reiki practitioner Fay Bailey spoke of the spirituality which lies 'within us and *makes us* a person'; kinesiologist Jan Ford Batey of 'dealing with issues of all the content in life from that aspect, the core of the person, the essence of the person'. Then there is Ofsted (1994), the school inspection agency of England and Wales, an organization which defines spiritual development as relating 'to that aspect of inner life through which pupils acquire insights into *their* personal existence which are of enduring worth' (p. 86; my emphasis).

The value ascribed to singularity goes hand in glove with the value ascribed to *freedom*. One cannot live one's unique life if one has to conform to an established order. By definition, established orders specify roles, duties, and obligations which apply to categories of people, not the person *per se*. To conform means being the same as at least some others. To live 'out' one's unique life, to be 'true to oneself', means finding the freedom, the autonomy, to be oneself, to become oneself, to 'turn' into oneself, to live one's life to the full. Hence the importance attached to activities which enable participants to experience a sense of liberation. Not permanent liberation – for that is *very* rarely promised – but enough freedom from the conformist authority of established orders to enable participants to listen to their 'inner voice' or 'true self' to live their own lives; to exercise *self-responsibility*.

Catering for the experience of inner-directed freedom, activities are participant-centred – in contrast to relying on what Taylor (1989) calls 'models without' (p. 376). This means that activities (in particular) are (relatively) *detraditionalized*; more comprehensively, are (relatively) *de-externalized*. That is to say, rather than inculcating the truths of established orders – what Hegel (1988) called the 'positivity' of many forms of religion, in evidence when agency is 'posited' for the individual by religious institutions (p. 98) – activities are typically experienced as *resources*: resources which participants can draw upon to 'fulfil' their own lives; resources which can be used in ways which are geared to 'what works best' for the individual lives of participants; teachings as resources rather than dictations. As the website presentation of *Common Ground*, the most important Californian directory for people interested in the unfolding quest, puts it:

> There are undoubtedly as many paths to personal transformation as there are people. Which is why, for the past 25 years, *Common Ground* has been a directory rather than a guide or handbook. We're not trying to tell you what all these things are, let alone which is best for you. We're simply providing access to resources. Whether a resource is useful to your personal transformation is a matter of attunement. (Common Ground Online, 30 January, 2003)

Thinking of the Kendal Project, spiritual healer Celia Forestal says:

> With healing you are using spiritual energy, for the nature of it is spiritual. But I don't preach my spiritual views. In general, the less said about it the better. But if they ask me about that then we may get into a really interesting conversation.

And reiki practitioner Fay Bailey affirms, 'I'm not a leader or master, I'm there as a guide'.

The importance attached to experiencing what one's unique, 'free' life has to offer means that attention is focused on the *here-and-now* – the immediacy of the experiencing self. Life before birth or after death is not of especial concern. Rooted in the *super natural*, spiritualities of life bypass that supernatural realm which exists before and after life in this world. Celebrating the moment, one of the great classics of the sixties counter-culture was Ram Dass's *Be Here Now*. In negative vein, and with an eye on the inner-life spirituality which he saw around him, Chesterton (1909) poured scorn on Matthew Arnold's 'Enough we live' (p. 128). Given the huge value attached to *experience* of spirituality-cum-sensory 'input' within inner-life spiritual circles, it is not surprising to find equally significant value attached to living in the present, rather than diluting what the moment has to offer by overlaying it with the past or too much of the future. The imperative of the present, 'the spirit of presentism', encouraged by practitioners, and being neatly captured in the lines of a traditional poem: 'Exhaust the little moment, soon it dies / And be it gash or gold, it will never come / Again in this identical guise'. The uniqueness of each passing, idiosyncratic moment – not replicating the paradigmatic past as faithfully as possible in the manner aspired to, say, by devout, conservative Muslims in Pakistan. T. S. Eliot's lines from *East Coker* serve to express the significance of immediacy:

> The knowledge imposes a pattern, and falsifies,
> For the pattern is new in every moment
> And every moment is a new and shocking
> Valuation of all we have been.

Mention of the term 'supernatural' prompts attention to that central term, *super natural*. Probably a more accurate designation than 'meta-natural' or 'metaphysical', this is certainly more accurate than the use, in this context, of the highly misleading term 'supernatural' – a term best reserved to refer to what transcends life in the here-and-now. Whether it is the life of the human realm or of nature as a whole, the great majority of holistic participants would resist the idea that spiritualities of life are reducible to the physical world as such. These spiritualities are *natural* – but go beyond the 'nature' which lies within the orbit of scientific investigation: whether past, present or future.

As for that absolutely central (analytical) concept, *authority*, around which so much revolves, suffice it to say for the moment that authority is primarily taken to lie with the realm which can be *most* directly, immediately, experienced – the depths of one's nature. So long as relationships are egalitarian, the spiritually informed authority of others or of the natural world as a whole are also important, but generally not so important as the unmediated source. And finally, thinking of *truth*, the authority of experience – most critically, spiritually suffused experience – is the key. 'It is a little-known fact that truth cannot be memorized', writes Barry Long in his *Knowing Yourself* (1983):

> Truth has to be discovered now, from moment to moment. It is always fresh, always new, always there for the still, innocent mind that has experienced life without needing to hold on to what has gone. (Preface)

Differences Within the Recurrent

The keywords serve to identify themes which run through spiritualities of life since the late eighteenth century (and before). However useful these keywords might be, they must not be allowed to mask the very real differences which also exist. The seminar spirituality of the 1980s, for example, might have had holistic themes, but it was considerably more dualistic than the mind-body-spirituality which is popular today. Basic themes, basic similarities, get played out in several major developments or waves: the inner-life spirituality of the Romantic Movement and its more immediate successors, the counter-cultural spirituality of the sixties, the seminar spirituality which reigned during the 1980s, the prosperity spirituality which probably peaked during the same decade, and the holistic wellbeing spirituality of today.

To enrich the picture of what spiritualities of life are all about, to place contemporary mind-body-spirituality in historical context by showing how various elements derive from the past of the west, and to start reflecting on questions to do with consumption, these developments are now all-too-briefly introduced. By drawing attention to variations, I also aim to avoid the charge of being an essentialist; that spiritualities of life are *just* one thing – a charge which has been rather unfairly levelled against *The New Age Movement* volume (Heelas, 1996a).[4]

The inner-life spirituality of the Romantic Movement and its more immediate successors

How did the Romantics envisage the sacred? Generally speaking, they looked beyond traditional, theistic Christianity. Some rejected most, if not all, of traditional Christianity. Some simply pushed Christianity to one side, treating it as more or less irrelevant. And some worked with a highly romanticized form of Christianity (for example, many passages of the 'early' Schleiermacher's *On Religion*, 1958, pp. 49–50). Providing a summary of the Romantic Movement, Charles Taylor (1989) writes of

> the gradual fading of a believable notion of cosmic order, whose nature could be specified and understood independently of the realization/manifestation of the current of nature in our lives. The old order based on the ontic logos was no longer acceptable. (p. 380)

What did the Romantics find beyond the orthodoxies of the mainstream Christianity of their time? Abrams (1973) identifies a fundamental, widely shared theme – 'highly elaborated and sophisticated variations upon the Neoplatonic paradigm of a primal unity and goodness, an emanation into multiplicity which is *ipso facto* a lapse into evil and suffering, and a return to unity and goodness' (p. 169). Or again: 'The myth is that of primordial man as a cosmic androgyne, who has disintegrated into the material and bisexual world of alien and conflicting parts, yet retains the capacity for recovering his lost integrity' (p. 155). As it can also be put, the Romantics worked with a 'myth' of change from life as non-differentiated to life as differentiated to life as de-differentiated.

The 'fall' from the original state of unity and goodness results in suffering. Suffering, for the Romantics, largely deriving from the sociocultural world they inhabited, is due to the fragmentation of life – fragmentation which the Romantics specifically attributed to political factors (especially in divided Germanic countries), to all the dislocations caused by the industrial revolution (Blake's 'dark Satanic Mills' being a familar example), and to the Enlightenment, the emphasis attached to the autonomous, the exercise of the will by way of the exercise of reason seen as serving to sunder the self from the remainder of its qualities.

At the same time, the fall from the original state of unity and goodness provides the opportunity for people to achieve a *higher* state of being: one which is 'higher...not only because it preserves diversification and individuality, but also because, instead of being a condition which has merely been given to man, it is a condition which he must *earn by incessant striving* along an inclined circuitous path' (Abrams, 1973, p. 185; my emphasis). (When the going gets tough, the Romantics get going! – the theme of suffering as good for the soul not exactly being conducive to valuing the cocooned comforts of some of the forms of wellbeing found today.) The quest for 'unity' – which Abrams describes as being for 'a unitive relationship within a man, as well as between man and nature and between an individual and other men, which has been lost and will be found again' (p. 246); which Hugh Honour (1979) refers to as the 'Romantics extoll[ing] the perfect union of bodies and souls in a love at once physical and spiritual' (p. 305) – requires the challenges which life throws up. Or to refer to Mark Taylor's marvellous book, *Disfiguring* (1992), and his discussion of the impact of theosophy on artists like Kandinsky and Mondrian, 'the goal of theoesthetics is union with the Absolute or Real, which underlies or dwells within every person and all phenomena' (p. 52). An Absolute, it can be noted, which is universal – thereby requiring the 'disfiguring' of the particular, ultimately its erasure.

Paradise lost, paradise regained – biblical influences are obvious. However, the Romantics typically accorded creative agency to the serpent of Genesis, envisaging it as that 'saviour' which explains the biblical lines 'And the Lord God said, Behold, the man is become as one of us' (Genesis 3: 22; see Abrams, 1973). The sacralization of life – not the Fall of so much orthodox Christianity. More fundamentally, the difference from the orthodoxies of theistic Christianity lies with the ontology, priority, and value of the sacred as immanent. Hence Abrams' (1973) book title, *Natural Supernaturalism*. An immanent frame clearly seen in Herder's 'life reverberates to life' and 'The artist is become a creator God', Novalis' 'The heart is the key to the world and life', Holderlin's 'one unified, eternal glowing Life', and Coleridge's 'primary imagination' as the 'living Power' (respectively cited in Taylor, 1989, pp. 369, 378, 371, 386, 379). An immanence equally clearly seen in Wordsworth's characterization of the poet as the person 'who rejoices more than other men in the spirit of life that is in him' (Abrams, 1973, p. 433), with Abrams writing that for the Romantics, 'Love...expresses the confraternity of the one life shared not only with other men but also with a milieu in which man can feel fully at home' (p. 431).

The presence of the sacred within this world helps explain why the Romantics attached such value to *unique* subjective-life experience. Quite simply, if the key to a great deal of Romanticism lies with an immanentist ontology of 'life'-cum-sacrality, most especially the 'life' of the individual Romantic experiencing and transforming it by learning from experiences of disunity as well as 'through' others and nature, the key necessarily involves the agency, the 'work' of the unique person. Only I can experience, and transform, my life. Only I as an 'original' can be creative. No one else can experience my unique creativity for me; no one else can express it, in my life, for me. 'Every Romantic work of art is unique – the expression of the artist's own personal *living* experience', writes Honour (1979, p. 20; my emphasis); and every 'successful' work of art is a realization along the path to unity.

Spirituality of life themes are clearly apparent: life-itself as sacred, the sacralization of subjectivities, the holism (as we would say today), the emphasis on the unique. And the 'expressivism' – that expressivism which Taylor (2002) describes as 'the invention of the Romantic period in the late eighteenth century' (p. 81). From the time of Rousseau (1712–78) and Herder (1744–1803) to the First World War and later, artists, composers, life-philosophers, novelists, poets, and 'orientalists' like Friedrich Schlegel (who coined the expression 'the oriental renaissance' in 1808) served as 'creators' – inspired from within, including 'experiences' from and 'of' the east or of 'traditions' like shamanism, to bring *life* to life. All replete with expressivistic spiritualities of life. The Romantics ultimately lived their lives through their art or 'philosophy'; their art is the art of life. Writing about Byron, Charles Whibley (1920) notes: 'He could not detach his work from his experience. His poetry was but his life transmuted into another shape' (p. xiv). The Romantics practised their spirituality through their art or life-philosophy, often informing their utopian 'Genius' – that is, their experience of the creativities of the life-within – by 'reflecting' on nature, the Wye above Tintern Abbey inspiring and 'unifying' Wordsworth, for example. Some dwelt in artist villages or colonies (including Worpswede where Rilke lived); or places such as Ascona, itself attracting people like Herman Hesse – even, with profound ambivalence, Max Weber on at least one occasion.

Although the Romantics of the Romantic Movement were few in number, 'popular romanticism', or 'romanticism in practice', took root during the nineteenth century. The *Naturmenschen, Jugendbewegung* (with its *Wandervogel* branch) and quite probably much of the *Lebensreform* movements provide illustrations (charted by Thomas Nipperdey's (1988) historiography of 'vagrant religion' and see de Ras, 2008). Spiritualities of life entered into realms like health, education and agriculture. Probably the most significant concerns health applications: the spa, homeopathy, osteopathy and chiropractic, for example. Setting the temper, Christoph Wilhelm Hufeland (1762–1836), friend and personal physician of Goethe, Herder, Schiller and Weiland, and who also was acquainted with Hahnemann, Gall, Fichte, Hegel and Schelling, published *The Art of Prolonging Life* (translated into English in 1797) and *Das Makrobiotik. Die Kunst das Menschliche Leben zu Vertlangern* (Kant wrote his own commentary). Macrobiotics is presented as a 'science' based on the principles of natural laws, prolonging life via diet, exercise, lifestyle, fresh air, sunbathing, cleanliness, stimulating travel and meditation. Hufeland also wrote articles about acupuncture, crainoscopy, hydrotherapy and homeopathy. Talk was of 'metaphysical spirit'. Dwelling with homeopathy, 'founder' Samuel Hahnemann (1755–1843) published his 'definitive' edition of the *Organon of Medicine* in 1842, the *heilkunst* ('art of healing') being envisaged as informed by 'the spirit-like vital force (*dynamis*)' or 'the life-force itself' which operates holistically (1982, pp. 14, 76). 'In the state of health', we read, 'the spirit-like vital force (*dynamis*) animating the material human organism reigns in supreme sovereignty' (p. 14); 'The organism is the material instrument of life: but it is no more conceivable without life-giving, regulating, instinctively feeling *dynamis* than this *dynamis* is conceivable without the organism' (p. 20). (Such is life!)[5]

Then there are educational applications. One can think of Rousseau-inspired Johann Pestalozzi (1746–1827) and Friedrich Froebel (1782–1852). Zurich-born Pestalozzi's *How Gertrude Teaches Her Children* was first published in 1801, the 'Pestalozzi Method' coming to fruition in his school at Yverdon (established 1805). Immanentism is well in evidence: 'entrust it [education] to the eternal powers of nature herself, to the light which God has kindled and kept alive in the hearts of fathers and mothers, to the interests of parents who desire their children grow up in favour with God and with men' (Silber, 1965, p. 134). So is what today would be called child-centred holism – the education of all aspects of the child by equilibriating the three elements, 'hands', 'heart' and 'head'. 'As "a little seed…contains the design of the tree"', Pestalozzi frequently commented. Briefly mentioning Friedrich Froebel, influenced by Pestalozzi as well as by the Romantics themselves, in turn becoming considerably more influential, he published his *Education of Man* in 1826. The first kindergarten was established in 1839; the first kindergarten in Britain (Hampstead) in 1854. In his *Autobiography* (1903), Froebel clearly saw 'dogmatic' forms of Christianity as an impediment, politely but bluntly stating: 'the naturally trained child requires no definite Church forms' (2007, p. 74). For him, 'Nature' – which includes the nature of the child – is all about 'the unity of her inner working, of her effective force' (p. 76); the objective of 'self-culture' is to seek out 'innermost unity', 'the spiritual' (p. 107). Later, there are Rudolf Steiner (anthroposophy) and Maria Montessori (theosophy) – both influential in educational circles today (Waldorf schools, for example; Montessori in Pakistan).

By the time of the First World War, Romantic-inspired subjective-life spirituality had clearly made its presence felt, most noticeably, it appears, in Germany. In Germany, vitalist, life-philosopher-cum-sociologist Georg Simmel (1997, pp. 20, 24), Troeltsch (1960, p. 794) and Weber (see Robertson, 1978) were among those who noted the fact. In France, so too did Durkheim (1971, p. 47); and in England, Chesterton (1909). Just to mention a couple of specific indicators of (relative) popularity, one is provided by the success of *Bibby's Annual*, a 'glossy', up-market magazine, run by a theosophical magnate based in Liverpool, which tended to focus on the spirituality of nature; another by the fact that George Cadbury could refer to 'mind, body and spirit' in a letter he wrote to the Prime Minister in 1916, the context of use strongly suggesting that the term had become (relatively) common currency. Without going into matters any more in the present context, it is reasonable to say that by 1914 virtually all the major themes and many of the activities found today were in evidence, with most directly descended from the Romantic Movement. Most especially, the dualistic theme that sacrality lies within the depths of life, the 'profane' with malfunctioning social, cultural and traditional arrangements.[6]

Holistic, subjective *wellbeing* culture – to use parlance from the twenty-first century – was reasonably well established, especially in the realm of alternative healing, but also in educational circles. (Whilst the theme of interconnection was widely abroad, Smuts did not coin the term 'holism' until 1926.) Since the language of consumption has been applied to wellbeing mind-body-spirituality today, should the 'classical' Romantics and their more 'practical' successors be thought of accordingly? Regarding the classical Romantics, not many of us today would consider this to be a wise move (other, that is, than in connection with their daily shopping and the like). However, the matter is not as simple as all that. Byron (1974), for instance, wrote:

> The great object of life is Sensation – to feel that we exist – even though in pain – it is this 'craving void' which drives us to Gaming – to Battle – to Travel – to intemperate but keenly felt pursuits of every description whose principal attraction is the agitation inseparable from their *accomplishment*. (p. 109; my emphasis)

Although a certain amount hangs on the significance of the term 'accomplishment', I think it is fair to say that we here see consumeristic indicators of the Romantic Movement – aspects which Colin Campbell explores in *The Romantic Ethic and the Spirit of Modern Consumerism* (1987): a volume which argues that Romanticism, as 'a castle of Romantic dreams' (p. 227), has played a pivotal role in the construction of consumer culture. On the other hand, it can surely be argued that the expressive, creative, artistic, philosophical, poetic, 'life-*work*' which lies at the heart of the Romantic Movement does not belong to the register of consumption: an argument to do with 'work' and 'ends', among other things, which will be developed later.

Romanticism, classical or popular, has a great deal to do with what can be thought of as 'autonomous holism'. At the same time, there is the quest for the unitary. The Romantics 'all strove to unite radical autonomy and expressive unity' (Taylor, 1989, p. 385; and see p. 382); the unique with the universal; self-expression with self-dissolution. The tensions are obvious.[7] Despite the importance attached to the quest for the unitary, however, the Romantics generally attached too much value to the creativity of unique selfhood to go all that far along the path which leads to the dissolution of the self – their *own* lives – into the whole (the unitary largely 'existing' in their creative, artistic expressions). The same cannot be said of the main eruption of 'inner-life', 'expressivist' 'romanticism' after the First World War – that which took place in the years leading up to, and during, the Third Reich. For here we find the full flowering of the idea that the whole is greater than the sum of the parts, with individuals, their unique subjective-lives, conforming – perhaps even dissolving – accordingly.

Nazi spirituality

During the 1930s, German biologist Bernhard Durken wrote, 'We are presently experiencing a spiritual revolution of powerful proportions' (cited by Harrington, 1999, p. 177). Inspired by Romanticism, among other sources, that 'transmutation' of inner-life spirituality which so pervaded the intelligentsia, 'explorers' and power-men-as-God of the Third Reich, meant that Romantic spirituality developed with a distinctive emphasis (Mosse, 2003). Holistic – but with the whole being more than the sum of the parts – the spirituality functions with transcendent authority. The 'whole', that is the *Volk*, of inner-life was transposed from the life of any particular, unique individual (other than power-infused leaders like Himmler) to serve as a unitary realm (Harrington, 1999). Mind-body subsumed by land-the-unitary, an important role being played by the experienced 'depths' of the deeply familiar 'land/scape'. (Darre, the Minister of Agriculture, promoted the fusion of 'blood and soil'.) In a manner reminiscent of Hegel's 'The truth is the whole', the totalized, reified sum of all the truths of the inner-life constituents thus served in life-as, dictatorial fashion, encompassing the (dutiful, etc.) individual to mould and hold him or her (although fewer women were involved in the 'revolution') as a powerful expression *of* the unitary. The unique is sacrificed for the whole. A life-as rendering of subjective-life spirituality, we can say – and one which strongly emphasized subjective wellbeing culture and provisions: the cruises, the holiday camps, the sports and athletics, the breeding of absolutely perfect bodies, the 'education' of the body more than the mind (a theme of *Mein Kampf*), the model villages and townships, the quality-of-life work floor and office design, the plan to turn Poland into one large 'garden', the heritage industry (including the 'aesthetically' evocative construction of ancient monuments), and so on. 'Strength *through* Joy'; or in reality was it more to do with the consuming pleasures of a wellbeing culture, not *all* that different from what we find today? The title of Shelly Baronowski's book is *Strength Through Joy* (2004); the subtitle is *Consumerism and Mass Tourism in the Third Reich*. As Anne Harrington charts in her *Reenchanted Science. Holism in German Culture from Wilhelm II to Hitler* (1999), 'Romantic' mind-body-spirit-earth themes became increasingly widespread during interwar Germany. Of particular note, naturopathic and homeopathic approaches were developed to contribute to the 'New German Therapy' (p. 186). And given that yoga was practised at Himmler's Wewelsburg Castle, there is little doubt that it was practised elsewhere: especially for the more elitist to pursue the quest to become 'god-men'.

Holistic spiritualities of life, it appears, thrived. However, with so much emphasis on '*volkische* wholeness', 'the cosmos of life' (Harrington, 1999,

p. 177), with the whole being more than the sum of its components, the holism of the Third Reich operated as a form of dictatorial spirituality – with anyone deviating from the totality losing some or all of their value. The quality of subjective-life might well have been enhanced for those members of the SS who engaged in the pagan rituals which Himmler was so devoted to, but enhancement involved surrendering the unique in favour of the 'transindividual' onto-whole (p. 177). De-differentiation *now* – rather than the myth-like time of the future of the Romantics.

The 'spiritual revolution' of interwar Germany, also propagated in other Germanic and Baltic countries, does not belong to the history of the development of spiritualities of life as I have characterized them. The discordant individual is swamped by the powerful *expression* of the whole; the concordant individual lives *as* an *expression* of the whole; one way or another, the whole *consumes* the individual. Inner-life immanentism there might have been, but this was an immanentism strongly tempered by forces beyond the individual: the *volk* itself, the pagan gods, 'empowered' leaders like Himmler, the *Fuhrerprinzip*, the forces discussed in the Nazi cultural magazine *Das Innere Reich*, with the first issue referring to 'this eternal Inner Germany, the "Holy Heart of Nations"' (Hale, 2004, p. 161); 'the indestructible life force of the nation' (p. 177). Subjective-life was *set* in this context ('Strength *through* Joy'); so was subjective wellbeing culture. With the (expected) collapse of the 'unique' among the masses, though, this totalizing, totalistic, totalitarian utopianism, this 'determination to create a new man' (Hitler, cited by Fest, 1974, p. 555), means that this kind of inner-life holism is taken out of the orbit of what we are attending to in this volume into another sphere. Indeed, Peter Levenda (2003) goes so far as to claim that 'There was no such thing as a "human spirit"'; 'there was only a racial [or 'Aryan'] spirit' (p. 294). Not the will-power of the individual (apart from, of course, that exercised by the super-elite); rather, the will-power of the superior whole (the engulfment of the individual by the wellbeing of the mass vividly conveyed by Leni Riefenstahl's film of Nuremberg Party rallies) (Salkeld, 1996). Furthermore, we most certainly do not find the theme of universalized humankindness. With the holism circumscribed by blood (or race), Himmler spoke for many when he announced, 'One principle must be absolute for the SS man: we must be honest, decent, loyal and friendly to members of our blood and to no one else'. Subjective wellbeing culture took the form of 'feeling right', '*being* right', when the 'right' is provided by the all-encompassing – whilst delineated – *Volk*: rather instructive for the comparative study of subjective wellbeing culture. 'Romanticism' with a sharp cutting edge wielded from above.

The inner-life spirituality of the counter-culture of the sixties

In his *Varieties of Religion Today* (2002), Charles Taylor writes, 'I believe, along with many others, that our North Atlantic civilization has been undergoing a cultural revolution in recent decades' (p. 81). Another 'revolutionary' in this regard, Talcott Parsons (1978), uses the term 'expressive revolution' specifically to refer to the sixties. Discussing the 'possibility' that 'a new religious movement of far-reaching importance' will develop (namely, what I am calling inner-life spirituality), he continues (albeit in 'Parsonseze'):

> If this does occur, it will be a major aspect of what I would call the expressive revolution. It would result in a tilting of the previous balance between the rational-cognitive components of our cultural orientation and the modes of its institutionalization in favour of the affect-expressive relative to the cognitive-rationalistic emphasis. (p. 320).

Basically a clash between the values and assumptions of the Enlightenment and the Romantic Movement, more accurately their legacies, the immense value accorded to self-expression meant that the sixties were precisely the reverse of that highly dangerous aberration, Nazi spirituality. In more secular mode, 'expressivism' is all about living life authentically – being true to one's 'own' life, and living it 'out' accordingly. In more spiritual mode, 'The good life comes to consist in a perfect fusion of the sensual and the spiritual, where our sensual fulfilments are experienced as having higher significance' (Taylor, 1989, p. 373). The hippies would have concurred enthusiastically.

Rooted in the longstanding expressive trajectory of modernity, the counter-culturalists of the later 1960s and earlier 1970s exemplified many aspects of whatever 'revolution' might have been underway. To the extent that the sacred was in evidence among the counter-culturalists, their 'imagination' tended to gravitate towards the inner-life; its potentials and expression. The historical record is too scanty for a clear picture to emerge, but it is reasonable enough to say that a significant number of the counter-cultural wing of the 'cultural revolution' despatched the Christianity they had been brought up with to turn to what I'm calling spiritualities of life. There is certainly enough evidence to support Hugh McLeod's (2007) assessment:

> For most counter-culturalists it was axiomatic that mainstream religion and churches were part of the conventional society which they had rejected... Belief in God, adherence to any formal code of morality, or loyalty to any kind of institution were often seen as ways of abdicating the individual's responsibility for self-realization, without any interference from external authority of any kind.

This turn to self-realization is hardly surprising. For the later 1960s did indeed witness a fairly radical shift of cultural values and associated modes of self-understanding – not just among the counter-culturalists, but more generally (Yankelovich, 1974). A shift from the conformist, 'stifling' thrust of the 1950s, when what mattered was matching one's subjective-life with the norms, rules, statuses, and roles of the established order (Kynaston, 2007), to the exercise of *self-responsibility* with regard to the development and expression of subjectivities themselves. (For who else can be responsible for one's *own* life-*as*-sum-of-experiences, available only to oneself?) Among sectors of the populations of many western countries, most especially the counter-culturalists, we find the intensification of subjectivities; the expansion of consciousness; the Dionysian spirit of self-exploration; the magic sought through hallucinogens and music; the 'revelations' of new horizons/new dimensions/alternative realities; new views of life, in one's head or by journeying to the east; the untrammelled; the liberated; the flowering of subjective-life: all came to be regarded – at least on occasion – as *the* key sources of significance: the essence of life with/in powerful states of consciousness. Not so much 'meaningful' as 'life-full', with a strong emphasis on open horizons, expansion; on intense experiences as the measure of what life should be *about* (even if the attempt to obliterate ego-awareness sometimes involved suffering, and took a number to the ultimate loss of the ego). Hence the main reason for the gravitation of the sacred to this 'interior' realm of being alive; why the founder of the influential *Whole Earth Catalogue* (regularly issued between 1968 and 1972), Stewart Brand, could affirm, 'We are as gods and might as well get good at it'.

With the importance attached to the liberation of the subjective-life from the *imposition* or internalization of conformist regimes, counter-cultural spirituality quite naturally took a dualistic form. Rather than emphasizing mind-body-spirituality as an integrated personal whole, this dualistic mode emphasizes the shortcomings, if not 'fallen' nature of those aspects of the self which have been 'acquired' from, that is determined by, the mainstream; those aspects of the mind, for example, which have been 'developed' by way of over-rationalized education. The mainstream of society – especially consumer culture and the income maximization complex – was seen as capitalizing upon the attachment or 'clinging' proclivities of the kind of life – the psychological slum – which the mainstream has constructed. Liberation from 'the policeman in my head', as hippies used to say, is called for; liberation from the cognitive processing of the mind, as LSD users often said of their quest to (in effect) destroy the Enlightenment; liberation from the 'machine' that runs our lives so appallingly (as Gurdjieffian-influenced enlightenment seminar leaders emphasized from the early 1970s); 'Leave your minds and shoes here', ran the notice outside the entrance to Bhagwan's ashram in Poona (an ashram which grew up to perpetuate the spirit of the 1960s), Bhagwan inside proclaiming, 'Off with your heads!' (Thompson and Heelas, 1986, p. 36). *On Having No Head* (1971) wrote Douglas Harding; *Cutting Through Spiritual Materialism* (1973) wrote Chogyam Trungpa, not simply rejecting consumeristic attachments to material goods, but also attachment to 'love' as it is experienced in the everyday world. There is a distinctly gnostic feel to the counter-culture – rarely radical world-rejection, but as much rejection of the polluting mainstream as feasible. A soaring of the spirit, the imagination, in the face of pedantry. The transgressive, not infrequently taking a *radical* form, for the sake of freedom of expression *and* the experiences the transgressive brings with it.

So far as I can see, hippies and other counter-culturalists did not use the language of 'wellbeing'. Neither was happiness *the* name of this 'game' of life. No doubt there were some who used spirituality as a means to the end of 'feeling good about oneself' (in a comfortable kind of way), spirituality arguably serving as a consumer good, but this does not capture the exploratory, boundary transgressing, learning-from-new-experiences, spirit of the age. Nor does 'healing' – older people might sometimes have turned to (often Romantic-inspired) alternative healing activities, but rarely the youthful, vibrant counter-culturalists. Instead, concern primarily lay with finding ways to allow the current of 'life' to take them beyond the ravages of the conventional to engage in adventure, exploration, experimentation (where will this take me?), going where it goes (or 'go with the flow'), moving beyond the confines of the mundanities of conformity, the mendacities, to experience altered, heightened states of consciousness, with some taking up Romantic themes to do with union, the radicalities of 'absolute' connection.[8]

Hedonistic consumption there certainly was. But many participants were 'spiritual' on one occasion, hedonistic on another. Even within the orbit of 'sex, drugs and rock 'n' roll', though, the ecstatic typically had greater significance than 'mere' pleasure. Certainly, the hedonism of the vulgar capitalism of 'straight' society virtually became a synonym for sin. And hedonistic self-interest was widely tempered by the expressivistic humanism of the time – the deeply felt concern for the North Vietnamese, love, the 'I-thou' relationships which Victor Turner (1974) describes as 'communitas', the 'sentiment of humankindness (p. 91); the 'spiritual solidarity' described by Parsons (1978, p. 318). (See Bernice Martin (1983), whose volume is the best academic work on the sixties, on the human/ity values of the period; see also Peter Berger and Richard Neuhaus (1970) on what they describe as those 'authentic humanistic impulses that offer great hope' (p. 49).)

'Dear Brothers and Sisters', begins a letter from a member of a commune,

> I'm female, nineteen, and a college drop out. Right now, I'm trying to keep from being *swallowed* by a monster – plastic, greedy, American society...I need to begin relating to new people who are *into* taking care of each other and earth. (Cited by Melville, 1972, p. 134; my emphases; see also Bruce, who somewhere cites a contributor to *Kindred Spirit*, speaking of how the world has become 'consumed by greed')

The primary source of consumption is clearly the totalized 'system': invasive, continually intent on consuming 'life'; to be cast off accordingly. An entirely different goal to the consumptive intentions of Nazi spirituality: the *volk*-system to consume individuals in the sense of 'taking them over'.

Seminar spirituality

If I had to sum up the sixties in a few words, they would be 'powerful, *significant* subjective experiences; pronounced "reality swerves" on occasion, revealing ...'. The same can be said for the seminar spirituality which grew as the sixties waned. The Sufi-like 'shift', best illustrated, as is done in Pakistan, by slightly but abruptly moving one's straight right hand, raised in front of one's face.

Whilst internalizing the sins of modernity ('the policeman in my head', for example), the counter-culturalists tended to emphasize the conflict between 'straight society' as an external force (the equivalent of Blake's 'dark Satanic Mills') and the truths of subjective experience as their primary source of positive significance. The dualism of seminar spirituality is more markedly internalized – as a conflict between the 'lower self' or 'ego' and the 'higher self' or the spirituality of the inner realm, with significantly less attention paid to the role played by the sociocultural sources of ego-problems or issues. If you like, seminar spirituality is more 'psychologized', with much more emphasis on the endogenous limitations of the 'mind'. At the same time, though, the dualism, the conflict between the 'lower' and the 'high' modes of selfhood, mean that holistic integration of all aspects of the person is not emphasized to the same extent as today. Having said this, however, seminar 'graduates' were not adverse to saying that experiences of their inner being flow through their being as a whole, thereby working to 'transform' the quality of the life of the mind.

Springing into life with the 'creation' of est (Erhard Seminars Training) in 1971, during the next twenty or so years an as yet uncounted number of seminars, or similar organizations, catered for considerable numbers of people: certainly more than 5 million, with the great majority in western settings. Employing a range of (often highly structured) techniques ('processes'), seminars 'provided the opportunity' to experience what lies beyond that mechanistic, conditioned machine known as 'the mind'. To experience the 'source', 'spirituality' or the 'God' within: with Erhard saying, for example, 'We have met the Creator and He is Us' (Rhinehart, 1976, p. 108). (Rhinehart's volume is the best ethnographic account of seminar spirituality.) 'Successful' est seminar 'graduates', namely those who have got 'It', come to appreciate the 'wisdom' of Werner Erhard's clarion cry: 'The organizing principle of est is: Whatever the world is doing, get it to do that' (cited by Bartley, 1978, p. 221). Bearing in mind that those attracted by seminar spirituality tended to be ex-counter-culturalists who had entered the mainstream as young professionals, perhaps to become yuppies, it can hardly be doubted that numbers of the more individualistic, the more self-centred came to appreciate consumption in terms *of* their spiritual awakening (or 'enlightenment', to use a participant term), enjoying getting this aspect of 'the world' to work for themselves. A mainstream-affirmation which is not exactly in the spirit of the Romantics. At the same time, though – and my own research during the 1980s, when seminar spirituality for the general public peaked, supports this – numbers of participants came to the 'realization' that the ego is a clanking Buddhist-like attachment mechanism, which is merely fuelled by the lures of consumer culture: a culture which does not cater for true expressivism. Indeed, a fair number of those most 'immersed' in seminar spirituality have moved on to work as holistic practitioners, or to work for development agencies such as the Hunger Project in countries like Uganda.

Individualistic prosperity spirituality

Then there are the more 'brash' – that is, considerably more world-affirming, 'go-getting', individualistic, 'magical' ('create your own reality') – forms of prosperity spirituality: teachings and practices which nurture and release inner-spirituality for rampant, avid success in the spheres of production and consumption; which ensure that you never have to drop whilst you shop; which are basically of a 'tap in, make out' nature. Typically providing 'inner-technologies' to enable participants to experience wealth creation and expenditure as the *manifestation* of inner-spirituality. Prosperity spirituality seeks totalizing, comprehensive holism. (Poverty does not belong to the 'whole' of prosperity consciousness.) Money *is* an expression of the spiritual dimension. Spirituality, the generative 'supply', is simply applied to income generation, spending and consumption as ends in themselves. Rather than the 'natural supernaturalism' of Abrams and the Romantics, this exemplifies what Trungpa calls 'spiritual materialism'. Rhonda Byrne's *The Secret* (2006), devoted to wealth (etc.), and not to be confused with Michael Berg's (2004) book of the same title devoted to a Kabbalistic 'being of caring', was number nine on the Amazon.com listing in August 2007. And activities like the staff wellbeing workshop run by London South Bank University to enhance inner powers for career success (Baty, 2007) can readily be found. However, apparently heavily consumerized forms of instrumentalized, means-end rendering of inner-spirituality of the 'God is unlimited...Shopping is unlimited' (Ray, 1990, p. 135) variety have waned in western settings (although most certainly not in countries like Nigeria), now being something of a shadow of themselves when compared with the 'go get it' 1980s and early 1990s: and this despite the waxing of spirituality in business life. Although the waning of prosperity inner-life spirituality means that detailed attention need not be paid to it in a volume which dwells on holistic, inner-informed wellbeing, the phenomenon provides a useful comparative frame of reference for exploring the relationships between consumption, interior – predominantly 'postmaterialist' – wellbeing, and spirituality.[9]

Wellbeing spirituality today

In western settings today, spiritualities of life are markedly holistic, albeit with a *personal* orientation. Whether it be group activities (of which yoga is the most popular) or one-to-one practices (of which homeopathy and spiritual massage are probably the most popular), or whether it be mind-body-spirit publications, the basic theme is very simple indeed: contact with, specifically experience of, the inner-realm enables spirituality to infuse life, transforming the quality of those aspects of one's being which have previously been divorced from the inner-life. Mind-body-*with*-spirit; emotions-feelings-somatic experiences-*with*-spirituality; the experiential aspects of all relationships-*with*-spirituality; and most comprehensively, wellbeing-*with*-spirituality. And with spirituality serving as the essential core of one's being, the realization can but only serve one's unique life of experience and expression.

Above all else, wellbeing spirituality is about the 'whole' *person*. Although the spirituality of nature is by no means absent, with Fodor and Fodor (1995), for example, writing that 'the ultimate goal is to feel at One – within oneself, within Nature, and with each other' (p. 7), there is less concern with connecting with the natural world than found among the Romantics and their successors; certainly less than found within Nazi culture. There is also *much* less concern with connecting with 'external' prosperity than is found in what is left of the prosperity spirituality camp. In fact, during the Kendal Project, we did not encounter any signs of emphatic world-affirmation of the prosperity variety. What is emphasized, though, is the *potential* for spirituality to flow through the person to render the person 'holistic' or integrated as mind-body-spirit; to provide 'harmony' or 'balance'; to 'heal'; to bring wisdom; to facilitate genuine wellbeing. And the potential is fulfilled when activities enable the spiritual flow to help overcome 'blocks', or dams, within subjective-life and the body. The dualistic orientation of seminar spirituality has faded from view.

Like the Romantics and the counter-cultures of the nineteenth century and the sixties, wellbeing spirituality practitioners typically work with a fusion of the expressivistic and humanistic. Unlike the Romantics, however, there are few signs of artistic, philosophical expressivism – so important for the Romantics as a mode of self-fulfilment, with poetry, for example, serving as the expression of, and contribution to, one's true and unfolding life. For practitioners, as well as for many of their participants, activities like yoga provide the vehicle, the 'paint brush'; and *personal* life is the work of art: a work, we shall emphasize, which is widely conceived to be relational rather than unduly individualistic or solitary. As for the anti-establishment thrust of previous counter-cultures, there has undoubtedly been a shift of emphasis from 'change-the-world' idealism to personal wellbeing and growth by addressing ill-being – although as I shall argue in the last chapters, this is not to say that wellbeing spirituality is largely reserved for the wellbeing of the person and the person alone. Henceforth refraining from using the rather ugly term 'practically spiritual', the fact remains that there is a significant practicality to inner-life spirituality today: wellbeing for the self *and* for and with others.

Summary

If it is true that subjective wellbeing spirituality today is largely, or entirely, a matter of consumption, then it is highly likely that so are great swathes of the expressivist trajectory of modernity. For although the 'Neoplatonic paradigm' which Abrams locates at the heart of Romanticism has almost entirely faded from awareness, it is clear that the romantic spirit is alive and well within wellbeing spiritualities of life: the themes of 'energy', holism, learning 'through' suffering or by tackling 'issues', among others. And it is equally apparent that many of the activities and applications found today are rooted in the history of romantic expressivism: most especially those to do with healing (as in spiritual CAM) and education.

A note on dualistic-holism today

The ideal for more radical world and mind rejecters is a holism bound up with inner-life spirituality itself, perhaps ultimately dissolving into the holism of the spirituality of the universal (a theme also found in passages of the Romantics). Whilst recognizing that the 'machine' that is the mind will never disappear, activities emphasizing mind-rejection or the experience of 'mind-distance', not infrequently coupled with, or reinforced by, more comprehensive world-rejection (during the counter-cultural sixties, for instance), are of very little numerical importance today. When it is found, the teachings and practices of dualistic-holism make a stand against the lures of consumer culture, consumption, 'mere' wellbeing.

Spiritualities of Life and Spiritualities within Religious Traditions of Transcendent Theism

Durkheim (1971) wisely notes,

> it is necessary to begin by defining what is meant by a religion; for without this, we would run the risk of giving the name to a system of ideas and practices which has nothing at all religious about it, or else of leaving to one side many religious facts, without perceiving their true nature. (p. 23)

The same applied to spirituality, perhaps even more so. For if the great majority of commentators are to be believed, it is virtually impossible to 'define' spirituality, let alone to identify different forms. This is not just a matter of spirituality, or those spiritualities, beyond the confines of Christianity. For the picture is complicated by the fact that spirituality, or spiritualities, are widely reported within *different* mainstream forms of religion.

Thus far, a main aim has been to ensure that we have a reasonably good idea of what spiritualities of life are all about. Another way of elucidating the meaning of the term 'spiritualities of life' is by comparing it with variants of spirituality which are found within major religious traditions. For the sake of brevity, attention is limited to Christianity. Very similar, if not identical distinctions can be made within other religious traditions.

To varying degrees, religious traditions take the form of 'life-as' religion (Heelas, 2002, p. 371). Grounded in the past, life-as religion provides detailed information about how one ought to live one's life. Beliefs, commandments, and ethical precepts are among the numerous vehicles which spell out the good life: the nature of the good itself, what has to be avoided if one is to live the good life, what should be done in order to live the really good life. Life-as religion tells one what one has to 'live up *to*'. The emphasis is on conformity, the 'match': being a good Christian by electing to live up to authoritative tradition.

Within the realm of life-as religion, spirituality – too – takes a general life-as form. In contrast to the spirituality of the inner-life, and the importance attached to freedom, uniqueness and expressivity, life-as spirituality has to do with experiences provided by tradition and God. For Alister McGrath (1999), '*Christian beliefs* interact with spirituality, fostering and encouraging *certain* approaches to the spiritual life and rejecting or criticizing others' (p. 25; my emphases). For Eolene M. Boyd-MacMillan (2006), Christian spirituality is all about transformation by way of embracing God. Regulation, probably relatively determinate construction, is in evidence in these spiritualities for life.[10]

Life-as spirituality is exemplified by what I shall call *transcendent spirituality*.[11] Found in conservative forms of Christianity which emphasize the otherness, power and glory of God, the authoritative nature of biblical text and the importance of obedience, this is a spirituality *of* the transcendent God. The contrast with spiritualities of life in the here-and-now is obvious. Another variant of life-as spirituality is found in forms of Christianity which incorporate an emphasis on experience. These combine the authority of biblical text and the otherness of God with the experiential immediacy of the Holy Spirit. For the born again Christian, the Holy Spirit has come to dwell at the heart of subjective-life. Transforming or healing subjective-life, there are certainly parallels with spiritualities of life. However, the *Holy spirituality* of the experience of the Holy Spirit takes place within life-as tradition. Accordingly, rather than the Holy Spirit being associated with the essentially inner-directed self-expression of spiritualities of life, it is associated with those experiences demanded or validated by scriptural authority. The third variant of life-as spirituality is found within liberal, humanistic forms of Christianity. Rather than emphasizing the texts of tradition, or the Holy Spirit, importance is attached to the sacrality of all people. This *spirituality of theistic humanism* has much in common with the humanistic spirituality of the inner life (most obviously linking spirituality with extensive relationality) – with the critical difference that the humanism is grounded in a transcendent Godhead. Finally, *immanent spirituality* is found in those forms of Christianity which most emphasize the God 'within'. As with the Quakers and many Unitarians, spirituality is found within the depths of life. With the importance attached to the idea that spirituality belongs to human nature, and with the importance which is attached to the idea that inner-spirituality can speak to and flow through the person, light-within spirituality is very similar to spiritualities of life – a major difference being that the freedom which is required to grow as a unique person – to be and become oneself – is restricted by the life-as ethicality (often of a strict variety) sustained by the God which is also 'without'.

Critical Reflections

Returning to spiritualities of life *per se*, to further aid our understanding of what they are all about, I briefly attend to three criticisms of the distinction between spiritualities of life and spiritualities/religions for life.

According to Jan-Olav Henriksen (2005), the distinction is between experiences determined or otherwise influenced by religious tradition, beliefs, doctrines and so on, and experiences which are somehow 'pure' manifestations of the depths of the interior life (pp. 75–6). In reply, as an academic I am certainly not committed to the belief that there is such a thing as a pure experience (or experiences) of inner-spirituality. I am committed, though, to making a distinction based on what is publicly available – the evidence provided by what believers or participants say. In *The Spiritual Revolution* we wrote of 'subjective-life forms of the sacred which emphasize inner sources of significance and authority and the cultivation or sacralization of unique subjective-lives' (Heelas and Woodhead 2005, p. 6). Rather than being based on agreement *with* the participant assertion that there *is* an (unmediated) inner source, the characterization is based on the nature of the assertion itself.[12]

Kimmo Ketola's (2005) criticism of the distinction drawn in *The Spiritual Revolution*, and developed here, has a rather different emphasis. As Ketola makes his point:

> Religion is something that requires you to live your life according to externally imposed expectations, roles, and duties, while – of course – spirituality is nothing of the sort! This sounds rather dubious, to put it mildly. The distinction between religion and spirituality as used in the book is exceedingly vague and ambiguous. (p. 290)

In reply, I am certainly not committed to the non-academic belief that inner-life spirituality somehow operates – in experience, let alone practice – without the help of 'externally imposed expectations, roles, and duties'. As I have argued elsewhere (Heelas, 2006a), and will also argue later here, it is perfectly possible for the researcher to draw attention to the operation of 'context setting' and performing rules, principles, cultural and/or practice-specific expectations, values, meanings and truths in yoga groups, for example. It is for this reason that we wrote of 'subjective-life *forms* of the sacred' in *The Spiritual Revolution* (Heelas and Woodhead, 2005, p. 6; my emphasis). However, whatever the role played by sociocultural factors, quite possibly sometimes exercising conformist pressure, the fact of the matter is that participants or 'believers', most especially practitioners, generally understand things differently. Talk is of being 'free spirits', being 'in tune with inner truth' or of 'living *out of* the spiritual dimension'. And by virtue of the fact that participant understanding takes such a detraditionalized, de-externalized nature, we are provided with the ethnographic reality which serves to ground the distinction between inner-life spirituality and life-as religion and spirituality.

As for the third criticism, Steven Sutcliffe (2006) writes of *The Spiritual Revolution*, 'I can find no clear, unequivocal definition of "spirituality"' (p. 307). The definition we offer, he claims, is 'fuzzy' (p. 308). If inner-life spirituality is so lacking in clarity, it would indeed be difficult to measure the extent to which beliefs (and activities) have increased in popularity; even to know what to study in connection with issues like consumption. Whether because of their aversion to 'belief' as opposed to experiencing experience, or because of the mystery they found *in* life, it is true that the participants we talked with during the research which informed much of *The Spiritual Revolution* volume (relatively) rarely tried to explicate or elaborate on what they meant by life-spirituality in and of itself. However, they were more than happy to talk about the depths of life serving as the key to bringing life alive, or about the ways in which spirituality was making a difference to their lives, including the values they experienced as being bound up with living the spiritual life. And this is the discourse which provides our fairly determinate characterization. One thinks of the biblical epistemological pragmatism, 'Ye shall know them by their fruits' (Matthew 7: 16).

Criticisms aside, I am convinced that there is a world of difference between inner-life spirituality and the spiritualities of life-as religion. Basically – or logically, if you prefer – they are incompatible. Logically, it is impossible to reconcile an inner 'god' which facilitates *self*-actualization, the expression of the uniqueness or originality of the person, with the transcendent, theistic God of life-as religion-cum-spiritualities, which emphasizes adherence 'to' and places limits on autonomous self-development and expression (notwithstanding the fact that one might have initially elected to take the conformist path). The 'god' within and the God without cannot serve at one and the same time as *absolute* and *different* sources of significance and authority. Neither, for that matter, can one reconcile a spirituality which is generally taken to flow through all that lives, where we 'are all god/s', and which is thus fundamentally egalitarian, with spiritualities bound up with and emanating from a hierarchically located Godhead on High.

Indeterminacies

To orientate the reader by focusing this volume as clearly as possible, it is helpful to bear in mind two indeterminate zones which 'surround' the primary subject matter.

Consider, first, the relationships with traditional theistic Christianity. As just indicated, logically speaking the sacred with an inner locus and the sacred with an outer locus cannot both serve as 'absolutely' different sources of significance and authority at one and the same time – especially if the outer locus is at the top of the power hierarchy. Hence Georg Simmel's (1976) observation, 'We all know the great polarization that has split the religious life of our times . . . : the split between Christianity and a religion which repudiates any historical content, whether it be undogmatic monism, or pantheism, of a purely spiritual condition not entailing any specific beliefs' (pp. 258–9). But with the notable exception of rational choice theorists, few would dream of arguing that human affairs are exactly logical, many also arguing that human affairs should not always seek to conform to the dictates of the exercise of 'enlightened', 'de-emotionalized' or disembodied reason. In practice, a great many of those participating in the networks, small groups, retreats and all those other activities operating on the 'edges' of theistic Christianity are more or less at one and the same time drawing on the two sources of authority and significance. The God within *and* the God without; the God within, not without, *and* the God without; an autonomous spirituality of the unique self *and* conformist spiritualities of theism; an egalitarian, pantheistic spirituality *and* a hierarchical, 'supremacist' form emanating from God on High: perhaps welded together by way of the language of 'mystery'; perhaps coexisting in creative tension; perhaps with a *supra*-logical 'synthesis' of the 'thesis' (transcendent theism) and the 'antithesis' (inner-life spirituality); perhaps 'selecting' the best of what the god within and the god without have to offer, to find some kind of experiential harmony; perhaps 'yoga in the aisles' coexisting in an uneasy relationship with 'worship in the pews'.[13]

Other than making the point that many of the arguments which follow in this book almost certainly apply to this zone betwixt and between inner-life spirituality and transcendent theism, further analysis is not carried out here. The same applies to a somewhat related zone of indeterminacy. Just as theistic Christian-cum-Romantic inner-life intersections have grown during recent decades, so have those concerning paranormal-cum-spiritualities of life. At least in Britain, paranormal 'activities' have traditionally attached considerable importance to contacting the 'other side' – the 'side' of spiritual power, agency and knowledge or wisdom; the side which largely transcends what is available within life in the here-and-now (including human paranormal-cum-spiritual capacities); the side which is between heaven and earth but which often owes something to contributions from both heaven and earth. Recently, though, paranormal fairs and other activities such as those held in spiritualist 'Christian' churches have to varying degrees and in varying ways incorporated or drawn upon holistic mind-body-spirituality. It is not at all easy to answer the question, 'Does this development belong to the camp of inner-life spirituality, or not?' Suffice it to say, for present purposes, a more extensive critical analysis of consumption and spirituality would certainly have to attend to this growing development.[14]

Onwards

We now move on from the nontheistic 'tradition' of inner 'enlightenment' to say more about the nature of wellbeing spirituality today: our substantive focus for addressing the 'consuming growth' debate. To re-emphasize a key point: if what is found today is consumeristic, then so, in various ways, is much of what has contributed to the present situation.

Chapter 2

Wellbeing Spirituality Today

The span of transcendence is shrinking. Modern religious themes such as 'self-realization', personal autonomy and self-expression have become dominant. (Thomas Luckmann, 1990, p. 138)

New Age beliefs and attitudes are now so widespread in our society and its culture as to effectively dominate all areas of life. (Colin Campbell, 2004, p. 40)

'There is a new market category called wellness lifestyle, and in a whole range of industries, if you are not addressing that category you are going to find it increasingly hard to stay in business', enthuses Kevin Kelly. This broad new category, Mr Kelly goes on, 'consolidates *a lot of sub-categories*' including spas, traditional medicine and alternative medicine, behavioural therapy, spirituality, fitness, nutrition and beauty. As more customers demand *a holistic approach to feeling well*, firms that have hitherto specialized in only one or two of these areas are now facing growing market pressure to broaden their business. 'You can no longer satisfy consumers with just fitness, just medical, just spa', says Mr Kelly. (*Economist*, 6–12 January, 2007, p. 51)

The Wellness Revolution. How to Make a Fortune in the Next Trillion Dollar Industry. (Paul Pilzer, 2003)

Take some time out for yourself and try a taster session or a talk from the Natural Health Care Team in the Chaplaincy Centre, including homeopathy and reflexology. Every day the Sports Centre is hosting taster sessions at lunch time, everything from salsa to yoga. (Lancaster University 'Staff Learning Festival', 10–15 July 2006)

...*the number of adherents (if that is not too strong a term for the consumers of cultic religion)* will decline. (Bruce, 2002, p. 79; my emphasis)

Since one of the main arguments I am addressing is that the growth of New Age spiritualities of life can be explained away as being largely – if not entirely – a matter of secularistic consumption of a superficial kind, I now provide a brief survey of some of the evidence for the recent growth of wellbeing spirituality, paying particular attention to some of the more significant sociocultural contexts where growth has occurred and the forms it takes in these contexts. Without going into matters in any depth, salient explanations are introduced when appropriate. (Salient because they are drawn upon later.) What follows thus provides an opportunity for saying something about where, how and why consumer activities *could* be in evidence.

Of particular significance, I chart some of the ways in which inner-life spirituality has permeated a great deal of the culture and its institutions. Generally restricted to counter-culturalists during the sixties, then the 'cultic milieu' which developed (including those more seriously involved with seminar spirituality), it now has a home within an albeit variegated cultural milieu. Writing in 1983, Martin Marty notes, 'religion has unmistakably and increasingly diffused through the culture' (p. 273). Since then, indeed since earlier, it has been the turn of spirituality to develop into something akin to a 'sacred canopy'. Certainly, inner-life spirituality has sprung up within influential mainstream domains of the culture, such as the press, perhaps relatively autonomously, perhaps influenced by more specialized holistic activities and publications. It has also entered 'nooks and crannies', specific sites like bed and breakfast establishments, Burnley College (Hopi healing in the one of the most deprived towns in Britain), Looking Well (a holistic centre located in a 'genuine' working people's town, High Bentham near where I live), or the Sports Centre of Lancaster University. In many parts of Britain, small villages or their environs are likely to have a practitioner or two. More generally, the expression 'mind-body-spirit' has entered the ranks of 'cultural belief'; so has the term 'holistic', now encountered in contexts as diverse as medispas and university mission statements, or for that matter, the *Dawn* newspaper of Pakistan, one headline running, 'Soomro [the Senate Chairman] for Holistic Approach to Combat Terror' (3 October, 2006, p. 19); and terms like 'inner-child' have become a staple of the middlebrow press and women's magazines.

In some quarters, it has become customary to discuss the numerical significance of 'spirituality' in ways which smack of exaggeration, often with the feel of the indeterminate, and tending to gain their effect by listing relatively *ad hoc* illustrations or by using poorly evidenced generalizations. In *The Making of the New Spirituality. The Eclipse of the Western Religious Tradition* (2003), for instance, James Herrick claims:

> For many Westerners, the long-prophesied new spiritual age certainly has arrived. The Revealed Word and its busy, personal God have faded into our collective spiritual memory, and bright new spiritual commitments encourage fresh religious thought. (p. 16)

'I have been *asserting* that a massive shift in Western religious attitudes has taken place', continues Herrick, then noting that 'perhaps some basic evidence of such a change is in order' (p. 17; my emphasis). Whilst going on to provide a certain amount of useful data, Herrick also makes statements of the kind, 'The pervasiveness of alternative spiritualities forcefully confronted Americans with revelations that Ronald and Nancy Regan sought advice from an (expensive) astrologer' (p. 17). The relative paucity of survey data, of information gathered by way of locality research, systematic interviewing and the like means that it is tempting to have recourse to this kind of statement. I shall do my best to avoid it.

What is Growing

With the development of the assumptions, beliefs, values and associated experiences of the autonomous self, especially during and since the sixties, *subjective-life* – so vital an aspect of the self-understanding of the unique autonomous agent – has unquestionably become an ever-increasing focus of attention and concern. (See Patricia Clough's edited volume, *The Affective Turn*, 2007.) Catering for subjective-life, fuelling the massive subjective turn of modern culture, perhaps in measure constituting elements of subjective-life, *subjective wellbeing culture* has thus entered a range of occupations, from shop floor assistants in major stores to spiritual therapists in hospices.[1] Careers where subjective wellbeing culture, in various forms and in various ways, has become a significant aspect of work, now add up to one of the largest – if not the largest – employment 'sectors' of contemporary modernity. And especially during the last decade or so, the development of the culture of subjective wellbeing has increasingly become very much part and parcel of the development of inner-life spirituality.

All cultures are bound up with the (subjective) wellbeing, or not, of their citizens. Subjective wellbeing culture is marked out by the *explicit*, sometimes highly elaborated, attention paid to subjective life. One sees this, for example, in the difference between the car ad that provides the objective facts (fuel consumption, number of cylinders, etc.) and those that declare, 'Experience', 'Experience the Difference' or 'The Drive of Your Life', with only a photograph. Clearly, you might be pleased about the fuel consumption figure. But the fact remains that the life of experience is not explicitly addressed in objective, impersonal promotions of the factual variety.

Those working within subjective wellbeing culture seek to align their provisions and activities with the elementary 'logic' of enhancing the quality of subjective-life. Within the constraints of brand identity or style, the fact that the subjective-life of any particular individual is unique means that provisions or activities are personalized or individualized as much as possible (or are left intentionally vague so as to be inclusive whilst being open to personal interpretation). The key is to enable people to *be themselves* (which is where the unique comes in) *only better* (which is where the enhancement of quality comes in) – a two-fold aim which is frequently advanced by encouraging people to go 'deeper' into their experiences of themselves to develop their qualities and circumvent their limitations (and especially for all those who regard life as unfathomable, there is plenty of scope for going deeper). '*Feel* the *difference*' or '"*know* the difference" *for* yourself' are perhaps the major litmus tests for wellbeing-cum-wellness in subjectivized mode. From child-centred, progressive or 'independent' education, to the manager-centredness of 'soft capitalism', to patient-centred nursing, to guest-centred spas and hotels, to the more individuated health and fitness clubs, to customer-centred shop floor assistants, to 'person'-centred call centre operatives, to viewer-centred reality TV shows, to reader-'engaging' or 'life-provoking' autobiographies and women's magazines, to advertising, to client-centred therapists, to life-skill coaches – provisions and services offer a wide range of ways of being yourself only better. The child-centred primary school teacher works in the spirit of Rousseau or Froebel to cultivate the particular abilities or 'gifts' of individual children and to help particular children to develop their own 'well-rounded' personalities; the therapist at the spa endeavours to work with her guest to facilitate the best possible experiences; those producing reality TV shows aim to provide as many opportunities as possible for the individual viewer to learn from the 'personalities', both how to avoid ill-being and how to be happy and successful as a person; those working for development agencies increasingly 'put people first' – their 'capacities', 'capabilities', their 'potential' (Nussbaum and Sen, 1993).

What has all this got to do with the growth of New Age spiritualities of life? Within the ranks of those supplying the provisions of purchasing culture, any good market researcher will be aware of the numerical significance of the inner-life beliefs of the kind reported by Eileen Barker and others (see below and the Appendix). Market researchers will know that the sales of newspapers like the *Daily Mail* or magazines like *O The Oprah Magazine* benefit from the inclusion of articles catering to the hopes of those with beliefs of a mind-body-spirituality variety; market researchers will know that 'spiritual' products sold in health and beauty shops are likely to appeal to those who think that holistic spirituality might well improve their quality of life. And in turn, the widespread presence of spiritually 'significant' provisions – not least the many books housed under the 'self-improvement', 'health and fitness' and, of course, 'mind-body-spirit' categories in the wellbeing zones of major bookstores – could sometimes be contributing to the number of people who 'believe' in inner-spirituality, perhaps by influencing all those who say they 'believe in something' or 'definitely believe in something' but who do not know what to call it; who have not wanted to pin it down or take away the mystery by applying an unrealistic 'label'.

'Capitalizing' on widespread 'beliefs' in what lies within and what this realm has to offer, many of the provisions and activities of subjective wellbeing culture have introduced holistic, mind-body-spirit themes. Sometimes these are well developed; sometimes they provide a 'taste'; sometimes they take the form of allusions to inner-life spirituality and hints of what it promises. Relative to the context of subjective wellbeing culture, inner-life spirituality is thriving. It adds to the 'better' or 'more' of more secular forms of subjective wellbeing culture by offering additional means to the end of the 'more'. Working from within the heart of the person, to flow through her or his personal life, it does not distract from the unique – the 'I am what I am' anchorage of so much of modern culture – and appeals accordingly.

Whether or not people are taken in by the advertising (etc.) of much of subjective wellbeing culture, what matters is that they have the opportunity to be 'taken in *to*' their subjectivities – and this leads some to the 'real thing' – activities like reflexology. The heartland of inner-life spirituality, today, is found within the holistic milieu. The milieu takes the form of *holistic activities* – activities which are run by *spiritual practitioners*. Some run small groups; others one-to-one activities. Adept in the arts of practising spiritualities of life of the mind-body-spirit variety, the focus of tai chi groups or one-to-one reiki sessions, for example, is generally orientated towards wellbeing-cum-'healing'-cum-health; the 'well-life'.

The assumptions and values of subjective wellbeing culture – the importance of subjective life; the positive, 'can do' way it is envisaged; the theme of exercising autonomy to develop, express and celebrate who you really are – are writ large in the holistic milieu. The affinities are close. Accordingly, expectations aroused by subjective wellbeing culture can serve to direct people to the specialized zone of the milieu itself. Here, they can engage in associational, face-to-face activities to go (yet) deeper into what is to be found in other areas of the culture. One reads about yoga and wellbeing (or 'wellness') in a popular magazine; one decides to 'work out' whilst watching a yoga DVD; one gets interested, buys a book or two and reads about *chakras*, energy flows, *kundalini*, and what yoga has to do with the purpose of life; one gets older and starts thinking about one's health and what one's life is all about; one exercises one's autonomy to find out what works best; one finally settles with a tai chi group; one 'realizes' things about oneself that one had not fully appreciated or known about before. Or again: a primary school teacher feels that she should really do something to prepare for the upcoming Ofsted inspection during which 'spiritual development' will be assessed; she introduces 'stilling' sessions; she experiences the effects for herself and observes the results in the classroom; she decides to join a meditation group.

Many of the practitioners and participants of the holistic milieu work, or have worked, in person-centred, wellbeing professions – nursing, education, counselling, therapy, HRD, and so on. Some become active in the holistic milieu because they have been unable to fulfil their holistic, person-centred, subjective wellbeing concerns within the workplace. Take NHS hospital nurses as an example. On the one hand, governmental policies direct them to respond to the 'spiritual needs' of their patients; on the other, they are terribly busy working to comply with scientific and bureaucratic procedures. A number of nurses who have been interviewed are seriously interested in their own 'growth', by working closely with others, and with what holistic spirituality has to offer their patients, but have become so frustrated with the iron cage of the ward, perhaps fed, especially the seemingly ever-increasing number of regulations, procedures and targets, that they have simply left or gone part-time – to liberate themselves by learning to become holistic practitioners in their own right (Heelas, 2006b).

Summarizing the evidence for growth rather more systematically, during the Kendal Project research we erred on the side of caution by working with a strict definition of what counts as belonging to the holistic milieu (Heelas and Woodhead, 2005, pp. 36–7). Our paradigmatic criterion of a holistic milieu activity is that it is run by a *spiritual* practitioner. Normally open to the public, activities are held in private. The milieu is comprised of specialized activities. That is to say, rather than taking place within and with reference to more encompassing sociocultural contexts like schools or companies, groups and one-to-one activities are 'self-contained'. All that is required is available within them. Taking place in a setting like a hired room which is not 'linked up' with surrounding (or other) settings, activities are specifically focused on what is taking place as people gather to make progress. Activities provide 'time-out'. Not taking place within and with reference to broader institutional contexts, institutional issues need not dominate. This characterization certainly serves to distinguish holistic milieu activities from – say –spiritually or holistically informed management training taking place *within* a company, and therefore open to all sorts of company factors (aims, 'philosophy', etc.).

Kendal Project research shows that during the autumn of 2001, 95 spiritual practitioners were providing the activities of Kendal and environs. During a typical week, 600 people were participating in 126 separate activities – comprising 1.6 percent of the population of the area. As argued in *The Spiritual Revolution*, there are very good reasons for supposing that Kendal can be taken to be representative of Great Britain as a whole. This means that slightly over 900,000 inhabitants are active on a weekly basis in the holistic milieux of the nation, of whom 146,000 are spiritual practitioners.[2] At much the same time, Church of England regular Sunday attendance was around 960,000 (Brierley, 2003, p. 8.3); as of 2005, for England, 870,600 (Brierley, 2006, p. 2.3). Thinking of the USA, using different sources of evidence (including recent surveys), our estimate is that between 2.5 and 8 percent of the population are involved in holistic milieu activities provided by spiritual practitioners. And in Britain, together with many other western countries, holistic milieu activities have grown during the last few decades – from being very few and far between in Britain in 1960 or 1970, to the number we find today.

One of the drawbacks of the research carried out during the Kendal Project is that we did not think through the *very* tricky problem of distinguishing holistic milieu activities from relatively 'specialized' activities taking place within the primary schools of Kendal, the local hospital and the like; or, for that matter, Kendalians participating in spiritual reflexology one-to-one sessions whilst on a cruise holiday: 'specialized', but with a good chance of the experiences, challenges and opportunities of life aboard entering into the sessions. For complicated reasons, I am now pretty firmly convinced that it not possible to identify a strictly defined holistic milieu of the kind we attempted to operationalize during the Kendal Project. Accordingly, for present purposes I am going to drop the tricky 'self-contained' criterion. I shall simply use the term 'holistic activities' to refer to mind-body-spiritualities, run by *spiritual*, *holistic* practitioners, *wherever* they are found.

Mind-body-spirituality wellbeing activities have become relatively widespread in a range of contexts where person-centred subjective wellbeing culture is in demand. These include hotels (of the more luxurious variety), spas (again, of the more upmarket variety), 'adventurous', New Age holidays (where the experiential adventures lie within), shops (like the 'therapy rooms' of the naturalistic outlet, Org, in Leeds), stores (Boots toyed with it, Harvey Nichols have done it), beauty salons, airports, prisons, (relatively) designated spaces in hospitals, general practices, Healthy Living Centres, meeting places for pensioners, (some) nursing homes, rehabilitation centres (tai chi at the Meadows), training or personal consultancy rooms in companies, lecture rooms in Colleges of Further Education (especially when the topics include beauty treatments, health and fitness), classes within Adult Education facilities, MA/MBA university courses (whether in state or private management or business schools), some restaurants and clubs, health and fitness emporia, the areas around bed and breakfast facilities in remoter reaches of the land, new social movements (in particular environmentalist), primary school quiet rooms, class rooms, assemblies and after-school activities, sporting and recreational activities (meditative forest walking, for example) and the meeting rooms of therapists and counsellors (although my own counsellor is primarily psychological-cum-humanistic, he nevertheless describes himself 'as God'). Then there are also enclaves within – or associated with – the United Nations (Mikhail Gorbachev and Maurice Strong's 'The Earth Charter', with 'sacred trust' placed in the 'interconnected[ness]' of the 'environmental, economic, political, social and spiritual challenges facing the world), government quarters, most especially departments of health and education, and to go further afield, INGOs and NGOs.

Before looking more closely at several of these settings, I should emphasize that the term 'wellbeing' (or the somewhat more health-focused term 'wellness') should not be taken to automatically evoke the ideas of the trivial or the consumeristic. True, the term is used in the sense of 'feeling good *about* oneself' – the 'feelgood' factor that one should experience after a pampering session at a spa. However, the term is also used in somewhat different contexts. Amartya Sen, for example, writes:

> The functionings relevant for well-being vary from such elementary ones as escaping morbidity and mortality, being adequately nourished, having mobility, etc., to complex ones such as being happy, achieving self-respect, taking part in the life the community, appearing in public without shame... The claim is that these functionings make up a person's being, and the evaluation of a person's well-being has to take the form of an assessment of these constituent elements. (1993, pp. 36–7)

As it might be said, much of what used to go under the rubric of welfare now falls under the rubric of wellbeing; or the shift of emphasis from the basics of traditional trade unionism to the subjective wellbeing and personal qualities of soft, 'participatory' capitalism. Much of expressivistic subjective wellbeing culture is humanistic – not just within national and international charities or other organizations, but also within (certain) shops on the high street and (certain) businesses. Although there are basic themes running through subjective wellbeing culture *per se*, the extent to which its products or services are so to speak 'taken in' in an arguably consumeristic manner, or the extent to which products or services have to do with the kind of more 'complex functionings' which Sen writes about, depends on context.

Google Data

For obvious reasons, this kind of data provides only a rough guide. Nevertheless, a simple search using Google serves to indicate the *relative* popularity of ways in which spirituality has come to be considered. At the end of January 2006, a straightforward search for 'spirituality and...' on Google.com resulted in the following figures: spirituality and health, 20,400,000; spirituality and business, 16,100,000 (with Peter Senge heading the list); spirituality and education, 14,800,000, spirituality and enlightenment, 2,200,000. A search at the end of January 2007, now using Google.co.uk, provides the same sequencing: health, 1,270,000; business, 1,200,000; education, 918,000 and enlightenment, 132,000. With this pulse of public, quasi-academic and academic interest in mind, I adopt the same sequence.[3]

Health

By 2001, almost half the general practices of England were providing access to CAM activities – those complementary and alternative forms of medicine which take a 'mind-body' form (approximately two thirds) together with those of a 'mind-body-*spirituality*' nature.[4] Almost one third of the

CAM activities were provided in-house by doctors themselves or their staff (Dobson, 2003). Much the same picture is found in the USA, one indicator being that 75 out of 125 medical schools, including Harvard, offer courses on CAM, including prescribing courses of action (Wetzel et al., 1998; and see Baer, 2004). Given that around a third of CAM activities incorporate a spiritual dimension, generally of an inner-life variety, it is apparent that the inner-life is by no means viewed unfavourably by considerable numbers of the medical establishment.

Within the sphere of public services, specifically the UK's National Health Service, government charters and plans state that nurses must attend to 'the spiritual needs' of their patients. Reflecting their own experiences-cum-beliefs, it is perfectly apparent that hospital nurses are increasingly exercised by the values and experiences of holistic, mind-body-spirit spirituality, their growing interest owing a fair amount to what patients are looking for in terms of their prior values, beliefs or expectations. Turning to hospices, cancer care centres (normally charities) and similar organizations, holistic spirituality is considerably more in evidence – almost certainly to the extent of having eclipsed Christianity. Cancer Care-Kendal, for example, provides an 'extensive range of complementary therapies', including those with a spiritual dimension; the Penny Brohn Cancer Care Centre (formerly the Bristol Cancer Help Centre) offers 'a unique range of physical, emotional and spiritual support', facilitating 'inner strengths and resources'. (See also Hedges and Beckford, 2000; Partridge, 2005, pp. 4–41; Heelas, 2006b.)

As for CAM itself, a considerable amount of research attests to its popularity. To mention several indicative findings, Toby Murcott (2005) reports that 'Half the population of the UK has visited an alternative practitioner' (p. 36), many of whom will be working with spirituality. And during 2007 it was widely reported that Britons spent £1.6 billion annually on CAM. As long ago as the mid-1990s, the New Age and kindred therapeutic practices of the USA – which will certainly have included a considerable amount that has come to be known as CAM – were generating around $14 billion a year from personal spending (Ferguson and Lee, 1996); and arrestingly, Raymond Tallis (2004) reports research which shows that 'By 1996, expenditure [on 'alternative therapies'] in the USA...exceeded the total amount out-of-pocket in the entire mainstream medical system' (p. 127).

Returning briefly to the UK, under the title 'Booming Subjects', *The Times Higher Educational Supplement* (19 January 2007, p. 19) places 'complementary medicine' first, undergraduate applications having increased by 36.5 per cent between the years 2005 and 2006; and, it can be added, rose by 31 per cent during the 2006–7 admission process (Paton, 2007).

'Nothing really matters except health', says Danish supermodel Helena Christensen. Surely a widely held evaluation, and one which helps explain the conjunction of spirituality with the wellbeing of health – one which directs us to the realm of health and fitness clubs, spas and the like.

Leo Hickman (2006) states that 'On January 1, 2005, there were 7,036,118 members of 5,486 public and private health and fitness clubs in the UK – 11.8 per cent of the population' (p. 5). Tom Dart and Jonathan Keane (2002) provide more information: 'Between 1994 and 1999 the value of the UK fitness market grew by 81 per cent', also noting that '14 per cent of the [American] population belongs to a health club' (p. 31). And Matthew Goodman (2006) notes that the health and beauty-spa market of Britain is valued at £1.5 billion. Every health and fitness club (or leisure centre) which I have visited to collect brochures (and this is now a significant number) provides holistic activities; interviews and other sources of information indicate that these are normally run by spiritual practitioners. These are the new cathedrals of so many of our towns and cities – externally bare, bland and monumental shells housing the life of health and fitness.

Remaining with the theme of capitalist services in the mode of relaxation, pleasure or rejuvenation (capitalist in that they almost always aim to make a good profit), the International Spa Association's (ISPA) definition of a spa transforms the Latin *salus per aquam* ('health from water') to an 'entity devoted to enhancing overall wellbeing through professional services that encourage the renewal of mind, body and spirit'. The Association reports that in 2001, 156 million spa visits were made in the USA, with $11 billion in revenue (up from $6 billion in 1999). Certainly, the more up-market (and utterly luxurious) spas of the USA, Britain, Bali or that world capital, Bangkok, and – indeed – those located all over the globe in uplifting places, have drawn on their market research (which presumably shows the popularity of the spiritual dimension of the life of wellbeing for the people they aim to attract) to invest considerable sums in catering for the spiritual expectations of their target clientele.[5]

Mainstream Business

In Madeleine Bunting's (2004a) estimation, 'what the "super-performance" companies require from employees involves a process of transformation of potential, of self-discovery and self-realization and transcendence of limitations, which springs directly from the New Age spirituality of the sixties' (p. 115). Within the context of what has come to be known as soft capitalism (Thrift, 2005), talk is of 'bringing life back to work', 'people come first', 'the learning organization', 'personal growth through work' – and, of course, 'unlocking human potential'. The state of being of employees is taken to be critical. The emphasis lies with work 'from the inside out'. So if called for, inner-life spirituality is quite naturally at home.

As indicated by the Google measuring rod, holistic spirituality has established a relatively significant presence within the heartlands of 'big business' capitalism: corporate cultures, trainings, weekend courses, talks, seminars and so on. Clearly, the Google figure for 'spiritual and business' will include businesses of an 'alternative' bent. However, the Google figure for 'spirituality and alternative business' is 1,970,000 – a relatively small percentage of the 16,100,000 items under 'spirituality and business'. Equally clearly, the Google figure for 'spiritual and business' will include Christian spirituality. However, my 2006 Google.com search provided a figure of 13,500,000 for 'New Age spirituality and business' (in effect 'out of' the 16,100,000 number) – compared with a figure of 1,700,000 for 'Evangelical Christianity, spirituality and business'.[6]

Moving to more solid ground, Douglas Hicks (2003) summarizes his study of USA companies by noting:

> One of the most significant and complicated developments in American religion that contributes to interest in spirituality at work and elsewhere is the rise of New Age traditions. Indeed, along with a new public Christian evangelicalism, New Age language *fundamentally shapes* discussions of contemporary workplace spirituality. (p. 31; my emphasis)

Significantly, Hicks also notes that 'the aging of the boomer-dominated workforce has been a prime factor of the rise of spirituality in the office' (p. 28) – significantly because many of these boomers, who have obtained positions of influence (especially in HRD, etc.), will previously have had contact with the spiritualities of the 1960s whilst they were at college. These are the people, one can surmise, who are likely to have faith in what lies within; the contribution it can make to the workplace. These are the people who organize or participate in the training, courses and seminars – the events which aim to release and optimize the resources of the inner-life; the spiritual 'energy', 'wisdom' and 'creativity' ('spark' or 'flair'). These are the people who read, and contribute to, the journals which have flourished, largely during and since the 1980s. These are the people who buy works by Peter Senge (for example *The Fifth Discipline*, 1999): minimally quasi-spiritual in approach, a person who has become increasingly spiritually orientated over the years, who refers to 'the spiritual revolution', and who is of *very* considerable influence as an advocate of the self-development focused 'learning organization'.

Ian Mitroff and Elizabeth Denton's *A Spiritual Audit of Corporate America* (1999) provides more evidence. Although the surveys and interviews of their project can hardly be said to address corporate America as a whole (a huge task!), this pioneering study is reasonably representative. Finding that the 'first choice of everyone we interviewed regarding what gave them meaning and purpose in their job was "the ability to realize my full potential as a person"' (p. 36), it comes as no surprise to read that 'Roughly 60 per cent, of the majority of those to whom Mitroff talked, had a positive view of spirituality and a negative view of religion' (p. 39). 'For these people', we also read, 'it is taken for granted as a fact that everyone is a spiritual being and that spirituality is an integral part of humankind's basic makeup' (p. 41) – with 'integration' and cooperation being highly valued.

Briefly mentioning spiritual activities (management training, etc.), the popular demand indicated by Google, together with the amount of material which has been written about spirituality and business (publications which have taken off since the earlier 1980s), suggests that many are interested in implementing what they have read about (perhaps by looking at the wealth of material in Robert Giacalone and Carol Jurkiewicz's edited volume, *Handbook of Workplace Spirituality and Organizational Performance*, 2004). Comparing the situation with the 1980s and earlier (which I endeavoured to chart in *The New Age Movement*, 1996), it is perfectly clear that there is *much* more activity taking place today – one source of information being all those journals which have sprung up catering for interest in what workplace spirituality can offer; in its effective implementation.[7]

Mainstream Education

I might have missed something, but it very much looks as though systematic investigations, whether by way of locality study or by way of survey, have yet to be carried out. A big job, which would require looking at syllabuses, teaching content and practice, assemblies, after-school activities, activities on university campuses, departments in universities (including management and health), colleges (including beauty and health departments), adult education, and so on.

All the schools of England and Wales are legally required to attend to the spiritual development of their pupils. David Bell, until recently the Chief Inspector of Schools of England and Wales, sets the tone when he says (it will be recalled) that 'spirituality has come into its own as encapsulating those very qualities that *make* us human' (my emphasis). More formally, to cite in full the definition of spirituality used by Ofsted (1994), the non-ministerial government department responsible for inspecting the standards of schools and teachers in England,

> Spiritual *development* relates to that aspect of *inner life* through which pupils acquire insights into their personal experience which are of enduring worth. It is characterized by reflection, the attribution of meaning to experience, *valuing a non-material dimension to life* and intimations of an enduring reality. (p. 86; my emphases)

It is then explicitly stated that '"spiritual" is not synonymous with religious' (p. 86). Going a little more comprehensively into the matter of the nature of the 'spiritual', probably the most useful document is Ofsted's 'Promotion and Evaluating Pupils' Spiritual, Moral, Social and Cultural Development' (2004). A web-based publication, it includes most of the relevant points. To pull some of them out, we read of the acquisition of 'personal beliefs and values' (pp. 10–11); 'the spiritual quest' (p. 11); 'the belief that one's inner resources provide the ability to rise above everyday experiences' (p. 12); 'the essence of being human, involving the ability to surpass the boundaries of the physical and material' (p. 13); 'a propensity to foster human attributes such as love, faithfulness and goodness, that cannot be classed as physical' (p. 13); 'the inner world of creativity and imagination' (p. 13); 'the quest for meaning *in* life (p. 13; my emphasis); 'the sense of identity and self-worth which enables us to value others' (p. 13); 'the human spirit' (p. 14); 'their *own* spirituality' (p. 14; my emphasis); 'a pupil's "spirit"' (p. 12); and of 'encouraging pupils to explore and develop what animates themselves and others' (p. 18). Vitalism alive and well today.

Although there are also more theistically orientated passages (partly so as not to leave anyone out), it is clear that the extracts I have provided associate spirituality with humanistic-cum-expressivistic values, and more than hint that many will find that the 'inner world' *is* important. Taking their cue from governmental documentation, it is certainly the case that numbers of teachers encourage inner-life spirituality. After all, schools are inspected, the Chief Inspector of Schools having the general duty of keeping the Secretary of State informed about spiritual – moral, social and cultural – matters. The emphasis is on spiritual *development*, frequently taking place within child- or student-centred contexts where holistic themes are in evidence, where a fair number of teachers are 'believers' (maybe holistic participants, even practitioners), with faith in 'spirituality' as a way of being inclusivistic enough to handle monocultural and multicultural issues; teachers who welcome relief from the routine focus on exam results. With these and other factors encouraging 'spiritual development' in addition to 'merely' teaching *about* spirituality, it is not surprising that inner-life, *experiential* activities are becoming more popular within the mainstream educational system.[8] Although I do not yet have systematic evidence, research to date in an area around Lancaster ranging from Blackpool in the southwest to Settle to the northeast suggests that many primary schools now provide yoga or tai chi for their pupils (and parents); some have special areas where pupils can go for creative, calming and holistic therapies. Certainly, local schools around where I live in the Yorkshire Dales (perhaps an unlikely setting in that many pupils come from traditional, Methodist farming families), including Ingleton Middle School and the Church of England Primary School which I serve as a member of the Board of Governors, are active.

Provisions

In 1998, Daniel Mears and Christopher Ellison (2000) carried out an innovative study. With a 60 per cent response rate to their telephone survey of Texas residents, they found that 22 per cent of respondents answered in the affirmative to the question, 'In the past year, have you purchased, read or listened to any "New Age" materials (books, magazines, audio or videotapes)?' (p. 297). What is especially important to note is that New Age themes are in evidence: 66 per cent of the 22 per cent of purchasers believe that 'spiritual truth comes from within', for instance (p. 300). The 'consumption', as Mears and Ellison designate it, of 'New Age materials' is predominantly by 'New Agers' (p. 300).

A great deal of hard evidence, collected by publishers and publishing agencies, supports the contention that the most noticeable area of growth of New Age provisions along the high street has taken place within bookshops (or shops which have a book section). Volumes addressing inner-life spirituality are becoming ever more numerous, one major chain in Britain (which must remain anonymous) selling something in the order of four times more mind-body-spirituality publications than those devoted to traditional theistic world religions. And in newsagents, magazines and newspapers contain increasing amounts of material on mind-body-spirituality. More systematically, unpublished research by Andrea Cheshire (2001), then of Lancaster University, shows that in January 2001, 56 of the 187 high-street shops of Kendal were selling New Age products – products which signalled, encouraged or aimed to facilitate holistic spirituality. Replicating the research in April 2003, Cheshire found that the proportion of these shops had risen from 30 to 45 per cent, with a number being serviced by companies specializing in New Age provisions. It is true that 'new spiritual outlets', as I call those 'alternative' shops specializing in New Age provisions, have not grown as fast as one might expect – but this is surely due to their being rendered relatively redundant by the 'mainstreaming' of such provisions within more conventional outlets.[9]

The Unbelievable

Probably the most arresting evidence concerning the popularity of New Age spiritualities of life is provided by the numerical significance of relevant 'beliefs'.[10] The findings from a number of countries are indeed rather unbelievable.

The RAMP (Religious and Moral Pluralism) survey of the late 1990s was carried out in 11 European countries. Of particular significance for present purposes, religious 'beliefs' were probed by adding an option to the kind of list which has long been in use. In answer to the question 'Which of these statements comes nearest to your own?' respondents were provided with the opportunity to select 'I believe that God is something within each person, rather than something out there'. Drawing on a range of sources, including Eileen Barker (2004 'Summary of Research Results', www.regard.ac.uk), respondents from the 11 countries provided the following responses:

Portugal (979 respondents)   39.1 %
Great Britain (1,423 respondents)   37.2 %

Sweden (1,007 respondents)	36 %
Italy (2,149 respondents)	35.9 %
Denmark (597 respondents)	35.2 %
Belgium (1,659 respondents)	30.8 %
Finland (758 respondents)	28.9 %
Netherlands (1,002 respondents)	26.4 %
Norway (480 respondents)	25 %
Hungary (979 respondents)	24.6 %
Poland (1,133 respondents)	18.4 %
Total	29 %

It is also noteworthy that in 6 of the 11 countries, percentages for the 'God within' are higher than percentages for the 'personal god':

Sweden	personal God = 18 %	God within = 36 %	difference = 18 %
Denmark	personal God = 20.1 %	God within = 35.2 %	difference = 15.1 %
Great Britain	personal God = 23.4 %	God within = 37.2 %	difference = 13.8 %
Portugal	personal God = 25.9 %	God within = 39.1 %	difference = 13.2 %
Belgium	personal God = 21.5 %	God within = 30.8 %	difference = 9.3 %
Netherlands	personal God = 23.4 %	God within = 26.4 %	difference = 3 %

Using 'I believe in a God with whom I can have a personal relationship' as a *rough* guide to belief in the theistic God of Christianity (and other traditions), and using 'God within' as a *rough* guide for inner-spirituality, the data *could* be taken as signifying a spiritual revolution of belief.

In the USA, Wade Clark Roof (1999b) draws attention to the fact that 'The Barna Research Group estimates that one out of five Americans, or 20 per cent, are what it calls "New Age Practitioners"' (p. 136). The importance of inner-life spirituality is also indicated by George Gallup and Timothy Jones's (2000) finding that 'almost a third of our survey defined spirituality with no reference to...a higher authority', a typical response being that spirituality is 'the essence of my personal being' (p. 49).

Although longitudinal comparison is somewhat tricky – not least because survey questions have tended to change over the years – it is safe to say that there has been a considerable increase in the number of people in Europe, and almost certainly the USA and elsewhere (including Australia and Japan), who have 'turned within' for belief. It is not an exaggeration to say that the inhabitants of a number of European countries are living through the most radical period of spiritual-religious change of belief since Christianity took root in their lands.[11] Without denying for one moment that there are problems with this kind of data, including the near-certainty that God within 'beliefs' does not always mean that respondents explicitly refer to inner-life *spirituality*, the findings can hardly be ignored. (For further discussion, see Heelas, 2007a, 2008a; Heelas and Houtman, 2008; Palmisano, forthcoming.) They must indicate something – almost certainly a *great deal*. And the fact that a broadly similar picture emerges from other surveys gives us some confidence that the findings are reasonably reliable (see the Appendix).

The numerical importance of inner-life beliefs among the general population of Britain and elsewhere is considerable. Obviously, though, buying a mind-body-spirit volume, let alone reading a mind-body-spirit article in a magazine or newspaper, could indicate interest or amusement rather than belief. Neither does participating in mind-body-spirituality activities within a relatively secular spa necessarily involve belief. Far from it. With only around half of the participants of the holistic milieu of Kendal according spiritual significance to their activities, the figure is likely to be less within spas. Nor, for that matter, need belief be involved when primary school teachers are leading 'centring' activities – neither for the teachers themselves nor for their students. Nevertheless, publishers and spa owners, for example, would not be interested in the holistic, spirit-body-mind dynamic if their market research had not led them to the conclusion that there was a market to be catered for; a 'cultural platform' to capitalize upon. Equally, businesses would not spend considerable sums on cultivating inner-life spirituality among employees unless employers had a good idea that it would be adopted (and prove effective).

The number and range of provisions and activities found in cultural-cum-institutional settings would not have proliferated as they have unless there was a receptive sector of the population; unless they were in tune with the beliefs, expectations, values or interests of a significant number of people. The 37 per cent of the British who apparently see God as 'inside each person' serves as a basis for provisions and activities to cater for, for spirituality to flow into new settings. And given the pretty solid evidence from a reasonable amount of research showing that inner-spirituality is associated with expressivistic values, higher levels of educational attainment and the person-centred professions (see chapter 5), there is little doubt that teachers, nurses, HRD personnel and the like are most likely to be 'believers', maybe contributing to growth in their sectors of expertise accordingly.

Concluding Thoughts

Earlier in this chapter I mentioned the fact that slightly over 900,000 inhabitants of Great Britain are active on a weekly basis in the holistic milieux of the nation. Numbers of participants swell if one includes those who experience their activities as spiritual even though their practitioners do not. Given the 'God within' percentage, and the likelihood that this is higher among those attracted by (say) more secular (body-mind) holistic forms of CAM, the number of participants of this kind could be considerable. Furthermore, there are those who 'participate' alone: yoga at home; life-meditation whilst walking; etc. Mike Savage et al.'s (1992) analysis of British Market Research Bureau data suggests that this number could be relatively significant for those health, education and welfare professionals who practise yoga (p. 108). As for beliefs, much hangs on whether one includes those humanistic expressivists who 'believe' in their 'true' or 'authentic' self; those who do not use the language of spirituality but who 'believe' in an inner, authentic self which somehow lies beyond society and culture. On the one hand, the idea of this true self most certainly smacks of the metaphysical (Shils, 1981, pp. 10–11; Tipton, 1982; Heelas, 2000, pp. 244–48). It is an interior self which has a great deal in common with the 'spiritual self'. One might say it is spiritual in all but name – Gilbert Ryle's (1963) 'ghost in the machine' comes to mind. On the other hand, though, the language of spirituality is not used; and perhaps other than serving as an inner source of wisdom, the authentic self of the mode of expressive humanism under consideration is relatively secular. The (healing, etc.) powers of the sacred are not in evidence. At the same time, however, the mode of selfhood under consideration is only *relatively* secular: various aspects of inner-life spirituality, such as the theme of holistic integration, could well be in evidence – 'psychological' integration of a 'magical' kind which scientistic psychologists would dismiss. In short, there is a spectrum between the spiritual self and the relatively secular, numerical significance varying in accord with where a line is drawn; and it has to be said that it is exceedingly doubtful that a useful line can be drawn between, say, the functionally (and to an extent metaphysically) similar ideas of 'unlocking human potential' and 'expressing one's spirituality'. (See also chapter 8.)

Drawing his discussion of religion and 'alternative' spirituality in Britain to a close, Bruce (1996) writes that 'in so far as we can measure *any* aspect of religious interest, belief or action and can compare 1995 with 1895, the only description for the change between the two points is "decline"' (p. 273). Whatever the very considerable virtues of Bruce's data survey in connection with the decline of traditional, theistic religion, in so far as 'alternative' spiritualities are concerned the evidence which has been presented shows that Bruce's assessment can be reversed – to run, 'the only description for...change...is "growth"'. 'New Age beliefs and attitudes' might not have become important enough to 'effectively dominate all areas of life', as Campbell would have it (to think of the quotation at the beginning of this chapter). But the flow through society and culture, as well as whatever 'independent "invention"' which has taken place, is of an arresting order. Even Gleneagles, that bastion of baronial establishmentarianism, has 'gone with the flow' – 'The Spa', 'recognized as the best hotel spa in Scotland following the Annual Conde Nast Reader Traveller Awards 2006', 'offers beauty care and therapeutic treatments for ladies and gentlemen, including the innovative ESPA holistic programmes in life enhancement and unique organic healing and therapeutic Ytsara treatments'. (ESPA treatments are as much for the 'inner self' as anything else.)

Spiritual revolutions – defined as beliefs and/or activities of an inner-life spirituality nature becoming more numerous than the beliefs and/or activities of life-as religion and the spiritualities of transcendent theism – have taken place, or might *very* well be underway, in a variety of contexts: book store chains, associational activities (the fortunes of the holistic milieu compared with the fortunes of the congregational domain), educational practices, mainstream health provision, mainstream business activities, personal beliefs, for example. But are these revolutions – or revolutions in the making – significantly 'spiritual'?

Growth: which means that more people have the opportunity to engage in 'spiritual' consumption than, say, in 1970. The pleasurable titillation of the spiritual massage; the healthy hedonism provided by the holistic spa; the glow that comes from believing that one is a spiritual being; the enchantment stimulated by the 'moving' spiritual autobiography; the purchased freedom provided by the spiritual adventure story; the pride felt in connection with the status display of the 'Tibetan' Buddha in the hall (that 'symbol of restrained good taste', as Mick Brown (1998) puts it). Or is this entirely fair, at least as an overall portrayal? Could it be the case, for example, that even the most 'trivial' of New Age provisions or services *can* serve to lead people away from whatever consumeristic processes are in evidence to 'deeper' things – *beyond* the orbit of 'merely' gratifying the individual? Then what about nurses and primary school teachers? Is it a matter of somehow dividing up the provisions and activities of New Age spiritualities of life into consumer and non-consumer dominated categories?

It is likely that a considerable number of those purchasing commodities are already of a spiritual disposition. Mears and Ellison's finding – that the 'consumption' of New Age materials is predominantly by New Agers – provides support. So does the consideration that those who purchase commodities are primarily middle class, expressivistic, and more likely to belong to the 'God within' camp than the 37 per cent for Britain as a whole; and are also more likely to see 'God' as a spirit or life-force than the typical person (the national average being 14 per cent – see the Appendix). Perhaps 'believers' are less likely to be consuming New Age commodities than non-believers. Perhaps they are more likely to be finding *spiritual significance* in what they buy, over-and-above secular self-satisfaction.

It can be argued that inner-life beliefs are sustained, perhaps developed, perhaps solidified, perhaps enriched by mind-body-spirituality provisions, let alone holistic activities. It can be argued that inner-life beliefs would not be so popular without the provisions (and holistic activities) – provisions (including magazine articles about celebrities and spirituality) playing an important role in acclimatizing, perhaps interesting, younger people, for example. It can be argued that provisions (and activities) would not be so popular without the beliefs, the popularity of provisions owing a great deal to the ways in which they resonate with beliefs, associated expectations, 'demand'. It could also be argued that *feedback* is taking place, commodities contributing to belief, belief encouraging appropriate purchases. But none of these possibilities are especially significant if the presence of spirituality really only means the presence of consumption.

Finally, although I have not gone into it in detail in this chapter, governmental agencies in the UK (most noticeably in the form of Ofsted and the NHS), and no doubt governmental agencies elsewhere, have had a role in encouraging some of the growth areas. This is taken up later.

Part II

The 'Consuming Growth' Debate

Chapter 3

The Debate

What is the spirituality revolution? It is a spontaneous movement in society, a new interest in the reality of spirit and its healing effects on life, health, community and well-being. It is our secular society realizing that it has been running on empty, and has to restore itself at a deep primal source, a source which is...at the very core of our experience. (David Tacey, 2004, p. 1)

...the close parallels between the two [a New Age-style worldview and modern consumerism]. (Colin Campbell, 2004, p. 40)

New Age discourse is continually redirected to address possible opportunities for consumption in the lives of participants. (Guy Redden, 2005, p. 239)

New Age spirituality would seem to be a strong candidate for the future of religion because its individualistic consumeristic ethos fits well with the spirit of the age. (Steve Bruce, 2006, p. 45)

The consumer, it appears, more or less makes the world go round. Capitalism works through 'consumer seduction' (Lyon, 2000, p. 39). The macro-economy of the globe is influenced by inflation, in turn influenced by rates of consumption. Voting patterns reflect consumer-orientated promises. At least from the time of Vance Packard (1957), followed by the influential Ralph Nader (Bollier, 1991), the 'active consumer' has been identified as the responsible citizen. Work ethics – in the workplace and at home – are indissolubly linked with consumer 'ethics'. For many, living life to the full has come to mean fulfilling the promises of consumer culture. Personal identities are linked with consumer provisions. Age, ethnic, national, class, gender, religious, community, 'tribal' and friendship matters are articulated and contested through patterns of consumption. An apparently ever-increasing number of activities and ideas – educational, aesthetic, romantic love, mainstream health provision, for example – have come to be envisaged in terms of the basic language of consumption: 'consumption' itself, 'consume', 'consumerism', 'consumerization', 'the consumer', 'consumer culture'. The term 'the consumer' has progressed in the direction of rivalling, even displacing, more traditional terms like 'the student', 'the audience', 'the client', 'the patient', 'the spectator', 'the purchaser', 'the customer'. Responding to a questionnaire, one of my undergraduates wrote 'I consume information'. For Habermas, 'the consumption of culture' more or less *in toto* is now widely in evidence (Calhoun, 1996, p. 21). Zygmunt Bauman recently published *Consuming Life* (2007), Benjamin Barber *Consumed. How Markets Corrupt Children, Infantilize Adults, and Swallow Citizens Whole* (2007) and Antonella Caru and Bernard Cova *Consuming Experience* (2006); and then there is Sara Henderson and Alan Petersen's edited volume, *Consuming Health* (2001).

Reflecting on contemporary culture, Karin Ekstrom and Helene Brembeck (2004) note, 'Consumer culture is a way of looking at, and seeking to derive, value in the world *that has far reaching consequences*' (p. 3; my emphasis) – fuelling the spread of individualistic, self-centred, 'emotivist culture' (MacIntyre, 1985, p. 22), it can be added; fuelling the 'ethic' that people should deploy choice on the basis of their own evaluations of their own subjectivities to satisfy their own preferences. As Ekstrom and Brembeck also note:

> Consumption (and consumerism) is gradually trickling into *all* areas of human life. It is closely related to all aspects of being human, and is – for good or bad – the foundation of human existence. (pp. 1–2; my emphasis)[1]

In similar vein, Colin Campbell (2004) argues, 'Since...more and more areas of contemporary life have become assimilated to a "consumer model" it is perhaps hardly surprising that the underlying metaphysic of consumerism has in the process become a kind of default philosophy for *all* of modern life' (pp. 41–2; my emphasis). For Zygmunt Bauman (1992), 'consumption' is 'steadily' becoming the 'moral focus of life' (p. 49).[2] And, at greater length, Jean Baudrillard (1988), who, it will be noted, goes so far as to claim that there is a cultural bond between consumption, happiness and being social:

> The consumer, the modern citizen, cannot evade the constraint of happiness and pleasure, which in the new ethics is equivalent to the traditional constraint of labour and production. Modern man spends less and less time in production, and more and more in the continuous production and creation of personal needs and of personal well-being. He must constantly be ready to actualize all of his potential, all of his capacity for consumption. He is therefore not passive: he is engaged, and must be engaged, in continuous activity. Otherwise he runs the risk of being satisfied with what he has and of becoming asocial. (p. 48)

Just as the language – if not the reality – of consumption has grown in significance during the last few decades, so, we have seen, have all those New Age provisions, activities and beliefs which locate the heart of spirituality within the depths of life in the here-and-now rather than within a transcendent, over-and-above-this-world source. Consumption is significant; spiritualities of life have apparently come to comprise a significant aspect of the 'sacred' – so what are the relationships between the two? Awash in a sea of consumption: can anything counter the rising tide?

At least since the time of Chesterton, scholars have clearly enjoyed using their acerbic skills to criticize 'alternative' spiritualities. Generally speaking, the 'reduction' to consumption strategy has been their favoured tool – for some, because it can be used in their war against the increasing significance of the 'sins' of capitalism; for others, to show that the sacred has taken corrupt forms under the influence of modernity. From G. K. Chesterton (1909), with his argument that 'god within' believers are consumed by self-interest (p. 136), to Christopher Lasch's (1980, 1987) equally forceful 'narcissism' critiques, to Zygmunt Bauman's (1998) even more forceful attacks focusing on 'consumer self-indulgence' (p. 70), to Jeremy Carrette and Richard King's $elling Spirituality (2005) with their 'capitalist spiritualities' and 'the promotion of unrestrained desire-fulfilment as the key to happiness' (p. 21), to Kimberly Lau's *New Age Capitalism* (2000) and Adam Possamai's (2005) 'hyper' consumption, New Age spiritualities have received something of a battering. The most radical of the frequently encountered claim that 'alternative' spirituality is privatized, selected and purchased in the consumer culture marketplace to serve as leisure-time self-gratification, is that New Age spiritualities of life *in general* are fully-fledged forms of consumption. Thus, for Possamai (2005), 'New Age is the consumer religion *par excellence*' (p. 49), those involved with 'alternative spiritualities . . . consum[ing] products for gathering and enhancing sensations' (2003, p. 31). For Lau (2000), even 'responsibility' belongs to the realm of consumption: in New Age circles, 'financial sacrifice is rewarded with the cultural capital and moral sense of having consumed "responsibly" – whether that means responsibility toward one's own personal consciousness and spiritual development, one's community, or one's planet' (p. 18).

In stark contrast, those active within inner-life circles generally avoid the language of consumption like the plague. Practitioners of the very large number of holistic activities currently available use terms like 'group members' or 'clients' to refer to their participants; browsing through the voluminous mind-body-spirit literature, almost entirely written by practitioners, one virtually never comes across the language – other, that is, than when consumer culture is criticized for diverting people from what really matters in life. This is hardly surprising. Such language has so many negative associations.

'The word "consume"', writes Alan Aldridge (2003),

> dates from the fourteenth century. Its original meaning was pejorative: to use up, destroy, devour, waste, squander, exhaust. 'Consumer' dates from the sixteenth century, with similar pejorative connotations. 'Consumption' originally referred to any wasting disease, before becoming the term for severe pulmonary tuberculosis. (p. 2)[3]

With an eye on present circumstances, Aldridge continues, 'The pejorative meanings associated with consumption, consumerism and "the consumer" are ammunition for cultural critics' (p. 3; see also p. 84). The term is used to refer to the trivialization of provisions in order to pander for the lowest common denominator, thereby maximizing profits; spoon-feeding or giving people what they want by making away with anything challenging – to please students, for example. In the words of Aldridge (2003) again, 'Much of the sociological literature ... paints a portrait of consumers as pathetically warped pleasure-seekers devoid of moral worth'. In short, according to this critical usage, 'Consumerism does not raise us up, it drags us down' (p. 25, 9).

Given these negatives, those researching or commenting upon mind-body-spiritualities can readily draw on the language of consumption – and associated subjectivities – as a powerful critical tool: my favourite exemplification being theologian Graham Ward's (2006) claim (previously mentioned in part) that the more that spirituality-cum-religion 'becomes commodified', the more it will

> develop forms of hyper-individualism, self-help as self-grooming, custom-made eclecticism that proffer a pop transcendence and pamper to the need for 'good vibrations'. By means of this 'spiritualism' – that is sensation hungry and the counterpart to extreme sports – a collection of religious people will emerge (are already emerging) who will be unable to tell the difference between orgasm, an adrenalin rush and an encounter with God. (p. 185)

The Debate and the Nature of Growth

There is, then, a pronounced contrast between all those 'outsiders' who apply the language of consumption, often in critical vein, and all those participants who steer well clear of the language of consumption (except, that is, to criticize the mainstream of modernity). This raises a fundamental issue, namely, who is right over the matter of whether New Age spiritualities of life largely, if not entirely, *belong* to that major feature of modernity – the core values and assumptions of consumer culture – rather than providing a counter-current, perhaps some kind of 'break' to make a stand.

I now list the interpretive options.

On one side of the debate the argument is that many – or virtually all – mind-body-spiritualities are deeply imbued with the spirit of consumption.

'Consumer culture', writes Mike Featherstone (1991a), 'uses images, signs and symbolic goods which summon up dreams, desires and fantasies which suggest romantic authenticity and emotional fulfilment in narcissistically pleasing oneself' (p. 27). Apparently sacralizing consumption, though in fact heavily consumeristic, in practice holistic spiritualities function to generate 'images, signs and symbolic goods' to evoke 'dreams, desires and fantasies': with the promise, suggestion or indication of fulfilment; with the promise of 'changing your life' or of enabling you to 'get a life' (to think of two major slogans of western culture); with the possibility of actualizing the veritable barrage of 'makeover' dreams-cum-'realities' proffered by the media ('makeover' being a sub-slogan of the 'changing your life' theme); with the possibility of at least doing something to match the *high* expectations which so characterize cultures in the west. (Jokingly, Terry Pratchett says he 'doesn't want to get a life, because it feels as though he's trying to lead three already'.) Although it might be accepted that 'producers' or 'suppliers' sometimes have honourable spiritual intentions, their consumers are seen as obtaining 'spiritual' highs of a 'merely' psychological variety. Especially when *taken* to be ultimate, the presence of inner-life spirituality products and services within consumer culture arouses hopes of 'perfect' wellbeing, 'spiritual beauty' (Cartner-Morley, 2001), wellness, pleasure, sensory experience. 'Magical' products and services serve to provide the opportunity to experience the 'best', the consummation of what consumer products and services have to offer – 'ultimately' suffused or heightened experiences. The consumer culture wing of modernity is epitomized; consumption is consummated, if not brought to 'completion', 'fruition' or 'fulfilment'; that utopianism so characteristic of so much consumer culture is at least assuaged. A 'cultural extremity' of consumer culture.[4] The self consuming itself – the self as the sum of consumer experiences, flooded 'with' spirituality, 'narcissistically pleasing' itself, a consummation of the self-absorbed – is at least on the horizon.

Whether used for critical purposes or not, the language of consumption is perfectly applicable. New Age consumers who do not recognize this are suffering from some kind of false consciousness or reality aversion syndrome. On the other side of the debate, one argument is that participants have to be listened to seriously when they explicitly reject the idea that their activities (or beliefs) have anything (much) to do with consumption. A complementary, albeit more significant argument, is that the *nature*, the *meaningful reality* of their beliefs, experiences, values and activities shows that spirituality – the 'ethos' (to recall the introductory quotation from Bruce), the ways it is held to work – transcends conformity to consumer culture, perhaps resisting it or reacting to it to facilitate or support the difference that *makes* a difference over-and-above what everyday consumer culture has to offer.

Then there is the possibility of some sort of middle way (or ways), one which recognizes that certain aspects of certain activities call for the selective use of the language of consumption, whilst also recognizing that other aspects should be portrayed in other languages, such as that of the ethic of humanity; languages which locate New Age spiritualities of life within and beyond consumer culture – without reducing to either.

Finally, there is the possibility that much of the debate can be resolved, or bypassed, simply by avoiding the language of consumption as much as possible – if at all – using other terms (like 'recipient') to make relevant points.

The importance of the debate: the salience of growth

Few, if any, scholars deny that mind-body-spirituality is a growing presence in the UK (or elsewhere in the west). As we saw in the last chapter, whether it be associational, face-to-face, holistic activities like yoga, tai chi or spiritual aromatherapy, inner-life spirituality within the realms of mainstream institutions like schools (especially primary schools), hospitals, hospices or companies (especially 'cutting-edge' businesses), commodities (including books, magazines and New Age artefacts), the (possibly) less tangible provisions of subjective wellbeing culture (including those provided by spas, 'wellness' or health and fitness centres), or beliefs in the general population, indices show growth, not decline. But *what* is growing? Is secular consumer culture consuming – that is, using or absorbing the 'sacred' like blotting paper – to provide an attractive bonus to fuel *its* growth, or are *spiritualities* of life 'consuming', now in the sense of (significant numbers of) participants having been 'taken over by', or 'absorbed by', the spirituality of being?

Growth raises issues for secularization theorists. Faced with the evidence, the strategy is to argue that growth is more apparent than real. Accepting that the 'offerings' of the 'cultic milieu' have become more popular (Bruce, 2002, p. 85), Steve Bruce (2006) argues, 'What matters for testing the secularization thesis is not the range of spiritual offerings being purveyed but the numbers who take them up and *the spirit in which they do so*' (p. 39; my emphasis); and the 'spirit' of 'New Age spirituality', he continues, takes the form of an 'individualistic consumeristic ethos' (p. 45).

Thinking of one of the two meanings of the expression 'consuming growth', the argument is that growth is largely, if not entirely, consumed: 'taken in' to be 'used up' by people, especially those absorbed by consumer culture. Rather than being spiritual in any 'serious' or 'significant' sense of the term, activities and provisions are a 'fag ending' of the sacred, if not essentially secular. The language of 'spirituality' takes its place alongside all those other expressions and devices which consumer culture uses to stimulate and satisfy desire. Using expressions like 'yoga highs for perfect wellbeing', mind-body-spirituality activities take their place alongside the 'I'm luving it' of the fast-food trade, the 'Because you're worth it' of the beauty industry, the 'Experience the drive of your life' of the car advert. Even if the growth of New Age spiritualities of life suggests that a spiritual revolution is underway – with inner-life spiritual activities and beliefs becoming, or having become, more important than those associated with the God of transcendent theism – it is far from being a *spiritual* revolution. A false dawn of the sacred; a travesty of the real thing. The consuming way, and away, of growth. The abortion.[5]

Thinking of the second meaning of the expression 'consuming growth', the argument now is that what is growing is able to be 'consuming'. As in expressions like 'consumed with anger', when *one* is 'taken over by' an emotion, the idea is that that the *realm of the sacred* is in the process of being 'taken over by' inner-life spiritualities. Furthermore, the argument is that many of those involved with particular activities, like meditation groups, are working to experience being consumed by what they take to *be* spirituality – rather than somehow consuming meditation or yoga simply to pleasure themselves. As a meaningful spiritual reality, growth is real.

The 'consuming growth' debate is important. The spiritual salience of growth is not simply a matter of academic curiosity. From an existential viewpoint, the significance of inner-life spirituality for participants is at stake. *Just* another kind of gratificatory consumption, akin to a good meal? Or Roof's (1999b) more precise 'thin...chicken soup' (p. 138)? Recalling what has been said in the Introduction, the significance of inner-life spirituality for relationships, including relationships with kin, friends and colleagues, is also at stake. *Just* an enhancement of the narcissistic, the self-absorbed? And from the sociopolitical, ethical and activist perspectives, there is the significance of humanistic ethicality. *Just* another kind of selfish consumption, dressed up as 'self-realization' but actually serving to sap the will to change anything beyond the self, including the ways the self has been instrumentalizing activities and people? *Just* a capitalistic tactic, an opiate diverting people from what matters in the world at large by seducing them with forms of consumption which actually harm the world – the poor who could be helped if resources were allocated differently; the environment if people did not fly off for mind-body-spirit spas on distant islands?

Religion

The 'consuming growth' debate also has a significant bearing on the study of traditional religion – although now with regard to the overall decline of Christianity in the great majority of countries in the west. On the one hand, it is argued that the consumerization of religion contributes to decline; on the other, to the stability or the growth of some forms of Christian tradition. Whatever the case, the matter of consumption and Christianity is not without importance.

On one, entirely plausible, Romantic-inspired interpretation, the verse from Genesis running 'For God doth know that in the day ye eat thereof, then your eyes shall be opened, and ye shall be as gods, knowing good and evil' is best interpreted by way of the verse which comes next: 'And when the woman saw that the tree was good for *food*, and that it was pleasant to the eyes, and a tree to be *desired* to make one wise, she took the fruit thereof, and did eat, and gave also unto her husband with her; and he did eat' (Genesis 3: 5, 6; my emphases). The first significant awakening of autonomy, which renders Eve and Adam 'as gods', derives from the satisfaction of desire. In the first instance, knowledge of good and evil is nothing to do with 'abstract' ethicality. In measure, it is more akin to the kind of knowledge or 'wisdom' provided by a consumer guide. Humanity begins with an act of consumption.[6] And one which elicits the wrath of God. 'I also will do this unto you; I will even appoint over you terror, consumption, and the burning auge, that shall consume the eyes, and cause sorrow of heart', reads a verse from Leviticus (26: 16). The initial act of consumption elicits another kind of consumption – from the God of the Old Testament.

Today, as swathes of Christianity in the west detraditionalize, intentionally or unintentionally shifting from the authority of the traditionalized past to come into alignment with the authority, values, (rational) choices and expectations of the more individualistic, arguably more consumeristic present, the locus of consumption has shifted correspondingly: from the Godhead to the person. In the words of Christian Smith (2005):

> The more American people and institutions are redefined by mass-consumer capitalism's moral order, the more American religion is also remade in its image. Religion becomes one product among many others existing to satisfy people's *subjectively defined* needs, tastes, and wants. Religious adherents thus become spiritual consumers uniquely authorized as autonomous individuals to pick and choose in the religious market whatever products they may find satisfying or fulfilling at the moment. And the larger purpose of life comes to be defined as optimally satiating one's self-defined needs and desires. (p. 176; my emphasis)

By and large, New Age spiritualities of life are further along the 'fully traditionalized'–'fully detraditionalized' (or 'post-traditional') ideal-type spectrum than virtually all forms of Christianity.[7] Being further along this spectrum, indeed sometimes reaching the end point of *the* detraditionalized (where there are no external voices of sacred authority for participants), issues to do with the significance of consumption are highlighted. Taking things more *or* less to the limit, the study of consumption and New Age inner-spirituality provides an excellent context for probing the language of consumption and the sacred. Accordingly, it is more than likely that conclusions drawn from the study of the more radically detraditionalized can contribute to the study of the (generally) less radical forms of detraditionalization increasingly found within Christianity in the west. Whether detraditionalized forms of religion or New Age spiritualities of life, though, the great danger is the much the same – fuelling self-centred consumption.

Some Challenges

It is one thing for believers to hold that their meaningful reality, especially when it is experienced or taken to be of ontological standing, is far removed from the consumeristic sins of excess-capitalism, far enough removed to resist profanation, abuse or dissolution into *de*-generative 'comfort'; far enough removed for their meaningful realities to 'work' in their lives and the world around them to make a difference. It is another for the academic to make the same kind of case.

One reason is that it is easy to find evidence which appears to favour the 'consumption of spirituality' interpretation. Rather than providing examples from western settings, which readers might have encountered already, I briefly turn east, to the arguably unlikely setting of Pakistan, where in fact New Age mind-body-spirituality provisions and services are *very* similar to those found in (say) Britain or the USA. Turning to Pakistan also serves to introduce spirituality in a country which is returned to in the Epilogue.

Government tourist promotion banners (December 2006) announce, 'Let the Spirit Take You' – a reference to the spiritual 'traditions' of the country. The Pearl Continental Hotel Bhurban, north of Islamabad, announces on a prominently displayed poster: 'Hospitality without a Break. A Spiritual High Atop the Mountains'. In Islamabad itself, ChenOne (a fashionable 'Changing Lifestyles' store) uses the slogan 'The Spirit Within'. Also within Islamabad, the Nirvana Day Spa & Salon proclaims 'A State of Spiritual Joy', a booklet reading, 'NIRVAVA has been designed to excite all your senses and take you on a path to wellness'. 'A sensory journey through the orient, a fusion of Balinese grace, Thai charm, Japanese elegance and everything in between' is promised, with 'body, mind and spirit' activities – like Elemis Body Therapy – 'soothing your soul'. 'Spirituality' serving to ice the cake of luxury, the jazzed-up subjective wellbeing culture in Pakistan? If true, I cannot resist adding, where there are surely better things to do.[8]

Illustrations like these – and I have a very considerable number from a range of countries, including Uganda – indicate, perhaps demonstrate, that terms like 'spirituality', 'spirit' and 'spiritual' have a role to play in consumer culture. As we shall see, the very tricky challenge – empirical and conceptual – is to establish where provisions, services or activities, together with those involved, lie with the predominantly consumptive (presumably as within the commercial setting of ChenOne) or the predominantly not (perhaps for some involved with NIRVAVA) spectrum. If indeed this task is (always) feasible.

A second challenge derives from the fact that so much of western culture – including 'western' culture found elsewhere in cosmopolitan places like Islamabad – favours the 'reduction' to consumption thesis. It has become virtually standard practice to proclaim that consumer culture is central to life in the west; 'mass-consumer capitalism fundamentally constitutes the human self', emphasizes Christian Smith (2005, p. 176). If so many of our lives are so dominated, perhaps constituted by consumption, by the purchase, by the experience of ownership or possession, then the expectation is that commodified forms of the sacred – in particular – will tend to fall 'victim' to consumeristic intake. Furthermore, precisely because we live in a 'risk society', we also live in a risk-averse culture. Hence the great popularity of the ethic of 'comfort': the infatuation with 'feeling comfortable'; the continual questioning along the lines of 'Are you feeling comfortable?'. (To make someone feel uncomfortable places them 'at' risk, with the same applying to oneself, not least if the 'just in case' protective conventions of political correctness have been transgressed, or if emotional-response features of harassment rules have been violated.) And with the valorization of comfort, it is only to be expected that many seek to experience comfort as much as possible – by being pampered by a mind-body-spirituality practitioner by entering the security of a holistic spa, for example. Mind-body-spirituality promises to enable participants to 'live "life" to the full': so why not fill it up with the nice and easy, and safe?

Colin Campbell (2004) asks whether 'the New Age worldview can be regarded as coming into existence as a consequence of extrapolation from the assumptions that underlie modern consumerism' (p. 40). The possibility is that New Age spiritualities of life add up to a capitalist-led phenomenon, the 'massive subjective turn of modern culture' (itself fuelled by capitalism among other factors) stimulating consumption (with providers catering for requirements of subjective life), thereby contributing to sales and the capitalist system (as well as the 'turn' itself).[9] The argument owes much to the consideration that knowing what you want from life is one thing; getting it is another. Consumer culture cultivates the 'knowing'. Within those high-street shops where subjective wellbeing products are on sale, the argument continues, the 'magic' of 'spirituality' is called into play to appeal to expectations, desires, wishes or dreams. 'Homeopathy, aromatherapy and a pharmacy. All from the experts in retail therapy' (Tesco); 'The Perfectly Balanced Range' (Waitrose);'Meditation Balm' (Global Gatherings); 'Miracle So Magic' (Lancome). And tending to concentrate on offering the magic of that product known as perfect wellbeing – well, as perfect as 'humanly' possible – specialized holistic activities have grown in popularity accordingly. There is little doubt that by encouraging the search for the experientially laden 'more', thereby widening the gulf between what one has and what one expects from subjective life, consumer culture plays a role in generating and sustaining holistic spiritualities.[10] Neither can it be doubted that there are those who swallow up 'spirituality' for the sake of psychological wellbeing: pleasuring the self rather than living out of spiritual reality. Given that the New Age can serve as a spirituality of and for consumer culture, especially in its subjective wellbeing mode, the challenge is to show when this is not (significantly) the case. What the purchase can – can not, does not – do for the inner life...

Remaining with Colin Campbell, a challenge is posed for his 'easternization of the west' thesis. The thesis is bold, even bolder than the spiritual revolution thesis offered by Heelas and Woodhead (2005). It is that,

> the worldview characteristic of the East is in the process of replacing the formerly dominant Western view – in other words, that metaphysical monism is replacing materialistic dualism. More precisely, it means that belief in a transcendental, personal god is giving way to belief in an immanent and impersonal one; that all dualisms are being rejected, whether that of god and mankind, mankind and nature, mind and body, or body and soul, in favour of generally holistic assumptions. (2007, p. 66)

As Campbell himself points out, however, when yoga in the west (the most popular 'import') is 'stripped... of its spiritual associations and purpose' – which is by no means uncommon – it is 'doubtful' whether it can 'justifiably be deemed to constitute an aspect of Easternization' (p. 34). Citing Steve Bruce (2002), the significance of the east is undermined by 'causal "consumerist" interest' (p. 31).

To refer to just one other challenge – perhaps the most significant of them all – holistic spiritualities of life *themselves* tend to lend themselves to consumerization. Falling around the detraditionalized end of the external–internal voices of authority spectrum, there is plenty of scope for participants to exercise their own say; pursue their own desires – which could well have been stimulated by the psychological dynamics of consumer culture. Being 'an essentially inward-looking endeavour', Stephen Hunt (2005) more than implies that this orientation is linked with 'consumerist trends' (pp. 154–6). What goes in goes in. Somewhat conversely, it is highly likely that most practitioners are fully aware of the power of the 'ego' – the realm of the 'lower self' – which takes participants away from going within to experience their inner-spirituality in favour of 'wrong' kinds of wellbeing (such as finding pleasure by being selfish); 'ego'-power which might well be exercised in favour of the 'externals' of consumer culture (such as purchasing for competitive status display). The challenge is thus to show that activities can work, *as* mind-body-*spiritualities*, despite their apparent vulnerabilities.

For Zygmunt Bauman (1998), '"self-improvements" movements' – including what I am calling mind-body-spirit activities – 'are aimed... at the training of "*perfect consumers*"; at developing to the full the capacities of the experience-seeking and sensation-gathering life of the consumer/chooser demands' (pp. 71–2) – capacities which serve 'a life devoted to the art of consumer self-indulgence' (p. 70). Is he right? Tackling yet another challenge – 'defining' consumption – we will shortly see that there is some truth to the 'consuming spirituality' argument. As chapters unfold, though, it should become increasingly apparent that the vague and elusive meanings of the key terms of the language of consumption enable them to function along what could well be the slippery slope favouring erroneous reduction to consumption.

The Nature of the Evidence

As the chapters unfold, it will also become increasingly apparent that a good deal of the argument hangs on what participants have to say. This immediately raises a whole series of doubts. Can't participants be evasive, perhaps embarrassed about what they are really up to – consumption? Aren't they likely to be biased or to exaggerate? Aren't social scientists perfectly justified in arriving at conclusions which differ from whatever 'truth-value' might be accorded by participants? And most fundamentally of all, can they be relied upon when they report *spirituality*?

The 'consuming growth' debate is big enough; the participant validity debate is much bigger, with many issues still left unresolved. Compressing some of the arguments as much as possible, let me begin with the last of the above questions, not least because it is the easiest to address.

As social scientists, we do not have independent access to 'spirituality'. By this I mean that *if* spirituality exists, it is *highly likely* that it exists as a state of affairs which lies beyond anything which can be studied, scientifically, by way of publicly accessible information. Regarding my use of the expression 'highly likely', it would be to beg the question of the reliability of participant discourse to *believe* what they have to say about the supra-empirical nature of spirituality or about it being 'Unknowable' (Bloom, cited in Heelas, 1996a, p. 225). I say 'highly likely' on the commonsense ground that it is highly *unlikely* that our evolutionary past has provided us with the mental equipment to understand more than a fraction of what is taking place within the universe – including states of affairs, such as putative spirituality, which are totally beyond our ken as empirical investigators. *However* skilled we become at empirical investigation, the likelihood remains – although, of course, not the certainty – that there is an Einsteinian 'more' which we simply don't know about. (Describing himself as 'pantheistic' in the fashion of Spinoza, Einstein wrote of 'the insufficiency of the human mind to understand deeply the harmony of the Universe') (Jammer, 1999, pp. 75, 121–2; cf. Vallentin, 1954). 'There are more things in heaven and earth, Horatio, Than are dreamt of in your philosophy' matches the bill to some extent: although Hamlet has to 'know' this to say it. In reply to the objection, 'But surely it is an act of faith to claim that the unknowable, the mysterious, will always remain?', my reply is 'Maybe, but especially with some humility, not a very significant one'. Certainly, participants are fond of saying things like 'The Tao which can be known is not the Tao'. Or as one participant said to me (quoting someone, I think), 'The universe is stranger than you imagine; the universe is stranger than you *can* imagine'. From the perspective of many participants, if the sacred can be comprehended it is not significantly 'more' than what our comprehension is capable of. From my own perspective, I have to say that it would be extraordinary if it were not the case that the sheer limitations of the human condition entail that *nothing* can be discounted about the nature of the realm of ultimacy. Akin to ants 'listening' to Mozart...

Faced with this situation, my 'wager' is that it is best to take participants seriously when they say that they are spiritual, or are in contact with a spiritual dimension. We don't have to believe the *ontological truth* of what they report, but it is appropriate to take their *word*.[11] With no independent access to spirituality *per se* (if it exists, that is), we are simply not in the position of, say, the social scientist studying class, when one can argue, for example, that a neighbourhood is working class (as evidenced by occupations, choice of newspaper, housing, etc.) *even though* they consider themselves to have moved 'up'. In other words, even if it were the case that spirituality exists, there is no objective reality (other than meanings) to test what participants have to say about it.

But what of the objection that participants are simply mistaken when they say, for example, 'spiritual healing will cure my terminal cancer' (then moving on to die); or, if they are prosperity orientated, 'chanting will "manifest" money' (then going broke)? As anthropologists like Evans-Pritchard (1937) have for long argued, the problem here is that spirituality (or magical powers) can only too readily be brought into play to render apparent falsifications non-falsifiable. Spirituality, the argument goes, protects itself: the death bed utterance, 'Well, the spiritual healing didn't work – that's because I didn't remain in contact with my spirituality for long enough'. How is the social scientist to dismiss *this* as mistaken?

For reasons like this, even that supposedly exemplary figure of the Enlightenment, Richard Dawkins, says, 'How do I know there isn't a spirit world? Well, I don't.' He is only prepared to say, 'It *seems* improbable' ('The Enemies of Reason', Channel 4, 13 August, 2007; my emphasis).

Of course, my wager does not stand in the way of research directed at trying to ascertain whether participants use the language of spirituality in a secular way, for instance referring to possibly secular referents like being in 'high spirits'. But this *depends* on what participants have to say.[12] If they mean 'good feelings', fine – 'spirituality' *is* secular; but if they mean something metaphysical, something other than the secular, then that is equally fine.

David Voas and Steve Bruce (2007) write, 'Spirituality is clearly religious (in a broad sense) to the extent that it involved non-natural forces' (p. 51). They also write, 'the descriptions of spirituality given by the Kendal respondents [deriving from the Kendal Project] seem to have little to do with the supernatural or even the sacred; it appears to be a code word for good feelings, the emotional rather than the material' (p. 51). My answer for now, and it is elaborated later, is that if the evidence supports a super natural (not supernatural) referent, then whatever the interfusion with 'good feelings', spirituality it is. After all, we are in the realm of the holistic.

Broadening our compass, Alasdair MacIntyre (1971) argues:

> Beliefs and actions are...intimately related, since it is a central feature of actions that they are expressive of beliefs; and this is not just a contingent fact about actions. An action is identifiable as the action *that it is* only in terms of the agent's intention. (p. 253)

Primarily advanced by the Wittgensteinian fideists, most noticeably Peter Winch (1963), and then by some of those of postmodernist persuasion, this kind of argument has considerable force, and has had commensurate influence. Take away the meanings of *getting married* in church and the bodies inside the church would be left with very little indeed – except chaos in all probability. Particular 'acts', like hitting someone, can *mean* very different things – thereby serving *as* very different forms of activity. (For an application of this anti-positivist argument to the issue of characterizing supposedly peaceful societies, see Heelas, 1989.) From a different perspective than the strict fideist, Michel Foucault nevertheless argues the key point: meanings are *realities*. As he puts it from a radical constructivist perspective:

> It would be wrong to say that the soul is an illusion, or an ideological effect. On the contrary, it exists, it has a *reality*, it is produced permanently around, on, within the body by the functioning of a power...on those one supervises, trains and corrects, over madmen, children at home and at school, the colonized, over those who are stuck at a machine and supervised for the rest of their lives. (Foucault, 1991, p. 29; my emphasis; cf. Rose, 1990)

To put it mildly, whether it be getting married, engaging with spirituality, or states of affairs such as the soul, *meaningful realities* are hard to ignore. (See also the useful discussion in McCarthy, 1979, esp. p. xi.) Applying the fideist approach to mind-body-spirituality, when holistic participants do not believe that their activities, or their intentions, are anything to do with consumption (for example), then their activities are *not* about consumption.

Advanced by Freudians, structuralists (in particular Lévi-Strauss), sociological symbolists (like Durkheim) and many other schools of thought, the counter-argument is that although participants might be telling the truth as they see it, we social scientists (or psychotherapists) can establish the real truth: the signified of the symbolic system, the hidden or disguised meanings, the latent functions which show that the 'authentic self' is nothing less than a cultural ploy, the false consciousness. (On the last, see MacIntyre, 1971, p. 217.) Applying this argument to spiritualities of life, the conclusion is clear: even though participants might insist that their meaningful reality has nothing to do with consumption, as social scientists we can *detect* that consumption is in evidence – thereby justifying provision of a reductionist account.

Rather than engaging with the philosophy of social science to settle the matter (which in any case is far from settled), a way forward has to do with what is involved in 'detecting' consumption, or aspects of consumption: *when* participants use different forms of discourse to characterize their activities. Detection is surely perfectly justified when social scientists, working with a 'checklist' of what counts as consumption, apply their list to activities to show that consumption (better, aspects of consumption) is in evidence. If someone is 'clearly' using participation in an activity as a way of boasting at the dinner table, we are entitled to note this as a consumeristic latent function – latent in that the person involved talks about the activity in other ways. The same general point applies to the participant who uses words like 'pamper', 'pleasure' and 'not spiritual', but is 'uncomfortable' with the language of consumption – for we are then surely entitled to apply the language.

However, to move beyond the participants' frame of reference requires *good* evidence: perhaps the participant letting slip; perhaps observational evidence; perhaps contradictions. What we social scientists should not do, it seems to me, is apply a checklist of what counts as consumption to 'read off' consumption simply or largely because of the checklist – rather than because of good evidence. To illustrate, just because 'purchasing' is on the checklist, and just because purchasing is in evidence, it is a mistake to judge this as evidence of consumption *when* the act of purchasing is understood – say – as buying a gift for a close friend or flowers for a grave. In other words, detection of consumption requires at least reasonably sound evidence showing that purchasing has consumer or consumer-like meanings: going beyond denial ('I'm *not* a couch potato', for example) to show that that is what the person 'actually' is. And as we shall see, it is the frequent absence of satisfactory evidence to support the move beyond the (non-consumeristic) participant's frame of reference which persuades me that it is often *better* to 'go along' with the participants.

But having said this, I fully accept that it is all very tricky. And to compound matters, we shall see in the next chapter that the language of consumption is indeed elusive. I, for one, am still uncertain about exactly what is involved in calling an act an act of consumption – if indeed any act is simply, or very largely, an act of consumption. Holistic participants, it is probably fair to surmise, are also pretty unclear. So to ask them about consumption might not elicit a very helpful (or comprehensive) response. After all, the majority of participants won't have thought as deeply about what counts as consumption as interested academics – meaning that they might well not 'know' how to respond to the academic's list of what counts as consumption. (The academic's list of 'consumer items', as it might be put.) As Colin Campbell makes the point, 'Most people rarely think of themselves as consumers. On the contrary, we tend to think of ourselves as "shoppers" or "customers," or engaged in "eating," "watching a film," "going on holiday", etc.' (personal communication). Furthermore, academic inquiry on the matter might well be thought offensive, putting participants off. And in addition, it has to be kept in mind that it is not uncommon for participants to use the language of consumption as a way of 'downing' those holistic activities which they do not approve of – without good evidence, and almost certainly in ways which should be handled with circumspection.

I have spent some time on the issue of participant understanding because it *really* matters. For policy makers, for instance, the question of what credence, what significance or weight, to attach to what people have to say about spiritual counselling in hospices is important; or what teachers and pupils have to say about 'spiritual development' and associated values (if any). On policy grounds alone, the marked contrast between all those holistic participants who steer well clear of the language of consumption and all those academics (and others) who apply the language in dismissive vein, requires critical scrutiny – hopefully arriving at a better idea as to who is right, and about what.

Above all, perhaps, the fact that social scientists are not in the position to know anything about spirituality *per se* – that is, *if* it exists – entails that we have to take the meanings, the meaningful activities, of participants into account. If we don't, there is very little to study. We would not even know that we were studying 'spirituality'.

Unless there is *good* evidence of some kind to move beyond the participants' frame of meanings, I proceed on the basis of what participants have to say. And the more frequently that any particular participant says – for example – that 'this spiritual healing is all about coming to terms with my anger, although I sometimes think that it makes me feel self-indulgent', the better. Meanings matter for social scientists. In answer to the question 'Meaning for whom?' priority has to be given to our subject matter – the meaningful experiences, values and activities of participants. Priority (even) when a participant insists that 'pleasuring the self' *is* spiritual. How do we academics know how to disagree?

There remains the consideration that it can readily be argued that spirituality *per se* does not have to be present for spiritualities of life to be efficacious. Placebos, as performative beliefs, could be at work enhancing subjective wellbeing. For many people, values – such as respecting others – are not taken to depend on spirituality for their efficacy. Meanings *qua* meanings matter.

Chapter 4

The Language of Consumption and Consumeristic Aspects of Mind-Body-Spiritualities of Life

There is nothing stable or obvious at all about consumption. (Karin Ekstrom and Helene Brembeck, 2004, p. 2)

People involved in Alternative Spiritualities are part of... consumer religions. They consume products for gathering and enhancing sensations... the consumption of 'sensations'. (Adam Possamai, 2003, pp. 31–2; my emphasis)

So what is to be made of the argument that consumption is alive and well, if not rampant, within the expanding spheres of spiritualities of life, perhaps leaving them as little more than empty shells of 'spirituality'? This is by no means an easy question to address in order to provide answers. For among other reasons, consumption is a slippery customer. More exactly, the language of consumption is multi-faceted, terms being ripe with connotations, with many spill-overs of meanings.

Richard Wilk (2004) makes two key points. First, the 'vague, undefined and intangible nature of the concept of consumption that most social scientists use in their work' (p. 11). Second, he writes that 'any enterprise that sets out to find an objective category of consumption as a simple category of objects or activities that is "out there" as a bounded and measurable group, is doomed from the start' (p. 24) – a point also made by Ekstrom and Brembeck (2004) when they write that 'consumption is elusive in that it is not possible to identify... some clearly demarcated practices' (p. 6). Accordingly, it appears that we are faced with a situation in which (a) the concept of consumption is obscure; and (b) that the application of any straightforward definition, or definitions – if they can be identified – to characterize the 'totality' of z or y 'out there' is destined to fail.

Looking more closely at the first of these points, in the introduction to their aptly titled volume *Elusive Consumption* (2004), Ekstrom and

Brembeck suggest that 'consumption is elusive in that it is not possible to identify one single definition' (p. 6). As a cursory look at the voluminous, largely sociocultural literature on consumption serves to indicate, the elementary language of consumption – 'consumption' itself, 'consume', 'consumerism', 'consumerized', 'the consumer', 'consumer culture' – serves a wide range of uses. As we shall see in greater detail in a moment, these include the exercise of choice, the act of purchasing, the 'act' of passive and superficial absorption, the utilization of products required to sustain life, the pleasuring of the self, and the affirmation or creation of identity. Of particular note, the language spans two very different kinds of end products:

> The eating and burning metaphors [widely abroad in the language of consumption] tell us that the inevitable result of consumption is ashes and waste, of little or no value, malodorous and filthy. [However,] there are some kinds of consumption that actually raise and increase the value of things... You buy a house on the market, and consume it very much the way you consume a car or a television set, but a house is usually more valuable after ten years than it was when you bought it. (Wilk, 2004, p. 21)

From the destructive to the constructive, from the passive to the active, from the superficial to the necessary: it is not just that the range of uses is wide; some, at least, are contradictory.

It might well be expected that the scholarly literature on alternative spiritualities or New Age spiritualities of life would have gone a considerable way in establishing the nature and significance of consumption within this New Age territory. Unfortunately, this is not the case. Typically, researchers use the language of consumption without spelling out what they have in mind. They might well indicate their primary definition, but what else they might – or might not – have in mind is left hanging in the sphere of implication. Expressions like 'the consumer', for example, are frequently encountered in the literature. Is this just another word for the 'primary' senses of 'the one who chooses' and/or 'the purchaser' (for example)? Or does it also imply self-gratification and/or status display (for example)? The matter is left unclear. 'New Age is the consumer religion *par excellence*', writes Adam Possamai (2005, p. 49) – but his *Religion and Popular Culture* (2005) does little, if anything, to spell out and demonstrate the states of affairs or processes which he has in mind, and therefore the extent to which they operate to justify the '*par excellence*'. 'The consumption of media and popular culture with a religious or spiritual content' is how one of the themes of a 2007 conference is formulated. With consumption taken to be operative, the reader is expected to know what this signifies. Would that this be the case for me! (Or is the theme left intentionally vague to widen appeal?)[1]

The casual way in which the *basic* language of consumption is employed, the lack of specificity about the *particular* senses which are discerned within – or attributed to – New Age spiritualities of life, and (it can be emphasized) the strong tendency to prioritize assertion over evidence, means that a great deal remains opaque. To compound matters, there is Wilk's second point. Like any other cultural provision or activity, those provided by New Age spiritualities of life are multi-aspectual. Their 'embodied' assumptions, meanings and values – namely, those provided within texts, chants, activities – are multi-faceted; the ways in which they are interpreted and 'experienced' by participants even more so. It might be possible to characterize *aspects* of a yoga group by drawing on *specific usages* of the basic language of consumption. But it could very well be the case that what is taking place within a yoga group, for example, is too 'rich' for the language of consumption to handle – a possibility, indeed strong likelihood, which can only be explored once the language of consumption has been applied precisely enough to show its limits.

In short, the vague use of the language of consumption, which is such a feature of the secondary literature, means that a great deal of the scholarly appraisal of New Age spiritualities of life fails to provide a determinate picture of the consumeristic aspects – the arguably consumeristic 'ways' – of these spiritualities.

Given this lack of clarity, a reasonable way forward is to draw on the literature in the fields of sociology and cultural studies to tease out some of the key meanings which have been ascribed to the language of consumption. Working through these 'marks', they are applied to address the question of whether spiritualities of life are – in measure – functioning consumeristically. Since the great majority, if not all, New Age provisions or activities are complex, especially when recipient understandings and experiences are taken into consideration, with many shades of 'embodied' and interpretive meanings, it must be stressed that the 'definitional' markers which follow should be thought of as indicating different *aspects* of the processes or activities under consideration – aspects which can also readily combine in various ways. Certainly, to apply a key meaning, or a combination of key meanings, should not be taken to mean that any particular provision or activity consideration is *simply* to do with consumption. It should also be borne in mind that (a) the use of some of the key terms is not limited to the language of consumption *per se*; (b) the list of key terms does not add up to a coherent whole; and that (c) until a great deal more research is done, and quite possibly not even then, we are simply not in the position to determine where many things – provisions like mind-body-spirit books and their readers, activities like yoga and their participants – rank on some sort of 'more consumeristic–less consumeristic' scale. Finally, whilst critical appraisals of how the 'keys' of the language of consumption have been applied to spiritualities of life receive preliminary attention now, most are returned to in greater detail in later chapters.

Markers

What can be involved in consuming something? Answers are legion. However obvious the answers which are now provided might be, the ways in which the key terms of the language of consumption have been characterized should help tackle 'elusiveness'; should enable us to reflect on how characterizations apply, or don't apply, to spiritualities of life. Drawing on the voluminous literature, markers – signals, keys, simply meanings or characterizations, if you prefer – include the following.

First, *the consumer envisaged as someone who has the freedom to exercise choice*. The connection between 'the consumer' and the person who exercises choice to live their 'own' lives is deeply rooted. Thinking of the important political dimension of this association, at least since Vance Packard (1957), and then Ralph Nader (see Bollier 1991), many have equated the consumer with the active citizen. Politicians like Margaret Thatcher play the freedom and liberation card by glorifying the subject as the 'sovereign consumer' or 'enterprising self', elevating the individuation of decision-making over and above being dependent on decisions made by others (Heelas, 1991, 1992a). Today, the Labour Party also caters for the value ascribed to choice by using the phrase 'the consumer' as often as is required to emphasize emancipating choice within the spheres of healthcare, education and public services in general (ESRC, 2006).

In connection with spiritualities of life, Bruce (1995) writes of provisions being supplied by way of 'a cafeteria counter', allowing 'consumers to make their own choices, not only about what is good or moral but also about what cures ailments and explains the nature of the universe' (p. 122). The self-referential, autonomous authority which Bruce ascribes to the 'consumer' is even more clearly seen when he states, 'New Agers maximize their returns by choosing what suits them best' (2002, p. 89; see also p. 77); by selecting what does most for them. Briefly assessing the significance of the role played by choice, together with the word-of-mouth factor, the most important organizational mode of New Age spiritualities of life takes the form of 'listings' – from the San Francisco Bay area's *Common Ground* (which began early in the 1970s) to guides to yoga or spas in national newspapers. What Jenny-Ann Brodin (2003) calls the 'matter of choice' (p. 381) is clearly widely in evidence, people 'shopping around' to decide what to do (or do next).[2] Holistic practitioners typically encourage their participants to elect to 'go by', or only 'stay with', what 'works for them' – that is to say, to exercise their choice on the basis of their experiences. And as we shall see later, the exercise of choice is by no means devoid of 'political' significance. However, the role played by choice is by no means all-pervasive. 'Belief' in inner-life spirituality is rarely, if ever, chosen. One might dearly love to *be* spiritual, but it is highly unlikely that any amount of conscious decision-making will bring this about. Coming to 'believe' – better, to have veridical experiences – is not like feeling the need for a vacation and going ahead and taking it. No doubt one can choose one's particular 'beliefs' once one 'believes'. No doubt one can put oneself in situations where one could have veridical experiences. But the 'active convert' literature notwithstanding, however hard one tries, needs or wants to move beyond the secular realm, nothing is likely to happen through will-power alone. One cannot elect to have *the* spiritually significant event (Heelas, 1996a, pp.181–200).

Second, *the consumer envisaged as someone who purchases things*. The close connection between the act of purchasing things and acting as a consumer is shown by the fact that the Central Statistical Office of the UK records 'patterns of consumption' on the basis of expenditure – expenditure which includes 'motoring and fares' and 'personal services' (Bocock, 1992, pp. 135–6); and consumer trends surveys report spending on things like private healthcare and private education. In connection with those mind-body-spirituality provisions and services which are provided by others, it hardly needs stating that they normally have to be purchased (Mears and Ellison, 2000). However, just as one does not have to pay anyone to pray at one's bedside, so one does not have to spend anything to meditate alone in one's home, to reflect on the spirituality of nature whilst walking in Wordsworthian mode or to practise yoga in a tranquil spot. And neither do primary school children, for example, have to pay anything when 'centring' meditations are run by their teachers. Furthermore, just as one cannot choose to believe or to have a spiritual experience (except, possibly, by taking LSD or the like in the right setting), one cannot buy belief or convincingly *spiritual* experiences.

Third, *the consumer envisaged as someone who is passive, therefore favouring ease of consumption*. For Adorno, 'Before the theological caprices of commodities, the consumers become temple slaves' (Arato and Gebhardt, 1982, p. 280). For all those working in the tradition of the Frankfurt School,

> a defining characteristic of consumers is their passivity. It marks the contrast between high and mass culture. High culture has active knowledgeable connoisseurs, mass culture has passive consumers. (Aldridge, 2003, p. 84)

Buy a TV on a state handout, slouch on the couch, have a *real* leisure experience; pay for it, have the orgasm; hand over, handed back – the easy mechanical transaction; the soma-ites of *Brave New World* – whose 'ladies', as Adorno (1967) puts it, 'converse only *as* consumers' (p. 76; my emphasis); let the suppliers do the work, I'll sit back and consume the product – experience – 'without effort' (Lasch, 1980, p. 151). From the 'classic', total passivity of the couch potato's reception of the 'ready-made', to the partial passivity of those whose goals and preferences are set and cultivated by consumer culture but who nevertheless exercise their consumer 'skills' (including a degree of choice) to obtain the best buy, to those who are consumed by powerful experiences – the passive consumer is variously envisaged. 'The "intentions" of the producers are simply absorbed whole and unmediated by the unsuspecting and passive "consumer"', write Miles et al. (2002, p. 3.); 'the theory of the autonomy and sovereignty of the consumer is thus refuted', writes Baudrillard (1988, p. 37) in his discussion of alternatives to conformity-to-input theory; the 'ideology that the meaning of life is to be found in buying things and pre-packaged experiences', writes Bocock (1993, p. 48) of 'consumerism'. 'Until graduate school', writes Stark (1992, p. 635), 'one is a consumer of knowledge – and one succeeds by learning about what other people think about various matters';[3] the decentred self, following the sensate flows of the emotion-'games' and tricks of consumer culture rather than exercising its own 'stand-apart', unitary authority. Basically, the externally preformed is replicated within to form the 'mindset'; the '*at* your leisure' *subject* of the easy and quick fix of consumption. (Not so far removed from how Enlightenment thinkers regarded the passive replication of tradition.)

In connection with spiritualities of life, depending on how one *happens* to feel, one simply 'buys into' neatly prepared offerings. It is all very 'comfortable'. In the words of Lau (2000), 'the commodified forms of these bodily practices [like yoga or tai chi] and their related products offer tangible ways of addressing . . . wellness through the easy mode of consumption' (pp. 9–10). Now in the words of Colin Sedgwick (2004), there are many who 'want the feelgood factor, but not the cost of commitment'.

Briefly assessing this kind of claim, certainly there are those who lie back and let themselves be pampered; who recline and let the New Age music wash over them; who buy 'this brilliant little gadget off the internet that does your meditation for you' – whilst you are sleeping, and so that you awake 'chilled, fresh, spiritual' (Wilde, 2005). Equally certainly though, to introduce a point which is returned to, many are far from passive or especially comfortable. One point can be dealt with now – namely, the idea that ease of consumption is greatly facilitated by the immediacy factor. For Lasch (1980), the 'demand' for 'immediate gratification' is one of the hallmarks of our times (p. xvi); to modify the 'We want the world and we want it now' of the Doors, 'I want the world and I want it now'; for Frederic Jameson (1991), 'instant pleasure' has become the game of life (p. 18). Frequently, New Agers have been accused of being too fast – expecting processes to work when 'traditionally' they have taken years to perfect (a point made, for example, by the Dalai Lama and Daniel Goleman, 2003). Whatever the relationship between speed and spiritual efficacy – and as academics we are not able to study the matter – the fact remains that a good case can be made for arguing that holistic activities can provide an opportunity for slowing down rather than speeding up.[4] Reading a book by the Dalai Lama on the tube; getting up early to practise yoga – what matters is not so much the 'space' (and certainly not the 'spaced out' space of the

1960s) as time-out: the time by myself, the 'time for myself' (cf. Black, 2004, p. 59).

Fourth, *the consumer envisaged as someone who has (varying degrees of) authority over the producer or supplier*. By virtue of the role played by choice in a market economy, producers or suppliers have to cater for the authority of the consumer or customer. To refuse to respond to the authority of choice is to run the risk of going out of business or not capitalizing on demand. Even the 'laid back' passive consumer likes quality. The 'commodification' of New Age provisions, writes Bruce (2002, p. 101), 'leaves the consumer in command'; or as he elsewhere puts it, 'the fact that the [New Age] revelation is paid for strengthens the hand of the consumer' (1995, p. 119). The fact that many provisions are purchased over the counter means that it is easy for the purchaser to decide to select another product (something which is not so easy to do when personal bonds such as loyalty or friendship are involved). Briefly assessing this claim, high-street shopping chains in the increasingly competitive subjective wellbeing market carry out market research to ascertain the scale of the demand for 'spiritual' products; to work out how to respond to particular requirements (Redden, 2005, p. 235); aspirant New Age authors might well be keeping an eye open for a new market niche; those writing mind-body-spirituality articles for the *Daily Mail* bow to the nature of the demand to try to ensure that the nature of their 'supply' matches the reader. And it is undoubtedly the case that Darwinian forces are at work in New Age circles: the ineffectual practitioner has to close down, for example. However, personal bonds frequently develop during the course of holistic practice, diminishing the significance of the rational or experiential pressure-through-choice of 'the consumer'; and, no doubt, authors build up loyal readers.

Fifth, *and in closely related vein, the consumer envisaged as someone who exercises autonomy to decide on the nature and significance of what is actually provided*. As Miles et al. (2002) argue,

> producers of commodities have little or no control, despite the rhetoric of marketing and advertising, over their deployment and use. Therefore we should not fall into the naive fallacy of assuming that the 'intentions' of the producers are simply absorbed whole and unmediated by the unsuspecting and 'passive' consumer. (p. 3)

Identifying 'the central tenet of the modern consumer ideology' as 'the assumption that personal experience and personal experience alone... constitutes the highest authority', Colin Campbell (2004, p. 40) highlights the point. In our pragmatically and experientially orientated times, 'consumers' who acquire ownership and freedom of use put their experiences to work to exercise their right to determine what they value about their purchases; their right to ignore the intentions of producers. As David Harvey (1989), with the 'death of the author' literature no doubt in mind – albeit ignoring all those attempts by producers-cum-suppliers to establish influential relationships with their customers – sees it:

> The cultural producer merely creates raw materials (fragments and elements), leaving it open to consumers to recombine those elements in any way they wish. The effect is to break (deconstruct) the power of the author to impose meanings or offer a continuous narrative... The effect is to call into question all the illusions of fixed systems of representation. (p. 51; see also Featherstone 1991b, p. 134)

In the New Age context, Bruce (2002) writes that 'consumers... are not locked into open-ended commitments of reciprocal obligation; they buy the book, tape or training session, and are free to make of it what they will' (p. 90); 'New Agers determine for themselves the extent of their involvement' (p. 94; and see p. 77; see also 'the purchaser decides the extent and nature of his or her commitment': Bruce, 1995, p. 119). Most graphically, to cite Bruce (1995) again, 'With everyone paying the piper, everyone calls his or her own tune' (p. 119). Briefly reflecting on this kind of claim, it is unquestionably the case that those purchasing New Age publications, music (etc.) have very considerable freedom to play their 'own tune': that many 'raid' books, for example, to devour all that is useful and to discard or strip away all that is deemed worthless; that in 'private' individuals decide what to make of the spiritual authors or 'ultimate' life-meanings they have encountered.[5] As we shall see, however, although the autonomy of the participant is catered for within associational activities, it rarely runs riot in anything approaching a smash-and-grab, anything-goes, sense. The practitioner has as much say as the participant – typically, more. Unless very specifically requested ('I'm only paying you for this session to have a good moan'), practitioners rarely relinquish all their 'spiritual authority' to capitulate to whatever their participants might be demanding. Paying to become a member of a yoga group purchases a certain amount of control, the right of self-expression via the experience of 'ownership' ('we all own the group, we are all responsible for its success') – but *you* do not own, let along buy, the group by virtue of paying up and going along.

Sixth, *the consumer envisaged as someone whose authority-by-way-of-autonomous-choice, and whose passivity favours ease of consumption, is catered for by producers and suppliers providing the consumer-friendly*. 'The key is to keep the customer satisfied' (Halpin, 2006) – not surprisingly *the* slogan of neo-liberal capitalism in selling mode (and Tony Halpin is talking about universities). More cynically, the key is 'pandering to the philistines'. To draw on a term from the *OED*'s definition of *consumere*, producers and suppliers aim to 'make away with' anything which is too challenging or off-putting. In the acerbic words of Curtis White (2004),

> this bland, no-thinking-required 'product' that passes for culture... a mainstream consensus that pleases everyone but moves, challenges or shocks no

one: ... from free-market ideology to TV arts programmes, New Age self-help and Oprah's Book Club. This is a book [*The Middle Mind*] for anyone who thinks culture should be a force for change, not just something to acquire and consume; who wants to reclaim the destabilizing power of the imagination – and start thinking for themselves. (Back cover)

Or as Lasch (1980) writes of the 'culture of commodities and consumerism', 'experiences formerly reserved for those of high birth, deep understanding, or much practical acquaintance of life can be enjoyed by all without effort, on purchase of the appropriate commodity' (p. 151) – once the preserve of the elite, the auratic is defiled by being replicated through mass production for the leisure pleasures of the masses.

To thrive by appealing to the lowest common denominators of the mass market, producers and suppliers – including political parties (the 'voting for values' questionnaire which has been used by the Labour Party), capitalistic universities using the language of equality and accessibility to ensure they have enough students, and even the royal family (Hardman, 1998) – use market research to pursue the strategy of beefing up the 'nice bits'; of 'modernizing'; of 'dumbing-down', 'selling *out*'. The student as consumer judges the previously 'inviolate' lecturer by way of the course assessment questionnaire; to provide good data to enhance promotion prospects, the lecturer meets the demand (for ease, enjoyment, etc.) by trivializing to spoon-feed. Thinking of the New Age in particular, the claim is that 'suppliers' are thoroughly consumer orientated. Their products and services are 'commodified, sanitized, and thus *neutralized* for easy consumption' (Lau, 2000, p. 12; her emphasis). Or, to refer to Bruce (2002), 'particular elements of the New Age easily lose their essence, through either the selective attention of the consumers or the cynical marketing strategies of commercial enterprises' (p. 103); we 'only' find 'an individualistic gutting of a rich variety of traditions' (1995, p. 119). 'Traditional' yoga is consumed by capitalism.[6]

Briefly reflecting on claims of this debased, defilement variety, there is no doubt that religious traditions are widely experienced by New Agers as being clogged up with unnecessary, often harmful, baggage: doctrines and dogmas, traditions of discrimination against women, and so on, all serving to detract from their shared spiritual core. There is also no doubt that world-rejecting, 'beyond-the-ego', 'purists' (like Chogyam Trungpa, 1973) consider the majority of western practitioners with distaste, guilty of reducing traditional eastern practices to 'convenience spirituality' – easy-to-do guides and activities serving the counter-productive attachments of the 'ego'. Eastern practices are judged to have become too simplified, too sanitized, too trivialized, too speedy, too self-centred a fashion to be other than working to reinforce what is wrong with life. Too much has been destroyed for the sake of comfort, too much has been 'used up' in order to please the participant, for them to be other than a travesty of what they ought to be. However,

Falun Gong is much the same in China as in the west; Vedanta for management in a luxury hotel in Chennai is no more or less consumer-friendly than Vedanta for management in Boston; Zen for wellbeing in Tokyo is little different from wellbeing Zen in London. More significantly (explored further in chapters 5 and 8), although participants have the authority to judge on the basis of what rings true in their personal-cum-spiritual experience and have considerable freedom to 'play their own tune', western-based practitioners exercise their spiritually informed *virtuosité*, their accumulated wealth of experiential authority, to practise in terms of what they take to be the *effective substance* of their 'eastern' (or more local) teachings – rather than simply staying with what they might consider to be the superficial preferences of those 'stuck' with 'the nice bits'. The autonomy of the participant rarely runs riot. Furthermore, it can readily be argued that to engage in 'tailoring' (much in the manner of the traditional Indian village storyteller), to adapt to, to take into account, to *respect* the values and expectations of participants is to facilitate engagement and effectiveness (Stark and Iannaccone, 1993) – an argument which can equally readily be enhanced by pointing out the ways in which 'appropriated' teachings and activities from 'traditional' settings are typically enriched by 'culture-friendly' – as indigenous – themes and practices: for example, the enrichment of many forms of shamanism by way of psycho-therapeutic sensibilities and processes. Certainly, from the practitioners' perspective, tailoring language for participants is defensible in that what matters is not remaining faithful to the 'certainties' of eastern (etc.) texts in the manner of the scholar, but using language in whatever ways – however 'uncertain' or suggestive – which are most effective for the evocation of experience.[7]

Seventh, *the consumer envisaged as someone who is content with the superficial.* Those academics and commentators who emphasize the passivity of consumers, intent on doing as little as possible to satisfy themselves, also emphasize the superficiality of involvement. For Bruce (1996), 'most [New Age 'products'] are consumed by people as a slight flavouring to their mundane lives' (p. 261). According to Carrette and King (2005), it will be recalled, 'What is being sold to us as radical, trendy and transformative spirituality in fact produces little in the way of a significant change in one's lifestyle or fundamental behaviour patterns' (p. 5). Briefly reflecting on this kind of claim, it is no doubt valid for many purchasers of New Age provisions. One certainly cannot discount the possibility that a large number of those who read mind-body-spirituality literature, for example, are content with a 'slight flavouring' (or might simply get bored). However, as we shall see in chapter 6 and later, much of what takes place is far from superficial or inconsequential.

And eighth, *'mere' superficiality aside, the consumer envisaged as someone who puts provisions or services to various forms of use.* Drawing on the extensive literature, deployment includes the following.

(1) *Vital requirements*. As Bocock (1993) notes, 'Consumption appears to be rooted in the satisfaction of purely natural, biological or physical needs' (p. 212). Material provisions are consumed for the sake of survival, to sustain life. If they are not available to be used up, the outcome is suffering or death. Briefly assessing this claim, some of those active within the inner-spirituality orbit have life-threatening conditions. In accord with Bocock's (1993) 'material use value' (p. 95) characterization, participants whose lives are at risk, who are seeking to prolong their lives, are engaging in consumption when they practise inner-spirituality healing. Whether by way of ingesting efficacious potions or tapping into the energy flow of one's practitioner, oneself or nature, spirituality is drawn upon to serve the end of life itself. However, one of the more surprising findings of the Kendal Project is that very few of those active in the mind-body-spirituality milieu of Kendal and environs were suffering from serious or terminal illness (Heelas and Woodhead, 2005, pp. 91–2).

(2) *Social and cultural currency*. Beyond matters of survival, consumption is frequently discussed in connection with social and cultural performance, display and identity. One's 'radar system... monitors the behaviour of other people and seeks to align [one] with it' (Aldridge, 2003, p. 71). Purchases are deployed to facilitate sociocultural progress: the conspicuous consumption of trading in a middle-range car for a more upmarket model, for example, demonstrating – and helping to construct – upward mobility and aspired status. Purchases are used to affirm one's position in life to one's peers: the wine bought for the middle-class dinner party serving to confirm that one belongs to a particular *habitus*. Purchases are used to distinguish one's way of life from that led by others: making sure that one lives in the 'right' neighbourhood, rather than getting mixed up with ways of life found in the wrong kind of locality (Bocock, 1992, p. 148). Purchases contribute to the cultural capital of the lifestyle expressivism of postmodernists (Aphonen, 1990). In connection with spiritualities of life, Lau (2000) writes that 'purchases [of 'alternative health'] reflect social status and class distinctions' (p. 17); 'identities become commodities to buy', 'purchased identities' in particular serving to signal 'elite culture' (pp. 13, 14, 17); journalist Anna Pasternak (1999) notes that 'The height of chic is to gain an audience with the Indian spiritual guru, Mother Meera, in Germany' (p. 3); a product line, *Yogitoes*, is promoted with the words:

> All Yogitoes products are available in a beautiful range of full-spectrum Chakra colours: Choose the hue to suit your mood. Each product features a signature orange zen dot at the end: They benefit your yoga *and they look cool!* (www.yogamatters.com; my emphasis)

Ways of life are reified by the sacred (Hunt, 2005, p. 170). Briefly reflecting on claims of this variety, it is perfectly reasonable to suppose that those engaged with spiritualities of life have social and cultural requirements.

Although many might be reluctant to talk about it, activities are used – for example – to affirm their way of life. 'I have a Reiki Master' could well go together with 'I am a caring person, a vegetarian. I value authentic, deep relationships and person-centred, rather than money-measured or grabbing occupations' (cf. Lau, 2000, p. 14). Those who buy provisions from high-street shops are arguably even more likely to use to their purchases to express life-values and interests: New Age enlightenment volumes in the lounge, with 'healing' foods in the kitchen serving to express a way of life which goes beyond the 'superficialities' of consumer culture at large. However, as we shall see in later chapters, it is highly likely that a fair proportion of New Age services – in particular – do far more than serve as social and cultural markers.

(3) *Personal display and identity requirements.* Here, 'individuals are governed...by a gyroscope attuned to internalized values' (Aldridge, 2003, p. 71), the aim being to align consumption with oneself; to find self-expression via material (and other) provisions. Discussing Simmel's seminal work on metropolitan life, David Frisby (1985) writes of the 'individual's struggle for self-assertion', a struggle which 'may take the form of stimulating a sense of distinctiveness' (pp. 131–2). Increasingly, as consumption becomes more 'individuated' or 'post-Fordist' (Urry, 1990, pp. 13–14; see also Heath and Potter, 2006, p. 20), products and services are used to express one's own uniqueness; one's own 'lifestyle' (Featherstone, 1987); to engage in 'self-branding'.[8] With regard to New Age spiritualities of life, Lau (2000) claims, 'these discourses ['around aromatherapy', etc.] sell the possibility of exchanging one's own bodily status for another, higher one through the use of alternative practices that promise to reshape and rework the body' (p. 15); consumption is used 'to create differential identities' (p. 16).[9] Briefly reflecting on this kind of claim, given the variety of activities provided by spiritualities of life practitioners, given the variety of products available from high-street shops, and given the individualistic values of western culture, it is only to be expected that activities and products are used to help meet the requirement of expressing or 'creating' the singular. 'Free spirits', those who do not like being 'labelled', seek out their own paths. Rather than participating in more popular forms of yoga, for example, they find a more obscure version. The unconventional is favoured over the conventional. To be the only one of one's peer group who knows about the new practitioner in the vicinity is pleasing. However, the consumption-for-the-sake-of-individual-uniqueness thesis should not be overstated. During any given historical period spiritualities of life are characterized by the recurrence of themes, the dominant theme today being holistic wellbeing (Heelas, 1996a, 2006a; Heelas and Woodhead, 2005; Aupers and Houtman, 2006). One of the characteristics of contemporary mind-body-spirituality is the operation of the 'blockbuster' – the spiritual volume which 'you simply must read'; another is the (sheer) repetitiveness of New Age music, a great deal aimed at evoking the experience of tranquillity; and so on.

Then there is what is being displayed, namely self-identity 'itself', what Adorno (1967, p. 78) thought of as 'pseudo-uniqueness'. The most frequently encountered argument concerns a form of possessive individualism: a materialistic individualism where the 'possessive' constitutes the individual. 'To have *is* to be', as it is sometimes put (Paterson, 2006, p. 52). Thinking of holistic spirituality, the considerable majority of participants (especially practitioners) are almost certainly 'postmaterialists' (Inglehart, 1990; Heelas, 1996d; Heelas and Woodhead, 2005). Some are 'post' because they devalue what the materialistic life has to offer – by downsizing, for example – to look for 'the more' of the personal or expressive; some retain a materialistic orientation, but are 'post' in that they are also looking for similar forms of 'the more'. Prosperity New Agers aside – and they have declined in significance since the early 1990s – few are satisfied with the identity of materiality.[10]

(4) *Hedonistic requirements.* Whereas the social and cultural utility values of consumption are primarily realized by way of public gaze and evaluation, the hedonistic aspect of consumption has a more immediate bearing on subjective-life. Rather than the emphasis lying with materialistic products (signs or images), the product is basically the vehicle for experience. Purchases are primarily valued for their 'production' of inner results – most obviously pleasure. The culture of this 'mode' of consumption is that of the desire-fulfilment of self-centred, self-interested, self-absorbed individualism. Consumption is about the 'narcissistic' self in Bauman's (2001) sense of the term, namely what takes place when desire 'has itself for its paramount object' (p. 13). Consumption involves 'immediate gratification' (Lasch, 1980, p. xvi). 'An ethic of hedonism, of pleasure and play – in short a consumption ethic' is held to be abroad (Bell, 1976, p. 63). 'Consumer culture uses images, signs and symbolic goods which summon up dreams, desires and fantasies which suggest romantic authenticity and emotional fulfilment in narcissistically pleasing oneself', to recall Featherstone's argument (1991a, p. 27).

This is the consumption of 'utilitarian individualism' (Bellah et al., 1985); of 'consumers [who] have needs that are created by people who then purport to satisfy them' (Aldridge, 2003, p. 2); more exactly, of those who are locked into the market economy in that their emotions, their desires, are stimulated by capitalist producers and suppliers in order to enhance the consumption of commodities. As for this 'mode' of consumption and spiritualities of life, it will also be recalled that Bauman (1998) believes New Age activities 'are aimed... at the training of *"perfect consumers"*; at developing to the full the capacities which the experience-seeking and sensation-gathering life of the consumer/chooser demands' (pp. 71–2) – capacities which serve 'a life devoted to the art of consumer self-indulgence' (p. 70). In measure, with their reference to a 'feelgood spirituality', Carrette and King (2005) join the ranks (p. 158). In line with Baudrillard's (1995) analysis of the Gulf War (*The Gulf War Did Not Take Place*), in line with de-authenticating and delegitimizing the *favelas* of Rio by treating them as an entertaining 'human zoo' (Hyde, 1997), in line with reducing Mount Everest to a luxury status symbol, replacing challenge and bravery with 'The Everest Experience' (Weaver, 1992), what takes place in the world is orchestrated so as to enhance sensation. Hence the popularity of New Age holidays ('A Journey to the Dragon Kingdom of Bhutan') and the appearance of theme parks such as the I Ching park in China, with its *Taiji* ('Ultimate Principle') pyramid (Parkins, 1994).[11] Briefly assessing claims of this variety, it is certainly true that participants are sometimes hedonistic. Princess Diana explicitly distinguished her 'pamper Diana days' from more 'serious' holistic activities (Heelas, 1999). With just 7.6 per cent of the respondents to a Kendal Project questionnaire stating that they were basically seeking 'pleasure, enjoyment or a treat' from their mind-body-spirit activities (Heelas and Woodhead, 2005, p. 91), it is clear there are not that many engaging in 'pamper me' events. That 92.4 per cent did not select this questionnaire option paves the way for one of the key themes of what follows in this volume: *more* is going on than the hedonistic.

Summary

Whether it be the exercise of choice, the act of purchasing, the passivity and ease of consumption, the authority of the consumer in the market, the autonomy of the consumer in connection with what is drawn upon, the provision of the consumer-friendly, contentment with the superficial, vital requirements, social and cultural currency, personal display and identity requirements or hedonistic gratification, it is perfectly clear that one or more, in various combinations, can be found within the general territory of spiritualities of life.[12] Whether harder or softer, well in evidence or less so, the empirical findings are frequently incontestable. It is perfectly obvious, for example, that purchasing choice is often exercised. It is also pretty obvious that what appears to be spiritual is sometimes so-to-speak 'consumed away': enter Harvey Nichols; talk with someone engrossed in retail therapy who says, 'I've been feeling low; I've just bought at handbag; I'm just going to Urban Retreat for a spot of Reiki to help me feel good'. 'Spiritual?' you ask. 'Good gracious, no.' Clear evidence for the 'consuming growth' argument...

But are the commonly used 'marks' of consumption as reliable as they might appear to be? Consider the exercise of choice. On the one hand, consumption (in the sense of 'taking in') can take place in the absence of choice (as in the traditional prison system, when prisoners did not decide to have porridge for breakfast). On the other hand, choice need not have much to do with consumption *in toto*. To say that someone who ingests a potion to commit voluntary euthanasia is engaging in an act of consumption is surely to misrepresent the overall significance of the act, doing the gravest injustice in the process. For the child-centred educationalist to encourage the choices of the child is not to treat the child as a consumer (neither is learning sacred texts by heart, with no choice in the matter). The fact that I decide which voluntary association to work with, which political party to vote for, which 'aims and values' to tick for a ballot paper for the Labour Party, shows that 'choice' is a broader category than anything which can reasonably be thought of *as* an act of consumption. That Huxley decided to ingest ('consume') LSD is *surely* not the sum of the matter. Or consider the purchaser. The 'consumer' – that is, the purchaser – very often does not consume, a considerable amount of shopping being for gifts. (And is the reception of a gift best thought of as an act of consumption?) Or consider a surgeon selecting, purchasing and using a specific instrument – to call this an act of consumption is surely to miss the point of much of what is going on. The same applies to the craftsman, using (not consuming) his newly acquired tool – albeit obtaining a certain 'hedonistic' delight whilst using it.

Whatever the value of 'marks' in guiding our attention to consumeristic aspects of holistic spiritualities of life, the one thing which these signs – quite naturally – do not do is guide our attention to other aspects of what might be taking place. The frame of reference provided by the language of consumption might make it easy, or relatively easy, to spot signs of 'consumption' – like the exercise of purchasing choice – in the territory of holistic spiritualities of life.

In his pioneering *The Invisible Religion* (1967), Thomas Luckmann writes of '"autonomous" individuals who are potential consumers of their ['sacred'] "product"' (p. 107); a recurrent theme of Reginald Bibby's *Fragmented Gods* (1987) is of the 'sacred' being 'reduced to consumption fragments' (p. 175). Together with the fact that these academics are not exactly clear about what they respectively mean by 'consumers' and 'consumption fragments', the main issue to hand is that they are even less clear about what – if anything – is 'left'. Bluntly, what are the characteristics of the aspectual – perhaps *sui generis* – qualities of meaningful spiritual life which transcend the consumeristic?

As I am sure the contributors to *Elusive Consumption* would agree, the apparently simple questions – 'When is an act *an* act of consumption as opposed to some other form of act?' and 'When is an act more to do with consumption than other acts? – have yet to be satisfactorily answered. Maybe purchasing and then studying Kant's *Critique of Pure Reason* is not an act of consumption. But what about an easy-to-read introduction to Kant, one which makes you feel good and status laden? On the other hand, what about reading a pulp novel which happens to make you think? Finally, maybe the 'When is an act *an* act of consumption...' question is misleading – the more useful approach being the one advocated by Marcel Mauss with his notion of 'the total social fact': teasing out as many aspects of 'the fact' as possible to try to gauge the significance of their 'weight' in any particular provision, service or activity. As we shall now see, though, this way forward does not rule out the possibility of determining a – if not *the* – paradigmatic case of consumption: use for utilitarian self-gratification. A determination which is of great value in identifying and analysing those aspects of New Age spiritualities of life which go beyond the consumeristic.

Chapter 5

The Sacred and the Profane: Spiritual Direction or Consumer Preference?

What is missing in the new surrogate religions is a spiritual discipline – submission to a body of teachings that has come to be accepted even when it conflicts with immediate interests or inclinations and cannot constantly be redesigned to individual specifications... eclecticism in general makes few difficult demands, as a believer can shuffle the ingredients to suit his requirements for psychic comfort. (Christopher Lasch, 1987, p. 82; my emphasis)

The decline of value consensus which is exemplified in the individualism and consumerism in the New Age. (Steve Bruce, 2000, p. 234)

To recap some key observations, by and large those studying, commenting upon or criticizing inner-life spirituality (or Christianity) are vague about their use of the language of consumption, most especially in providing empirical evidence to show that a particular aspect of 'consumption' – say purchasing choice – is in fact operating in conjunction with other aspects of the provision or activity under consideration: aspects which might, or might not, be accurately described by using the language of consumption. The fact that activities – on which I concentrate henceforth – are 'purchased' once people have 'shopped around' could imply a great deal about consumer use: passivity, contentment with ease and blandness, using *up* for self-indulgence, the exercise of unadulterated self-interest, above all the gratification of consumptive 'preferences'. But need this be the case?

To test the 'reduction to consumption' thesis, we first have to go further in pinning down 'the elusive' to arrive at a more determinate picture. Critically, we have to find workable ways of determining those aspects of spiritualities of life which, if any, do not deserve to be characterized in terms of the language of consumption: at least not in any of the 'serious' senses which that language has to offer.

On Pinning Things Down

A brief excursus into Durkheim's *The Elementary Forms of the Religious Life* (1971) is called for. On page 47, the most important in the book, Durkheim provides his famous definition of religion:

> A religion is a unified system of beliefs and practices relative to sacred things, that is to say, things set apart and forbidden – beliefs and practices which unite into a single moral community called a Church, all those who adhere to them.

Higher up on the same page – and this is what gives the page its particular importance – Durkheim writes:

> There still remain those contemporary aspirations towards a religion which would consist entirely in internal and subjective states, and which would be constructed freely by each of us.

This 'religious individualism' (p. 47), he also observes, is associated with 'private religions', religions 'which the individual establishes for himself and celebrates by himself' (p. 45) – to the extent that when they take root, 'there will be no other cult than that which each man will freely perform within himself' (p. 46).

Looking more closely at the first, much better-known, of these two definitions, Talcott Parsons (1968) provides a useful elucidation of the meaning of the 'sacred'. Contrasting it with the 'profane', he writes:

> ...the profane activity *par excellence* is economic activity. The attitude of calculation of utility is the antithesis of the respect for sacred objects. From the utilitarian point what is more natural than that the Australian should eat and kill his totem animal? But since it is a sacred object, this is precisely what he cannot do... Thus sacred things, precisely in excluding this utilitarian relationship, are hedged about with taboos and restrictions. Religion has to do with sacred things. (p. 412)

Contrary to Frazer's view of totemism – 'a magic production and consumption club', as Freud (1938, p. 179) summarizes it – totems belong to a realm which is sacred precisely by virtue of the fact that it operates over-and-above the desires or needs of the individual. As supra-self sources of power and authority, existing before and after the this-worldly life of any particular person, totems are set apart from individual interference. They are grossly violated, cease to *work* as they should as sources of power and agency, if they are consumed. To work *as* the sacred, the sacred must remain inviolate. You cannot argue with the sacred *per se*.

For Parsons, as for Durkheim, consumption is the exemplary manifestation of the profane. More precisely, utilitarian consumption, namely the use of provisions or activities – especially when the sacred is involved – to cater for individual self-interest, is taken to be paradigmatic of what counts as the profane, as profanation.

This Durkheimian/Parsonian legacy remains firmly in evidence today. By no means infrequently, scholars elucidate what they mean when they apply the language of consumption to forms of religion and – especially – New Age spiritualities of life, by thinking in binary terms. Whether explicitly or implicitly, whether justifiably or not, the Durkheimian sacred of 'true' religion is used as a touchstone, a point of contrast to highlight the 'profane', the 'less-than-true', if not the secular.[1] Thus in his discussion of 'new forms of this-worldly religion', Stephen Hunt (2002) writes:

> ...it may be argued that little of what now passes as religion, particularly in its new forms, has any great substance, any great degree of spirituality.... consumerism...locates meaning not in the things held sacred but in the *profane pursuit of self-gratification*. Religion is thus reduced to what it does for individuals in this world and not in the next. It will tend to advance a philosophy of human potential, health, and wealth – whatever the spiritualized clothing it is dressed up in. It will be void of an abstract system of morality imposed by divine being which demand human obedience. The tendency will be to play down beliefs that the divine impinges its will upon this world. (p. 43; my emphasis)

The imperative values of the 'true' religion of Durkheim's 'moral community' include obedience, adherence, duty and obligation (the last explicitly contrasted with consumption by Davie, 2004, p. 78; 2006, p. 27), commitment (contrasted with consumption by Bibby, 1987, p. 169), deference, dependence (rather than the inappropriate exercise of self-responsibility), surrender, submission, obligation, self-discipline, self-denial (Bauman 1998, p. 70), self-sacrifice, dutiful service, faithfulness, certainty, security, and perhaps above all else piety and conformity. The ultimate goals of believers are provided by the way of life laid down by the sacred – an eternal way of life which must be aspired to in this world. To ensure that the sacred works for life in the here-and-now and the hereafter, the often 'costly' challenge (Pickering 1968, p. 83) is to resist the profanities of utilitarian consumption, working instead to live up to the requirements of the sacred to ensure that it does its work.

Jean Baudrillard (1988) argues, 'Traditional morality only required that the individual conform to the group; advertising "philosophy" requires that they now conform to themselves' (p. 13). Thinking of a topic on which Durkheim wrote extensively, when the authority and practices of the teaching *profession* are in practice, students 'conform to' – more accurately, aspire to – inviolate standards. Students become 'consumers' when they exercise their authority (via course assessments, student representation, etc.) to attempt to ensure that their courses conform to their own expectations, pleasures, self-interest. In similar vein, the difference is between the person conforming *to* – matching *up* to – the true religion of the sacred moral community and the person who seeks to ensure that religion conforms *to* – caters for – his or her *self*: an internalization of authority which means that what religion might offer is filtered through, altered by, quite possibly curtailed by, the capacities, the abilities, the desires, the self-understanding, the horizons of the 'believer'.

What, then, of Durkheim's 'religion which would consist entirely in internal and subjective states, and which would be constructed freely by each of us'? Written as his own last major publication, *The Elementary Forms of the Religious Life* has little to say on the matter. Given what he writes elsewhere about the pervasiveness and dangers of utilitarian or 'egotistical' individualism, however, it is reasonable to suppose that he would have associated this kind of individualism with the 'religious individualism' of his second definition. Whatever Durkheim might have had in mind, it is certainly the case that the 'private religions which the individual establishes for himself and celebrates by himself' provide ample scope for 'sacralizing' those 'internal and subjective states' which constitute them – 'states' which presumably include the promptings of self-interest and the desires of consumption, and which therefore would not appear to belong to the realm of the sacred as Durkheim characterizes it. The indestructible-as-incontestable, the non-negotiable, appears to have evaporated.

Since Durkheim's time, 'those contemporary aspirations' which he saw around him, and which surely had much to do with the popular romanticisms of his time, have of course developed into all that we find today: all the New Age spiritualities of life dwelling on 'internal and subjective states' rather than being couched in terms of the inviolate, transcendent sacred of Durkheim's first, most influential definition. And a number of scholars have indeed explicitly associated this form of the sacred, *if* that is what it can still be called, with the paradigmatic consumptive activities of utilitarian individualism.

Surveying the literature, Hunt (2002) writes that 'new spiritualities... are constantly influenced by the fads and fashions of today's culture... They thus tend to be *void* of all that is usually appraised as a *true* religiosity that *adheres* to an unchanging morality, belief and practice, and endures through the generations as an unquestioned "rock of ages"' (p. 212; my emphases). From the Durkheimian perspective, the 'fads and fashions' of (consumer) culture eradicate the sacred. With participants exercising their choices on the basis of those needs or desires which they feel by virtue of the operation of the psychological 'logic' of ways in which consumer culture values, expectations or promises are promoted, and with participants selecting those provisions or services which provide the most consumer-friendly ways of meeting their needs or desires, spiritualities of life become a matter of utilitarian *preference writ large*. Rather than 'really' improving life by challenging, changing or disciplining preferences in the fashion of 'true', 'impervious' religion-cum-spirituality, provisions and activities are selected to be used to satisfy the *given* of the desire-seeking case. Adapting or conforming to the 'needs' of the 'consumer' (Hunt 2002, p. 34), rather than vice versa, the authority of the utilitarian consumer is very much in evidence. The greater the extent to which spiritualities of life are *about* utilitarian preference and consumption, the lesser the extent of the Durkheimian sacred – and, accordingly, the lesser the extent that the growth of the provisions and services of inner-life spirituality can work as the Durkheimian sacred is supposed to work: according to the sociological point of view under consideration, that is.

In *The Economy of the Earth*, Mark Sagoff (1990) introduces his chapter on 'Values and Preferences' with the *New Yorker* and the Devil:

> A *New Yorker* magazine cartoon depicts the Devil introducing newcomers to hell. 'You'll find there's no "right" or "wrong" here', he tells them, 'just what works for *you*. (p. 99)

The Devil is most attracted by the most popular. As befits a detraditionalized modernity, with 'truth' reduced to the pragmatism of 'what works for *me*' rather than being provided by authoritative narratives or traditions, the Devil's job is to be as devilish as possible. He thus contradicts his promise, dashing hopes by going to the heart of what really matters. As Sagoff puts it, 'His goal is to defeat or frustrate preferences insofar as he can' (p. 99). Given the pre-eminent value ascribed to the 'no rules, only choices' nature of emotionally driven, 'how you feel about things', relativized consumer culture of many of his captives today, the Devil does not have to bother very much with 'absolute' values beyond the emotional life (Ewen and Ewen, 1982, p. 250).

On first sight, the Devil is just waiting to have a field-day with those currently participating in mind-body-spirituality activities. Rather than being dictated to by strict, conformist, transcendent renderings of the sacred-as-inviolate, the authority of participants would appear to be considerable indeed. Kendal spiritual practitioner Beth Tyers (homeopathy and massage) emphasizes, 'I certainly don't have a fixed faith or dogma which I adhere to'; Kendal shiatsu practitioner Jenny Warne stresses, 'it's very much the person working with you, we don't want to be something we impose on somebody else ... and the more the person can actually be involved in the process, the better it is really'; William Bloom stresses that practitioners should 'Listen with care and enable people to clarify and own their *own* psycho-spiritual development' (www.williambloom.com; my emphasis). Practitioner observations of this kind are legion. The freedom, the 'space' accorded the participant; the extent to which the participants are encouraged to engage in self-reflection, monitoring themselves, carrying out their own 'internal conversations'; the respect accorded the words of participants, those 'free spirits'-in-the-making; the value practitioners ascribe to participants testing 'what works in their own experience'; the significance attributed to the authoritative reality of those experiences which inform judgement (*de gustibus non est disputandum* – 'there is no disputing about tastes', as Campbell, 2004, p. 33, emphasizes); the moral or expressive 'individualism' which is widely in evidence (Houtman and Mascini, 2002); the fact that practitioners sometimes serve those who have turned away from being dependent on doctors in order to exercise their own self-responsibility to heal and express themselves: there would appear to be ample opportunity for preferences, even whims, to be well in evidence. Taking points of this kind on board, Bruce (1995) can therefore argue that there is little or no 'binding tradition' within New Age quarters (p. 119); that unlike the tradition-sustained forms of the sacred of transcendent theism, 'There is no corresponding power in the cultic milieu *to override individual preferences*' (Bruce, 2002, p. 99; my emphasis; cf. Hunt, 2002, p. 40). It appears that Durkheim's 'consist *entirely* in internal and subjective states' characterization (my emphasis) is by no means inapplicable today.

Practitioners at Work

So how are we to argue against the claim that holistic activities are frequently, if not virtually always, mere vehicles – nay, excuses – for the gratification of preferences? What, if anything, lies 'beyond' utilitarian, self-interested, self-absorbed consumption, to provide participants with the opportunity to go beyond their 'mere' preferences? I now bring Durkheimian and other arguments to bear to criticize the claim that associational activities – especially from the perspective of practitioners – are reducible to utilitarian consumption.

An obvious way of arguing against the profanation thesis is to draw attention to the multifarious ways in which activities are *orchestrated by* their practitioners. Russell Keat (1992) suggests,

> the basic meaning of being a consumer is that the meaning, value, etc. of the 'object' concerned is seen exclusively in terms of how its 'receiver' understands, interprets, judges, etc. it – in terms of 'what it did' for him/her, of its significance for him/her, of how it related to his/her particular projects, aims, needs, etc; rather than in terms of how its provider or producer regarded the object in these respects, and/or what meaning, etc. the object itself possessed, a meaning that it might gain by virtue of its position in relation to a certain tradition, practice, etc. (p. 1)

Using Keat's language, I argue that the 'receiver' is by no means running the show in the great majority of holistic activities. Rather than the death of the 'provider', the practitioner is the 'conductor'. Bearing in mind that participants generally pay to be 'served' by, or engage with, practitioners, practitioners normally have a certain standing, a reputation (most typically passed on by word of mouth) for being good at their job. They are seen as having spiritual expertise, an expertise acquired by virtue of their being more practised; of their being 'more in touch with their spirituality'. For participants, practitioners have a measure of 'in-built' authority. Since most practitioners are skilful (for if they were not they would soon go out of business), and often allude to the fact that their skills are due to their years of experience in acquiring spiritual virtuosity, wisdom, and 'depth', their authority is enhanced during activities themselves. Their expectations also come to bear: expecting progress from participants, participants increasingly expect to progress themselves – and in at least some cases accord with what is expected of them. Furthermore, participants look to their conductor. Frequently experiencing themselves as stuck in their lives, they are looking for help to move on. In order to get in touch with *true* spirituality, to find the *true* source of ethicality, spiritually orientated participants (in particular) seek guidance, helpful assessments or 'judgements' to enable them to recognize misleading, ego-generated experiences from those emanating from the 'real' source. And more basically still, in most activities assistance is required simply to learn *how* to practise.[2]

The authority and spiritual wisdom of practitioners, which in a basic sense *are* the activities they orchestrate, means that participants are not left bereft of guidance, suggestions, cues. 'Take anything you're told as a *suggestion*, not solid advice', says one practitioner. Affirming the importance of freedom, self-expressivity and self-exploration, emphasized within holistic activities, 'strong advice' of the 'If I were you . . .' variety is avoided. But 'suggestions', gentle 'direction' or 'orientation', the 'wink', the 'nudge', the non-verbal communication are called into play to *help* participants: the wisdom of the more 'experienced' serving the less experienced, those who are more 'artificial' or 'plastic', to indicate whether they are on the right path, the progressive path. And as anyone who has participated in 'non-directive' counselling or psychotherapy, let alone mind-body-spirituality activities, will know, the 'suggestion' ('Why don't you consider dropping that mask you put on when you meet people who frighten you?'; 'It might be a good idea for you to think about your childhood before we next meet'; 'I'll only mention it in passing, but it might be worth reflecting on the humility you have told me you show in your relationships') has an uncanny habit of taking root. For example, 'advice' provided by a spiritual practitioner played a role in one participant firming up his conclusion that 'I don't need the cars and fancy ties and all those trappings that consumed me once': a kind of outcome which is not at all unusual.[3] Strong advice of the 'If you don't experience the life-force flowing through your back pain there must be something wrong with you' or 'If I were you . . .' variety is not typical; subtle, 'person-tested' advice is. Encouragement when things are going along the right lines, then mutual affirmation when things are going really well, can readily be effective.

As the conductor, the practitioner is primarily responsible for orchestrating the ethicality, ethos, expressivity, emotional tone, the sentiments of the practice.[4] This can be considered in connection with what Charles Taylor (1994) has to say about 'recognition':

> Our identity is partly shaped by recognition or its absence, often by the *mis*recognition of others, and so a person or group of people can suffer real damage, real distortion, if the people or society around them mirror back

to them a confining or demeaning or contemptible picture of themselves. Nonrecognition or misrecognition can inflict harm, can be a form of oppression, imprisoning someone in a false, distorted, and reduced mode of being. (p. 75)

A primary aim of practitioners is to enable participants to 'be themselves'. To recognize themselves, each other, their practitioners as they 'truly' are; to *be* with each other – together with their practitioners – in what Martin Buber (2004) describes as the 'I-thou' mode of being. Caring and sharing, giving and taking, opening up, expressing and confessing, seeking advice or help, exercising the arts of recognition and relatively non-judgemental acceptance (a more appropriate term than 'forgiveness'), showing respectfulness (although not respectability), being trusting, 'allowing yourself to be known' (as one participant told me, citing Arthur Miller), being as non-competitive as possible, listening as carefully as possible ('while you are concerned with an opinion about a person', writes Barry Long (1983, p. 6), 'you cannot listen and might miss the truth'): so personal, often intimate or intersubjective, almost always affect-laden reciprocal bonds tend to develop, with people 'cherishing' one another.[5] On the one hand, these bonds mean that one-to-one clients or group members are unlikely to be any *more* 'in command' than their practitioners. On the other, since the practitioner is crucial for the 'unison', the *cooperation* or musical co-subjectivity of the orchestra, the practitioner remains the person who is most *at* work in connection with the activity as a whole. Utilitarian, consumption preferences could enter into the orchestration – only significantly, though, if they are included in the orchestration of the conductor.

The Significance of Taylorian 'Horizons'

For that great philosopher of forms of expressivism, Charles Taylor (1989),

> Our normal understanding of self-realization presupposes that *some things are more important beyond the self*, that there are some *goods or purposes* the furthering of which has significance for us and which hence can provide the significance a fulfilling life needs. A total and fully consistent subjectivism would tend towards emptiness: nothing would count as a fulfilment in a world in which literally nothing was important but self-fulfilment. (p. 507; my emphases)

Durkheim's 'no other cult than that which each man will freely perform *within himself*' might very well 'tend towards emptiness', most noticeably the emptiness of the egotistical self, a self somehow using holistic activities and/or provisions to provide self-indulgent, perhaps rather vacuous 'fillings'. But times have moved on. Of the 200,000 or so separate holistic associational activities run by mind-body-spirituality practitioners in Britain today, it is fair to say that the great majority are well-honed (or relatively well-honed) *ways* of facilitating growth, 'by' and through those who are active within particular activities.

Of these ways, I now argue that the role played by 'horizons' is central. According to the *SOED*, a horizon is 'The boundary-line of that part of the earth's surface visible from any given point; the line at which earth and sky appear to meet'. Less to do with physicality, another of the definitions offered runs, 'The boundary or limit of any circle or sphere of view, thought, action, etc.; limit or range of one's knowledge, experience, or interest'. Following *Roget's Thesaurus*, the words which come to mind are 'distance', 'edge', 'limit' and 'view'. Following Eliza Fodor of the Meditation Centre in Dent, 'Horizons expand' (2002 leaflet). Horizons can limit; equally, to broaden horizons is to open new things up – which could be significant enough to work towards.

Thinking of those things which are 'important beyond the self', Taylor draws on Romantic themes to develop the notion of 'horizons' (a term used in a number of his publications, including *The Ethics of Authenticity*, 1991). Drawing in turn on Taylor, I now explore what horizons have to do with the orchestration of holistic activities. Horizons are meaningful; indeed, as illustrated by the work of Casper David Friedrich, for instance, ripe with significance. Viewed from afar, horizons hint at, perhaps express, perhaps even reveal, the allure, the 'gravitational pull' of what lies within them or beyond. Horizons can serve to take you out of yourself – leaving your everyday restrictive view of the world to pursue visions. Beckoned on, experiencing challenges, opportunities, the life-enhancing *en route*, counter-culturalists of the 1960s took the 'magic bus' from Amsterdam or London for the journey to the east, encountering new vistas, new openings, new experiences in the process. The horizon in view ever recedes; the quest for what *could* lie beyond the visible horizon never ceases. In the process, though, the experiential life is enriched. Assuming that you have decided to go in the right direction, and/or have been guided there, consciousness 'expands' as one travels through the initial 'view' towards the horizon, and expands even more if the horizon takes a form (like a range of hills) which provides another perspective on what the world has to offer.[6]

From the viewpoint of practitioners, participants are typically seen – better, 'experienced' – as living in terms of unduly restrictive, narrow horizons. When they look out to see what life has to offer, participants (especially newcomers) tend to work within a relatively circumscribed frame of reference. Some, for example, might tend to limit the pleasurable to the measurable: to what money can demonstrably buy. Others might be content with 'getting on as best they can', by living with, tolerating, their lack of dynamism or their shyness. In astronomy, the term 'horizon' is used to refer to the limit of the theoretically possible universe. Within holistic activities, the job of the practitioner is to help participants cast doubt on or undermine, perhaps assist in demolishing or bypassing the 'theoretically' impossible; to open up *vistas of significance*; to bring more into view. The job of the practitioner is to encourage participants to travel from the 'narrow-minded' expectations of what (many) take to be the theoretically, empirically, psychologically, realistically possible, towards the beckoning, more expansive experiences promised by what comes into 'sight'. Practitioners serve as *beacons*, signalling, pointing or *directing* the way to more distant horizons; beacons which encourage participants to 'move on' to appreciate, to (more) *fully* experience, what 'life' has to offer. The New Age shaman enables participants to go where they have never been before: the inner recesses of their consciousness where they find sacred 'symbols' or imagery, serving as a new, liberating horizon of significance – perhaps helping individuals address relationship 'issues'. A one-to-one practitioner might serve to enable her participant to see that it is possible to have reciprocal relationships in the context of 'duty'-bound care. The undoubted skill of most practitioners lies with their ability to reveal, open up, those horizons which 'take you out of yourself' to provide new perspectives – not least beyond that vision provided by the monetary version of 'man is the measure of all things' positivism, associated with the limited goal of satisfying preferences by way of secular consumption. The skill is to enable participants to question their restrictive horizons; to release themselves from mundane routines or 'blocks' which stand in the way. Rarely 'literalizing' or spelling out the nature of horizons in the language of the 'ought' (as with 'this is the horizon you ought to aim for'), the 'opening up' process caters for the freedom of the participant. At the same time, though, the practitioner is there is provide 'bearings' if they are called for. Participant: 'I couldn't possibly be like that'; Practitioner: 'Try it this way and *see*'.

In *Martin Eden*, Jack London writes, 'She would never have guessed that this man who had come from beyond her horizon, was...flashing on beyond her horizons with wider and deeper concepts'. The ultimate horizon of holistic mind-body spirituality is expressed by experiences *of* the spiritual realm. For the seeker (the practitioner as well as the participant), this is the horizon which beckons in experience. Just as the visual horizon of the seafarer constantly recedes, so does this spiritual horizon: the flotsam and jetsam of everyday life, which continually interrupt the spiritual quest, take care of this. However, since the horizon expresses the spiritual realm, seekers perpetually experience it as 'flashing on' with what spirituality has to offer. As with many of the works of art of the Romantics, that familiar quality of horizons – the (apparent) intersection of the earth and the sky, or the sea and the sky – 'flashes', illuminates the message of the unitary. Today, the spirituality 'behind' the horizons of everyday circumscriptions manifests itself through the ultimate horizons of what caring for or enabling others, being cared for or enabled oneself, loving and being loved, health, tranquillity, peace, harmony, 'balance', energy, vitality, *can really* be like. In short, horizons, and what they express (especially via their beacons), beckon you on, open up directions in life. Travel to the island on the horizon; stay at the New Age centre; travel beyond what you normally expect of life; pursue what you find.

To *reach* the horizon which expresses the spiritual realm *per se* is to *enter* it for the rest of your life. However, like their Romantic precursors, few if any participants today think that *this* is possible. Life in the everyday world generates too many diversions, pitfalls, materialistic temptations, along the route. But this should not detract from the key point: that for many active within the holistic milieu, spiritual horizons 'call', practitioners serving as revealing lighthouses – which are relatively rarely focused on lighting up the world of secular purchasing culture. Ultimately, spiritual horizons are meant to serve to inspire; to enable participants to move past their limited frames of reference; to take them out of their 'normal' selves. Of particular note, a pivotal feature of the horizons of good practice is provided by the horizon of Buberian 'I and Thou' relationships: the 'work' that has to be done to move beyond the 'appearance', the 'dress', the 'presentation of self', the 'ego games', the 'defence mechanisms', the 'It' of the 'I-It relationship as Martin Buber (2004) calls it, to enter the openings, to fulfil the *visions* of the 'I and Thou' dimension of life. Overall, glimpsed by the spiritual seeker through the mountains of the ego, that ultimate horizon, the spiritual dimension, with all its promise, serves to set the journey. So long as horizons are in place, Chesterton got things wrong.

MacIntyrian Practices: The Authority of Activities

Most practitioners are *practiced* practitioners. To remain in work, they have to be 'experienced' as 'experts'. They know what to do, and when to do it. Albeit serving the goal of autonomous self-realization, much of *substance* is brought into play by practitioners through 'their' work and the ways in which events are orchestrated. To help ensure that 'their' activities work as effectively as possible, frames of reference, practical rules, 'principles', 'how to' instructions, structured ways of growing (required to deal with harmful ego-attachments), hypothetical imperatives of the kind 'if you want it to work, *do it*', even 'taboos' to prevent activities from being disrupted or damaged too much, are (variously) in evidence.

To advance the analysis, we can consider what Alasdair MacIntyre (1985) has to say about the notions of 'a practice' and 'a virtue'. 'By a "practice"', he writes,

> I am going to mean any coherent and complex form of socially established cooperative human activity through which goods internal to that form of activity are realized in the course of trying to achieve those standards of excellence which are appropriate to, and partially definitive of, that form of activity, with the result that human powers to achieve excellence, and human conceptions of the ends and goods involved, are systematically extended. (p. 187)

And concerning virtues:

> A virtue is an acquired human ability the possession and exercise of which tends to enable us to achieve those goods which are internal to practices and the lack of which effectively prevents us from achieving any such goods. (p. 191)

Generally speaking, holistic, mind-body-spirituality activities are MacIntyrian 'practices'. Internal *goods* are in evidence, for example spiritually informed health. Internal goods are *realized* by way of *appropriate* activity, which in turn develops *virtues*. And human *conceptions* of ends and goods are systematically *extended* – for example by being inspired by new horizons of experiential-cum-existential significance to come to experience what it is to be 'truly' wise in one's relationships. What matters is doing what is required for the practice to work, for instance by obeying 'ground rules' for the sake of the 'goods' of the practice – freedom and authentic self-expressivity. (A most helpful analysis of how 'disciplinary' rules serve the goal of liberation or self-expressivity is provided by Steven Tipton's (1982) discussion of what he calls 'rule-egoism'.) Unhelpful preferences and other states of mind, namely those which disrupt the *point* of good practice, have to be gently (in exceptional circumstances, not so gently) 'handled'. Those who are apparently content to languish in their 'comfort zone', whilst showing clear signs of having 'issues' which they (awkwardly or hesitantly) want to address to become 'truly' at ease with themselves, will be 'nudged' into action. Accordingly, practitioners are likely to say things along the lines of, 'If you want it to work, all you have to do is do *this* – don't worry if it makes you feel uncomfortable to begin with'; 'Don't clog up your mind with worries and doubts'; 'Live with your boredom to allow it to work'. *Requirements* – not *duties* – are taken to be operative. Guided by their practitioners, participants are not encouraged to dwell on 'restrictive' or disruptive preferences-cum-beliefs of the 'I'll *only* be happy when I look beautiful' or 'All I *really* want is a luxurious house' variety. The holistic 'goods' of practitioners count against this; so does their concern to guide participants *within* – rather than (further) into the material world; so does the *experiential* thrust of practices, with participants being discouraged from indulging in their (perhaps deeply engrained) *beliefs* about beauty or luxury; so does one of the basic themes of holistic practitioners – that spirituality flows through all that lives – participants with selfish, racist, elitist life-values or tendencies being urged to try out other more holistically encompassing approaches to life.

As a 'socially established *cooperative* human activity' (MacIntyre, cited above; my emphasis), a key feature of good practice within holistic activities is cooperative learning and growing (c.f. Crossley, 2004), Taylor (1994) serves to make the point:

> On the intimate level, we can see how much an original identity needs and is vulnerable to the recognition given or withheld by significant others. It is not surprising that in the culture of authenticity, relationships are seen as the *key*

loci of self-discovery and self-affirmation. Love relationships are not just important because of the general emphasis in modern culture of the fulfilments of ordinary needs. They are also crucial because they are the crucibles of inwardly generated identity. (p. 81; my emphasis)

Holistic participants enter into contexts where the emotional *reality* almost invariably requires being 'emotionally transparent and literate about [one's] own processes – actively seeking and welcoming feedback from others' (Bloom, 2006). Also in the words of Bloom (2004):

We celebrate the fact that we may be wrong.
We warmly welcome opposing views.
The more different from us you are, the better we like you.
We trust that the universe is just fine with all this diversity and change.
These are our beliefs and core values – value them or not.
We are interested in you, whatever you feel or think about us. (pp. 43–4)

However utopian this passage might appear to be, it emphasizes the importance of difference for inwardly generated identity and 'authenticity' (Heath and Potter, 2006, p. 270). The same encountering the same is not all that helpful. For activities to work as well as possible – which is what spiritual practitioners, in particular, are aiming for – participants (together with practitioners) 'should' be prepared to doubt themselves in the *light* of others; 'should' be open to learning from the 'views' of others; 'should' welcome the opportunity of revising their own 'views' of themselves especially in view of the experiences of others – thereby extending their appreciation of what life has to offer; 'should' appreciate the opportunity of *recognizing* what is wrong with their own lives by seeing what is not working in the lives of their co-participants; 'should' be prepared to show their trust in others by acknowledging their failings – thereby encouraging others to reciprocate in trust. Taking place within the context of relatively coherent, cohesive and 'established' activities, honed by practice, good work thus serves as a powerful learning experience of interchange – 'those standards of excellence', including honesty and openness, which serve as the 'point' (the internal goods) of MacIntyrian practice encouraging participants to 'move on': 'beyond' disequilibriating (perhaps materialistic, perhaps personal) attachments; beyond their distorted, their bad habits of the heart – which no one is ever entirely free of. 'Life', not undue materiality or distorted relationality.[7]

As good practice, the authority of the group member or one-to-one client is negotiated within (many) face-to-face holistic activities, taking its place together with the expertise of those spiritual *virtuosi*, the practitioners. It is quite likely that happenstance 'preferences' are incompatible with the good practice being pursued. Generally speaking, the 'ethic' of 'what you want is what you should have' does not rule the roost. Mere preferences are rarely allowed to run riot, transgressing the 'control' of the guidance of the practitioner and her or his orchestration of practice. Hanegraaff (1999), for example, surely overstates his case when he writes that '[New Age] religion becomes *solely* a matter of individual choice' (p. 153; my emphasis). Provided by practitioners who consider their activities to be of spiritual significance, associational activities are 'sacred' in a way which is akin to the Durkheimian sense – albeit serving the expression and development of the uniqueness of the lives of participants rather than the conformist order of traditional religion with its transcendent Godhead. Activities are inviolate in that if they are 'profaned', treated without respect, or severely disrupted, they are very unlikely to be experienced as working – especially by participants who are spiritually committed. Bruce's (1995) point that 'With no comprehensive and binding ethical code, in the New Age there is always the danger that pursuing self-growth actually means pursuing self-interest' (p. 120), and Lasch's (1980) more radical point concerning 'the dead end of narcissistic preoccupation of the self' (p. xv) cannot be discounted *in toto*. But in connection with a great many associational activities, where relational receptivity and expressivity are so significant for good practice, we can already see why the danger is by no means as great as is often supposed. The extent to which practitioners serve as influential 'role' models remains open to debate (debate which awaits further ethnographic and social psychological research). What we can say, though, is that practitioners take primary responsibility for the *quality* of their practices, including guidance with regard to the ethos of expressivity and receptivity and the value of 'growing' through and with others; including instructions with regard to the 'how to' of practice, indications about how their facilitatory rules contribute to 'life'. After all, this is what many participants expect – and pay for: good practice, with its valued ends and experiences serving as an end in itself, rather than bad practice, serving as the means to external ends which do not chime with the practice itself.

Durkheim's 'Religion of Humanity'

Recalling the importance which Charles Taylor ascribes to the point 'that some things ['goals and purposes'] are more important beyond the self', it is apparent that not everything expressed by way of spiritually informed horizons or visions need be of equal significance. Take 'perfect' health or wellbeing, for example. This could be sought just for oneself, and no doubt this is sometimes the case. Even in instances like this, though, the 'beyond the self' could very well be in evidence – one's 'own' health or wellbeing taken to enhance the quality of what one has to offer others (perhaps as simply as by being happy).

What lends credence to this theme of 'wellbeing for others', and what – more generally – provides a powerful argument against the 'the profane pursuit of self-gratification'/'consumer preferences' treatment of holistic activities, is that the ethic of humanity is widely abroad within New Age spirituality of life circles.

To briefly refer to the ethic in its more 'secular' mode, the ethic is a mode of evaluation and decision-making which is driven by the claim that there is a universal or unitary 'humanity'. The core value of the ethic lies with life itself and its basic attributes. What we all share by virtue of the life of humanity lies beyond all differences, whether biological (pigmentation, for instance), ethnic, religious, gendered or national, etc. Since we are all humans, we are all fundamentally equal; since we are all humans, we are equally entitled to the same freedoms to develop and express ourselves. Other values, including respecting the dignity of the other, respecting the other by telling the truth, applying justice equitably, flow accordingly. Acknowledging that no one human being is the same as another, the respect accorded to the other goes together with the value of freedom: the freedom for people to 'live out' their humanity in their own way – so long as life itself, the freedom of others, the dignity of others, is not unduly at stake. The ultimate value assigned to life itself by what is surely the dominant ethic of the west (and in other parts of the world) means that it is not surprising that Durkheim (1971) called the ethic the '*religion* of humanity' (p. 46; my emphasis).

In explicitly sacralized mode, the ethic of humanity in expressivist mode of self-understanding serves as *the* most significant ethicality of spiritualities of life. The sacred is located within the depths of the shared life. To think of an important Kendal Project finding, 82 per cent of questionnaire respondents agreed with the statement that 'some sort of spirit or life-force *pervades all that lives*' (Heelas and Woodhead, 2005, p. 25; my emphasis).[8] In common with more 'secular', formalistic renderings (the UN's Universal Declaration of Human Rights, for example), there is a universal core to life – a core which expresses or 'manifests' itself through the unique life-experiences of particular individuals by virtue of the (relative) freedom provided by the ethic. In common with more 'secular' renderings, only now informed by the spiritual dimension, the fact that we are all spiritual beings, of fundamentally equal value, means that it is vital to strive to be as open, honest, trusting, caring and respectful with others as possible. Where the sacralized ethic differs, however, is that it speaks 'from the heart', not 'out of' duty. That is to say, rather than the ethic operating in terms of the requirements, demands or threats of rationalistic, codified, legalistic prescriptions – as befits its development with the Enlightenment – the values of the ethic are experienced as flowing from what it is to *be* true to life: as befits its development during and since the Romantic movement. An 'emotionalistic' rendering is in evidence, value-informed and affect-laden 'sentiments' (a term favoured by Durkheim) flowing from within ('my heart goes out to you') as befits expressive ethicality.[9]

With around 80 per cent of mind-body-spirituality associational participants reporting 'belief' in inner-life spirituality, and with the values of the ethic of humanity so widely in evidence in inner-life circles, the ethic can be experienced as functioning as an inner-directed, that is expressivist, form of the Durkheimian sacred. It is an experientially laden form of metanarrative – 'meta' in that it is *experienced* as transcending, going over and above, narratives of reason. It provides a 'horizoned' promise, to do with living in the spirit of truth, honesty, wisdom, love, harmony, understanding (in the sense of *being* understanding), empathy and openness; the spirit of enablement or care, of looking for the best in others, appreciating others and what they have to offer, of relating with others through emotion-laden ethicality (a much better expression, in this context, than 'emotional intelligence'), of forgiveness, compassion, and the integration of life – not just 'spirit' as in the casual sense of 'let us get this sorted out in the spirit of reconciliation', but in the profound experiential sense of 'true' spirituality. Infusing the values of the ethic of humanity with sacrality, this 'articulated spirituality', 'spiritual code', 'spiritual ethicality' or 'spiritual direction-finder' is experienced as serving as the key litmus test of ways of life: the key test of what is appropriate or inappropriate; of authenticity and inauthenticity; of good practice. According to this litmus test, for example, many participants experience, or re-experience, the 'truth' that it is much more important to be in tune with oneself, *for* others, than to be 'consumed' – taken over – by one's looks, by how one *appears* to other people. You cannot expect much from yoga if you treat it as a display of radical chic rather than an unfolding 'life-vista' making a difference to those around you – or so your yoga practitioner is likely to remark. For practices to fulfil their potential – that is, to open up horizons to experience more of the 'true' life – there is no point in indulging in the 'you' whose preferential 'truths' of self-interest come from, are limited to, materialistic consumer culture. To be guided by the truths of the pregnant ethicality of so much of inner-life spirituality, the 'you' of the 'what works for *you*' has to be encouraged – if indeed it needs encouragement – to *go beyond* the 'you' of narrow horizons, the 'promises', 'hopes', aims, targets, of secular routine – to work with and for others.[10]

It remains to emphasize the important point that many participants report experiencing the values – the 'timeless truths' – of the ethic of humanity as emanating from the sacrality of the interior life. The values are experienced in expressive mode. Unless they emanate from a spiritual realm which really exists, the values must be internalizations, subjectivizations, of the ethic as it operates within society. Whether or not it has been acquired by virtue of socialization, the fact that the values are typically experienced as coming from within, 'from the heart', by way of the voice of the 'inner child', or through the promptings of 'inner' conscience, means that they are one's 'own' – in the sense of being experienced at first hand – values. Rather than being experienced as restrictive duties, obligations or responsibility, the values are an aspect of one's self expression. The value of freedom is not undermined.[11]

Bruce's Self of Preferences?

The importance Bruce attaches to individual preferences within the cultic milieu (as he often calls it) prompts the thought that for Bruce the participant (or practitioner) is little more than the sum of her or his preferences. A good way of undermining the claim that holistic spiritualities of life (in particular activities, which I continue to dwell on) are little more than consumeristic preferences writ large is to show that the 'preferential' aspects of the selfhood of those involved are nowhere near as important as Bruce (and others, like Bauman) would have it.

A difficulty immediately rears its head. Use of the term 'preference' can only too readily run out of control. Most generally, as exemplified by use within rational choice economics, the term refers to choices between alternatives, alternatives being ranked according to preference or 'taste'.[12] Somewhat more specifically, the term can refer to a stronger liking or predisposition – as with 'my own preference is for good literature, but if absolutely necessary I'll read anything', or as with 'my preference is to stay at home, but I have to go out to work'. The term can also refer to less determinate forms of liking – as with 'both kinds of chocolate are nice, but I'm inclined to favour the dark variety'. Whether it be likes, desires, needs, inclinations or tastes, the term is applied in connection with a range of forms of choice.

To cut things down to empirically useful scope and applicability, I follow what I *think* lies at the heart of the way Bruce, among others, uses the term. (I emphasize 'think' because use is generally pretty indeterminate.) Whilst undoubtedly used in connection with subjectivities, like desires and tastes, the term primarily refers to those choice-prompting experiences which belong to that aspect of being known as 'utilitarian individualism' – the 'life devoted to the calculating pursuit of one's own material interests', as Bellah et al. (1985, p. 33) put it. (They could well have added 'one's own material-*cum-subjective* interests'.) In other words, 'preferences' have their primary, paradigmatic home in those aspects of the self which have become bound up with the 'truths' of a great deal of shopping culture, including associated media presentations: preferences prompted by advertising; preferences which you feel are your own but which would not exist in the absence of purchasing culture (or consumer culture, if you prefer); preferences which translate into concrete choices on the basis of your expectation that the selected items will work for 'you' – when the *you* is the consumerized you.

Accordingly, preferences can be distinguished from other modes of choice or agency: the urging of one's conscience, one's heartfelt sense of having to go out of one's way to help another, one's decision to take on one's responsibilities or duties, one's 'inner voice' suddenly urging, 'this is the person I *must* marry'; one's intuitive sense that 'this really is not the right job for me'; the shock of discovering that an intimate friend is living a lie; one's realization that 'I simply must do something about my life' – to join a tai chi group. In these, and many other ways, then, the life of any particular individual is rarely, if ever, a totality of consumerized preferences. There is much to be said for 'the human beyond preferences'! And more empirically, there is much to be said for the arguments of those like Amitai Etzioni (1990): 'There is more to life than a quest to maximize one's satisfaction'

(p. 13); less politely, as it can be put, people are not merely the sum of their preferences – with large appetites.

With the possible – some might say highly likely – exception of those attracted to holistic activities taking place within settings like spas and hotels, selves of a strongly consumerized bent are almost certainly few and far between in most holistic, associational contexts. Practitioners and participants are mostly drawn from the ranks of predominantly expressive, rather than utilitarian, 'individualists' – people for whom the utilitarian mode 'leave[s] too little room for love, human feeling, and a deeper expression of the self' (Bellah et al., 1985, p. 33). Those attracted generally have a 'post'-materialist outlook, some (but not many today) making considerable efforts to cut the materialistic aspects of life to the bone in counter-cultural fashion; some (but probably not all that many today) attaching considerable value to what the material world has to offer whilst also wanting 'more' (the best-of-both-worlds 'yuppies' of the 1980s); some (the majority) exercising moderation with regard to the materialities of life, to concentrate on the (relatively) non-materialistic goals of living the more harmonious (less cluttered as less materialistic) life – the 'quality of life' life, where quality is found through friendships, golfing clubs, walking, relaxed gift shopping, 'going for a drive', good-quality food – and above all, being as authentic as possible, as true as possible to what one has learnt from one's life experiences – especially as one enters the time zone where one's sense of morality is likely to loom ever larger, focusing one's attention on what really matters in life: the personal, interior life, not the external 'trappings'; perhaps, as death approaches, the living spirit coming ever more important while the 'shell' of one's disintegrating body becomes of ever less value.[13]

Those attracted to holistic activities are largely mid-life women, many with good educational qualifications, many with expertise in person-centred relational careers like nursing, primary school teaching, many (probably of a significant numerical order) having downsized, with a great many committed to expressive-cum-'humanistic' values or ethicality – being true to oneself and growing through relationships, for example; finding self-fulfilment by helping others to grow. As is only to be expected, many of those attracted *already* hold many of the key values and 'beliefs' of associational settings (Heelas, 2006a, p. 231; and see below), thereby contributing to the cultural substance of the associational. Those nurses or primary school teachers, intent on exploring their self-identity by seeking to become more secure, 'centred' or 'experienced' in themselves – for the wellbeing of others (Heelas and Woodhead, 2005, pp. 98–107) – are not the kind of people who are in much danger of suddenly changing their life-values to leap into hedonistic self-interest and absorption; to leap from caring values to become grossly individualistic; to apply some kind of cost-benefit analysis to suddenly exclaim, '*I'm* worth it' and take up yoga accordingly. Far from it: productivity for the sake of money, many consumer culture commodities, the glorification of the 'I' are rarely 'truly' valued by the people under consideration, not infrequently being seen as a cause of 'dis-ease', disequilibrium, the unbalanced life. And as we have seen, to the extent that utilitarian self-aggrandizement comes into evidence, then to that extent practitioners are likely to get to work to serve as beacons to 'open up', reveal or illuminate broader, spiritually infused horizons. Furthermore, even if participants are exploring their own selfhood, it is highly likely that the majority do so because they want to become better people for others – for the wellbeing of others (Heelas and Woodhead, 2005, pp. 98–107).[14]

In some kinds of activities, if participants ask to be pleasured they will get a good pampering or 'seeing to'. Many of those purchasing mind-body spirituality publications are surely intent on 'simply' having a good read or time. But the treatment of holistic activities as part-and-parcel of the self-gratifications of consumer culture 'preferences' clearly has its limitations. The role played by that experiential pragmatism which is driven by utilitarian preferences must not be overemphasized; not all 'preferences' – if that is what they are – are equally 'right' (that is, effective for the 'good' life). Participants with consumeristic, 'mere-pleasure', selfish, greedy, anti-humanitarian preferences or attachments are like to be encouraged to 'move on' by 'going deeper' – or simply move on by leaving. Many find that their sense of liberation from the rat race of keeping up with the fashions and trends of consumer culture, achieved in the first instance by downsizing – going part-time, taking up voluntary work or turning to less well-paid albeit person-centred careers – or by retiring (approaching a quarter of Kendal participants), can be complemented with activities catering for the liberation of personal and intra-personal 'growth'.[15]

For Taylor (1991), 'the powerful moral ideal...behind self-fulfilment is that of being true to oneself' (p. 15). For him, the core value underpinning the ethics of authenticity is that 'everyone has a right to develop their own form of life, grounded on their own sense of what is really important or of value' (p. 14). The right to become an 'authentic' consumer of the *de*-limited realm of consumer culture preferences is not what (many) associational activities are all about. To emphasize this point, if the 'you' of 'what works for you' were of the consumerized kind, we would expect to find a great deal more of the 'practise this – earn more money – have more to spend' variety of prosperity, utilitarian, 'enterprising' (as in 'enterprise culture') New Age activity.[16] Instead, holistic activities work with expressivist-humanist experiential-cum-cultural assumptions, values, 'beliefs' and practices, thereby catering for, whilst being 'solidified', mutually reaffirmed, by those with a similar, if not identical, outlook. (A nurse responding to a primary school teacher after a tai chi session, saying, 'That is amazing; I experienced a profound sense of integration at exactly the same time'; '...the most exciting thing on this journey is finding your own thoughts are the same as someone else's', as an interviewee told one of my research students, Janet Eccles.)

Under the Spell of Modernity

Adapted from the title of a volume by Stef Aupers, *In de Ban van Moderniteit* (2005), the phrase 'under the spell of modernity' serves to direct our attention to arguably the most important ways in which holistic activities provide a *solid base* – and one which transcends utilitarian consumption.[17] Typically, participants enter holistic activities *with* the key values and assumptions which they then encounter through participation. They come with the values and assumptions of the ethic of humanity. They come with the values and assumptions of expressivism, most especially that of the authentic or true self. They come with the values and assumptions of a postmaterialist outlook on life. They arrive with their moral individualism – an individualism framed in terms of the ethicality of expressivistic humanism. And as we shall see in the next chapter, they generally come with at least a modicum of 'belief' in the spirituality which lies within. Furthermore, although the evidence is not so conclusive on this point, it is highly likely that many arrive with prior 'experience' or 'knowledge' derived from mind-body-spirituality literature or other sources of information. Prior 'beliefs', values, assumptions, quite probably experiences in many cases, undoubtedly play a role in 'solidifying' holistic practices. Speaking much the same language, mutual affirmation takes place between participants. A feedback process occurs during participation, between that which is prior – and the commitments which go with it – and that which is encountered, a feedback process which contributes to the plausibility of what is provided by holistic activities: most especially the plausibility of the 'more' – the greater 'depth', the greater efficacy of inner-spirituality – which is encountered.[18]

'The New Age lacks [a] solid base', writes Bruce (2002, p. 101). Others also claim that the activities are under-institutionalized. Far from it. The continuities between what participants bring with them and what they engage with alone ensures this. To say that holistic practitioners and participants are 'under the spell of modernity' might be to exaggerate the point. What this expression indicates, though, is that those concerned are under the spell of what is promised by major assumptions and values of modernity: what is promised by becoming 'truly' authentic, spiritual, expressive, caring and so on. And this is where practices come in. Meaningful activities, which precisely because of the nature of their meanings serve to articulate, amplify and explore values and assumptions *through action*.[19] An action-based learning environment. One where the 'experienced' truths of practices have to be taken seriously if participants want to get anywhere. One in which one can go 'deeper' into what it is to respect others by 'listening' and responding to what they have to say about their activity-revealed experiences; a learning environment in which one becomes more aware of the extent to which one's self-expression has been hampered by one's bodily movements, one's tone of voice, one's defensive ego-games...

The basic point cannot be emphasized enough. Values *are* deeply embedded in virtually all practices; the practising bodies (c.f. Crossley, 2004). Values in action enable change, typically embedded by virtue of practitioners talking along the lines of 'To get anywhere, it's really important for *you* to try your very best to say what you really mean' or 'What I'm about to show you is a practice which will enable *you* to respect what lies beneath aggression'.

The spiritually informed, humanistic-expressive values and assumptions of holistic activities, taken to be *of* the sacred and articulated and explored through authoritative practices, with relationality, skilfully authoritative orchestration and beckoning horizons in action as well: rather than being insubstantial or precarious, good practice is substantive and cohesive. At least when practices are in full swing, they are effective in ways which cannot be captured by using the language of consumption: not unless one wants to treat the ethic of humanity in this way, that is. Plenty of spiritual direction and – through good practice – discipline here, meaning that activities are fit for the future: themes developed in later chapters, when additional points are provided. The *Substantive*.

Conclusion

For Bruce (1995) the New Age 'illustrates the zenith of individualism' (p. 122) for Ward (2006), we find 'hyper-individualism' (p. 185); for Possamai (2000), New Agers are 'the perfect individualists of religion' (p. 368); and for Possamai (2003), 'a strong detachment from systematized belief and practice' is in evidence, with 'an extreme form of individualization' (p. 40). Prompted by their (necessarily) individualistic 'preferences', 'everyone calls his or her own tune' (to recall the words of Bruce, cited in the last chapter). As I have argued, rather than the application of a simple binary opposition – 'principles come before feelings' for transcendent theistic tradition (Combe, 1998), 'preferences instead of principles' for New Age spiritualities of life – something different is going on in holistic activities. Something different which *involves* the cultural values of the expressivist ethic of humanity, the ethic of relationality, the articulation of inner-spirituality-cum-the-true-self, the role played by horizons of significance, the 'principles' (and other characteristics) of practices, the ways practices with their embedded values are orchestrated, and last – but by no means least – the presence of so many postmaterialists. Something different, which goes a long way toward explaining why New Age spiritualities of life do not lapse into spiritualities of consumeristic preference. Although holistic activities do not operate with the 'external', theistically sustained doctrines, orders, injunctions, commandments and duties of 'strong' tradition, they *do* operate as orchestrated repertoires, whose 'performance' strongly discourages ineffectual, or counter-effectual, refuge in an uncritical, non-reflexive 'I'm happy *simply* doing what *happens* to do most for me'. 'What you want to have is what you should or must have' – by no means *necessarily*! The vistas provided by spiritually informed horizons of expressivist-cum-humanist significance – horizons opening up ever more vistas with their directions and opportunities – see to that. So does the fact that the 'I' of 'You don't make up the rules, I do' is customarily replaced with the authority of 'experiential tradition'.

And even if the positivistic or atheistic social scientist is justified in claiming that the ultimate (sacred) 'author' or 'composer' of inner-life spirituality does not exist, there remains the 'conductor' or the 'harmonizer' – the practitioner who relishes the opportunity of enabling participants to go beyond the mundanities of the grasping, attachment-laden materialism mindset to open up 'new dimensions'; the practitioner who far from relishes the prospect of participants dismantling practices to use them in any way they happen to wish – thereby diminishing or destroying their efficacy. Thinking of the observation made by Lasch, cited at the beginning of this chapter, the person-centred approach of practitioners means that 'individual specifications' are taken into account – but especially in group activities, and practices are not 'constantly redesigned' to suit the individual. (This would result in chaos in groups.) Practices have an ethical 'weight', so to speak, of their own; practices have been honed over time, the honed, so to speak, being the honed.

The back cover of Crook et al.'s *Postmodernization* (1992) provides the statement that we are witnessing 'the collapse of culture into a postmodern cafeteria of "styles"'. Taking a cue from the Quakers, the form of *holistic spiritual meetings* (or gatherings), where people come together to practise, enables them to chart a course between the conformity of traditionalized, theistic transcendent religion, where Durkheim's classic definition of religion has its home, and antinomian individualism where utilitarian preferences are able, indeed likely, to run riot. At least for engaged seekers, the sacred of holistic activities is inviolate. As the key constitutive aspect of MacIntyrian good practice, it cannot be questioned, altered or changed or ignored for convenience. To persist in praising racial intolerance during a one-to-one spiritual healing course (for example) would be to miss the point of the practice, thereby destroying it for oneself, probably others; rendering it inefficacious. Just as the 'secular' ethic of humanity brings its illiberal edge into play when its key 'sacred' values are disregarded (UN agencies being prepared to sacrifice life to prevent genocide, for example), when holistic activities themselves are too threatened, the toleration of holistic milieu practitioners is replaced by action ('If you really *want* to persist with your racism, please don't come back').

Ultimately, mind-body spirituality is not about personal contentment – that is, the satisfaction of those subjectivities stimulated or aroused by the more capitalistic aspects of everyday life. By definition, expressivists are looking to express themselves by broadening their creative horizons. To cater for them, to cater for the quest for the fullness of life, to cater for body, mind *and* spirit, horizons have to be expanded. Practitioners (themselves often working with other practitioners) facilitate the expansion of experience – rather than just catering for participants within their comfort zone.[20] Hence the importance of spiritual direction for the best route to the horizon – and beyond. The 'better' the horizon, the 'better' the vision, the 'better' the practice, the 'better' the living of life. Those intending to participate might well 'shop around' to select the activity which they think is best suited for them. But *active* participation could well mean that significant 'suitability' is only appreciated when participants have dealt with those more self-indulgent '*I* want to feel good' aspects which might have contributed to initial appeal – but which have subsequently transpired to be disruptive barriers or attachments. In any case, the 'you' of the 'what works for you' is most frequently the 'you' of a humanistic-expressivist, postmaterialist orientation, already well on the road beyond those who find the pleasures, the 'truths', of much of life via consumeristic, utilitarian, materialistic culture. The 'you' of expressions like 'what works for *you*' or 'what does most for *you*' can mean so many things: the person testing out a new sport; the person trying out a new musical instrument or a new novelist. The 'you', it seems, need not mean the consuming 'you' of consumption. And given the nature of the 'you' that is emphasized by holistic participants in continuity with their prior values, 'beliefs' and assumptions, rather than the 'you' of the utilitarian individualist mode having to be constantly overridden, it is relatively inconspicuous – a point taken up in chapter 8.

One thing is for sure. In much of the associational realm, experiential ethicality – where feelings, 'principles of spiritual efficacy', values and – no doubt – 'beliefs' so-so-speak fuse in the experience of activities guided by the 'good' practitioner (who is far from 'dead', as with the 'death of the author'), relatively few 'pipe' – or rather consume – as they like. Other than those who have sought out practitioners who are happy to serve consumeristic preferences, the self of narrow, restricted horizons, valuing life within the circumscribed, valuing consumption according to the sway of consumer culture, is not the name of the game.[21]

Although additional evidence is required, which will be provided in due course, it is fairly safe to arrive at a couple more conclusions. One concerns Taylor's (1991) point that 'Issues where we were meant to accept the dictates of authority we now have to think out for *ourselves*' (p. 81; my emphasis). Holistic activities, we have seen, hardly operate with 'dictates'; and neither do they leave participants alone. The second concerns Taylor's (1991) point that for self-centred, highly individualist expressivists, 'there is nothing there beyond the self to explore' (p. 90). The operation of the ethic of humanity, alone, counts against this (with the anti-relational unlikely to be attracted in the first place, or to stay). A humanistic ethicality is surely not a consumptive ethic: most certainly not when it is put into practice to contribute to the lives of others; when the 'me' serves the 'we'. To treat the values of the ethic of humanity as 'marks' of consumption would be strange indeed.

Seneca famously observed, 'Mirrors were discovered in order that man might know himself.' Within holistic practices, 'mirrors' are other people, reflecting one's activities to encourage self-reflection. In addition, one sees oneself in others and one learns from the lives of others. And above all else, others – most especially practitioners – serve to enable spiritual direction.

Chapter 6

The Matter of Personal Significance: Profaned Superficiality?

Much of what passes as spirituality is as thin as chicken soup and as transparent as celestine profits. (Wade Clark Roof, 1999b, p. 138)

Spirituality isn't instant soup. (Adi Bloom, 2007)

Spiritual drumming has been saving and changing my life. (Undergraduate student, Lancaster University)

Experience the difference. (Paul Heelas)

The mix of ingredients is too unstable to hold together, to provide a coherent explanation of things or even a coherent answer to the personal difficulties that attract people in the first place. (Christopher Lasch, 1987, p. 80)

Rather than simply a pretext for the ransacking of other cultures, the individualist and perennialist philosophies of New Age and alternative spiritualities can be a source of personal meaning that supports and enables multiple values and ideologies. (Stewart Muir, 2005, p. 101)

It is not just that those favouring reductionism emphasize consumption. There is also a strong tendency for theorists to emphasize the *superficiality* of consumption. Steve Bruce (1996) writes that New Age 'products' are 'consumed by people as a slight flavouring to their mundane lives' (p. 261); Christopher Lasch (1987) of 'spiritual stew' (p. 80); Terry Eagleton (2007) 'New Ageist claptrap' (p. 40).

One of the strongest arguments against applying the language of consumption – most especially terms used to highlight the supposed superficialities of utilitarian, hedonistic individualism – is that many of those participating in holistic activities are trying to do something about, transform if not change *significant* aspects of their experiences of themselves. Rather than being lightweight or inconsequential, I now argue that many activities '"make" a difference': most noticeably when they address challenging 'issues' by ways which themselves can be challenging. Obviously, the arguments of the last chapter against the claim that utilitarian preferences run riot come to bear here. For the less that untrammelled preferences – perhaps fuelled by consumer-culture expectations, promises or desires – are in evidence, the less likely it is that easy-to-use acts of consumption are operative. In other words, the greater the significance of the 'Durkheimian'-like sacred, the less the likelihood of activities being superficial in the sense of indulging those feelings which people *happen* to have when their minds-bodies-emotions are engrossed by the everyday secularities of purchasing culture.[1]

The case for *experiential* significance now has to be made more comprehensively. The focus in this chapter is on the 'inner-life', the subjective life; on how participants experience themselves. More 'externally' orientated, practical or applied aspects of spiritually informed selfhood, including more on self-evaluation, self-understanding and motivation, are looked at in later chapters.

Before proceeding any further, I should emphasize that I am not focusing on the highly controversial matter of whether holistic spiritualities 'really' work – in the sense of really curing physical illness, for example. There is no need to dwell on the bearing of 'real', that is 'hard' scientific evidence, in connection with bodily changes: whether providing the case for improvement, regression or no demonstrable change. Fully accepting that physical changes can have a bearing on how holistic participants are feeling, the scientific research is too detailed, too contradictory, to enter into here. Furthermore, the research is probably not of all that great a relevance. Provided with a list of reasons for originally trying the activity in which they had participated during the last seven days (or the most significant of these activities if they had participated in more than one), respondents to the holistic milieu questionnaire of the Kendal Project were asked to rank them in order of significance. Just 3.4 per cent selected 'dissatisfaction with mainstream medicine', even less – 0.8 per cent – 'to complement mainstream medical treatment'. True, 13.9 per cent selected 'bodily pain or illness'. But few were seriously ill. Thus in response to the question, 'How would you describe your state of health these days?', 3 per cent answered 'poor' (the 'Soul of Britain' questionnaire finding was 6 per cent: see Heald, 2000), none reported 'very poor' (the respective figure for Britain was 2 per cent), whilst approaching 75 per cent replied 'very good' or 'good' – this last percentage strongly suggests that significant numbers are intent on further enhancing the *quality* of *experienced* health or fitness (stress levels, etc.) rather than curing or even preventing physical illness (Heelas and Woodhead, 2005, pp. 91–2). In addition, there is the consideration that there is not an especially strong link between bodily condition and experiential significance: even when holistic participants are seriously ill, they often report (high) quality experiences.

Julie

Julie has been suffering from breast cancer. She says:

> I believe art therapy saved my life by giving me the opportunity to get in touch with *my authentic self*. This part of me *is now allowed to have a life*. The part that existed before was *a highly developed false self*. Every year it became harder and harder to do everything that I thought I should do. I felt as though I was running to stay still. My will power forced me to go on and my body forced me to slow down. But I had no respect for my body even though I had breast cancer. I continued to ignore my body's messages until one day I scattered into tiny pieces and my self-sufficiency, my bravado, my achievements trickled out of my body as I sobbed and shivered. I could not hold in any more suffering.
>
> I was having psychotherapy, creating images with my mind, but in art therapy my mind was not in charge. It did not control the paint or glue. I interacted with it by relating to whatever materials I had chosen. It was like meeting someone new. The materials would have their say, be whatever they were, show their qualities and I would make a connection, engage with them. Images emerged from an inner world that I had lost touch with. It was here that I discovered my values, my priorities and came to understand that I had sacrificed them for the most *urgent demands of life*. As time went on it was here that I examined the parts of myself that had been scattered, and I reclaimed those that I recognized as authentic.
>
> These fragmented and lost parts appeared week by week on the paper. It was a process of gathering – my grief, my desolate childhood, my feminine qualities, divinity. They were brought to my centre, later I mixed with a pulse of light and leaps of joy.
>
> Art therapy is not for producing a picture for anyone else, it is about being spontaneous, allowing something deep inside to express itself, to make its mark. I believe that the body knows how to heal itself, redress the balance. Feelings are processed and expressed without the involvement of the ordinary mind. So I mix, glue, teat, and fix together. I construct sculpture and structures which represent me as I change. Recently, I made 'well' my being which reached down into the watery depths and stretched up higher than a spire to bubbles of joy. (Cited by Connell, 2001, p. 105; my emphases)

For Julie, art therapy has nothing to do with satisfying the 'preferences' (if that is what they can be called) of what she came to understand to be her false self. It has to do with liberating herself from its attachments (previously the supposed most urgent demands of life) for much more important ends. It is highly unlikely that this is the kind of activity (and experienced 'belief') which Wade Clark Roof has in mind when he writes that '*much* of what passes as spirituality is as thin as chicken soup' (my emphasis). Would one use the language of consumption to characterize participation in creative art lessons in schools? If not, would you then apply it to people like Julie? My answer: given her circumstances, it is even more ridiculous to think of her therapy in terms of consumption than art lessons. Indeed, if Julie is included within the register of consumption, what is not to be included? Would it not leave us in the situation of having to say that we can all consume pretty much anything?

Julie's testimony serves to do two things. First, attention is drawn to how spiritually infused practices *are* able to act; to what *can* be done to provide experiential significance: in her case surely of an *existential* order, over-and above a fortifying rich, nourishing, chicken broth, let alone a thin gruel. And second, the testimony serves to introduce the point that rather than being all that exceptional, it is very much in line with what has been reported by people participating in many of the activities where spiritualities of life are at work in similar, or relatively similar, circumstances. For as inner-life spirituality becomes increasingly available within care centres, hospices, the 'terminal' or rehabilitation wards of hospitals, general practices and some nursing homes, for instance, participant testimonies like Julie's are becoming increasingly frequent (Barraclough, 2001; Heelas, 2006b; Partridge, 2005).

From the Record

'Pre-experience' intentions

All I have in mind by the term 'pre-experience' is what holistic participants refer to when they talk about their motivations or expectations prior to participation. What has this to do with experiential significance? The answer basically lies with their *intentions*. To explain, few people – certainly very few of those belonging to the holistic milieu who responded to the Kendal Project questionnaire – can hold up their hands and say, 'My life is working; I am perfectly content with the way it is'.[2] Given that those attracted to holistic activities almost always have (relatively) serious, challenging or demanding 'issues', it is perfectly reasonable to suppose that they often intend to tackle them. When a 'burnt-out' person decides to participate, it is quite likely that that person will gravitate to an appropriate activity; when people with 'a mental handicap' turn to yoga, they turn to the appropriate kind (Bullard, 1988, p. 4). I am not for one moment suggesting that there is always a perfect match between what holistic activities offer and the 'issues' of those attracted, but even when there is not it is likely that prior 'issues' will 'come up': during a tai chi group discussion, for example, whilst practising at home, or whilst reflecting on the activity on has been practising. After all, 'only connect' is the definitive characteristic of holistic spirituality. And what can be more valuable than connecting the fundamentals of one's being with the fundamentals of one's 'issues'? Hence the significance 'from' intentions.

Now to the nub. Given that the 'issues' which participants intend to tackle are likely to 'come up' during, between or on completion of their participatory activities, and given the fact that activities themselves typically serve to 'reveal' additional issues (typically working from the somatic to the emotional to further within), the challenges facing participants, their related intentions or motivations, *imbue* activities with existential significance. Assuming that 'issues' are of a serious or relatively serious nature – to do with matters of 'life' such as the 'dis-ease' generated by looking after an elderly, solitary parent – activities are *suffused* with a significance which far transcends mere status display or hedonistic gratification, for example. As has been argued elsewhere (Heelas and Woodhead, 2005, pp. 83–94), those attracted to holistic, mind-body-spirituality activities are often seeking something other-and-above the 'therapies' provided by the over-the-counter provisions of subjective wellbeing culture. Dissatisfied with anti-ageing lotions, customers go to mind-body-spirituality spas. Other people are seeking ways of compensating for problems at work – nurses, for example, frustrated by the suffocating iron cage of the ward ('Number of inspections "choking life out of the NHS"', runs a recent headline), a cage which leaves little room for being caring, by turning to activities where caring flourishes (Heelas and Woodhead, 2005, p.103). Often with the encouragement of practitioners, 'issues' will tend to emerge during practices; will be reflected upon; could well be discussed. In short, what this boils down to is that the purpose of many of those who decide to participate is to find ways of making a difference to their lives; of healing their 'wounds'; of defusing their worries. Pre-participatory motivations and expectations, namely what people are looking to *do*, accord significance to *what* they do. For Julie, the significance of art therapy is inseparable from her already having had cancer. And, it can be emphasized, when important personal matters are at stake, effective activities are called for, their effectiveness then contributing to that personal wellbeing shown by testimonies like Julie's.[3]

Evidence from Kendal and Environs

Asked to 'Indicate your most important reasons for originally trying this [current] activity or therapy', the 237 respondents to this particular question of the survey distributed to the participants of the mind-body-spirituality activities of Kendal and environs provided the following 'first choice' results: 'health and fitness', 23.2 per cent; 'looking for spiritual growth', 19.4 per cent; 'stress relief', 15.2 per cent; 'bodily pain or illness', 13.9 per cent; 'looking for personal growth', 13.5 per cent; 'pleasure, enjoyment or a treat', 7.6 per cent; 'life crisis (such as a relationship break-up, bereavement or job loss)', 6.3 per cent; 'time out of daily routines', 5.5 per cent; 'to meet like-minded people', 5.1 per cent; with the remainder of selections being under 5 per cent. With the major exception of 'looking for spiritual growth' taking over from 'health and fitness' to take the number one spot, much the same sequence appears in response to the request, 'Please indicate the most important reasons that you are now involved in this activity or therapy': a clear indication that 'issues' are addressed during practices.

Bearing in mind that just 7.9 per cent placed 'pleasure, enjoyment or a treat' as their first choice, experiential significance is indicated by at least several of the other percentages. In addition, we also asked an open-ended question: 'What would you say are the three most important problems facing you, personally, these days?' Answers to this question – which have only recently been analysed in some detail – do not provide an entirely satisfactory account of pre-participation problems: after all, the questionnaire was distributed to active participants. However, bearing in mind that the majority of the problems listed are almost certainly of a long-term nature, and bearing in mind that most participants (other than many practitioners) have not been participating for all that long, I think it is fair to conclude that participant problems are reasonably informative in connection with their pre-participatory self-understanding. The findings certainly serve to indicate what could very well come up during activities – to imbue practice with significance.

Analysis to date shows that relationships are of greatest concern (cf. Heelas and Woodhead, 2005, p. 105). Concerns are serious. Many of the relationship 'issues' have to do with the health of kin, in particular elderly parents. Others have to do with the lack of relationships – loneliness or feeling isolated. Concerns about the state of society or the world are of second greatest importance. Again, they are far from trivial: 'corporate greed', 'world injustice', 'lack of values'. Fitness and health follows next, with a fair number of serious matters: 'long-term recovery', 'mobility', and 'diabetes', for example. Just to mention the next most important matter, work-related issues basically revolve around the theme of there being too great a workload for respondents to be able to exercise their own abilities, their own unique gifts, satisfactorily. In short, with few exceptions, the great majority of holistic participants report significant personal difficulties or challenges, which helps explain the attraction of holistic activities and their significance for them.

Participatory Experience Itself

It is terribly easy to cast one's net to collect positive participant testimonies. Some are very positive indeed. Julie can be recalled. Or we can think of the Lancaster student who had been feeling desperately lonely after her arrival from Japan who wrote in an essay, 'spiritual drumming has been saving and changing my life'. In similar vein, there is Henry Dent-Brocklehurst, stating, 'I was feeling very low. But meditation saved my life' (cited in Wolff, 1997,

p. 3). More modestly, a Bristol 'Buddhist' affirms, 'I can determine my life now; I do not feel at the mercy of things going on around me or my own negativity. I am beginning to see myself as I am. You begin to see a much truer picture of yourself' (cited in Wigmore, 1985). Another testimony is noteworthy in that 'conversion' is claimed. Having crashed her car, in the process inadvertently killing her mother, Catherine Lucas (2005) later started 'therapy'. As she puts it:

> And so my search for healing gradually revealed itself to be a spiritual journey. Because whilst most psychotherapy stops at the level of the mind and the emotions, the spiritual journey connects us to the source of that indwelling happiness and wholeness – the great mystery we so often refer to as God. (p. 7)

Testimony from journalist Anna Pasternak (1999) serves to indicate emotional significance. Participating in Foster Perry's 'hummingbird therapy', 'a spiritual science that is akin to shamanism' (p. 34), Perry 'triggered deep seams of grief with a sentence' (p. 35). As Pasternak reports:

> If...you feel you have been living below your potential on every level – particularly emotional – I can't recommend Perry highly enough. It seems as if I have wiped a decade of unhappiness from my system and feel as I used to: confident, optimistic and happy. (p. 35)

And as Perry told her, 'Finally, you've realized that you can have what you want in life. You can be yourself and be happy.' Then we can think of Marco, a Dutch businessman who left his mainstream workplace to found the New Age centre Marlin:

> ...why I left business life. When I felt that I had to work on the basis of my intuition, or my feelings, this became a problem... It was just not accepted that such a thing as intuition existed. I had to base my accounts on numbers and figures. I couldn't bear that any longer. Now I want to do work that feels right. (cited in Aupers and Houtman, 2006, p. 207)

Somewhat more systematically, data from the Kendal Project holistic questionnaire provides something of a picture. Asked to reply to the question, 'How important is spirituality in your life?', 38.1 per cent answered 'very' on the 1 (not at all) to 10 (very) scale we used. Responses from 70.8 per cent fell between points 6 and 10. Asked to reply to the question, 'Which of these statements comes closest to your beliefs?', all bar 13 per cent 'believe' in some form of the sacred. Asked to select the 'best description of your core beliefs about spirituality', all bar 11 per cent selected choices which show 'belief' in spirituality, the great majority showing 'belief' in the inner-life form. And spirituality certainly appears to be about important things. For example, 76.9 per cent say it provides 'special healing powers'. On the reasonable assumption that spirituality has something to do with the 'meaning and purpose of life', it is also noteworthy that in response to 'How often, if at all, do you think about the meaning and purpose of life?', 60 per cent stated 'often', 31 per cent 'sometimes', 8 per cent 'rarely' and 1 per cent 'never'. Directly comparable 'Soul of Britain' results run 38 per cent 'often', 33 per cent 'sometimes', 19 per cent 'rarely', 10 per cent 'never' and 1 per cent 'don't know' (Heald, 2000).

The most convincing testimonies of all are provided by the 'real' thing, ethnographic films. The most graphic that I know shows a sannyasin who is about to die at Medina (an ashram of the Bhagwan Shree Rajneesh movement), a TV ethnography showing how peaceful he was as he moved on 'in the spirit of Bhagwan'. Dying itself is 'transformed'. Documentaries collected over the years illustrate the experiential, often existential significance of holistic activities in ways which simply cannot be captured in print.

The significance of personal testimonies is also demonstrated by the fact that they play a crucial role in attracting people to holistic activities (Heelas, 1987; Heelas and Seel, 2003). Testimonies serve to appeal, to diminish the uncertainties of those considering participation (Brodin: 2003, pp. 381, 386–7). If testimonies alluded to the superficiality of particular practitioners, they would rapidly go out of business. 'Produce the goods or else', to put it bluntly. In addition, evidence of experiential significance might be sought by formulations presented on flyers and websites (for example a Rebirthing brochure stating, 'We will look at thoughts and beliefs that no longer serve'), and testimonies provided by books published by practitioners (ten or so volumes from Kendal practitioners alone) and others (especially in the business and spirituality territory, as well, of course, 'fictional' accounts). There is also the academic publication, researchers providing verbatim accounts together with interpretative ethnographic material. Stewart Muir's (2005) interpretation of the ways in which Australian 'aboriginality' is drawn upon in New Age circles provides a good illustration of this last, Muir writing of 'the attempt to incorporate the missing or alienated part of oneself' (p. 146); of being 'inspired by' indigenous teachings and practices (p. 245); of 'an endlessly renewable source of meaning' (p. 243). On the grounds that actions speak louder than words, experiential significance is also seen in the behavioural consequences of participation. Resources would not be allocated to mind-body-spirituality management trainings unless there was at least some evidence of their efficacy, perhaps with regard to motivational issues; teachers would not be interested in working with holistic spirituality unless they found that it worked in practice – considerations developed in later chapters.[4]

Critical Reflections

Intentions, expectations, hopes, sometimes desperate hopes, testimonies and the other kinds of evidence which have been all-too-briefly introduced, all count against the experiential inconsequentiality claim. This said, the fact remains that not everyone will be convinced. Positivistic and not so positivistic social scientists will raise some pretty obvious objections. The most obvious of all concerns the issue of representativeness. The objection is that the evidence is selective. Although the evidence of the kind which I have been drawing upon might show that experiential significance is considerable, it does not include instances of superficiality. It does not show the ratio between the significant and the superficial (or, indeed, the positively negative). Another problem concerns the reliability of participant testimonies or reports. It can readily be argued that books published by practitioners, for example, provide camped-up, exaggerated accounts, including the 'good' at the expense of the 'bad'. Yet another problem is that it can readily be argued that positive testimonies own little or nothing to active participation. Consider the 'meaning and purpose of life' findings. True, they are considerably higher than the national data. But the possibility remains that they could be due to participants already being more interested in exploring the 'meaning and purpose of life' than most people.

Reflecting on the first of these objections, the ideal would be to carry out a research project which (a) systematically explored experiential significance for participants and (b) systematically explored experiential significance for participants and ex-participants. To the best of my knowledge, the first of these aims has yet to be adequately addressed. I do not know of research which systematically studies all the participants of all the yoga groups of a particular town (for example), using a questionnaire, then interviewing a representative sample of respondents. To the best of my knowledge, neither has the second of these aims been adequately addressed to date. Unless ex-participants are interviewed (etc.), we are left with the problem of bias: that is, of not taking into account the fact that those who find activities too superficial (or negative) simply leave, leaving us with a biased sample of those who have remained with activities. As for the second objection concerning reliability, I think that common sense it called for. Unless we can somehow devise a magical litmus test to distinguish between the 'authentic' testimony and the (variously) distorted, the only way forward is to exercise very considerable caution indeed when drawing upon sources of information like interviews with journalists (when participants could aim to impress). However, who is to disbelieve people like Julie?

We are a long way from establishing the numerical importance of the experientially significant and insignificant. What is pretty incontestable, though, is that the former *is* in evidence. And most probably in considerable evidence. For who would pay 'good money' for a bland 'soup' – one too 'thin' even to provide a good dose of pleasure?

There remains the worry that participants are so-to-speak bringing the benefits they report with them as they come to participate, rather than experiencing the benefits through active participation. Building on what was said in the previous chapter, about the continuities (expressivistic, humanistic, egalitarian) between holistic activities and the more general values and assumptions of (most) participants, it can be added that there is a very strong likelihood that most participants are *already* spiritual. On the one hand, all bar 11 per cent of Kendal holistic questionnaire respondents selected options which show 'belief' in spirituality, the great majority showing 'belief' in the inner-life form. On the other hand, only around 50 per cent regard their current activities as being spiritually significant. This makes it likely that around 40 per cent 'arrive with' spirituality. Furthermore, there is a consideration deriving from the fact that around a third of the adult population of Britain are reported as 'believing in' the God within, not without (chapter 2). Those attracted by holistic activities typically belong to that sector of the population – expressivistic, postmaterialistic, person-centred, egalitarian, mildly or non-competitive in spirit – which almost certainly has a much higher percentage of 'God within believers'. (See chapter 5; also see Inglehart and Welzel, 2005.)

Thinking of the seminar spirituality which flourished during the 1980s, seminar experiences were clearly powerful, powerful enough for conversion to occur (see, for example, Heelas, 1996a). Although conversion cannot be ruled out *in toto* – and indeed examples have been provided earlier in this chapter – it is extremely unlikely that it is widespread today. For many participants, though, what is almost certainly happening is that 'issues' are addressed, recast, reframed, re-experienced; that horizons are expanded; that spirituality is 'deepened', that 'insights' are experienced, that the quality of relationships is enhanced, and so on (matters which are returned to later in the volume).[5] Quite simply, unless something was happening – over and above the superficial – it is terribly difficult, probably impossible, to explain why holistic activities are growing. Why should participants continue to practise, whilst spending money (and time) in the process, unless they experienced benefits or progress? Found the meaning of healing? Experienced the healing of feelings? Felt the difference of the healing?

For Lasch (1987), 'a spiritual stew does not make a synthesis, and the indiscriminate eclecticism of these movements provides an important clue to their lack of staying power' (p. 80). Yet according to Stewart Muir's (2005) research, New Age incorporations from 'other' cultures '*can* be a source of personal meaning that supports and enables multiple values and ideologies (p. 101; my emphasis). Much too much has been made of the instability and incoherence of the radical *bricolage* which is supposedly going on; of the idea that the sacred has been fragmented, 'deconstructed' into loose elements which are left to the individual to attempt to 'integrate' (if the person attempts to at all) according to the sole criterion of personal preference. Enriching what was said in the last chapter about the orchestration of the consensual by the practitioner, ethnographies like Muir's provide additional evidence that there is sufficient coherence to enable participants to have experiences which they value. Practitioners do not 'ransack' other cultures; they exercise their skill to craft activities which draw upon those 'experienced' elements from 'other' cultures which chime with the values of expressivistic-humanistic spirituality. To say that Julie's art therapy (which draws on various sources) is not coherent enough, rich enough, to serve the cause of existential significance is simply not true. As befits their trade, practitioners – with their participants – aspire to be experts at making connections. 'Only connect' lies at the heart of their practice: which makes it difficult to see the significance of Bruce's (2002) claim that 'The New Age is eclectic to an unprecedented degree' (p. 105).[6]

As Wouter Hanegraaff (1999) makes the point, 'New Age religion[s]... provide exactly what religion has always provided: the possibility of ritually maintaining contact with a more general meta-empirical framework of meaning, in terms of which *people give meaning to their experiences* in daily life' (p. 152; my emphasis). Testimony after testimony after testimony: evidence is provided which is a far cry from Bruce's claim (already cited) that New Age 'products' are 'consumed by people as a slight flavouring to their mundane lives', or Wade Clark Roof's 'thin as chicken soup' claim. Although 'impact' varies considerably from activity to activity, participant to participant, 'slight flavouring' is certainly not in evidence in what a colleague wrote to me after having taken an Advanced Diploma in Psychodrama at Findhorn – 'it took me three weeks to recover from a five-day residential, such was the *raw power* of the collective unconscious in the group process, and of transference and counter-transference' (personal communication; my emphasis). Neither is it in evidence in journalist Anna Pasternak's (1999) report of her encounter with 'soul retrieval' with Foster Perry of 'hummingbird therapy', 'trigger [ing] deep seams of grief with a sentence' (p. 34). Nor is inconsequentiality in evidence in all those TV programmes which have been documenting what can *only* be called the existentially significant. ('Faith in the Future: The New Age', shown in the 1990s, provides a good illustration, especially the footage of a shamanic, inner-exploration group.) And neither will it be in evidence in the future, when 'issues' really become significant for the baby-boomers who came of age during the 1960s and now face old age.

As a final critical reflection, it is interesting to see that reductionists are by no means agreed about what is taking place. For in contrast to the 'thin as chicken soup' brigade, there are those who emphasize the climatical. Bauman belongs to this camp. For him, 'If the religious version of the *peak-experience* used to reconcile the faithful to a life of misery and hardship, the postmodern version reconciles its followers to a life organized around the duty of an *avid*, perpetual... consumption' (1998, p. 70; my emphasis). For him, it is perfectly in order to write of 'the orgasmic experience of the postmodern sensation-gatherers' (p. 70) – a theme also taken up by Graham Ward (2006) with his point that the 'sensation hungry' are attracted by alternative spiritualities, people who are looking for the 'orgasm', the paroxysm of desire (p. 185). To reduce to the orgasm is surely not to reduce to the superficial. Something must be amiss when such divergent, whilst summary assessments of significance are abroad.

Conclusion

The spirit of a great deal which is taking place within holistic activities is not the spirit of 'one-dimensional' consumption (Smith, 2005). The 'ends' of the intentions, hopes and expectations which are largely in evidence are not those of the utilitarian individualism of hedonistic gratification. It is surely noteworthy that only 7.6 per cent of respondents during the Kendal Project reported 'pleasure, enjoyment or a treat' as an original reason for participating. This alone suggests that *more* is going on than can be adequately captured by the language of consumption-cum-capitalism. 'Health and fitness', 'looking for spiritual growth', 'stress relief', 'bodily pain or illness', 'looking for personal growth', 'life crises', 'emotional support or human contact', 'dissatisfaction with mainstream medicine', 'to complement mainstream medical treatment', even 'time our of daily routines' and 'to meet like-minded people': these reasons for initial and subsequent participation suggest that activities are no more 'consumeristic' than those provided by the gym, the health and fitness club, the general practitioner, the psychotherapist, or the elderly people's club – if they are consumeristic at all.

Seeking to go deeper into what life is all about is no more (and quite probably less) a form of superficial consumption than seeking profundities by way of classical music or novels. Working hard by dedicating oneself to infinite tai chi is no more a form of superficial consumption than seeking the truth as an industrious student or academic. 'Listening to one's inner wisdom' to act on this basis is no more a form of superficial consumption that 'heeding one's conscience'. Practising spiritual tarot to discern what is wrong with one's life need not be any more a form of superficial consumption than going to a psychotherapist or taking a psychometric test during a job interview. Trying to avoid being self-centred by practising aikido is no more a form of superficial consumption than having an open self-revealing discussion with one's wife. Practising rebirthing to 'develop awareness, sensitivity and self-confidence . . . a developing sense of physical safety, of trust in relationships' (cited in Heelas and Woodhead, 2005, p. 29) is no more a form of superficial consumption than participating in a Christian 'small group'. Seeking to become more loving, caring, compassionate, trusting, open and reciprocal is no more a form of superficial consumption than seeking to develop these qualities with one's family or friends. Going to a spiritual healer to deal with chronic back pain is no more a form of superficial consumption than going to a GP (who you might have gone to already). Seeking to provide better palliative care in a hospice by way of New Age spiritualities of life is no more a form of superficial consumption that seeking to provide better palliative care by way of more secular forms of counselling or interpersonal psychology. Seeking to implement the injunctions of Ofsted bearing on 'spiritual development' by encouraging primary school children to meditate in nature or to practise yoga is not more a form of superficial consumption than an inclusivistic school assembly. Learning to take better responsibility for oneself is not any more a form of superficial consumption than acquiring this at an AA meeting.

The significance of the 'issues' which are discussed in a great deal of the mind-body-spirituality literature, the significance of the 'three most important problems facing you these days' discerned during the Kendal Project, the significance of the reasons provided for participating and continuing with participation, the significance which practitioners find in their activities – a considerable amount supports the contention that many are seeking to change aspects of their lives, and at least in measure succeeding in doing so. Certainly going beyond the orbit of the passive, pleasuring-the-self mode of life, the significance of change itself is provided by the most useful of the evidence: positive personal accounts of meaningful experiences which are not sensibly thought of in terms of the language of consumption.

Another way of looking at the matter of triviality is to think of expressions which are frequently used in holistic circles. They include: feeling uplifted, a sense of integrity, unburdening the past, dwelling on the present, feeling less selfish, feeling more centred or balanced, finding oneself, feeling more hopeful, feeling more self-fulfilled, a sense of greater self-esteem or confidence, deeper self-understanding, feeling *good* about oneself, feeling a greater sense of purpose, becoming more open-minded and open-hearted, becoming more caring, feeling healthier, feeling more empowered, being more happy, feeling more alive than ever, understanding anger better, living a richer life, feeling more relaxed about life, feeling 'good enough', gaining insight into issues, appreciating that life is good, going with the 'flow' of life, becoming aware of how happy one is, taking 'time out' to reflect, overcoming a sense of separation from others, feeling more energized and motivated, feeling more valued, feeling more trusting and forgiving, being more expressive, being more honest, being more loving, coming to terms with the past, becoming a 'better' person, feeling good about one's body, and forgetting oneself, release of tension, placing 'proving oneself' in perspective, feeling a sense of liberation, perhaps shifting the emphasis from 'taking in' to 'giving out'.

Feelings and 'beings' galore; feeling in measure being the being.[7] However, expressions of this variety hardly belong to the register of consumption, to the language of the trivial. Generally speaking, they are best regarded as a relatively modest contribution to Schiller and Weber's theme of 'reenchantment'. Maybe not often the 'life-changing' experience so frequently reported when gap-packers return from a first visit to India, but to say that the New Age works 'no wonders' (Lasch, 1987, p. 82), or to write of the 'flakiness' of spirituality (Roof, 1999b, p. 157) as though it were a certain kind of chocolate, is to detract from what holistic spirituality can offer to the lives of participants, and indeed often delivers. The nurse who feels repressed at work, who revitalizes herself by way of holistic activity, who then tries to integrate what she has found with her patients... Would you use the language of consumption to characterize creative art lessons in schools? If not, would you still apply it to people like Julie? For that matter, would you apply the language to the famous actress who says, 'It's more about walking into your own creativity, discovering what you are like inside and what you want to say to the world'. And what of the experience of the 'healthy death'? (Surely worth dying for...)

I have to admit that the evidence for significance, sometimes profundity, is reassuring. Frequently more than 'the spice of life'. I would hate to think that I've been spending much of my life studying the airy-fairy. Important intentions, commitments, valuable experiences, though, are clearly in evidence: which leads to the next topic – working *for* what practices have to offer.

Chapter 7

Work: Consumptive or Productive?

Snow White's education is itself a commodity, the consumption of which promises to 'fulfil her creative potential'. (Christopher Lasch, 1980, p. 152)

Don't ask questions – that was the first rule for a quiet life with the Dursleys. (J. K. Rowling, 1997)

...artifice was considered by Des Esseintes to be the distinctive mark of human genius. Nature, he used to say, has had her day... In fact, there is not a single one of her inventions, deemed so subtle and sublime, that human ingenuity cannot manufacture. (J.-K. Huysmans, 1959, pp. 36–7)

Doing nothing sucks. Doing nothing sometimes has terrible consequences. (William Bloom, 2006, www.williambloom.com)

The consumer orientation contrasts with the idea that most things worth doing require work to do well. Consumers watch other people play baseball, rather than learning to play themselves. (Robert Wuthnow, 2005, p. 44)

When I tell my students that there are those in governmental and educational quarters who say that students are consumers, they tend to get upset. 'We might be consumers when we go shopping or eating in Lancaster', they reply, 'but here at the university we are working.' Although I only have a handful of interviews with mind-body-spirituality practitioners to draw upon concerning the point, I strongly suspect that practitioners in general would think that it is an insult to describe their group members or clients as consumers. Connoting as it so readily does the idea that their participants are using spirituality up, absorbing it like blotting paper, without doing much, if any, work, the language of consumption is regarded to be inappropriate, perhaps a hurtful insult. In the eyes of practitioners, participants are not passengers – certainly not if they want to move forward.

As we have seen in the last two chapters, the sacred dimension of mind-body spirituality can provide valuable 'additions', over and above the everyday world. The key argument of this chapter is that for the sacred to work, the difference it can make has to be worked at – the opportunity critically being provided by way of practices.

Consumption and Production: General Considerations

Most comprehensively, consumption has to do with 'taking in', production with 'making out' – making something out of something. Or so the academic literature indicates. Marx's observation, 'Consumption is...immediately production' (in Clark et al., 2003, p. 252), serves to highlight the fact that production always requires an input. The apparently necessary relationship between 'using up' and production means that it is not surprising to find that a great deal of what is discussed under the head of 'consumption' in the voluminous literature in fact has to do with – broadly conceived – 'production'. In contrast to the passive consumer approach, the active, positive or creative (so-called) consumer is at work: performing, expressing, producing, making, crafting. Duc Jean des Esseintes, of Huysmans' *Against Nature* (1959), agonizes over what to purchase to create the perfect aesthetic for his utopian milieu. One does not simply '*become* one's own designer product' (Ward, 2006, p. 185; my emphasis), one has to work at it. For Richard Elliot and Kritsadarat Wattanasuawan (1998), 'the *search* for self-identity is a key determinant of postmodern consumption' (p. 131; my emphasis). For Jonathan Friedman (1994) and Daniel Miller (1998), commodities are used for the production and performance of selfhood. For 2005 Health Secretary John Reid, 'New Labour...will develop a politics of consumerism...[which] ensures that the consumer, *who is determined to shape her own life*, is also aware of her potential *contribution* to the wider systems on which she depends' (Webster and Jameson 2005; my emphases). For Celia Lury (1996), consumer culture is an important context for everyday creativity, including the creation of social and political identities. In the spirit of Timothy Leary's *The Politics of Ecstasy* (1970), Shane Blackman (2004) writes of the cultural politics of substance consumption.[1] The implementation of the 'to have is to be' strategy might involve ready-made, quite possibly standardized, purchased components, but how they are selected, assembled and deployed in particular circumstances is rarely limited to replicating the initial provisions or services (Harvey, 1989, p. 51). The autonomous authority of the purchaser comes to bear, utilizing the possibilities, the evocations, of the pre-packaged.

Holistic Activities at Work Within

Possibly the best argument against the most damning, the most popular version of the 'reduction to consumption' claim – namely the idea that

Work: Consumptive or Productive?   153

spiritualities of life are basically, largely or entirely all about utilitarian individualism in receptive, self-centred, hedonistic mode, passively absorbing whatever is pleasurable without contributing anything, turning off the input when it becomes boring, paying for ready-made experiences without doing anything much – is that participants who 'want something to happen' typically *work* to *change* the ways they experience and understand themselves, others and the world around them. Maybe not the 'four years of meditation, prayer and study cut off from the world in a Dumfriesshire retreat' reported by Michael Smith (1993), but work it is. The emphasis lies with the *doing*, not the *using* or the *relying*.

Writing about 'spiritual' people who 'quest' beyond 'organized religion', Pastor Colin Sedgwick (2004) claims, '"I want the feelgood factor, but not the cost of commitment" – that, in reality, is what such people are saying'. With breast cancer, Julie would be profoundly perturbed. For Julie, change does not just happen. Whatever she might use (up) – like paint – she has to do something. Asked to describe the 'three most important problems facing you, personally, these days', respondents to the associational milieu questionnaire of the Kendal Project referred to things like 'sharing life with a husband who has health problems', 'growing old', 'constructive use of my free time to be useful still in society', 'elderly relative care', 'helping my daughter sort her life/health/relationships to achieve a happy life' and 'stress and pressure'. As we have seen in the last chapter, the holistic – ever-flowing, encompassing – nature of mind-body-spiritual associational practices means that there is a strong likelihood of these problems, especially those to do with relationality, 'coming up' during one-to-one or small group activities. Participants are thus provided with the opportunity to *do* something about their 'issues'. Assuming that they realize that the everyday same, more of the same, is not exactly a recipe for change, their interest, enthusiasm, commitment and desire are likely to be called into play. Motivated to do something about their issues, they work at it. Indeed, they *have* to work at it – for unless I am very much mistaken, few spiritual practitioners think that they, and they alone, can *supply* change.[2]

For many, associational practices provide a – sometimes *the* – key vehicle for 'good work'. Holistically speaking, 'dis-ease' must always have a cause. At the end of the day, major contributory causes lie with society, culture, socialization, and the choices one has made and continues to make about how to live one's life with regard to the externals of life (a rush-around lifestyle choice, for example, generating internal disequilibrium, manifested as an aching stomach). At the beginning of the day, *the* cause lies with/in oneself. Simply, one is not 'in touch' with spirituality – neither one's own, nor the spirituality of the lives taking place in one's surroundings or the world. The pressing task, in other words, is to 'get in touch'; is to enable the spirit to flow – and this is where practices come in. Only then can one develop as a 'whole'; only then can one fully 'realize' what it is to be an authentic agent acting in and for the surrounding world; only then can one 'truly' improve the quality of the lives of others; only then can one 'move on' to tackle the causes which lie with disequilibriating socio-cultural factors. Or so it is experienced by practitioners and their 'good' participants.

Whereas the work of everyday purchasing activity, for example using 'consumer guides' to work out what to buy (Aldridge, 2003, p. 143), is often directed to the end of satisfying established (or relatively well-established) *recurrent* 'appetites', needs or desires, the work within holistic associational activities is typically to the end of *changing* unsatisfactory 'attachments', 'appetites', needs or desires – for example, those belonging to what Julie came to realize was her 'false self' – by making contact with, or making deeper contact with, the spiritual dimension of life. And at least from the perspective of practitioners, as well as more 'experienced' participants, this is not such an easy thing to do. Bad habits of the heart – replete with ill-being, internalized by way of socialization, sustained by and reflected in the bad habits of everyday life – are deeply ingrained. To prise oneself away from the 'prizes' which the 'lower self' awards itself to feel secure or comfortable (such as overdoing the exercise of power on receiving promotion to compensate for lack of control, insecurity, fear) requires real effort. Holistic mind-body spiritualities today might not emphasize the 'tyrannical', regulatory hold of the 'ego' or 'lower self' to the extent that has often been the case in the past (Heelas, 1996a, pp. 18–20). Nevertheless, spiritual seekers today come to appreciate the skills of their socialized selves in resisting change – in effect what Anna Freud wrote of under the title *The Ego and the Mechanisms of Defence* (1968); come to appreciate that one cannot 'really' change one's externally manifested harmful habits until they have been illuminated by what lies within. ('Externally' in the sense of being manifested from within, *through*, whilst beyond one's body.)

Challenges have to be faced and worked through (breast cancer, especially its deeper significance, in the case of Julie); challenges have to be revealed (for example, when repressed anger is 'discovered' to be a root of back pain). Sheer physical work is often called for to engage in 'good' practice to experience change, as in many forms of yoga, for instance – see Iyengar (2005) on the 'tough' (p. xvi), on the 'sweat' (p. 24). There is the sheer concentration required to meditate or 'still' effectively. 'Issues' have to be worked at in order to 'come to terms' with them by placing them within a broader context – not least the spiritual aspect of life. Practices might not be as severe and demanding as those adopted by the spiritual *virtuosi* of the traditional east; with exceptions like some Gurdjieffian groups, few practices today are as challenging as the confrontational seminar spiritualities which flourished during the late 1970s and then the 1980s.[3] However, with their intention to improve or change their lives, it is highly likely that relatively few participants are *long* content with passivity; activities which 'please everyone but move or challenge no one' – to slightly modify the citation from Curtis White provided earlier. Even in holistic spas, I surmize, few spiritual practitioners are content with their clients in passive mode, seizing opportunities to encourage 'real' work.

Yoga of Discipline (2006) write Swami Chidvilasananda and David Katz. The great German countertenor and mystic, Andreas Scholl, says, 'Real enlightenment takes an effort, and people don't want effort' (Ashley, 2000). As we have seen, few of the asssociational, face-to-face activities around and about today are primarily focused on enlightenment as an end in itself. For good practice, though, virtually all require *active*, really active involvement. Just as one will not get very far if one visits one's relatively secular person-centred therapist and remains silent for session after session, so one will not get very far if one plays the couch potato 'game' whilst visiting one's spiritual homeopath. As an MA student of mine has said of her first-hand experience of spiritual homeopathy, 'You have to put something into it; you have to bring something yourself'. Palmistry, provided at the Pearl Continental Hotel Burban (north Pakistan), is described as 'about bringing balance to all areas of body-mind & soul'. To 'Take control of your life by understanding your strengths and weaknesses', clients are encouraged to engage in guided, often distressful, introspection: recognizing, 'returning' and working through disturbances which have been repressed – to release 'The Star in You'. The stagnant self, stagnating in its dammed-up pool, is not the name of the game.

Work is required for *productive* participation: cognitive-work; emotion-work, verbal-work, learning emotion-scripts (to be cynical), perhaps struggling to say the unmentionable to others; working at exercising self-responsibility, working oneself at revealing oneself in 'public'. As the title of David Dunning's book – *Self-Insight. Roadblocks and Detours on the Path to Knowing Thyself* (2005) – implies, it is not easy to 'go within' – one argument being that we all erect 'psychological barriers' precisely to avoid the fears which we think we need to avoid but which we actually need to encounter. Recalling Bocock's (1993) characterization of consumerism as the 'ideology that the meaning of life is to be found in buying things and pre-packaged experiences' (p. 48), for participants to insist on remaining with the 'pre-packaged' (if it is available, that is) is to remain with the static – leaving practitioners waiting for signs that the creative life of growth is emerging. In the spirit of romanticism, for those seeking the 'more' of change, challenge – not pampering – is called for. As participant testimonies like Julie's serve to demonstrate, a great deal can then be 'learnt'; a great deal can change. Those who 'are *called upon* to be true to themselves and to seek their own self-fulfilment' (Taylor 1991, p. 14; my emphasis), namely those (expressivists-cum-postmaterialists) who swell the ranks of those active within holistic mind-body-spirituality practices, have to seek, have to feel and think about themselves more 'profoundly', if they are to fulfil the promises of the activities they are engaged in – as well as their own promises. And although practitioners, with their practices, might be considered to be of great, quite probably vital, assistance, ultimately no one other than oneself can pursue the inner quest. The *very* 'moral ideal behind self-fulfilment', namely 'being true *to oneself*' (Taylor, 1991, p. 15; my emphasis), means that only the participant can find what truly matters: the inner realm that no one else can experience as profoundly and vividly as oneself; that no one else can grasp in all its 'sum of one's life-history' depth, uniqueness and immediacy. Holistic questing thus calls for the exercise of self-responsibility, the exercise of self-discipline to monitor and address one's state of being – to prize oneself away from the glittering – but sham – prizes to discover, within, what only the self can truly discover about its Self.

Work is most especially required for productive participation when it is too late to do much, if anything, about what have become the basic circumstances and conditions of one's life. Whether due to the decisions one has made during one's lifetime, whether due to more inevitable states of affairs such as the ageing process itself, one apparently has to live, then die, with the consequences: the 'dis-eases' which have been generated within oneself. Under these circumstances, inner-work really comes into its own. As we have seen in the last chapter, although it is unlikely that many expect to be cured of those dis-eases which manifest themselves in the physicalities of their being, the intention of doing something about the experiential is widely in evidence among those who become involved with holistic activities when they are seriously ill or approaching death. When the cost of failure is high – that is, *not* learning to live with cancer, *not* acquiring the context to approach death with equanimity – the 'cost' of work is likely to increase. Consequentially, one is likely to put more effort into it. The significance of what one is doing is of paramount importance; one's commitment is correspondingly high. Hence the amount of inner-work which takes place in settings like hospices. Here, in particular, Bruce's (2002) observation – that commitment is 'slight' in New Age circles – is inapplicable.

In an article called 'Dialogue with Life', Lin Fang-ju (1995) writes of the importance of being truthful, honest and 'blunt' with one's self-appraisal, of being self-critical, of having illuminating conversation with oneself. What needs to be emphasized is how difficult it is to move beyond the delusions or half-truths we all live with. Cynics aside, who see practitioners (psychotherapists, etc.) busily constructing difficulties to ensure that their assistance is required for reasons of income and professional standing, we surely all know from personal experience that a very close friend (say) can help one confront the repressed or disentangle the confused. Knowing oneself, the path of self-discovery, *is* hard work. What also needs to be emphasized is that there are so many holistic activities. Very considerable skill is required for 'good' practice: the 'internal' monitoring of the states of being of one's partner by discerning the significance of movement (especially important in activities like spiritual aikido); learning how to concentrate to clarify or quieten the mind (especially important in the various meditations); acquiring positional skills (especially important in activities like yoga), and so on. With so much work to do, it is not surprising that on average all those participating in the holistic activities of Kendal and environs had previously been involved with six of the activities we asked them about – together with their current activity or activities. And this does not include what they were doing at home or elsewhere.

A pre-prepared sandwich of experiences on a plate? Hardly. Bad habits of the heart – the proximate cause of dis-ease – have a habit of clinging on.

Into the World: Holistic Activities at Work Within *and* Without

Shifting the focus from inner-work to work which takes place through, whilst going 'beyond', the person, we now enter the public world.

John Elster's (1986) Marxist-based analysis of that central theme – 'self-realization' (equivalent to Taylor's 'self-fulfilment') – helps shed light on the productive aspect of spiritualities of life in the public domain. Elster argues that 'at the centre of Marxism is a specific conception of the good life as one of active self-realization, rather than passive consumption' (p. 97), self-realization being 'the full and free actualization and externalization of the powers and abilities of the individual' (p. 101). 'Self-actualization', *then* 'self-externalization', is of the essence. To illustrate the difference from consumption, Elster writes:

> One may train one's ability to enjoy poetry or wine, but the use of this power is not part of the public domain. It is consumption rather than self-realization. One may, however, externalize the power by interpreting poetry for others or taking up the occupation of wine taster, in which case the activity becomes a potential vehicle for self-realization. (1986, pp. 102–3)

Although self-actualization is required for self-realization, until 'externalized' or turned into 'actuality' (p. 102) it remains an act of consumption. As for what it is for something to be 'externalized', Elster writes that self-actualization has to have 'an external goal' or 'purpose', that it has to be seen to be 'performed more or less well' (pp. 99–100), for it to be self-realization rather than consumption. Elster then provides examples: the classics from Marx, namely art and science (p. 112); people 'stretching and growing as human beings' in the 'challenging' workplace (p. 113); the themes of 'self-realization for others' and 'production with others' (p. 119) – the latter involving what Marx and Engels describe as 'the free development of each [as] the condition for the free development of all', and being illustrated by way of 'the players in an orchestra' (p. 121).[4]

The analysis enables us to highlight the extent to which the activities of spiritualities of life have to do with 'productivity' in the public world. Rather than involving the (supposed) 'consumption' of self-actualization when it occurs without self-externalization, activities are deeply infused with practicality. Whether it be the primary school classroom, the management training, the personal relationship, or relationships with nature, 'external' goals – which serve, or should serve, as 'goods' within MacIntyrian good practice or as Taylorian horizons 'beyond the self' – are in evidence: what it is to be a 'true' manager, for example; or what it is to be a 'real' teacher, nurse or spiritual therapist, working to introduce, sustain or improve holistic practices in primary schools, hospitals or hospices. So, too, are ways of gauging 'productive' achievement or progress (the Ofsted inspection of spiritual development, for instance) – a point to which we return.

The analysis also helps us see the extent to which the activities of spiritualities of life have to do with productivity within – better, the crafting of – the 'private' world. The argument is that inner-work, where the emphasis lies with self-actualization (and supposed consumption), is crucially bound up with the 'way' of 'externalization'. Elster's point – 'One may train one's ability to enjoy poetry or wine, but the use of this power is not part of the public domain. It is consumption rather than self-realization' – detracts from the fact that it is often difficult, sometimes impossible, to train one's ability without engaging with others: others who contribute feedback, a frame of reference for self-cum-other evaluation or appraisal, guidance and so on. The idea that there is such a thing as 'self-actualization' without externalization (thereby supposedly taking the form of 'consumption') would appear to be strange. Certainly, it does not have much (if any) applicability to holistic activities of life. One works on oneself *by* expressing oneself to one's practitioner or group, this enabling one to 'test' oneself; one works on oneself as a player in the 'orchestra' that is the yoga group with much the same kind of 'horizon' of good practice, harmonization or 'flow' as in an orchestra itself. At least to begin with, one is not going to be especially productive in 'producing' one's inner-self alone – and indeed might end up as 'a morass of subjectivity' (Elster, 1986, p. 106). Solitary meditation, etc., might well come later, after associational practice. However, it is not really practised alone: memories or routines, acquired from others, are 'in mind'; and when it takes place without prior associational practice, the person meditating will presumably have learnt about 'what it is to meditate' from conversations, books, articles or DVDs.

Whether it be relating with others, or more specific activities such as teaching, counselling, managing, nursing, healing, caring or working as a 'cultural creative' (Ray and Anderson, 2000), or, of course, holistic milieu activities themselves, that paradigmatic example of self-realization for Marx – art – is here the art of life; the art of crafting one's life, or craft work, within what are experienced to be sacralized frames of significance: oneself, one's encounters with the spirituality of the world.

Complementing Elster's succinct analysis of self-realization via paid work, relationships and so on, Colin Campbell (2004) provides a thought-provoking and illuminating analysis of New Age themes in connection with modern consumerism itself, most especially shopping. His basic argument is that 'the activity of consuming...has become a kind of template or model for the way in which citizens of contemporary Western society have come to view *all* their activities' (p. 41; my emphasis) – activities including New Age: at least, that is, in that there are 'close parallels' between 'a New Age-style worldview and modern consumerism' (p. 40). However, he explicitly rejects the idea that modern consumption means that 'we are all victims of a selfish materialism and acquisitiveness' (p. 42). A great deal of modern consumerism has to do with much more elevated concerns than these. In a (relatively) detraditionalized world, where the verity-cum-reality of 'emotional states' (p. 34) contributes so much to a sense of self, the 'I shop therefore I am' or the 'we are what we buy' (or 'who we buy', if one employs an entourage for status purposes) themes of 'modern consumption' – providing customers with 'the basic certainty of their existence' (p. 33) – cannot be ignored. Arguably more importantly, neither can the 'I shop in order that I might discover who I am' (p. 33) theme, with 'our reaction to products' helping us to '" discover" who we "really are"' (p. 33).[5] Without going into the analysis in further detail, Campbell thereby moves to his point that shopping often takes the form of 'retail therapy' (p. 40). Shopping provides the opportunity for customers to throw off their inhibitions, express themselves, exercise the authority of their 'tastes', refine their tastes, *work* at discovering themselves (p. 41); 'feel...uniqueness' (p. 31); and – perhaps – 'create... identities' (p. 30). Rather than a panacea for, a diversion from, self-ontology issues, shopping can provide solutions (p. 42).

'Certainly, shopping does indeed commonly (although obviously not always) resemble therapy as New Agers understand that term', writes Campbell (p. 41). To the extent that shopping 'produces' or facilitates the effects that Campbell argues for, he is surely right. But does this mean that the New Age is basically a matter for the language of consumption rather than productivity'? I think not. Agreed, shopping serving to provide secular products or the provisions of 'promotional spirituality' belonging to the subjective wellbeing range, together with holistic activities *per se*, involve aspects of 'consumption' (consumer choice, the purchase, etc.). But much of Campbell's account of modern consumer culture (including New Age) is surely more *appropriately* described by way of the language of insight, self-exploration and creativity, Elster's self-realization, with Campbell himself now working with the notion of 'craft' (paper in preparation). Much of what is called 'consumption' has to do with the activity of bringing one's 'true' identity *out*, rather than forging an identity through or in terms of the externals which are *bought and brought in*. Locating consumer culture within the romantic, expressivist trajectory of modernity, Campbell's 'elevation' of much of modern consumerism is best read as supporting the case that the New Age is much more productive than is allowed for by the consumptive, utilitarian satisfaction of preferences, the emotions *of* consumer culture perspective.[6]

Work Itself

The most obvious place to look for evidence that inner-life spirituality is productive rather than consumptive is to look at what takes place within the realm of paid work. On the one hand, it is true that consumption is very much in evidence within the workplace. For Marx, just as 'Consumption is...immediately production', so 'Production is...immediately consumption' (in Clark et al., 2003, p. 252). Raw materials are used, often used up, during the production process; and more arguably, as Marx puts it, the individual 'expends [his abilities], uses them up in the act of production' (p. 252) – a theme explored more recently by Paul du Gay in *Consumption and Identity at Work* (1996). On the other hand, though, production is not consumption. Consumption might often enable production, but the dynamics, *purposes*, values, meanings are too different for the two to be the thought of as the same or similar.

Of all the ways in which spirituality enters into the lives of some of the 28.94 million people employed in Britain, I concentrate on what I'll call 'targeting spirituality'. Whilst a longstanding feature of the workplace, recent decades have seen an intensification of 'the culture of "the target"': a proliferation of terms and mechanisms, an extension of the scope; an enhancement of the 'efficacy'. Generally speaking, the shift has been from basing pay on the job *to* be done (the 'mere' job description) to basing pay on how successfully the job *has* been done.[7] Targets, together will all their apparatus (performance indicators, performance-related pay scales or bonuses, etc.), might appear to be a strange context in which to find spirituality at work. After all, many of the sins of the contemporary workplace are laid at the door of target achievement. Some telephone travel agents only get paid if they meet the targets which have been set for them – with all the anxiety this elicits. Within the university sector and elsewhere, 'priorities' function rather like juggernauts: one lumbers into view (rather more speedily if down hill), stands throbbing for awhile, then slowly moves on; another appears, then another; sometimes several are lined up at once. The result? Feelings of confusion, inadequacy, stress, chaos; and inefficiency. Set by aspirations generated by published league tables, targets are blamed for grade inflation in schools and higher education (Mansell, 2007). Thinking of the NHS, targets are blamed for the impoverishment of the 'personal touch', nurses, for example, having to spend less time with their patients. More generally, targets are blamed for the impoverishment of life in the workplace by virtue of the fact that targets entail the measurement of performances. Ignoring the sign which Einstein had hanging in his Princeton office – 'Not everything that counts can be counted, and not everything that can be counted counts' – the target-setter has to prioritize the measurable (say, income generation within the university sector) over the less readily measurable (say, creative teaching). The culture of the target, it can be said, is inherently reductionistic. Furthermore, for ease of accountancy and accountability the life of the employee is typically focused on *narrow* targets (so many sales, so many clients, so many students) to the exclusion of (supposedly) irrelevant aspects of what it is to *be* at work. The self at work virtually *becomes* the *means* to the end of the target which is being aimed for. A mere resource. Life *as*: All rather ironic, given that the great slogan of 'soft capitalism', that form of capitalism which puts people first, is 'bringing life back to work' – life in all its richness (Heelas, 2008b).

Despite all these drawbacks, perhaps because of some of them, the culture of the target can provide a home for inner-life spirituality. Like darts, in many regards archery exemplifies the target. Eugen Herrigel's somewhat contested classic, *Zen in the Art of Archery* (1953), explains the connection with inner-life spirituality:

> By archery in the traditional sense, which he esteems as an art and honours as a national heritage, the Japanese does not understand a sport but, strange as this may sound at first, a religious ritual. And consequently, by the 'art' of archery he does not mean the ability of the sportsman, which can be controlled, more or less, by bodily exercise, but an ability whose origin is to be sought in spiritual exercises and whose aim consists in hitting a spiritual goal, so that fundamentally the marksman aims at himself and may even succeed in hitting himself. (p. 14)

Growth through *expression*: that great theme of the Romantics, namely creative work, it is worth emphasizing. Archery provides the opportunity for expressing what one is and what one is capable of becoming – in order to hit the target with greater and greater accuracy. In the process, one has the opportunity for cultivating, exercising, one's mind-body spirituality; one's 'balance', one's 'focus', one's practical spirituality. Practice makes perfect; expression makes perfect one's practical spirituality (recall Elster on 'training'). During the process one also has the opportunity for gauging self-development – simply by using the target as the measure. What I call the self-work ethic is in evidence: by working (at archery) one works on oneself, with outcomes serving to assess inner and outer 'results' at one and the same time. The more one practises, the greater one's progress is likely to be. (And the less practice appears to work, the more that work is called for.) As for one's motivation, the more one values the cultivation of what lies within, the more one appreciates that to work for results in the external world is but the means to the end of what really matters.

In relatively secular mode, call-centre work provides a good illustration. Typically, personal development profiles are drawn up for newcomers. Targets are set. Newcomers are 'encouraged' to appreciate the importance of unlocking and expressing their 'potential' to carry out their emotion labour as effectively as possible (Dormann and Zijlstra, 2003). Through their work on the phone, together with associated trainings, employees work on themselves (with the rewards this brings) to be more effective phoners (with the rewards this brings). Thinking of explicitly spiritual work, managers, those working in the expressive, creative, caring, educational professions, can take courses which promise to unlock their potential, perhaps their spirituality – expressed (or applied) in the workplace to enable them to meet their 'own' targets. Sometimes, spirituality is instrumentalized to the extent that target attainment becomes more or less the end in itself, with few consequences for the development of 'much' of the person. More typically, though, targets are of such a nature as to serve as broader 'horizons', calling for the development of the person as a whole. To illustrate, a target like creating an advertisement by the end of the year requires inner-life spirituality – that *is* the expressive professional or cultural creative person involved – to flow through a range of personal qualities. In the company which I have studied in depth, Programmes Limited, even the 'narrow' aim of meeting telesales targets was experienced as functioning in this kind of holistic, encompassing way (Heelas, 1992b, p. 157; 1996a).

The productive self, the productivity of the self, the 'production' of the self: the language of consumption is simply not a useful way to talk or write about targeted spirituality. The same applies to other applications of spirituality in the workplace, for instance among those working in hospices who 'believe' that what matters is being spiritual themselves, expressing this with those they are 'working' with, enabling the 'cared' to be as spiritual as possible, and enabling the 'cared' to 'expressly' reciprocate. Or again, among those whose work involves encouraging spiritual development within schools: teachers working on themselves to be in line with their target of a good result when the Ofsted inspectors come; teachers working with their pupils accordingly.

No doubt some would argue that consumption is in evidence when spirituality is 'working out'; working in and working out; the spiritual work-out. They might draw attention to the consumption of the good feelings aroused by target attainment, for example. However, this kind of argument can be applied to all kinds of work, including the relief felt by the Romantics after the struggles typically experienced as they wrote, painted or composed. To throw the anti-consumption argument into stark relief, for the spiritually-inspired today, work is akin to the work of the Romantics themselves: through *expression* at work, and through how others respond to it, enrich it with meanings, one learns more about oneself, one's drawbacks, one's 'gifts'. Especially if trainings and courses are provided by the 'learning organization', one has the opportunity to hone one's abilities, deal with one's 'blocks', *find out more about oneself*, become more alive. For the spiritually-inspired at work, self-cultivation comes with self-expression in tandem with going within. In short, New Age spiritualities of life can serve to 'enrich' the employee, the self-work ethic alone plausibly helping 'enrich' the organization. And if this does not convince, there remains the consideration that according to participant accounts, holistic activities within, or associated with, the workplace can function to contribute to wellbeing; enthusiasm, perhaps harmonious working relationships; the 'buzz of energy' of what Lynda Gratton (2007) calls (successful) 'hot spots'. Above all, 'bringing life back to work'. Not living to work or working to live, but working in order to live a richer life within the workplace; and perhaps living with the 'lessons' elsewhere in life. Or so it seems.

Conclusion

Recalling the citation from Christopher Lasch at the beginning of this chapter, Snow White's education might have been a 'commodity', 'the consumption of which promises to "fulfil her creative potential"', but what counts as true fulfilment within the great majority of mind-body-spirituality practices does not work like this. Recalling the brief extract from J. K Rowling's novel – '*Don't ask questions* – that was the first rule for a quiet life with the Dursleys' – Harry Potter remains unenlightened, makes no real progress, within the restrictive confines of the repetitive bourgeois 'quarter-life' of the Dursleys until he enters Hogwarts School of Witchcraft and Wizardry. To acquire his skills, Harry then has to get to work. Holistic milieu practitioners expect – or hope – that their participants will take on the responsibility of getting to work to 'find their lives'. The typically implicit working assumption is: 'Your everyday routines don't appear to have worked; far from it; as you well know, they have left you with ill-being; unless you want to continue living an unfulfilled life of "poverty," something different is required; you already know in your heart what you could become; you *can* let your intentions off the leash; give the practice a try; you will have to work to experience anything of true value *according* to the practice.' Elster is surely correct to argue that the notion of consumption does not lie at the heart of what self-*realization* is about. That in effect, the significance of the sacred *owes a great deal* to it being put to work – a topic returned to when we look again at the transposition of the inner-life into action in the world. As for des Esseintes – practices better than nature ...[8]

To pull things together, work also has a bearing on a matter discussed in chapter 5, the 'solidity' of holistic activities. As Durkheim long ago argued in *The Division of Labour in Society* (1984; orig. 1893), the simple point is that by working together, by relying on one another, people come together. Reciprocal bonds are developed, all the more so when work is for a significant shared goal. Rather than that 'parcelling-out of the Soul' to which Max Weber refers (cited in Grant et al., 2004, p. 265), cohesiveness is enhanced through relationality.

Part III

To Work Beyond the Consuming Self

Chapter 8

A 'Fag Ending' of the Sacred or Fit for the Future?

> *Rather than see the New Age as an antidote to secularization, it makes more sense to see it as a style and form of religion well-suited to the secular world* (Steve Bruce, 2000, p. 235)

> ... *the emergence of secular spiritualities.* (Wouter Hanegraaff, 1999, p 152; his emphasis)

> *We are entering a new aeon,* governed *by a new ethos and a new spirit.* (David Tacey, 2004, p. 16; my emphasis)

A 'Last Gasp' of the Sacred?

The idea that spirituality – whether inner-life or not – represents some sort of 'last gasp' of the sacred is becoming increasingly popular. For Penny Marler and Kirk Hadaway (2002), for example, 'some marginal Protestants who readily admit they are "less religious" say they are "spiritual" by *default*. It is *what is left*: a residual spirituality that is described as something less, something "naked," or less "powerful"' (p. 297; my emphases). Focusing on what I am calling spiritualities of life, for David Voas and Steve Bruce (2007), 'Unconventional spirituality is a symptom of secularization, not a durable counterforce to it' (p. 43). One of the reasons they put forward to support their case is that 'Much of what is called "spirituality" seems to be merely pseudo-science' (p. 51). A similar argument is that spirituality 'seem[s] to have little to do with the supernatural or even the sacred; it appears to be a code word for good feelings, the emotional rather than the material' (p. 51). The outcome is clear. Envisaging 'spirituality' as 'a label for a ragbag of beliefs and practices that have slightly exotic origins', they conclude that 'participation ... is becoming less rather than more like religious activity' (p. 52). Then there is the argument elsewhere emphasized by Bruce himself: that a great many of the activities and provisions which are a growing presence are consumed – 'used up' – for the sake of the 'profanities' of consumption. Treating spirituality as something to be drawn upon as a means to the end of consumption, it will be recalled that Bruce argues that 'most' [alternative religions] are consumed by people as a slight flavouring to their *mundane* lives' (1996, p. 273; my emphasis). Again, 'In this cultic market place [the annual Mind, Body and Spirit convention in London], the individual consumer is sovereign. You select which bits work for you' (Bruce, 1993, p. 10). *As* a 'consumer', the 'you' of this self 'indulges' (p. 10) *itself*. Here is a great example of a secularization theorist using the 'tool' of consumption to help explain away the growth of the 'sacred'.[1]

Quite clearly, the greater the extent to which the kind of argument which Voas, Bruce and others advance is true, the greater the extent to which the 'spirituality' of the spiritual revolution (more specifically, of particular spiritual revolutions which might be underway or completed in various sociocultural territories) becomes a matter of catering for whatever temptations or desires are *already* in evidence on the consumption front – ensuring that 'revolutionary' change is nothing of the sort. Growth of anything much, other than a quite highly instrumentalized 'spirituality', is more apparent than real; little is developing which can contribute to the ways in which spirituality can be experienced as making a qualitative or behavioural difference to life: to what life is *about*; to *living* life; to living *out* one's life by *acting* accordingly.

Blanket Reduction?

The fag-ending claim is *exemplified* by those who treat all, or virtually all, holistic provisions or activities as consumer items. What I am calling 'blanket coverage' is clearly seen in the work of Kimberly Lau (2000), for example. For her, 'alternative health practices' – broadly equivalent to New Age spiritualities of life – are very much part of 'the contemporary consumer landscape' (p. 7). For her, *even* the most committed of participants is engaged with acts of 'consumption' (p. 11):

> One might practise yoga with the intention of creating a leaner, stronger body or one might move to a yoga commune where the philosophy behind yoga offers a complete lifestyle; one might eat at a macrobiotic restaurant occasionally or one might follow the strictest macrobiotic diet. It is only at the most radical ends of the continuum that practitioners create seemingly whole alternatives to the familiar structures of everyday life...And yet, even the more radical interpretations of these bodily practices open themselves up to the processes of commodification. A way of life *becomes* another commodity to consume and sell. (pp. 7, 17; my emphasis)

Fit for the Future? 169

Like Bauman (1998) and Lasch (1980, 1987) – and to a considerable degree Bruce (2000, 2002), Carrette and King (2005, p. 19), Redden (2002, 2005) and others, Lau applies the language of consumption to the New Age in a comprehensive way, blanketing out, 'stubbing out' anything which *might* deserve to be treated otherwise. New Age spiritualities of life are considered to be *entirely* about consumption; they *are* a form of consumer 'spirituality'. And this means that they are not fit for much of a future other than filling up the consumeristic self.

Naturally, it is perfectly in order to use the language of consumption in comprehensive, blanket fashion when 'marks' of consumption serve to characterize more or less everything that is going on. Equally naturally, though, to reduce spiritualities of life to the language of consumption *just because* of the justified applicability of markers like commodification, shopping around or the display of status, is bad social science. It is to leap in to act like a bull in a china shop, ignoring anything – specifically, the operation of the inner-life rendering of the 'Durkheimian' sacred – which *might* be present, which might be *irreducible* to 'the passive consumer', the 'slight flavouring' of the 'mundane lives' of participants, the hedonistic 'ease' of 'consumption'.

The nature of any particular activity or provision, the talk of any particular practitioner, the intentions of any particular participant: they are likely to be too *aspectual* – too complicated, with too many meanings or purposes involved for one-dimensional characterization – for serious consideration not to be given to the presence of the irreducible. And as I am arguing in this volume, a considerable amount is irreducible to the language of consumption. At least for those who experience or sense inner-life spirituality as a meaningful reality, an inviolate source of significance is in evidence. For this to be expressed in their lives, practices have to be followed; work has to be done. For the sacred to work, it must provide something over and above everyday life – that life which, being associated with the instillation of dis-ease, can hardly be expected to provide the solutions. It must provide something apart from everyday life, rather than something sucked into, and profaned by, the exigencies of the workaday world. For the holistic to satisfactorily enter everyday life, to be existentially-cum-practically significant, it is widely held to be vital to engage in practices – in groups, on a one-to-one basis, or alone – informed by the horizons, the 'goods' of the sacred: vital because according to New Age understanding of the human condition, it is only to easy to rest content with customary habits of the heart – warts and all.

Minimally, when the experience-cum-reality, the expression of inner-life spirituality, is in evidence, that is, when participants talk about inner-life spirituality as being *in* their experience, values and expression, blanket-coverage claims are wrong. When appropriate, characterizations drawn from the language of consumption (such as the consumer as the purchaser) might be in order. But they have to take their place alongside all those other characterizations which apply in particular cases and to particular aspects: 'healing', 'caring', 'empathic understanding', 'self-fulfilment', 'a sense of purpose', 'seeking the truth of my being', introspective reflection for wisdom, the acknowledgement of and 'liberation' from bad habits, and so on. And when existentially significant states of affairs of this variety are in evidence, *and* when they are experienced as emanating from the inner-life rendering of the 'Durkheimian' sacred, they could well have as little to do with the gratification of 'any old preference', the 'art of consumer self-indulgence' (Bauman, 1998, p. 70) or consumptive success 'in the material world' (Bruce, 1995, p. 102), as those transcendent, theistic forms of religion which also seek to lift adherents beyond the self-interested greed of possessive individualism. Self-fulfilment can certainly bring pleasure and hedonistic consumption if Lasch is correct about what he says using Snow White as an illustration. But the likelihood of this being the case is greatly diminished when the *point* of practices is provided by a spiritual realm which expresses or articulates basically supra-consumptive values such as enabling others to flourish, practices themselves serving to encourage participants to 'shift' away from those secular attachments – such as undue consumption of the wrong kinds of food – which are problematic; and which, if perpetuated, are only likely to make 'dis-ease' worse.

Worldly Rather than Spiritual?

Readers might agree that blanket-coverage claims are incorrect. It could still be the case, though, that a considerable number of activities are a fag ending of the sacred in that they are 'this-worldly'. More exactly, they are directed to *secular* ends, including those to do with consumption.

'In much New Age spirituality', writes Bruce (2002), 'therapy is the manifest, not the latent, function. Good health, self-confidence, prosperity and warm supportive relationships are no longer the accidental by-product of worshipping God; they are the goals sought after through the spiritual activity' (p. 85). What is most important about a great deal of 'alternative' spirituality today, it might well be concluded, are the secular ends which it serves. Also attending to the New Age, Wouter Hanegraaff (1998) argues in much the same vein. 'Its own foundations consist of an already thoroughly secularized esotericism' – one which 'increasingly shows symptoms of being annexed by liberal *utilitarian* culture' (p. 523; my emphasis); one which involves this-worldly types of holism; one which, indeed, involves 'the emergence of *secular spiritualities*' (1999, p 152).[2]

Bruce and Hanegraaff are among all of those who quite rightly emphasize the 'this-worldly' orientation of spiritualities of life today. Briefly recalling Kendal Project questionnaire findings, the five highest 'reasons for originally trying' responses turned out to be 'health and fitness' (23.2 per cent), 'looking for spiritual growth' (19.4 per cent), 'stress relief' (15.2 per cent), 'bodily pain or illness' (13.9 per cent) and 'looking for personal growth' (13.5 per cent) (Heelas and Woodhead, 2005, p. 91). Just 7 per cent of respondents considered spirituality to be 'overcoming the ego' (Heelas and Woodhead, 2005, p. 30), a percentage which indicates that few are intent on seeking 'enlightenment' – as an end in itself – when enlightenment to taken to require liberation from ego-attachments. Furthermore, although 19.4 per cent prioritize 'looking for spiritual growth', the holistic nature of their activities means that it is highly likely that this is often bound up with the aim of enabling spirituality to flow through their lives – to 'heal' their this-worldly 'issues' to do with ill-being.

More evidence, if it is required, of the this-worldly orientation of so much of what is taking place today is provided by the fact that mind-body-spirituality provisions and services are abroad within the relatively secular and widespread culture of subjective wellbeing (Heelas 2006d; Heelas and Woodhead 2005, pp. 84–94). Commodified provisions and activities – including health and fitness clubs, spas, the health and beauty literature, the 'experiential' holiday – explicitly promise to serve the goal of, the means to the end to, enhancing the quality of subjective-life. The 'spiritual' dimension is often included to promise 'the more' which the denizens of subjective wellbeing culture are typically seeking. And for many, 'the more' promoted by way of 'spiritually' imbued provisions or services – of 'extreme beauty', 'perfect health', 'perfect happiness', 'perfect wellbeing', more modestly of 'increased vitality', 'greatly reduced stress', feeling *really* good, let alone 'the more' of 'spiritual' status display – certainly would appear to belong to this world.[3] Furthermore, it is highly likely that a great many of those active within subjective wellbeing culture more or less ignore the spiritual dimension. Given that only around half of those active in the specialized, face-to-face holistic activities of Kendal and environs understand their activities to be of spiritual significance (Heelas, 2007b, p. 74), it is virtually certain that the percentage is lower for those who are content with buying mind-body-spirituality literature (for example) rather than participating in the more person-focused activities of spiritual practitioners.

A great deal of subjective wellbeing culture, not least promotional use of 'spirituality', belongs to the secular register of emotion, desire, want and taste. Capitalistic providers, it might well be concluded, titillate purchasers by adding a spiritual dressing – to cater for this-worldly ends. 'You can't buy a bar of soap these days without being promised a spa experience', writes Ian Penman (2006); 'You can't have a spa experience without being promised a spiritual experience for your psychological wellbeing', we might add. To the extent that the New Age provisions and services of subjective wellbeing culture are simply or largely about fulfilling the experiential, secular promises of the culture – about feeling good, displaying status or individuality, about providing people with whatever consumer-culture experiences they happen to want, about pandering to their desires – with only lip-service, or less, paid to the experienced-cum-'believed' reality of spirituality, then to that extent provisions and services *are* secular. They are not grounded in the scientifically inexplicable, a realm which is beyond the pale of this-worldly inquiry.

For many holistic participants, including virtually all practitioners, however, it is not accurate to say that spiritual activities – or spirituality itself – are 'consumed' in the sense of being used for *secular* ends. This is especially the case for those participating in face-to-face associational, spiritually significant activities. As befits activities taken to be 'comprehensively' *holistic* in nature by those concerned, the aim is for health and fitness to be experienced as *spiritually-informed* health and fitness; stress relief as the restoration of *spiritual* wellbeing; and so on. Holistically speaking, in other words, spirituality is understood to flow through the secular realm of ill-being, that is, all those aspects of one's life which are 'dis-eased' or out-of-balance precisely because they have yet to be 'touched' by spirituality. This is a flow which transforms ill-being into wellbeing by 'completing' the mind-body-spirituality nexus. A flow which sacralizes the whole. For many, then, the cultivation of spirituality matters – perhaps not *per se*, as an end in and of itself, but as a matter of enabling spirituality to flow through life. As Marion Bowman (1999) puts it, 'much ... is essentially about looking after the *spiritual well-being* of the individual self' (p. 182; my emphasis). As might also be emphasized, a *spiritual* sense of purpose, meaning-in-life, 'depth' of relationships, experiences of creativity. Unless we are to discount participant understanding, unless we can somehow establish that participants are not telling the truth, this is not secular. And even among those who are not participating in face-to-face associational activities run by spiritual practitioners, the fact that around a third of adult Britons apparently 'believe' in inner-life sacrality means that it is likely that numbers of those who participate in mind-body forms of CAM, or who purchase mind-body-spirituality literature, often think of themselves, perhaps experience themselves, with some reference to spirituality.

It is certainly true that the this-worldly orientation of so many holistic activities means that we cannot argue that the 'other-worldliness' factor, the quest for spirituality as an end in and of itself, serves as a stand 'against' secular ends, thereby not being secular spiritualities. If the meaning of the term 'secular' is taken to be worldly rather than spiritual, however, it remains the case that the great majority of applied spiritualities of life are *spiritual-cum-worldly*, not worldly *per se*. What spiritual elitists or, if you prefer, virtuosi, like Chogyam Trungpa (1973) dismiss as 'spiritual materialism' – including love as commonly experienced – remains spiritual in self-apprehension. Just because ends – like the relatively frequent 'issue' of dealing with back pain – are secular *until* spirituality comes to bear does not mean that the spirituality which flows through them becomes secular. Instead, the back pain – more precisely, how it is experienced – is sacralized.

To take the argument further, Bruce (1995) argues that the New Age is 'directed to helping consumers ... succeed in the *material world*' (p. 102;

my emphasis). Bruce might be right to attach importance to 'this-worldly' ends. But is materialism in such evidence?

As we have seen in chapter 5, most of those attracted by holistic spiritualities of life hold postmaterialist, expressivist values. Although few reject materialism to the extent of the counter-culturalists of the 1960s, few are rampant materialists. With the fading of prosperity spirituality in many western countries (chapter 1), those who tap into spirituality for its utility value generally do so for postmaterialist, quality of subjective-life ends. 'A life devoted to the calculating pursuit of one's own material interests... leaving too little room for love, human feeling, and a deeper expression of the self', which, it will be recalled, is how Robert Bellah and his colleagues characterize utilitarian individualism, is not for them (1985, p. 33). The person going to a holistic spa, quite probably already holding holistic 'beliefs', is much more likely to be concerned with the quality of her psychological-cum-somatic life than anything else. To recall the five highest rankings of the Kendal Project questionnaire data on reasons for original involvement, namely 'health and fitness', 'looking for spiritual growth', 'stress relief', 'bodily pain or illness' and 'looking for personal growth', post-materialist, frequently *non-materialist*, quality-of-life concerns are in evidence, with little if anything to do with success explicitly identified as success in the material world.[4]

Probably a clinching argument against the idea that New Age spiritualities are put to work for this-worldly ends, with spirituality rendered secular by virtue of the fact that it is *used* for these ends, derives from Durkheim's understanding of the sacred. As we saw in chapter 5, for Durkheim, the more the sacred adapts to the secular person-cum-world rather than vice versa, the more the sacred ceases to be sacred. However, Durkheim considered totemism to be of a sacred order – *whilst* serving the good of the community. That totems have a utilitarian aspect certainly does not entail the profanation of the sacred. Indeed, one might say that if the sacred does not have utility value, if it is not that which is required for certain 'needs', then it is of little or no value. Drawing on N. J. Demerath (2000), Hunt (2005) argues precisely this: 'the sacred is nothing if not a statement of function' (p. 168) – Hunt then drawing the obvious conclusion that this means that 'several strands of the New Age and self-spiritualities' *are* sacred (p. 168). And not just the New Age. For the functionality of the 'sacred' – as a state of affairs whose authority and power *must be kept intact*, rather than consumed by way of the authority of the consumer – is surely why we do not apply the word 'secular' to *most* of the activities provided by the religio-spiritualities of the world; namely, all those which are primarily put to use for apparently 'secular' ends; namely, all those which draw on the power of the sacred as a (often *the*) means to the ends of consumption, production, wealth or status creation.[5] In a nutshell, characterized substantially and functionally, the sacred is there *to* be used; and rather than the sacred being secularized, this means that the tendency is for secular features of life in the everyday world to be sacralized (see chapter 9). As if the sacred is only that which is worshipped or otherwise addressed in and of itself.

New Age spiritualities of life *are* 'this-worldly' – they *belong* to the *life* of this world (for many, the life of any other world as well). But this does not mean that they belong to the secular world. Inner-life spirituality is located 'within' the secular world, that is, the world which has yet to be touched by the inner spiritual dimension and which is only rarely considered to be too 'negative' to ever be touched. Grounded in the spirituality of the life of this world, the only way that activities can become secularized is for spirituality *itself* (and therefore its applications) to become secularized: a consideration to which we now turn.

Spirituality Itself as Secular?

If the preceding argument is correct, the practical, this-worldly thrust of New Age spiritualities of life does not entail that they are secular. But if the 'spirituality' which serves as the means to the ends of consumption (or making money, etc.) is not at all spiritual, then of course neither is the entire means-ends nexus. A real fag ending – more accurately, an extinguished butt: serving a future devoid of sacrality.

David Voas and Steve Bruce (2007) argue that 'the descriptions of spirituality given by Kendal respondents [to the questionnaire sent to those participating in holistic activities] seem to have little to do with the supernatural or even the sacred' (p. 51). For Voas and Bruce, the descriptions demonstrate 'pseudo-science' (p. 51). However, very few respondents use the language of 'science' to legitimate their spirituality, for example. Talk of the 'deep inner self' and 'inner knowing', or statements like 'The more you get in touch with your true nature, the more peaceful and loving you will be', do not belong to the language of science, 'new' science or even pseudo-science. 'Creative intelligence', 'the wisdom of the inner-child', and other renderings of how the inner-life is held to provide knowledge and ethicality, do not belong to the scientific register. The vitalism experienced at the heart of life – the chi, ki, yin and yang, prana, the 'vital energy' concentrated in the chakras, or, more generally, the 'life-force' – is not considered to be the same as anything which scientists have been able to find or find in the future: thus being 'metaphysical' (Coulter 2004, p. 113; cf. p. 103; see Bechtel and Richardson, 1998, on vitalism). Generally speaking, although the chakra system, for example, is thought of as 'natural' in the sense of lying at the heart of what life is by nature, it is explicitly distinguished from the 'merely' physical realm. Furthermore, many nurses turn to spiritual CAM precisely when the limitations of scientific medicine call for *another*, additional or alternative approach to healing. Leading figures of the medical establishment would not be engaged in forthright criticism of CAM if it were otherwise.[6]

Bearing in mind that around half of the respondents surveyed during the Kendal Project did not appear to attribute spiritual significance to their current activities, Voas and Bruce (2007) quite correctly observe that generally speaking the least spiritual of the activities – as gauged by the self-understanding of participants – are expanding the fastest (pp. 51–2). Incontestably, here is evidence to support the view that – in measure – the New Age is moving in the direction of 'mind-body-feelings' secularity. At the same time, however, the number of those experiencing the spiritual significance of their activities is growing (Heelas, 2007b, p. 75) – with many of the (increasing) number of practitioners, and no doubt the more active, regular, 'immersed' participants, in particular, being consumed *by* the spiritual dimension.[7] And slightly over 80 per cent of questionnaire respondents agree that 'some sort of spirit or life-force pervades all that lives' (Heelas and Woodhead, 2005, p. 25). Taking into account the consideration that it is highly likely that many of a more 'mind-body-emotions' persuasion consider themselves to be *working* to experience the *more*, the additional, the different, the (relatively) inexplicable, the *supra*-scientific holistic connection to deal with their 'issues', 'mere' accommodation to secular consumption is surely not in much evidence.

Does consumption secularize the sacred or is it already secular? My answer to the first part of this twofold question is that this can happen, but only when spiritual 'believers' somehow lose faith in spirituality whilst continuing to use it for purely secular purposes. My answer to the second part is that everything depends on what participants have to say. Recalling the argument at the end of chapter 3, if participants say that there is a 'subtle energy (or energy channels) in the body' – which is what around two thirds of holistic participants of Kendal and environs maintain (Heelas and Woodhead, 2005, p. 25) – and if participants equate this with a spirituality, a spiritual 'magic', which is clearly capable of operating over and above what is scientifically possible and/or which exists beyond the empirical frame of reference, we have to take their word for it. Furthermore, as understood by practitioners (in particular), mind-body-emotions holism is not strictly secular. And neither is the true, inner self of more humanistic renderings of the ethic of authenticity: the highly optimistic, Pelagian, Rousseauian, view of human nature, beyond all conditioning, would be regarded as a utopian 'no where' by most scientists and many philosophers: a 'no where' of Gilbert Ryle's (1963) ghost in the machine – 'minds are . . . merely ghosts harnessed to machines' (p. 21) as he puts it. (See also chapter 2.)

One might blanch at the idea that Amida Spas, advertised in the *Daily Mail* with the words, 'A haven of tranquillity, the therapy rituals combine ancient Eastern philosophy with Western technology', have anything to do with spirituality. My students frequently cannot believe it when they see things like 'vision therapy' or 'art therapy' included on the list of holistic activities in Kendal and environs (Heelas and Woodhead, 2005, pp. 156–7). However, 40 per cent of those practising vision therapy say it is spiritual, as do 35 per cent of the art therapy participants. Some of those visiting Amida Spas will almost certainly think the same.

It has to be accepted, though, that there is a spectrum running from the obviously secular to the obviously spiritual. When one reads of 'these divine dishes that both delight the palate and capture the imagination' (the Marriott in Islamabad also referring to 'culinary avatars'), of 'Good Spirits' (a headline in connection with Warwick University monies from Smirnoff) or of an article entitled 'Spirits sag as the sense of isolation on the farm deepens', one can be pretty sure that one is in the realm of the secular (although less obviously so with the last example). At the other end of the spectrum are statements of the kind, 'My spirit is immortal', meant literally. In between lie the less indeterminate: intermediary usage, illustrated by examples like: 'Live8. The biggest spiritual event ever... The core of the experience is both celebratory and moral – "spiritual" by any other name', 'Perfect time for a getaway to improve the mind and spirit', 'a threat to spiritual integrity, gentrification that will drive out the poor', 'songs of the spirit', and 'She is spiritual; she is so deep'; or, from the National College of School Leadership, 'Spirituality is the journey to find a sustainable, authentic and profound understanding of the existential self which informs personal and social action'.

With applications ranging from the vodka bottle and its consequences to the spirit of mind-body-spirit, the word 'spirit' enables the words 'spiritual' and 'spirituality' to function in different ways in different contexts. Unlikely to be applied to the drinker (although there is Gurdjieff with his spiritual drinking), the language of spirituality can certainly be applied to what appears to be the intermediary zone of the 'moving', 'uplifting', the existential. So to the key question: to what extent does talk of an apparently intermediary nature – common among holistic participants, with observations like 'it was such a moving, spiritual experience' – signify 'true' spirituality, that is, a state of affairs beyond the scientific, empirical register? For the greater the extent to which this is the case, the greater the extent to which holistic spiritualities of life move beyond the secular.

Until much more research is done, the answer is that we don't know. However, we do know that 'true' spirituality is widely abroad among holistic participants. Like Wordsworth's 'imagination', enabling the poet to move from the finite to the infinite, holistic practices enable participants to transcend the limitations of secular experience-cum-comprehension to what they experience as the 'truly' spiritual. Forever beyond the compass of science, of 'merely' human knowledge, scientific advance can never 'catch it'. To say that the term 'spirit', even 'spiritual', can refer to the secular does not involve a contradiction in terms. To say that 'true' spirituality is secular is self-contradictory. And spiritual 'believers' who use the language of spirituality to differentiate themselves from those who are content with the scientific (or pseudo-scientific) frame of reference, who use the language to emphasize the importance they attach to experiencing *the different*, to make a difference, *resist* the secularity which awaits the final consumptive gasp of the cigarette; and which appears when it is stubbed out.

In Praise of Subjective Wellbeing

Another way of combating the fag-ending judgement is to argue that subjective wellbeing culture, even in apparently 'junky', 'lowest common denominator' mode, is by no means necessarily devoid of value. In contrast to those (typically elitist academics) who would argue that the presence of mind-body spirituality within subjective wellbeing culture, in particular shops and spas, shows the extent to which it has capitulated to the indulgent, the ego-trip, the counter-case is that subjective wellbeing culture need not be without more significant forms of value – which people are prepared to pay for.

The Harvey Nichols chain of stores lies at the very heart of well-heeled purchasing culture in Britain. An 'exemplary' subjective wellbeing zone, 'Urban Retreat' is at the back of the store, at least the one located in a prime site within central Manchester. The 'consultation' and 'therapy' rooms – offering mind-body-spirituality services – are behind the desk of the staff, who look remarkably like nurses. Beyond the stereotyped joking which can readily be elicited when the 'sophisticated' see the 'nurses' and their wealthy clients, however, it *could* be the case that the private one-to-one encounters with spiritual practitioners are similar to less obviously joke-inspiring holistic activities, such as those drawn upon by 'real' nurses. Both could be helping to put anxious or distressed people at ease, for example.

To lend credence to this possibility, I briefly enter the territory of consumer culture studies. For it is frequently argued that significance *can* be found in what elitists look down upon, perhaps dismiss, as consumer-laden, commodity rubbish. Setting the tone of this brief discussion, John Fiske (1989) argues:

> Popular culture is not consumption, it is culture – the active process of generating and circulating meanings and pleasures within a social system: culture, however industrialized, *can never be adequately described* in terms of the buying and selling of commodities. (p. 23; my emphasis)

In similar anti-reductionist fashion, albeit with a sense of irony, Betty Friedan (1965) cites an advertising executive who says, 'American housewives can be given a sense of identity, purpose, creativity, the self-realization, even the sexual joy they lack – by the buying of things' (p. 181). Executive hype you might think. But then there is the frequently advanced case – here summarized by Bocock (1993) – that 'many people's sense of *identity* is now bound up with their patterns of consumption rather than their work roles' (p. 109; my emphasis); the 'to have is to be' (Lury, 1996) or 'who are what they buy' claims; the argument that *meanings* have more to do with what people consume that what they produce; the Lévi-Straussian argument that 'Commodities are not just objects of economic exchange; they are goods *to think with, goods to speak with*' (Fiske, 1989, p. 31; and see Campbell, 2004); food for thought, one might say. Then there is the more empirically grounded literature: Paula Black (2004) on the beauty industry and the phrase often heard in salons – '*making* the best of yourself' (p. 52; my emphasis) – 'a glib phrase which disguises a large amount of complex knowledge' (p. 181). 'Pampering' is by no means the whole of the story (p. 58) – a theme also addressed by Debra Gimlin in her *Body Work* (2002): a volume about the ways women 'beat the beauty trap' (as it may be put) – one major 'issue' being the fact that many fear dying less than getting fat (p. 4) – by, for example, 'renegotiating meanings of body and self, even when aerobics provides little actual physical change' (p. 51).

Until more research has been done on mind-body-spirituality activities in spas, stores like Harvey Nichols, 'holiday' venues, company weekends and so on, until more research has been done on how people treat New Age artefacts – such as the Buddha in the living room – or on how mind-body-spirituality literature is read, we remain in relative ignorance. Rather than assuming, in elitist fashion, that services or provisions are of little or no 'real' value, however, I think that we have a duty to see if existential or other forms of significance are in evidence. My own *very* strong hunch is that careful, and tricky, research will show that use of a £3.99 feng shui kit, with the packaging promising to align your garden with the natural forces of life, is by no means *always* reducible to some kind of trivial pursuit, 'instant soup' in the garden, a pleasuring of the self: perhaps instead contributing to a sense that one's garden provides a tranquil refuge from the chaos of the outside world. For one client, beauty therapy is a 'form of work'; for another person, obsessive pampering (Sharma and Black, 1999). For one reader of 'pulp' spirituality, an entertainment jag; another, the experience of 'truth'. For one person, junk; for another, a haven or illumination. This is not relativism, it is reasonable ethnography. Apparent junk, spiritual *kitsch*, should never be automatically discarded in the fashion of the elitist; value might well lie there; and to add another consideration, junk could be a gift. (See Colleen McDannell's *Material Christianity* (1996) for a first-rate analysis of Christian artefacts along these lines.)

Akin to those who see eastern traditions providing a path from more graspable levels to the less intangible, apparent junk with its 'mumbo-jumbo' (Wheen, 2004), the apparently pleasure-focused, can provide a starting point for the more significant (Heelas and Seel, 2003). Disillusionment with the promises of more secular versions of subjective wellbeing culture, together with the satiation factor, can lead to 'the deeper' – rarely the *more* superficial. Contact with the deeper, offered by associational mind-body-spirituality activities, and (perhaps less frequently) by way of literature, can open up horizons to be explored. And with the possible exception of the *strictly* indulgent, even the relaxing pleasures of holistic 'pampering' – lying back to let the 'happy' energy flow through to sooth – are not simply acts of indulgence for the busy person seeking to recharge daily life.

In Praise of Happiness

Happiness is very much on the wellbeing agenda. A 2007 happiness survey, the first to be carried out by the government, finds that 'most of us are happy' (Branigan, 2007, p. 8): David Cameron with his (Bhutan-inspired) 'It's time we focused not just on GDP, but on GWB – general wellbeing' (Elliott, 2007); lessons in happiness for 11-year-olds in the state schools of Britain (Harris, 2006); the *Journal of Happiness Studies*, 'devoted to subjective wellbeing'. Economists are at work; for instance, Luigino Bruni and Pier Porta's *Handbook on the Economics of Happiness* (2007); so too are the philosophers and political scientists (Lane, 2000); and there are major newspaper articles (Elliott and Newell, 2006).

According to the best comparative study of happiness on a global scale, 'High-income countries are particularly likely to show increases: 88 per cent of them show rising levels of happiness'; 'favourable existential conditions nourish a sense of human autonomy, which promotes a sense of subjective well-being' (Inglehart and Welzel, 2005, p. 130). Together with other factors, it looks as though subjective wellbeing culture is doing its job.

Drawing on Kendal Project findings, those active within the holistic milieu of the town reported somewhat higher levels of satisfaction with their health, their home life and their working lives than the national average (Heelas and Woodhead, 2005, pp. 106, 92). Living in a country which is already 'happy' according to the Inglehart and Welzel index (2005, p. 141), it thus looks as though they are somewhat happier than many adults. It is then easy to claim that these are people who are already happy 'enough', it being indulgent for them to seek yet more of the happiness quotient from holistic activities.

As a recent YouGov poll shows, although most Britons are satisfied with their overall personal wellbeing, most are also unhappy about specific things – like corruption in politics (Smith and Gadher, 2006). One counter-argument against the indulgence claim is that holistic activities have enabled participants to experience greater happiness about relatively specific things which *matter*. As we saw in chapter 6, many have worrying 'issues'. And at least in measure, these issues can be put into perspective, experienced more positively or resolved through participation. A related argument is that happiness (or satisfaction) about their home and work lives owes something to participation. Consider, for example, the person who recharges her batteries by going to a tai chi group twice a week, also practising at home, thereby enhancing the quality of her working life. It is not indulgent to deal with pressure, stress or irritation in this way. Another possible counter-argument derives from Baudrillard's observation (cited in chapter 3): 'The consumer, the modern citizen, cannot evade the constraint of happiness.' We might *be* happy, but we can never be happy enough. Relative to what happiness could be, relative to our 'right' to be happy, we are unhappy. Holistic activities could help bridge this gap. Or is this indulgent?

Most fundamentally, is it possible to argue that the importance attached to happiness (satisfaction, pleasure) in subjective wellbeing culture (specifically, mind-body-spirituality provisions and services) should not be automatically dismissed as that key sign of the fag ending, namely self-indulgence? Whatever the standing of European and North American countries on Inglehart and Welzel's index, the fact of the matter is that we are often unhappy, sometimes for long periods of time, entailing that to experience happiness or pleasure is not exactly a bad thing. In our frequently humdrum, stressful or jaded lives, happiness or pleasure is not a bad experience for the soul, the 'spirit' – perhaps serving to inspire, perhaps serving to emphasize the positive aspects of life, perhaps highlighting what is wrong with life to focus attention on what needs to be done, perhaps enhancing the quality of relationships, perhaps simply paving the way for *being* joyful. Hummingbird therapist Foster Perry's 'You can be yourselves and be happy' (Pasternak 1999: 35) would certainly meet with the approval of the Dalai Lama, with his *The Art of Happiness* (1998). Indeed, a great many spiritual 'masters', both in the east and in the west, attach very considerable importance to the value of happiness, often pleasure and satisfaction. For them, happiness *belongs* to the spiritual life. (Recall the Dalai Lama's 'basic spirituality'.) It is a noble gift, a capacity of mind-body-spirit to be nurtured, in particular by focusing on what you have, including relationships, rather than on money as the key means to, and measure of, happiness. To be 'happy with life' means being at peace with oneself, finding rhyme and rhythm or integration; being cheerful with others and receiving cheer back. Then, the 'joys of life'. Rhetorically, why on earth shouldn't happiness and pleasure belong to the sacred? Why shouldn't these experiences take a form which serves as a bulwark against the fag ending of the pleasures of the selfish? In defence of happiness: for the holistic person happiness is not end in and of itself – that is, when it is experienced as flowing through one's life to serve both oneself *and* others.

In defence of 'junk', even if 'tacky' consumption is involved – lying back, letting the 'happy' energy flow to sooth and tingle – happiness, pleasure, treats as ends in and of themselves are not a trivial matter. In defence of 'junk', even if 'tacky' consumption is involved, a spicy, pleasurable taste can serve as a starting point, opening up the way for higher things. After having read Boots' 'Time to Treat Yourself' and made a purchase or two, after having decided to 'make the best of oneself', one could very well feel better about oneself, with all the consequences. In praise of the smile! What is wrong with pampering sessions, the sense of wellbeing, when so many of us are so hard at work? What is wrong with holistic happiness during retirement when so many have to recuperate from their working lives to restore 'life' to life? As long as the 'hedonistic' does not translate into greed, harmful selfishness and lack of concern for others, what is so amiss?

One thing that the postmodern turn, as a valorization of aspects of the ethic of humanity, has emphasized *ad infinitum* is the egalitarian value of respecting others (Benhabib, 1992, p. 2; Heelas, 2005). Often influenced by the 'turn', many of those working in the field of consumer studies have taken this on board. It is highly likely, if not certain, that the most 'junky' of the holistic is simply *not* junk for some, perhaps many; that it has real significance which transcends the 'me, me, me' of the thrust of subjective wellbeing culture in utilitarian, self-centred, self-preoccupied, possessive, calculative, egocentric, or compensatory 'I'm worth it' mode (cf. Health and Potter, 2006, pp. 100–37). The 'little things suit little minds' mentality of the elitist must surely not be allowed to obscure what holistic purchases or participants, if listened to, could often have to say. For example: 'I have realized that to be truly happy I must stop taking my happy pills and deal with the root causes; I might not get very far, but at least I'll have the satisfaction of having worked at it.'

Casual Usage and a Bad Name

Many of the ways in which the language of consumption has come to be used in sectors of the scholarly literature on spirituality (and religion) have served to heighten the impression that holistic spiritualities of life are a fag ending of the sacred. This is because a considerable amount of the deployment of the language of consumption is casual, if not vague. Even though this causal usage is not often explicitly aimed at making the 'fag ending' argument (as exemplified by 'blanket coverage' use of the language of consumption), by giving this impression it serves to give undue prominence to whatever capitalistic aspects might be present – thereby doing injustice to those forms of the sacred which are in evidence. And this leads the reader to the idea that holistic spiritualities are only fit for a future of consumption.

Growing out of the 1960s, a great deal of postmodern or postmodern-influenced 'discourse' takes the form of passive consumption. Terms are plucked out of the array – that obscurantist term 'nuanced' (typically used to justify the significance of laboured, inconclusive 'texts'), the 'hyper-' this and 'hyper-' that, 'interrogate' (which simply sounds authoritarian, if not aggressive or demeaning), 'inscribe', and much of the language of consumption (most especially 'postmodern consumer culture') – to be used for the sake of fashion. Like so many others terms associated with postmodern 'thought', we might say, the language of consumption has become a consumer good – one which has been consumed by many within the academy, perhaps taking them over.

It is pretty certain that postmodern – '*out of* fashion' – factors help explain the popularity of the 'consumeristic' use of the language of consumption among those studying spirituality – and religion. More generally, there is a strong tendency for the term 'consumption' to replace, or tend to replace, 'use' or 'need'; the term 'consumed' to replace, or tend to replace, the 'used'. The kind of claim made by Steven Miles et al. (2002) – 'Everything we do, see, hear, and even feel appears to be connected in some way to our experience as consumers' (p. 1) – is in measure due to how easy it is to use the language of consumption. Succinctly put by Amartya Sen, the underlying point is that 'It is possible to define a person's interest in such a way that no matter what he does he can be seen to be furthering his own interests in every isolated act of choice' (in Nussbaum and Sen, 1993, p. 322; see also Dalai Lama and Cutler, 1998). Even when I engage in the most altruistic or loving of acts, I can still question the role played by self-interest; can still ask myself, 'What am *I* getting out of it?' The wants/needs/self-use/utility value 'card' is easy to play. Bearing in mind Demerath's Durkheimian argument, namely that the sacred is there to be used, the utilitarian aspects, the ways in which the sacred is adapted or adopted to cater for human 'needs', seem to call out for the application of the language of consumption.

Just because someone desires, wants or needs a good university education, perhaps thinking 'Which course is most likely to do most for me?', does not (necessarily) mean that this is *just* a consumptive business. The same point applies to a good holistic 'education'. Casual usage of the language of consumption, however, all too readily means that whatever 'more', over and above consumption, which might be in evidence becomes obscured, perhaps lost.

Given that terms like 'needing' and 'using' can be applied to so much of human life – the surgeon needing to use a particular form of equipment, the yoga teacher feeling that she needs to encourage her group to use a new *asana* – the language of consumption is utilized accordingly.[8] The combination of fashionability and ease of use, facilitated by the 'elusiveness' discussed in chapter 4, goes a long way toward explaining why the language of consumption – 'consumer demand', 'the consumer of commodified New Age products' and the like – is so commonly used in MA essays, doctorates, articles and books on New Age spiritualities of life. Despite that supposed virtue of the postmodern sensibility, namely, paying attention to the 'nuanced' by way of the 'nuanced' to recognize, specify, respect, perhaps valorize difference, terms drawn from the language of consumption are typically applied casually, with vagueness in evidence. What *exactly* does Bibby (1987) have in mind when he makes (frequent) reference to 'religion [encompassing spirituality] as a consumer item'? Grace Davie (2004), who emphasizes the change 'from obligation *to* consumption' (p. 78), refers to our 'culture of consumption or choice' (2006, p. 27), writes of the person attending church 'to fulfil a particular... need in my life' (p. 27), and writes of 'close similarities to the leisure pursuits of the secular world' (2001, p. 106). What *exactly* are the 'close similarities to the leisure pursuits of the secular world' which Davie has in mind? Many others, especially those who emphasize the marketing, 'supply-side' of religion and spirituality, attach considerable importance to the ways in which spirituality and religion adapt to cater for the 'needs' of 'consumers'. To what *extent* do they reduce spirituality or religion to the meeting of needs? What is implied by those who write of 'spiritual *shopping*'? When the language of consumption is applied to spiritual massage, does the phrase 'the consumer' merely refer to the fact that someone has paid for spiritual massage or does it also refer to the massage itself? Even though it is sometimes fairly easy to spot the primary sense of any particular application of the language of consumption – 'the consumer' as one who chooses, for example – I, for one, am often left scratching my head about what is implied; even more importantly, what is *not* in the mind of the author.

To remain puzzled is not too bad a thing. But casual, vague usage can be dangerous. When the meanings of terms like 'consumer' or 'consumption' are not specified, mental associations or semantic connotations are let off the leash. To simply refer to holistic participants as 'consumers' can only too easily bring to mind the wrong signals: that they are hedonistically pleasuring themselves, when in fact they are doing nothing of the sort – perhaps even working to counter the hedonistic. To use the term 'spiritual commodity' might accurately describe the purchasing aspect of what is taking place – but without further qualification could well imply that commodities are things which are used in a 'pre-packaged' fashion, which might be incorrect.

Given the danger of erroneously tarring spiritualities with the brush of misleading or inappropriate meanings, when terms like 'consume' are applied to an aspect (or aspects) of an activity or provision, it is imperative to *specify* their meaning, to justify their applicability whilst showing their limitations, to show how they coexist or interplay with other meanings, in short to make aspectual *distinctions* to acknowledge or recognize the multifaceted nature of what might very well be taking place; indeed, which is virtually certain to be in evidence. For someone who is wrestling with their experience of cancer whilst also using their spiritual art as a status symbol, the language of consumption is applicable – but primarily, perhaps only, to this symbolic aspect of their participation.

Even with precise, empirically justified use, the language of consumption remains dangerous. The language has so many powerful, negative connotations for so many people that it is perhaps best avoided altogether – all the more so in that it is most forcefully used by critics favouring blanket coverage rather than (systematically) looking for evidence of other aspects, and whose portrayals can help confirm the (possible) prejudices of students, for example. Accordingly, I originally thought of calling this book 'On Banning "Consumption"' – a polemical step too far, I have come to appreciate, in that in would curtail what we should be aiming for: as rich a language as possible to tease out the aspectual. The fact remains, though, that it is much 'safer' – that is, more open to critical debate, and less likely to involve the unjustified incorporation of negative baggage – accurate and determinate, as well as easy, to replace 'the consumer' with 'the purchaser' when appropiate; 'consumer choice' (Bowman 1999, p. 185) with 'people making purchasing decisions'; to replace Bruce's (2002) 'consumer in command' (p. 101) with 'reader in command' or 'participant in command'; when circumstances require, to replace 'consumer-friendly' with 'culturally appropriate', 'conspicuous consumption' with 'displaying status'; to replace 'the consumer' with 'the seeker', 'consumer culture' with 'purchasing culture' (Heelas and Woodhead, 2005, p.164); to find other or additional ways of talking about 'spiritual shopping', 'supermarkets' (Lasch, 1980, p. 14), 'the supermarket approach' (Duffy, 1998), the 'spiritual marketplace' (Van Hove, 1999), the 'spiritual supermarket' (Lyon, 2000), the 'hypermarket' (Bowman, 1999, p. 188), the 'smorgasbord' (Rubin, cited by Lasch, 1980, p. 14), 'spiritual disneylands' (Heelas, 1994), 'circus' (Bhagwan, cited by Heelas, 1994), 'fair' (Corrywright, 2003, p. 88), (perhaps) the 'supra-market' (a term used by Eileen Barker), the ubiquitous 'pick and mix' ('counter') (Bruce, 1993, p. 3; Hamilton, 2000), 'religious consumption à la carte' (Possamai, 2003; and see Bibby, 1987, p. 80) rather than the 'set menu' of the traditional church, the 'cafeteria', with David Spangler (1993) suggesting that when the New Age is compared with traditional Christianity, it is 'more like a flea market or country fair' (p. 77). As for the recently popular term 'spiritual *capital*' (for example Zohar and Marshall, 2005), the less said the better.[9]

Clearly, the operation of the market plays an important role with regard to the advertising, demand, supply, commodification, costing, product differentiation and product bunching, etc. of many provisions and services (Redden, 2005). Equally, though, to make too much play of the language of the market (even metaphorically) is to run the risk of overemphasizing particular aspect/s of what is taking place – and, of course, deflecting attention from the very considerable number of activities (and 'beliefs') which do not enter the market.[10] As for the consumptive obsession with the language of serving food, although there are positive associations (healthy eating, etc.), this root 'metaphor' of consumption (Wilk, 2004, pp. 17–19, 20–1) also carries many negative associations: unhealthy junk food from the cafeteria, conspicuous consumption if not gluttony with the self-service of 'as much as you can eat', and so on. It is also implied that spirituality – like food – is 'eaten up': misleading in that 'spirituality' is generally considered to be inexhaustible.

Summarizing Raymond Williams (1976) on the language of consumption and the cultural power of capitalism, Aldridge (2003) writes:

> 'Consumer' and 'consumption'... have become the dominant terms through which we conceptualize our relationship to all manner of goods and services. *Relevant distinctions are in danger of being lost.* (p. 3; my emphasis)

The richer the language we use the more likely it is to 'bring out', specify, those aspectual complexities which are so often ignored when researchers unintentionally or intentionally contribute to the 'fag ending' argument by making a meal out of the languages of the market, shopping, food (etc.): employed out of fashion, and readily (if not explicitly) importing shrouds of – often inappropriate – baggage of a negative kind rather than referring to any 'trails of glory' which might be in evidence. The ways in which so many academics (and others) have used the language of consumption to date only too promptly serves to mask, obscure, ignore and demean aspectual distinctions which – if made – could *very* well serve to reveal the *limitations* of the hegemonic tendencies of casual use; as well as the hegemonic claims made by authors like Lau with their blanket coverage.

In a nutshell, aspectual distinctions have to be made to escape from the stranglehold of the hegemonic; to arrive at a more accurate picture of what is growing by distinguishing as best we can that which is 'consumed up' and that which serves the 'life' of the spirit; to gauge the extent to which spiritualities of life have resisted capitulation to those 'capitalistic desires' embedded within the capitalist system, the profanities of self-interest, the 'merely' secular, consumptive habits adopted in the search for quality of life; to ascertain the spiritual significance of the growth of New Age spiritualities of life by exploring how spirituality operates in various ways in various contexts; basically, to explore the extent to which New Age spiritualities of life are not compromised by the market economy.

With an eye on the next chapter, where I argue that inner-life spirituality can serve to provide counter-currents, arguably a 'counter-cultural' stand against some of the excesses or distortions of capitalistic modernity, it must be emphasized that *the* great danger of casual, vague use of the language of consumption is that it only too easily results in, or encourages, ill-treatment. That is to say, it generates a misleading impression of the extent to which mind-body spiritualities are capitalistic: a form of colonization or academically driven imperialism, which does not help those advancing the cause of the counter-current and what it can offer the future. It does not help policy makers arguing the case for more holistic activities to be provided for pensioners or for a more pronounced shift towards spirituality in schools. The perceived, experienced value of tai chi for mid-life professional women is clearly diminished if they end up feeling that they are gullible consumers. Primary teachers might be put off from providing meditative 'quiet rooms', stilling practices, or after-school yoga. The commitment of nurses to the holistic practices they hear about whilst studying at university could be undermined. The political will to nurture holistic, humanistic spirituality – in evidence in UK governmental quarters as well as elsewhere – could be sapped. It is not exactly inspiring for teachers to gain the impression that the 'use value' they attribute to spirituality is in fact part and parcel of the fag ending of the sacred. Neither does it do much good to point out that the supposed placebo effect of activities is due to the internal consumption of opiates, triggered by performative expectations or beliefs (Devlin, 2007). To 'expose' what is 'really' going on in this kind of way could serve to diminish or destroy the effectiveness of certain spiritual CAM 'beliefs'-cum-activities. The experiential value of the mind-body-spirituality form of CAM could well be discredited in the eyes of doctors: unless, that is, they accept that 'imagined' wellbeing *is* wellbeing; that 'imagined' stress relief or the lifting of depression is just that.[11]

Making distinctions, recognizing rather than obscuring differences within the realm of the holistic, is important. Given that it is easy, and more ethnographically accurate, to use other terms when appropriate, it seems to me that Campbell's use of the language of consumption, for example, by no means always provides the best way of characterizing what he is portraying. Following his analysis, would it not be better to characterize swathes of so-called 'consumer culture' by emphasizing the language of 'self-discovery', for example? The creative purchaser? To the extent that they are studying and interpreting *something else*, there is no need for researchers to use the language of consumption. The use of the term 'church' in the title of Nurit Zaidman's recent article, 'The New Age Shop – Church or Marketplace?' (2007), might be problematic. But at least it directs attention away from the 'mere' marketplace.

The Volume Thus Far: Pulling Things Together

I now draw on some of the main points made in this chapter, as well as pulling together some of the key points made earlier, to come to as determinate a conclusion as possible at this stage.

John Elster (1986) writes of 'consumption, understood in a broad sense that includes aesthetic pleasures and entertainment as well as consumption of goods in the ordinary sense' (p. 97). Among other things, I have been arguing that general, broad, inclusivistic, vague or casual use of the language of consumption, especially by the elitist (the 'holier than thou', 'I know better than you' brigade, sustained by a 'little things for little minds' mentality) only too readily brings the baggage carried by the language to bear when it is inappropriate, thereby contributing to the impression that New Age spiritualities of life are a fag end of the sacred. By *dwelling* on the elementary point that one or two of the 'marks' of consumption are frequently in evidence, the significance of what lies over and above the 'consumptive' is neglected. And by neglecting the 'deeper', less visible aspects of what is taking place within the spa, the reader's mind, the yoga group, the reductionistic literature has the unfortunate consequence of *contributing* to the *image* of the colonization of capitalism. And if holistic activities are 'a good thing', harm results.

Obviously, some will insist that holistic activities are not a good thing; that it is fine to hasten the fag ending by emphasizing the consumptive. Our primary task as social scientists, though, is to provide as accurate an account-cum-interpretation of what is taking place in the world as possible – not to contribute to stereotypes or misleading climates of opinion. With Marx's 'consumption is *immediately* production' in mind, for this reason alone it is *highly* unlikely that any one act is ever *an* act of consumption, an act of consumption through and through. The teasing out of the aspectual is essential for this reason alone. And since it very much looks as though holistic activities of life benefit a great many participants 'themselves', as well as how they engage with the world around them, it is all the more important to identify and explore what activities have to offer over and above the consumptive – as well as the number of activities and the number of their participants.

For Bruce (2006), it will be recalled, 'What matters for testing the secularization thesis is not the *range of spiritual offerings being purveyed* but the *numbers* who take them up and the *spirit* in which they do so' (p. 39; my emphasis). The spirit of this observation is spot on. Unlike Bruce, though, I think that the range of 'offerings being purveyed' does matter. Since 'offerings' only stay in existence because they attract people, they serve as an good index of popularity; even though 'supply' contributes to 'demand', it also reflects 'demand' (compare Bruce, 2006, p. 45). And as we saw in chapter 2, there are almost 200,000 separate holistic milieu activities in Great Britain, provided by some 146,000 spiritual practitioners, with many more activities available in contexts such as primary schools and mainstream businesses. As for the 'numbers who take them up', as of 2001 slightly over 900,000 inhabitants of Great Britain were active on a weekly basis in the holistic activities of the kind we counted during the Kendal Project (Heelas and Woodhead, 2005, p. 53).[12] And as for 'the spirit' of those involved, among other things I have argued that the quest for the 'different', to make a difference, serves to resist the strict secularity which awaits the stubbing out of the cigarette.

A state of affairs akin to the inviolate Durkheimian sacred only works within and for 'good practice' when it is not profaned, rendered blasé, by being subjected to monetary or any other form of the utilitarian individualism of self-interest. To work, spirituality is understood and *experienced* as serving from over and above the secular – thereby being able to do something about this-worldly 'issues'. There has to be something *more* than the mundane to make a *difference* to life – especially when the mundane has generated the 'issues', or failed in the task of addressing them. Crudely, the same working on much the same is hardly effective; to keep the customer satisfied is to keep the customer satisfied (see Heelas 1994). Even those more 'yuppified' expressivists – who seek the very best, the ultimate 'more' of perfect wellbeing or quality of life by turning to holistic, mind-body-spirituality activities – are highly likely to encounter the requirements, the 'demands', of their practitioners: encouraging them to do what is necessary for the sacred to do its work. Alexis de Tocqueville wrote of people 'enclosed in their own hearts' (quoted in Taylor 1991, p. 9); Christopher Lasch (1980) of 'the dead end of a narcissistic preoccupation with the self'

(p. xv). If participants of holistic activities remain consumed by their own hearts of narcissistic desires, rather than 'exploring' themselves through intimate, revealing encounters with their practitioners, they might as well leave – or so their practitioner might hint. Assuming they do not leave, the transformative significance accorded relationality could serve to ameliorate the more anonymous, impersonal aspects of life in capitalistic modernity, for instance.

Thinking of Carrette and King's (2005) 'the promotion of unrestrained desire-fulfilment as the key of happiness' (p. 21), it is now safe to draw the conclusion that holistic activities do not exactly *promote* the *unrestrained* satisfaction of any old desire. Neither does the very language of 'desire' capture what is often 'experienced' as 'flowing out of' inner-spirituality. As befits the unique life-histories, the unique past-present-future circumstances of participants, flow is experienced in different ways – for those whose 'issue' is low self-confidence, as confidence-raising; for those whose issue is pressure, as relaxing; for those who tend to be intolerant, greater toleration. But at heart this spirituality is *about* the 'realization' and expression of truth, honesty, openness, wisdom, love, harmony, integration, life-affirming vitality, the quality of the inner life, and wellbeing: the bringing of life to life (chapter 6). It is experientially significant for the participant, and, as we shall see more closely in the next chapter, 'flowing' beyond the interior life to find expression in everyday life – thereby providing further evidence against the fag ending argument. The multi-functionality of what 'comes out' of holistic activities must not be neglected at the expense of what might 'go inside' to satisfy the desires of the everyday self.

To the extent that 'marks' of 'consumption' are in evidence in the realm of holistic activities, a great deal hangs on what, say, purchasing is *for*. Whereas the raw act of consumption, in the sense of 'taking in' to 'use up', is meaning-independent in the lives of the non-human, among humans 'taking in' is fundamentally (or also) *about* meanings: meanings to do with purposes, intentions, commitments, ends; meanings which can turn the raw act into any number of forms of significance. To provide a vivid example from the 1960s, people consumed, that is ingested, LSD. But to what end? When the goal was 'spiritual' experience, it is highly debatable that the ingestion is best thought of as primarily to do with consumption. 'Consumption immediately becomes production' – for a purpose: medicine for treating a bad heart, for instance. As for holistic activities today, we have seen that critical ends are provided by the spiritually grounded values of expressivistic humanism. What matters is *becoming* aware, in 'experience', of what being truly loving or caring or happy is all about, and acting accordingly. The preferences of the secular self – so emphasized by rational choice theorists – encounter the authority of *substantive* values, values which are experienced as flowing from the depths of life, as bound up with one's true self; values which inform many of the ends of life.[13] To seek to value others in the best possible manner, to aspire to express one's feelings as honestly as one can: whatever 'marks' of consumption might be apparent, the orchestrated activities are goal-directed. Primarily, substantive values – serving to provide a framework of aims, aspirations, validations, inspirations – function to help inform life, 'direct' action, rather than somehow being 'used up'. Relatively trivial senses or 'marks' of consumption do not justify the reductionism claim, that is when the senses are trivial relative to other aspects of participant understanding. To reduce to one or two aspects as though other aspects were not there... Whatever the role that subjective wellbeing culture might play in prompting some to 'go deeper', the humanistic *values* of so many holistic activities alone serve to differentiate them from much of so-called consumer culture (cf. Campbell, 2004, p. 40): values which judge excessive, especially materialistic, consumption as selfish or hedonistic.

Fit for the Future

If mind-body spirituality is thoroughly mired in the junkyard of the 'merely' indulgent, if holistic activities are too poorly organized to have anything other than a short shelf life, if critics (with academics largely setting the pace) succeed in shifting public and governmental opinion away from the relatively or very favourable assessment, then the future is far from promising.

An effective ethicality

Steven Tipton (1982) notes, 'The expressive style of evaluation appears somewhat ambiguous regarding its use of a deontological or a teleological theory of right acts' (p. 284). The latter is seen in the importance ascribed to finding out 'what works for me'. As a form of pragmatism, truth would appear to be relative to the test of (successful) experience. The deontological 'theory' of what counts as a right act is seen in the importance ascribed to those 'timeless truths' which are 'experienced' as emanating from within. Whether these 'truths' derive from the internalization of cultural formations by way of socialization or derive from the spiritual realm itself, spiritual participants take them to be part and parcel of their true, authentic selfhood.

Accordingly, the teleological aspect of the ethicality can (or 'should') function in terms of the test of experience provided by this inner self. In answer to the question, 'Works for what?', the answer is, 'A particular self-mode of selfhood'. To put it starkly, the truth of what 'works for me' crucially depends on the 'ultimates' – the 'cannot-be-questioned' values of the expressivist-humanist 'experiencing me'. What rings true *is* the ethicality; what works in experience is what works *for* authenticity; what works in experience is what works in terms of the humanistic expressivism of the depths of the participant. Rather than being 'ambiguous', as Tipton suggests, the complex coheres. Coherence is also seen in the fact that although it has sometimes been claimed that the ethic of humanity and the expressive ethic tend to clash – the former emphasizing 'the same', the latter 'the unique' – the very fact that the operation of the expressive ethic serves to express an authentic self which is so to speak laden with humanistic values means that clashes are minimized. Furthermore, with the values ascribed to freedom and respecting the other, the ethic of humanity is typically 'open' enough, or flexible enough, to permit a *very* considerable degree of unique self-expressivity.[14]

Daniel Bell's (1976) criticism – that the self is taken as the basis of cultural judgement, more exactly, that 'acting out of impulse' has become 'the touchstone of satisfaction' (p. xv) – is of limited applicability to holistic participants. For the greater the extent to which the values of their spirituality are in tune with widespread humanistic and expressivistic cultural values, the greater the extent to which they are unlikely to be self-interested, with 'purely' individualistic, self-contained 'touchstones' in evidence. The (great) majority of participants are simply not capitalistic, utilitarian selves. With their values embedded in their self-understanding as expressivistic humanists, participants think and experience themselves accordingly. The 'body of teachings' (Lasch, 1987, p. 82) embedded in holistic practices, discussions, literature (etc.) serves to reinforce the message. This is not an 'ethical no-man's land' (York, 2001, p. 367). Holistic activities are not settings where there is 'no room for the controlling influence of truth'; where 'an endlessly fragmented labyrinth of unlimited choices' results accordingly (Possamai, 2003, p. 37). The teleological consequences of action normally accord with the deontological nature of action.[15]

A balancing act, a 'tuneful' act

Even if it is accepted that holistic activities typically offer much more than those aspects which can be characterized by the 'marks' of consumption, with growth being more than the growth of a fag end, the fact remains that a fair number of academics judge inner-life spirituality to be precarious, and for this reason alone not fit for the future. The reason for the judgement is simple. The values of freedom, spontaneity, uniqueness, being true to oneself, and epistemological – better, experiential – individualism count against coherence or stability.

Anyone involved in running activities which cater for self-expressivity has to face the challenge of ensuring that their activities retain at least a degree of integration. Self-expressivity can become anarchical. Self-expressivity can serve to disguise the selfish. Self-expressivity can function to undermine good practices, perhaps to the extent of their collapsing into the disordered. And there is a long tradition of commentators claiming that expressivist activities frequently succumb to the 'wrong' kinds of expressivism. Emphasizing freedom – required for self-expressivity – the activities do not provide enough guidance or 'regulation' to handle the 'deregulated', disruptive expression of the 'ill-informed' self. Following Arnold Gehlen – that great pioneer of this tradition of analysis-cum-evaluation – Peter Berger et al. (1974) write of the 'precariousness' of 'under-institutionalized', expressivistic, 'secondary institutions' (p. 168). In much the same vein, Bruce (2002) argues that the deregulated individualism found in New Age circles means that the number of adherents will 'decline' (p. 79). And reflecting on the longer-term prospects of the New Age, Hunt (2005) draws attention to the consideration that there is too little cohesive substance for effective transmission over time: 'Much depends on their pick 'n' mix form of belief and practice. These would be hard to sustain over generations, since personal belief systems would have to be reinvented again and again' (p. 169). In short, holistic activities have no staying power.

The challenge continually facing practitioners (in particular) is to exercise their skill – their 'skilful means' (Pye, 1978) – to cater for autonomy, freedom or self-expressivity on the one hand, whilst providing enough 'input' to enable participants to experience 'a difference' on the other. The greater the structured input (what Adorno called the 'administered life') (Jarvis, 1998, p. 72), the greater the risk of undermining the moral individualism of self-fulfilment; the less the input, the greater the risk of not providing the guidance, the *help* required to enable participants to move beyond their 'blocks', 'barriers', 'stuckness'; to counteract those lures of the selfish life which never go away; to tackle those things which are hard to face on one's own.

Detailed analysis of how the balancing act which is required is 'played out' would take another book. With some activities more structured than others in this regard, variation would have to be taken into account.[16] More significantly, we need to move on from the 'assertive' social psychology of those working in the Adorno-Foucault tradition: a tradition which asserts that 'authorial' authority-cum-power is all-powerful, working through meaningful realities, but without providing sound evidence and without explaining the psychological processes involved.[17] Unlike the sale of New Age commodities – where despite the rhetoric of marketing and advertising, producers have little or no control over their deployment and use – it *could* be the case that on occasion the intentions (etc.) of the holistic practitioner are 'simply absorbed whole and unmediated by the unsuspecting and "passive"' recipient, as Miles et al. (2002, p. 3) make the point. Taking practitioner/participant understanding into account, however, and also bearing in mind the fact that self-reflexivity and questioning are strongly encouraged in most activities, it is *much* more likely that social psychological processes enter into the guiding or 'influencing' dynamic in ways which are *much* less transgressive of the autonomous values which participants bring with them from what they value of their everyday lives. Whatever, the fact that participants are 'determined' to be free – maybe in that sense of the word which is in line with Foucault, but *certainly* in the sense of their *own self*-determination – helps counter the Foucault-inspired objection that 'autonomy' and 'autonomous choice' are subverted by implicit regulatory, 'pre-formed' or constructivist processes. (See Crossley, 2004.) *Yoga. The Discipline of Freedom* (1998) as Barbara Miller's title proclaims.[18]

By far the most illuminating analysis of the exercise of authority and the associated ethicalities of New Age activities, Steven Tipton's *Getting Saved from the Sixties* (1982) serves to enrich the picture of the 'balancing act'. My own, more modest, contributions (e.g. Heelas, 1996a, 2006a) might also be referred to; as can chapter 5 of the present volume (where attention is drawn to the role played by 'horizons', of especial note in that they are directive without being impositional). The literature on egalitarian Christian 'small groups' is also relevant in interpretive and theoretical regards (see, for example, Wuthnow, 1994). For present purposes, though, it suffices to emphasize just two points. First, the evidence of growth serves to speak for itself. If holistic activities were as precarious or 'infirm' as has been claimed, if the 'author' is as ineffectual (dead?) has been suggested, if participants are left to themselves to the extent which has been claimed, the fact of growth is virtually impossible to explain.[19]

Second, there is the argument that practitioners have a pretty easy time balancing freedom and their 'authority', charting a course between the pitfalls of unfettered freedom and restrictive conformity to render their activities fit for the future. As we saw in chapter 5, the typical participant *already* holds expressivistic, humanistic, postmaterialistic values, with at least a degree of spiritual 'belief'. Mid-life or older women, often with, or having had, careers in the expressive professions, do not make the life of the practitioner especially difficult (except, perhaps, by way of professional scrutiny). It is not as though Lasch's narcissistic preoccupation with the self is much in evidence, with *self*-glorification taking precedence over respecting others. It is not as though utilitarian individualistic renderings of 'you must have what you must have' or 'I'm worth it' rule the roost. It is not as though the Hobbesian or Freudian 'problem of order' is much in evidence; namely, the problem that freedom releases antinomian, conflictual passions or drives, taking 'the lid off the id', with all its consequences. The values, assumptions and 'beliefs' which enter holistic activities with their participants are very similar to, if not identical with, those embedded in the practices and spirituality of the great majority of activities. Accordingly, the *sustenance*, sustainability, harmonization, the viability, the plausibility of activities and their practitioners are greatly enhanced. With much the same values, many participants have much the same overarching approaches to life, with all the implications this has for unity and coherence. Even if there is no such thing as inner-spirituality, the strongly internalized, deeply socialized values of participants are at work – maintenance enhanced by the veridicality of the internalized being mediated by way of what is taken to be the 'ultimate' authority of the spiritual dimension: a dimension which is not experience as performing a regulatory, duty-bound role in that it comes from the (albeit quite possibly socialized) heart. (See Amitai Etzioni's (1990) illuminating analysis of the role played by internalized values and the consequences of participation in what he calls 'the response community'.) Finally, a considerable amount of holistic activity takes place within mainstream institutions – contexts where good practice really matters; contexts where holistic activities are provided in connection with commensurate values, goals, purposes and targets. The patient-centred, 'whole-person', caring values of the NHS, for example; the values and assumptions embedded in Ofsted's emphasis on humanistic spirituality. Rather than 'precariousness', inner-life spirituality is here sustained by institutionalized arrangements, perhaps structures.

Conclusion: Fit for Work

I think a rather good case can be made for concluding that holistic activities are neither over-socialized nor under-socialized; and, it can be added, there is little or no evidence that they are comprehensively de-socializing. *Contra* Bruce (2002), holistic activities are substantive and cohesive enough to serve as an appropriately 'solid base' (p. 101). The crafted balance is just right, it seems, for freedom-loving humanistic expressivists to find that difference, that difference which also requires direction; to exercise self-reliance with a guide. Then there is that most elemental of points: the 'balancing act' is greatly assisted by the fact that the value of freedom is enhanced by virtue of the limitations of disciplines. Unalloyed freedom without its other is tantamount to vacuity, and certainly raises no 'growth challenges'. And just as discipline is good for freedom, so release from the unnecessarily restrictive is good for the experience of liberation.

When required, the meaningful realities of holistic activities are set fair to continue trumping consumption. Without the wilder, utopian dreams of Victor Turner (1974), this is 'normative'-cum-existential communitas in action. Relationality, solidarity, perhaps effective 'solidity' of purpose – not infirmity. Values which are not reducible to consumption in any sensible sense of that language. Values of expressivistic humanism suffused by what are *taken* to be experiences of inner-spirituality; the significance of experiences of the sacred for the profoundness of the 'existential'; the very real work that has to be done in the context of spiritual direction – this does not look like a fag ending to me, let alone a discarded butt. It is set fair to grow, with significance. So long as people continue to become participants, that is.[20]

Holistic activities can run as smoothly as clockwork. As the conductor, a measure of authority is exercised by the practitioner. But since the 'belief' among many of those participating is that all are equally spiritual at heart, this is fine for those who seek to 'get the best from *life*'. And when tensions do appear between the authority of the practitioner and the authority of the participant/s, creative dynamism, spice, is added to what is taking place, and people have the opportunity to critically reflect on what authority or power means to them – including the virtues of a middle way with others.

After all, if activities should become too suffocating, participants can just stop going along.

At the heart of it all lies a particular understanding or evaluation of the 'self'. Discussing the 'ideal of authenticity itself', Taylor (1994) writes:

> ...it calls on me to discover my own original way of being. By definition, this way of being cannot be socially derived, but must be inwardly generated. But in the nature of the case, there is no such thing as inward generation, monologically understood. (p. 79)

As he continues, the solution to this conundrum lies with the fact that

> human life is fundamentally *dialogical* in character. We become full human agents, capable of understanding ourselves, and hence of defining our identity, through our acquisition of rich human languages of expression...In the culture of authenticity, relationships are seen as the key loci of self-discovery and self-affirmation. (pp. 79, 81)

Leaving aside the consideration that inward generation is possible if spirituality actually exists, the heart of the matter is that many of those active in the New Age zone of the culture of authenticity have internalized the expressivistic-humanistic complex by virtue of the way they have been brought up, practised enabling or helping them to 're-experience' the ethicality 'from within', so-to-speak 'monologically'. The goal of 'making the best of life', 'becoming all that one can be' for oneself and others, is served by the test of 'inner' experience – value-laden experience which helps direct life accordingly. Enough of the targets 'set' by consumer culture...

There is nothing miraculous about inner-life spiritualities 'speaking' with the voices of the cultural values in which they are set. The internalization of the authority of the voice *of* the authentic self as a socialized sociocultural construct sees to that. That is, if inner-life spirituality does not 'really' exist, and probably, perhaps certainly, even if it does. A dynamic which is fit for the future of particular values in the world, values replete with spiritually suffused sentiments – giving (descriptive) substance to John Fiske's claim that 'culture, however industrialized, can never be *adequately described* in terms of the buying and selling of commodities' (cited by Paterson, 2006, p. 30; my emphasis). And at the individual level, Julie (and all those she typifies) does not consume; she is not a capitalist. Instead, her spiritual art therapy transports her into a personal culture fit for her own future. Most decidedly not a fag ending. Equally decidedly, at least for me, a rich view of human capacities, abilities, and quality of subjective life. Whatever the plausibility of Colin Campbell's (1987) innovative argument that the 'spirit' of modern consumerism owes a considerable amount to 'the Romantic ethic', Romantic antecendents were clearly about much more than the consumeristic. And it is this 'more' which is most in evidence, today: other, that is, than for the 'dream merchants' of the consumer, for profit, industry.

Chapter 9

Inside Out

> ... *the culture of competitive individualism, which in its decadence has carried the logic of individualism to the extreme of a war against all, the pursuit of happiness to the dead end of a narcissistic preoccupation with the self.* (Christopher Lasch, 1980, p. xv)

> *The only way to achieve true joy and fulfilment is by becoming a being of sharing.* (Michael Berg, 2004, back cover)

> *Cultic religion lacks the social significance of the church and the sect.* (Steve Bruce, 'The Failure of the New Age', 2002, ch. 4, p. 79)

> *[Socrates'] mission is useful for the city – more useful than the Athenians' victory in Olympia – because in teaching people to occupy themselves with themselves, he teaches them to occupy themselves with the city.* (Michel Foucault, 1988, p. 20)

> ... *the great current of life.* (Charles Taylor, 1989, p. 376)

> *The new age is simply a symbol representing the human heart and intellect in partnership with God building a better world that can celebrate values of community and wholeness.* (David Spangler, 1989, p. 1)

> *It grows out of the individual person from an inward source, is intensely intimate and transformative, and is not imposed upon the person from an outside authority or source.* (David Tacey, 2004, p. 8)

A standard argument runs that after the political activism of the sixties, and after the failure of the counter-culture to change swathes of the mainstream for the better, activists and fellow alternative travellers retreated into themselves and disengaged so as to attend to developing the quality of their own lives. This is the 'flight from politics' which Lasch, more than anyone, has documented and bemoaned – a flight clearly seen in the importance attached by the seminar spirituality which developed out of the sixties, to carrying out highly focused inner-work to 'transform' experience of the mainstream institutional order rather than explicitly endeavouring to change the organization of the mainstream itself.

As we have seen, more recently it has also become a standard argument to claim that contemporary forms of holistic, wellbeing-focused spiritualities of life are ineffectual – for what they do for the person; and, more glaringly, for what they contribute to relational, social or cultural life. I now look more closely at the critical claim that inner-life spirituality does little to address the major spanner in the works of life: all the adverse consequences which are taken to result from the emphasis on 'the economic', exemplified by the neoliberal capitalist system. I begin with a brief summary of some of the 'sins' of capitalism – sins which one might expect inner-life spirituality to address. This provides the context for going further into the matter of how holistic spiritualities of life enable participants to make a *stand* against many of the defects of the mainstream, a stand which serves as a basis for action. Holistic participants are certainly encouraged to 'go within' – beyond the 'outside', in. However, they are not encouraged to stay within; which in any case is *exceedingly* hard to do. *Inward looking for the outward bound* is what the great majority of holistic activities are all about. To the extent that the evidence permits, I shall also address the question, 'How much does "going within" *matter* to the world *around about*?' Answering that it does matter, that it can make a difference, the conclusion to be drawn is that a politics of wellbeing is emerging.

Some Perceived Sins of Modernity

If critics of modern times are to be believed, there is a great deal to make a stand against. It is widely maintained that liberal values – individualism, freedom and the pursuit of happiness – mean that the person 'is the best judge of his own welfare' (Sagoff, 1990, p. 99) – with all the negative consequences which flow when the individualism is that of the self-possessed or absorbed variety. MacIntyre (1985) argues that 'we live in a specifically emotivist culture' (p. 22), one where the 'reduction of morality to personal preference' (p. 20) is widely in evidence, one where people *consume* other people; that is, use them to fulfil 'desires without a concern for any good but their own' (p. 24). This is a culture where morality has become a matter of individual taste; where morality has come to mean 'the path that leads to emotional satisfaction' (as an article in Pakistan's *Dawn* newspaper puts it); a culture rife with moral subjectivism; a culture where the rightness of desires is tantamount to desires having rights; a culture where feelings – most noticeably, today, feeling 'comfortable' or 'uncomfortable' – have come to exercise very considerable 'ethical' authority – in the eyes of some, including myself, sometimes exercising psycho-ethical tyranny; an emotivist culture which, taken to its *reductio ad absurdum*, results in kinds of judgement like 'murder is wrong because it makes me feel distressed' or 'hanging is good because I enjoy watching it'.[1]

In similar vein, Herbert Hendin (1975) argues that we live in an 'age of sensation', an age 'marked by a self-interest and ego-centrism that increasingly reduces all relations to the question: What am I getting out of it?' (p. 86); a raiding of the sociocultural realm, and the world of nature, to satisfy the self; the Byronic quest for sensational sensations. More recently, R. W. Fevre (2000) presents the case for the 'demoralization' of western culture, a process which is driven by 'the only things that common sense trusts', namely 'sensations' (p. 82). Especially among postmodernists, it has become a commonplace to claim that our personal world of preferences, desires, dreams and needs, the last term often serving to legitimate desires (Walter, 1985), has undermined or weakened the realm of 'traditional' values, 'rights and wrongs' via the process of consumer-driven, 'for me not for the sake of the established order', process of this form of detraditionalization (Crook et al. 1992; Heelas, 1996b). Stimulated and – in measure – satisfied by consumer culture, the needs and desires *of* this culture ensure that the tradition-grounded value previously accorded to 'thrift' has come to be replaced by the spendthrift; self-discipline by self-indulgence (Lasch 1980, p. 64; see also Bell, 1976). Culture as a *supra*-self *order* of truths, virtues, values gives way to a culture where 'truths' are provided by, or expected from, the goals, promises, experiences of the 'dismal' life of capitalism: that 'cultural monstrosity'; that 'spoilt brat of affluence'; that 'junk culture' engaged in 'ceaseless acts of *profanation*' as Margaret Archer (1990) summarizes a body of literature (p.102; my emphasis). Generated by the capitalist system for its own ends, possessive individualism quite naturally generates selfishness.

'All fixed, fast-frozen relations, with their train of ancient and venerable prejudices and opinions are swept away, all new-formed ones become antiquated before they can ossify. All that is solid melts into air, all that is holy is *profaned*', runs one of the most famous passages of *The Communist Manifesto* (Marx and Engels, 1985, p. 83; my emphasis). Liquid, secularized modernity. Although Marx and Engels do not specifically attribute profanation to the development of consumer culture, favouring instead the role played by the 'constant revolutionizing of production' (p. 83), academics have increasingly emphasized the role played by consumption.

Of particular note, money – that great tool to enable the satisfaction of needs and desires – is held to exercise a corrosive effect on 'higher' values. The argument cannot be better put than by Georg Simmel (1978):

> The more money becomes the sole centre of interest, the more one discovers that honour and conviction, talent and virtue, beauty and salvation of the soul

are exchanged against money, and so the more a mocking and frivolous attitude will develop in relation to these higher values that are for sale for the same kind of value as groceries, and that also command a 'market price'. The concept of a market price for values, which, according to their nature, reject any evaluation except in terms of their own categories and ideals, is the perfect objectification of what cynicism presents in the form of a subjective reflex...Whoever has become possessed by the fact that the same amount of money can procure all the possibilities that life has to offer must also become blasé. (p. 256)

Revolving around the value ascribed to money, especially by those prioritizing the values of utilitarian or possessive individualism, the 'commodity frontier', as Arlie Hochschild (2003, p. 40) calls it, moves on to colonize more and more – Hochschild herself dwelling on what her book title identifies as 'the commercialization of intimate life'. Schor (2003) bemoans the 'commodification of childhood'; Adatto (2003) the 'selling out of childhood'; Davis (2003) 'the commodification of the self' itself. Kel Fidler (2006), the vice-chancellor of Northumbria University, UK, states, 'Students today do not see university as a privilege so much as a commodity they buy'. Leading National Union of Students representative Gemma Tumelty notes, 'we are beginning to see a situation in which a university degree is seen as a commodity – where you get what you pay for' (Shepherd, 2006). Returning to intimate life, increasingly, emotions are commodifed. Madeleine Bunting (2004b) suggests, 'Emotional engagement, energy and time are finite resources – the more they are *invested* at work, the less there is available at home' (p. 2; my emphasis); the price of regulative emotion-work is reflected in the energy used up by airline hostesses; the price of emotion-work, it might be added, also being reflected in a certain loss of authenticity or 'reality'; of 'genuine', that is 'natural', spontaneity.

To apply the value of money to determine the value of any number of things, critics maintain, is to devalue them. To literally purchase a university degree is to debase it; it is to let the money do the work, not the student, with all the implications this has for self-development. To engage in what has come to be known as 'transplant tourism' can brutalize other people. To purchase a body part from an executed criminal is to take away dignity (and perhaps encourage the execution in the first place). To 'value' your friend as a utility, with monetary implications (such as treating your 'friend' as a means to the end of promotion) is to instrumentalize, mechanize the friendship. To engage in 'self-branding' is to engage in a 'strategy of cultivating a name and image of ourselves that we *manipulate* for economic gain' (Davis, 2003 p. 41; my emphasis) – the self as a series of commercialized stratagems. When 'self-understanding is mediated by the consumption of goods and images', to cite from Joseph Davis again (2003, p. 41), the self is in danger of becoming one dimensional – largely on the material plain, thereby losing sight of a great deal of the other ways of being human. Drawing on another famous passage from *The Communist Manifesto*, the rise of the bourgeoisie has drowned the most heavenly ecstasies of religious fervour, of chivalrous enthusiasm, of philistine sentimentalism, in the icy water of egotistical calculation. It has resolved personal worth into exchange value. (p. 82)

On Not Making a Stand

For Stephen Hunt (2005), 'The key question is whether the New Age is essentially culture-resisting or culture-conforming' (p. 154). He speaks for many by continuing to note that 'aspects of both can be discerned, although the general tendency is towards cultural conformity'. Hunt also claims that the New Age today is 'more subject to consumerist trends' than during the counter-cultural 1960s (pp. 155–6). Then there are those for whom he does not explicitly speak – those who claim that the New Age has more or less entirely capitulated to conformity, with the consequence that it does not provide that difference which is required to make a difference. Far from it. By being so immersed in consumer culture, and, in measure, business culture, New Age spiritualities of life in fact contribute to the sins of capitalism. (See also Carrette and King (2005) on 'the silent takeover of *all* aspects of life by the corporate word and the interests of capital', including 'spirituality': p. 170; my emphasis.)

As we have seen, it is claimed that New Age spiritualities of life contribute to capitalism. Practitioners (and others) have 'sold out'. They sell 'out' to their market; their aim is to sell out; and they have sold out on 'true' spirituality. The creativity of capitalist enterprise is witnessed in the proliferation of 'new' mind-body-'spirituality' provisions within subjective wellbeing culture, aimed as a seductive bait to fuel the purchase, to fuel consumption; holistic activities are served up as a promising means to the end of recharging, reenergizing, 'empowering' managers for commercial, wealth-creation, shareholder, ends; publishers try to ensure that mind-body-spirituality books are composed and presented to maximize sales.

On these and other fronts, New Age spiritualities of life have been consumed by consumer culture and not via the kind of 'self-developmental' shopping to which Campbell directs attention. For some within the workplace, inner-life spiritualities contribute to how work has become an all-consuming way of life. Spiritualities of life certainly appear to be an adjunct, an extension of capitalism. The growth of holistic activities serves capitalist ends. Despite the best efforts of a few practitioners, the offerings of their quite possibly fashionable activities are swallowed up. Subjective wellbeing culture engorges itself.

It is not difficult to make the case that many of the holistic provisions and services of subjective wellbeing culture are mired in the excesses of consumer culture: jetting off to a luxurious 'meditation spa' at the up-country Four Seasons in Bali, thereby helping destroy the ozone layer; spending money on this kind of thing without caring for others; putting one's own pleasures first, rather than contributing to INGOs; falling for the 'magical' promise to be yourself 'only better' via consumption; celebrating being 'worth it' in a calculative 'after what I've done I've *earned* it' sense; ignoring political activism, perhaps any form of politics, in favour of personal wellbeing; becoming captivated by the 'soma', the dynamos of seduction, operating within consumer culture under the control of manipulative producers and suppliers. The untrammelled consummation of consumptive capitalism. The imperialism of needs. A 'new' form of exploitation. A 'new' form of quietism. 'New' dealers in emotions, stimulating the quest for the juicier and the juicier.

Directing her sights on the 'impotence' of the 'culture of modernism', Margaret Archer (1990) notes that this means it cannot 'criticize nor redirect post-industrial society' (p. 102). For Bauman (1991), 'The most seminal of privatizations was that of human problems and of the responsibility for their resolution' (p. 261). He also argues that 'adamant and uncompromising privatization of all concerns has been the main factor that has rendered postmodern society so spectacularly immune to systemic critique and radical social dissent with revolutionary potential' (p. 261). By this he means that more and more people have shifted their attention from major public issues to those personalized 'social' issues taking place in their vicinity; those which affect their immediate wellbeing. Social issues have become private concerns, with concern for others – remoter from oneself – suffering accordingly. Rather than acting as a 'citizen' to address the sociocultural roots of issues, emphasis lies with the inward looking. Attention is focused on the solutions of self-gratification or interior rebalancing. Dissent is psychologized, internalized, depoliticized. The self is too busy saturating itself with as many pleasurable, 'healthy' experiences as possible to really care about major 'external' issues; the lures of consumer culture explain the demise of the counter-cultural as a force to be reckoned with; the decline of protest movements; the decline of *alternative* ways of life.[2]

The Kendal Project questionnaire distributed to holistic participants provides evidence which appears to support the picture of middle-of-the-road conformism. Most pertinently, asked to locate their political views along a 'Left' to 'Right' spectrum from 1 to 10, the mean is 4.5 – very slightly to the Left. With the 'Soul of Britain' survey reporting a mean of 5.1 (Heald, 2000), it is clear that Kendal participants are only a little more inclined to radicalism than many of the general population. And this fits in with the (supposedly) denuded nature of their practices. Focused on the shift from dis-ease to wellbeing, whatever ethical principles practices which might have been provided in 'the past' of (say) yoga, such as negative evaluations of materialistic attachments, are dropped. As Carrette and King (2005) make the point, yoga has been '*recoded* in the terms of modern psychological discourse and the individualistic values of the western society from which the mindset originates', in the process losing much of what made it 'genuinely counter-cultural, transformative and challenging to western cultural norms' (p. 117); or as one of my students, Aleisha LaChette, puts it, 'yoga has been enfolded into the Western culture of capitalism and individualization that inactivates much of its power as a true political strategy' (2006). Rather than providing an alternative to capitalist culture and society, yoga provides new contexts, new choices, new promises to facilitate the expansion of capitalism; to make more money for New Age and other companies. And, of course, the commodification which is involved is seen as playing a key role in focusing attention on what can be measured, *evaluated* by money – and little else.

According to this perspective, the market is hard at work at the colonization of the 'sacred' by way of commodification, the cultivation of the pleasure principle, the cultivation of highly self-centred hedonism, the transformation of the 'existential' self into the consuming self (Adorno, 1973). Whatever ethical stands might have been provided by spiritual activities in the past have been replaced by the requirements of solace, contentment, pleasure. A milder form of recreational drug-use provided by the 'new' opiate of wellbeing, with 'comfortable' wellbeing taking the form of an 'ethical' imperative. Political engagement is not the name of the game. *If* there is a new world, it is within – and shallow at that. The sociocultural, family circumstances, the real 'root' causes of ill-being, are of little concern. So long as I can find ways of feeling okay, perhaps together with my closest, nothing else matters very much; so long as I am in touch with my spirituality, all will be well within this all-important circumference.

Counter-Currents

It appears that holistic activities are an entirely implausible candidate for a new form of 'counter-culture'. I now argue that although the 'counter-culture' of today is nothing like as 'counter' as that of the 1960s, it nevertheless runs 'counter' to a number of key features of capitalistic modernity. In common with the 1960s, 'It all starts with self' (to recall Shirley MacLaine). Rather than ending with the interiorities of some of the sixties 'freaks', though, *expressive* spirituality – together with spiritually imbued, humanistic values and outlooks – so to speak moves from the self to the relational; to the 'public' realm; into use. However else it might be experienced, spirituality *flows*. After all, this is a key feature of what it means to call it holistic – the integrative. It is held to flow through the person (the intra-dynamic). It flows from the person into the relational – entering into the spiritual person's self-expression with others and their interactivity (the inter-dynamic). It thereby enters into 'public' contexts, like teaching in schools. Spirituality flows to 'encompass', to 'incorporate' what it touches. Not a stoic humanism, but an 'inspired' flow of life.

Flowing from the self, spirituality is not normally experienced as flowing from a self replete with 'authenticity' derived from consumer culture and its advertising (Adorno, 1973). As argued in the last chapter, the dynamic is 'outside in' (via socialization) and then 'inside out' (via expression), the ethicality of humanity, for example, being internalized and then expressed 'from within'. Bearing in mind the possibility that ontological spirituality also contributes to the process, what we can say is that the socialized individualism of the authentic, true, spiritual self serves as a kind of spirit 'possession' from within, informing or directing life without. With holistic integration encouraged during practices, Weberian 'inner values' (Robertson, 1978, p. 120) help inform emotional expressivity. Durkheimian 'sentiments' – namely authoritative, ethically laden, emotionally charged, motivational values – are nurtured. Claims like Gill Edwards' (1993) 'If you complete these steps, the essence of what you want *will* arrive' (p. 79), have to be understood in this context. That crucial aspect of spiritual currents, the flow of sentiments, serves to direct (validate, etc.) life according to their nature: Victor Turner's (1974) 'sentiment of humankindness' (p. 91); the 'oughts' of expressivism.[3] (see also Roberts, 2007.)

With the major exception of commodification as an aspect of consumption, I am henceforth going to resist further engagement with the 'reduction to consumption' thesis. With the conclusions drawn towards the end of the last chapter in mind, the only sensible course of action is to proceed on the grounds that what experiences of mind-body spirituality and associated values *can* bring to life-in-experience goes beyond the simply (or largely) consumptive. In other words, a Durkheimian-like sacrality is at work within holistic activities (and possibly for many non-practising 'believers'); conversely, values are not completely 'subjective', a matter for individual choice.[4] A stand can be made, a point which is now placed in context by looking at various currents associated with inner-life spirituality.

First, *the current 'staying in'*. This is the current of Kant's hermit (cited in the Introduction). This is the current which Chesterton (1909) saw around him, operative within Christianity as well as beyond it: a current of inner-directed individualism generating what he described as 'social indifference' (p. 248). In Weberian language, in its more radical form this is the current of 'other-worldly asceticism', progressive disassociation from this-worldly sentiments or attachments tending to an 'acosmicism' of indifference to the condition of the world (Robertson, 1978, pp. 129, 125; and see Bellah, 1999). In less radical form, it is the current of 'inner-worldly' spirituality, with 'brotherliness' being more in evidence (Robertson, 1978, pp. 129, 125; see also p. 128). Albeit to varying degrees, world-rejection is a key component of the dynamic of the inner quest for both forms. Other than the ways the sins of capitalism render the inner quest yet more challenging, sins are ignored. The outside world is only called upon to provide the essentials of life. Basically, the self 'stays in'. Although present today, this kind of ever-deeper spiritual current is not found within the realm of wellbeing spirituality. The reason is simple. Wellbeing spirituality is holistic. With spirituality experienced as flowing through life, including life with others, gnostic tendencies are held firmly in check.

Second, *the consuming current*. Diametrically opposed to the current of world-rejection, the emphasis here very much lies with 'spirituality' flowing from provisions and services to enhance self-gratification and pleasure; the hedonistic. With the self absorbed with itself, turned in on itself, this current shares a major characteristic with inner-worldly asceticism. The self stays in, enclosed in itself with no concern for addressing the sins of capitalism (other than the fact, for the second current, that not enough consuming pleasures are available from it). Fuelling capitalism, affirming what consumer culture has to offer, the greater the emphasis on the intake, the less the likelihood of the self moving from the inward to the out. As I have noted in previous chapters (particularly chapter 2), with relatively few signs of the 'outing' of the prosperity self in evidence today, this kind of 'spiritual' current is not especially important. It is certainly present, but must not be overemphasized. Relatively few practitioners focus on strongly instrumentalized, prosperity applications of spirituality. Within companies, the spiritual development (some would say the construction) of systematically commercialized or commercial selves – at the expense of other aspects of selfhood – is rarely talked about as such.

Third, *the current through subjective-life*. Here, I am thinking of the difference that inner-life spirituality can be experienced as contributing to the quality of one's experiences of or within oneself: from the somatic to the emotional to the mental, and now over and above what utilitarian consumption has to offer. Since this is a topic which has been considered earlier in the book (especially chapter 6, where Julie's account of her self-experience, self-knowledge and sense of meaningful control highlights the matter), the only point which remains to be emphasized is that so far as I can ascertain this current is rarely experienced as 'staying at home' – locked within the self. For to enhance the quality of one's subjective-life – the quality of the back 'pain' in experience, to feel more 'spirited' about life – generally goes hand in glove with *self-expression*: a consideration now turned to.[5]

Fourth, *the current through familiar life*. Generally speaking, to feel 'better' *about* oneself is to express oneself accordingly. To be 'better' with others, perhaps taking some of the strain out of one's marriage; perhaps being more cheerful or relaxed at work; perhaps expressing more affection for one's children. To experience 'resolution', or to come to terms with the kind of 'issues' discussed in chapter 6, is to take at least a step towards *being* in the position to make more of a contribution to those around you. Familiar relationships within the home, with close kin, with neighbourly friendships, with intimate friends, with close colleagues at work: all benefit. From the malfunctioning 'we' of the marriage to the 'me' – and then inside out again, so to speak. With a few noticeable exceptions, including the research of Kim Knibbe (2007), the evidence here is not what it could be. However, on commonsense grounds alone ('Smile, and the whole world smiles with you'), it is perfectly reasonable to suppose that New Age spiritualities of life often make a significant contribution to the quality of the familiar life. It is highly likely that to 'transform' the back pain translates into behaving somewhat differently when one is with (close) others.

For Richard Sennett (1977), 'The reigning belief today is that closeness between persons is a moral good' (p. 259). Also for Sennett, the more the self is 'privatized', 'the more difficult it is for us to feel or to express our feelings' (p. 4). Spiritualities of life can get to work. Furthermore, a fair amount of evidence – presented in Heelas and Woodhead (2005) as well as in previous chapters here – suggests that many participants believe that other people are essential for growth. Alan Aldridge's (2003) comment, 'The quest for self-actualization is not necessarily incompatible with a desire for deep social relationships with others' (p. 74), does not do justice to how self-actualization 'best' takes place: 'through' others. Whether or not other people are also self-consciously spiritual, they too are experienced as spiritual at heart. The current is reciprocal. 'Without them we would not have been ourselves', runs part of the dedication at the beginning of Gregory Bateson and Mary Catherine Bateson's *Angels Fear. An Investigation into the Nature and Meaning of the Sacred* (1987). Hence the importance of inner-life spirituality in the context of opening up to others and vice versa; reciprocal sharing and caring. As is sometimes said in holistic circles, relationships are 'generative'. De Tocqueville's 'enclosed in their own hearts' hardly applies.

For Max Weber,

> The fate of our times is characterized by rationalization and intellectualization and, above all, by the 'disenchantment of the world'. Precisely the *ultimate* and most sublime values have retreated from public life either into the transcendental realm of mystic life or into the *brotherliness of direct and personal human relations.* (In Gerth and Mills, 1997, p. 155; my emphases)

This 'brotherliness' has little to do with the 'acosmic benevolence' and love of which he also writes (p. 330). For rather than being 'detached' and universal, brotherliness is clearly bound up with immediate relationships. The meaning of 'brotherliness' has to be discerned from Weber's contention that, 'What is hard for modern man, and especially for the younger generation, is to measure up to *workaday* existence' (p. 148). 'The ubiquitous chase for "experience" stems' from this (p. 148). Disenchantment, 'experience', and the *ultimate* value of brotherliness.

Fifth, *the current through the 'public' domain*. Weber's reference to 'workaday existence' leads us to everyday life – typically still familiar, but taking place within realms like the civic, the economic, the educational. For Steve Bruce (1995),

> whatever it does for how those involved feel and think about the world, the New Age has far fewer behavioural consequences than sectarian religion. There is *little or no impact on the world at large*. The state, civic society, the polity, and the economy remain unaffected. (p. 118; my emphasis)

New Agers, it seems, are Thatcherites, in that they, too, devalue 'society'.

Leaving Bruce's comparison with sectarian religion to one side for the moment, one thing which requires emphasizing at this point is that how one feels and thinks about the world is highly likely to have 'behavioural consequences'. To recall R. D. Laing's point, made in *The Politics of Experience* (1967), which I drew on in the Introduction, 'Our behaviour is a function of our experience. We act according to the way we see things' (p. 2) – the corollary being that 'Taking action is a vital part of bringing our consciousness into form and making a real change' (Gawain, 1993, p. 8). One does not have to turn to social psychology to back up the point that how we understand ourselves, experience ourselves, evaluate ourselves – and each other – is *the* prime motor of how we act, not least in connection with the sociocultural order. Marx and Engels (1985) might have raised the rhetorical question, 'Does it require deep intuition to comprehend that man's ideas, views and conceptions, in one word, man's consciousness, changes with every change in the conditions of his material existence, in his social relations and in his social life?' (p. 102), continuing:

> What else does the history of ideas prove, than that intellectual production changes in character in proportion as material production is changed? The ruling ideas of each age have ever been the ideas of its ruling class. (p. 102)

But unless one wants to virtually abolish human agency, 'consciousness' matters. And so attention is directed to those public territories where spiritualities of life are at work in connection with 'consciousness' and associated activities: in schools, hospitals, hospices, businesses, and so on.

As of now, the evidence of 'behavioural' – and other – change might be relatively scanty. But it is there: the introduction of courses on spirituality and nursing in universities, for example; or the implementation of inner-life management trainings. Furthermore, unless activities of this variety were judged to be efficacious, considerable sums of money would not be spent on developing spirituality within public spheres, whether financed by the government or by the private sector. In short, the available evidence strongly suggests that spiritually informed humanistic expressivism is helping to make a difference: helping to 'bring life back to work'; helping to humanize the workplace by encouraging equality of expression; helping to ameliorate the stresses of life in the fast lane; contributing to the quality of life of the ill or dying; fostering the value of equality among primary school children to help combat racism; contributing to social rejuvenation by way of Healthy Living Centres; providing the opportunity to reflect on the disadvantages of being over-competitive or over-ambitious; providing the opportunity to reflect on the drawbacks of continually feeling that one has to prove oneself, to oneself as well as to others; and so on. The currents at work.

Sixth, *the current through the 'counter-cultural'*. Rather than comparing holistic activities today with Bruce's sectarian religion, I briefly compare like with like. A useful comparison is with the counter-cultural spirituality of the sixties. For this comparison directs our attention to the matter of whether there is anything significantly counter-cultural about contemporary mind-body-spirituality activities (and provisions). Are there any signs of attempts to develop alternative ways of life to bypass the sins of capitalism in the fashion of the communards of the 1960s?

On first sight, the answer would appear to be 'no'. There seems to be a world of difference between the sixties counter-culturalists and the middle-aged (or older) professional (ex-professional, retired) women who tend to populate the holistic milieu today. On second sight, though, there is the consideration that around a third of those participating in the holistic activities of Kendal and environs, with the same percentage probably applying to the holistic activities of the nation, consider themselves to be 'a child of the sixties'. More fundamentally, there is the consideration that there are strong value continuities between the present and the sixties. In an especially significant passage of what is surely the best volume on the counter-cultural sixties (and its more immediate aftermath), Bernice Martin's *A Sociology of Contemporary Cultural Change* (1983), we read:

> What it 'countered' was not so much *traditional cultural values* as the contrasting hemisphere of instrumentality and power, work and politics. The counter-culture was historically continuous with the *humanistic/expressive values* of the traditional cultural elite. (p. 21; my emphases)

Essentially – and a great deal of evidence supports this – the counter-culturalists and the participants of holistic activities today share the same, or very similar values – the humanistic/expressivistic. For the sixties counter-culturalists, expressive-cum-human values played the major role in generating the rebellion against the mainstream, humanistic values in particular generating opposition to, frequently hatred of, the inequalities they saw in the hierarchical orders of 'straight society' or the establishment: the racism, the gender inequality, the violence against the victimized North Vietnamese (see Berger and Neuhaus, 1970). And as we have seen, holistic activities today typically attract the humanistic, the expressivistic. At the same time, though, the contemporary situation is far from being counter-cultural in the sense of attempting to develop, or succeeding in developing, alternative ways of life. Virtually all holistic participants today live in middle-class dwellings, not in communes. Very little attention is paid to seeking out new 'comprehensive' ways of life, provided by inner-life new religious movements, for example.

The 'Counter'-Culture Today: Gentle Flows

Are we witnessing a spiritually grounded politics of wellbeing values? Rather than having an articulate politics affirming the capitalist mainstream – perhaps excusing or justifying the apparent sins of capitalism – the majority of holistic participants have a politics of wellbeing which involves some sort of stand to 'counter' the derelictions of the mainstream. Unless one is going to capitulate to the sins to indulge in them, or unless one is to ignore them, some sort of stand has to be made.

Leaving self-indulgent consumers to one side, the stand is primarily afforded by the humanistic-expressivistic value complex. A value-laden 'stand' to *make* a stand: one which serves to illuminate the sins of productive and consumptive capitalism and which enables action to be taken. A stand which identifies 'restrictive practice' due to syllabus regimes in schools, for instance, and prompts some kind of response. A stand which sensitizes participants to the detection of the slightest whiff of harassment or bullying and serves to contribute accordingly. A stand which works with, or within, the system to identify, and act upon, the inhuman of the corporate world. A stand which frowns on excessive hedonistic consumption. A stand which counteracts the perpetual lures of the life of the material world and status display. A stand which could well be associated with valuing non-violence, pacifism, and can translate directly into voting over issues like the invasion of Iraq or the defence of animal rights. Perhaps a stand against the artifices of emotion-work in favour of authenticity. Certainly, a stand in favour of self-responsibility and authoritative control – finding this connection with health by visiting CAM practitioners rather than simply depending on that external authority known as The Doctor, for instance. Of particular note, 71 per cent of respondents to the Kendal Project survey of holistic participants think that economic growth is 'mostly harming' (rather than 'mostly helping') humanity, a clear indication of a post-materialist orientation. Furthermore, in answer to the question, 'What would you say are the three most important problems facing you, *personally*, these days?' (my emphasis), a significant number bemoan the sins of the mainstream: typically in a somewhat toned-down version of the judgemental language of the sixties. And virtually all are environmentalists or 'earth-concerned' in one way or another.

The kind of forceful, radical critique characteristic of the sixties is not in evidence among most holistic participants. Although the street protests against governmental policies over Iraq have surely included the holistically orientated, the protests do not match those of the sixties, especially those aimed at equality or the liberation of Vietnam. The dualistic view of the self of the sixties – the self as contaminated by the sins of the system as *opposed to* the true self – is nowhere near as apparent today. Nevertheless, it is easy to spot critiques and critical responses to the capitalistic mainstream: sometimes relatively implicit, very often devoted to small-scale matters, very often relatively gentle. Those whose expressivistic and humanistic values and life-leanings have been stamped on by the 'chain of being' of the McKinsey-esque managerial, 'bow to those above, dominate, and bully if you can, those below' system – which is increasingly coming into evidence – are especially vociferous in their attacks. Especially when they are in the process of being squeezed out of work by the value clashes they experience. Upper-echelon workers who feel that rather than 'getting a life' through the 'learning organization' of their company have lost their 'life'; school teachers who are too burdened to be child-centred; nurses who are lost in paper, who are spending a great deal of their time striving to obtain scientistic, measurable targets: who accordingly neglect the less-than-measurable, namely the patient (Aupers and Houtman, 2006; Heelas, 2006b).

Bloch (1998) argues that in alternative 'movements, emphasis is placed not on strong organizational ties or explicit political agendas, but on advancing new communication codes that challenge existing social controls and dogma' (p. 115). Rarely with the same anger, on occasion the ferocity, of the hippies/political activists of the sixties, the critique of major features of capitalistic modernity continues. Often taking place in the classroom, the common room, the personnel or HRD offices, or similar settings, the ethical struggle between the values of 'the system' and the values of humanistic expressivism have certainly *not* died away, with the politics of inner-life spirituality playing a role when, for example, an HRD department seeks to introduce inner-life, humanizing management trainings.[6]

Margaret Archer (1990) draws attention to those like Daniel Bell who claim that 'Junk culture is the spoilt brat of affluence, but in its ceaseless acts of profanation and unprincipled celebrations of novelty, it also denies the possibility of *any debate on the Good Society* predicated as that must be on enduring, if contested, principles and on rational discourse for their contestation (p. 102; my emphasis). If holistic spirituality were to be largely, or entirely, a matter of 'junk culture', it could not provide the basis for debate. Since it is by no means entirely a matter of 'junk' (whatever that is), holistic participants have a *sound* basis for articulating their views. Prince Charles, with his strong romantic, holistic orientation provides an exemplificatory illustration, the holistic informing his public announcements on agriculture, architecture, CAM, the environment, interfaith dialogue, painting, and the natural (Lorimer, 2003).

It might even be argued that the gentle path – gentle relative to the sixties – is more effective than radicalism. Radicalism readily generates forceful opposition (this dynamic probably serving as a major factor in the demise of the counter-culture during the early 1970s). By definition, radicalism preempts that gradual, progressive change which – it can readily be claimed – works best in the longer term. It can also be argued that it is best to start with the self. That rather than believing in big ideas, big political strategies, big utopian promises, it is more advisable to *work out* from the self; to work out from those 'micro' experiences and experience-laden values which make a difference to one's own life, those around you, those who can team together (in a small company, for example) to try to make a bigger difference. Inside out.

Without enough 'hard' evidence to make a conclusive case, I have been suggesting that a politics of expressivistic, humanistic values, underpinned or informed by the sacred in the form of inner-life spirituality, serves as a form of counter-culture to combat the sins of capitalism: a counter-culture strengthened by virtue of well-qualified people leaving their mainstream, often person-centred occupations to become practitioners. Unlike declining, liberal or humanistic forms of traditional religion, it can be added, the *expressivism* of the spirituality provides what is probably 'the vital difference'. Religions of humanity are not exactly renowned for their expressivism. With this poorly represented, they are unable to 'tune in' with what so many people are looking for – more viable ways of being true to themselves; of *acting* authentically by expressing their authenticity.

Finally, attention can be drawn to another strength of the counter-currents under consideration. Unlike seminar spirituality, for example, we saw earlier in this book that there is little evidence that holistic activities (let alone provisions like books) serve to convert; to perform relatively radical forms of change (Heelas, 1996a). Holistic activities today do not function as a kind of emotion machine, changing subjectivities in the way which is often claimed by Durkheimian social constructivists or cognitive behavioural therapists. As we have also seen earlier, most of those who come to participate are already 'believers' of inner-life spirituality. Most already hold expressivistic and humanistic values, with corresponding evaluations of their emotions – better, sentiments. The kind of radical or fairly radical change implied by the term 'conversion' is thus rarely in evidence.

Rather than assuming that this is disadvantageous, it has its advantages. For holistic activities frequently *amplify* previous convictions or tendencies, amplification or *magnification* serving to *reinforce*, *consolidate*, perhaps validate what is *good* about existing ways of life; serve to encourage the translation of 'beliefs' and values into practice. Holistic activities are built on a firm value-base, and can function accordingly. Consider postmaterialism. Given the available evidence (the number who have downsized, for instance, or attitudes to economic growth), many of those coming to participate in holistic activities are of a postmaterialist bent. They have come to appreciate that what can be measured, and thus purchased or invested, is not the sum of life. They 'realize' the value of what cannot be bought. For them, there is 'the more' of the more intangible – like 'feeling centred'. Although it is highly unlikely that the postmaterialist orientation is generated by holistic participation, it *is* highly likely that the orientation can be reinforced or cultivated. The 'garbage' of what could be bound up with undue, 'decentring' attachment to, indulgence in, materialistic consumption being placed under scrutiny. In any case, the lure of life in the material world and associated selfish tendencies always requires attention. To provide another illustration, those participating in mind-body-spirituality forms of CAM, who are already health conscious, will almost certainly be encouraged to become yet more health conscious (including the health of the environment), altering aspects of diet and 'lifestyle' accordingly. Or again, those attracted could well be provided with the opportunity for reflecting on their humanistic or expressivist values: putting them to the test of experience ('how did I feel when I did not give money to the street person?'); perhaps validating an approach when value-tension exists ('Yes, I should care for myself more rather than devoting myself to others quite so much'); and probably experiencing a greater 'spiritual depth' to value-laden subjectivities like 'being loving' and being 'truly expressive'. What is considered to be the 'good' life is reinforced; temptations to deviate are diminished.

The Issue of Commodification: The Mastery of Money?

Commodification: the issue which crops up time and time again during discussions after talks or lectures. The fact that so many holistic activities and provisions have to be paid for prompts critics to think that capitalism has won the day. Using Arlie Hochschild's (2003) term, the argument is that the 'commodity frontier' has extended to encompass much of what goes under the term 'New Age spiritualities of life'. The (apparent) failure to resist the 'frontier', the scant attention paid to developing non-commodified alternatives, leads critics to think that holistic participants are quite content to have sold out to capitalism; even that participants assume that money can purchase spirituality. Commodification runs counter to any counter-cultural stand. It is victory for the commercial 'outside in'. It demonstrates capitalism using its powers to the full, commodification of the sacred contributing to the consummation of capitalism itself.

To overemphasize the case, I now argue that by and large *commodification does not matter* (much). Although the 'inside out' flow of life frequently takes place within settings where time (etc.) is money, this does not invalidate the point that non-capitalistic counter-currents are operative.

'Commercial relations are the dominant mechanism determining such access [to groups, etc.] in New Age circles', writes Guy Redden (2005, p. 234). As he also notes, 'If "seekership" is the dominant mode of participation, it is – in material terms – primarily effected through selection and consumption of commodified goods and services made available by New Age businesses' (p. 240). Nothing to dispute here. However, he elsewhere claims that the New Age 'transmits *ideology* through commodity exchange' (2002, p. 44; my emphasis). This begins to smack of the kind of monetary reductionism which Marx and Engels (1967) noted with alarm – as when they claimed that bourgeoisie economics has 'reduced the family to a mere money relation' (p. 82). In other words, Redden is at least implying that the transmission of 'ideology' is by way of the purchase: that you get what you pay for; that what the supplier provides *depends* on the depth of your wallet; that money more or less determines the nature of transactions. This is an illustration of the (adverse) consequences which so many find in what Cathryn McConaghy (2000) sees as 'a central feature of contemporary colonialism', namely 'cultural commodification' (p. 50). That you have to work to experience spirituality drops out of the picture.

'Are there some things which money should not buy?' asks Michael Sandel (2003, p. 77). Essentially, postmaterialists or expressivists – who are *much* more likely to be attracted to spiritualities of life than materialists or utilitarian individualists (see chapters 1 and 5) – are those who have realized the limitations of the purchase; who have realized the value of that which cannot be purchased. The reduction or exclusion of a great deal of life to 'only' that which money can buy is not for them. To varying degrees, and in varying ways, a stand is (typically) taken against the excesses of 'monetary positivism', namely, prioritizing the value of currency as *the* measure. Postmaterialists-cum-expressivists would concur with Jonathan Sacks (1990): 'the human being as consumer neither is, nor can be, all we are'. Few are interested in cultivating the kind of 'commercialized self' which Hochschild (2003) detects in her analysis of (often, New Age-orientated) self-help literature; few are intent on developing the kind of enterprising self which Paul du Gay (1996) found within the companies he studied. Few would liken themselves to those students who would exercise their authority to 'pay the piper [to] call the tune' (Marcus, 2006).

Given the amount that has been written on commodification and the purchase – what can, should not and cannot be bought – I am only able to dip into matters here. (The special issue of the *Hedgehog Review* (2003), 'The Commodification of Everything', contains much of analytical purchase.) Fully accepting that Simmel's 'blasé' can be found – money counting to provide the culture capital of the 'absolutely fabulous' Buddha in the hall, for example – a great deal of what is going on within spiritualities of life cannot be reduced to monetary exchange, *to* what money can buy. With it being widely accepted that it is fine to pay for yoga (for example), it is true that many do not make a stand with regard to the 'commodity frontier' in this kind of regard. But this does not mean that many think it is possible to buy what *goes on* during practice. Just as pretty well everyone agrees that 'Money can't buy you love' (only a semblance or travesty of it), so have I never come across anyone who claims that money, and money alone, can buy you spirituality. 'You get what your pay for' – fine for a Lexus, not so fine when a university degree is treated as a commodity, and considerably less fine when one tries to purchase spirituality, for you won't get anything (much) at all. As they are understood and *experienced*, love and spirituality – let alone tranquillity, wisdom, a sense of being 'centred' – transcend the capacities of cash flow. And it has to be emphasized that practitioners frequently exercise their arts to 'open up' the significance of what lies beyond the limitations of the competitive, monetary frame of reference – the life circumscribed by *attachment* to wealth accumulation or 'the consumptive' – thereby making a stand against 'colonization' of the hedonistic.

Furthermore, contrary to what many of my students think (for example), I have never come across any evidence of participants thinking that payment makes an iota of adverse difference to the authority or experienced authenticity of – say – yoga, let alone the 'halo' of the practitioner. 'I have to pay for yoga? Fine!' Indeed, it is highly likely that payment actually increases value, a sense of ownership, a sense of authority among participants – an 'investment' signally that they want something to happen; and one which contributes to their commitment (which Bruce (1996, p. 273), it can be noted, thinks is 'slight'). In addition, participants generally appreciate the fact that payment tends to be relatively modest (that is, relative to activities like psychotherapy); that practitioners have to make ends meet; that practitioners are hardly 'in it' to become even reasonably wealthy. Neither is there any evidence, that I know of, which suggests that 'exchange value' means that practitioners join the ranks of those referred to by Marx and Engels (1967) when they wrote,

> The bourgeoisie [dominated by the 'callous "cash payment"'] has stripped of its halo every occupation hitherto honoured and looked up to with reverent awe. It has converted the physician, the lawyer, the priest, the poet, the man of science, into its paid wage-labourers. (p. 82)

The 'halo' of the practitioner depends on her skill; her arts of life. She does not want to lose her halo, not least because her halo signals that rather than dumbing down she is working with that degree of skill and 'knowledge' which deserves respect; which works.

Having noted 'the encroachment of commodification into almost every aspect of life', the author of the Introduction to a special issue of the *Hedgehog Review* (2003) then makes the point that '*the very character of life* seems increasingly consumeristic and commercial' (p. 5; my emphasis). Money might be a prerequisite for participation in most groups and one-to-one holistic activities, but I do not for one moment think that the *monetary factor* means that the very character of life within activities is affected. Cash enables entry – perhaps for a six-week course. What goes on after entry is *not* a matter of a cash nexus – with the exception, that is, of a few miserly types, who, no doubt, will be encouraged to get to work on their 'issue' with money. To think that self-expressivity – the expression of one's unique feelings, so central to many holistic activities – is somehow 'forced' into commodifiable form in the fashion of training a sales assistant how to 'smile' is to miss the point. To think that expressivistic values, the values of the ethic of humanity, can somehow be commodified, *subjected* to money flow – well, together with the implausibility of this, I know of no evidence. Experiences-cum-understandings of authenticity, justice, deep selfhood: where is the evidence of the impact of 'commodification'? Where is the evidence for the calculative instrumentalization or 'maximization' of friendships or working relationships between practitioners and participants? Other than a few instances, where is the evidence that money is the Master? To pay the piper certainly need *not* kill the tune.

Asking the question, 'If a commodity is a product, something that can be bought and sold, then in what sense can the self be commodified?', Joseph Davis' (2003) answer is, (a) 'that self-understanding is mediated by the consumption of goods and images...We know who we are and we judge the quality of our inner experience through identification with the things we buy'; and (b) that 'self-commodification involves the reorganization of our personal lives and relationships on the model of market relations' (p. 41). There is undoubtedly some truth to this when New Age products are purchased. But as noted in chapter 4, however hard one tries, one cannot choose to be spiritual, decide to be spiritual, buy 'belief'. (A similar point can probably be made with regard to attempting to buy happiness – the more you try, the less likely you are to be happy: cf. Lane, 2000, pp. 59–76.) There are some things which money cannot buy – and the reality of spirituality, which cannot be commodified *per se*, is one of them. What takes place within holistic activities is not a commodified, spiritual version of an organ transplant. Self-understanding and experience are primarily 'mediated' by the practitioner and the practices; the 'reorganization' of personal lives and relationships which might take place flows from the activities – with 'market relations' playing a very small role indeed, if any.

The market so clearly has its limits; the reduction of spiritual growth to what money can buy is so clearly misguided, as is the application of monetary positivism – only valuing what is measurable; the very idea that emotions are commodified, when all one's efforts, all one's work, is directed at being as 'natural' as possible (let alone the fact that emotions, *per se*, are not priced); the very idea that money is the measure of life rather than life-growth through self-expression and interaction. Small wonder, then, that holistic participants rarely express any concern about the 'commodity frontier' encompassing their territory; of money coming to be treated as the measure of success. There is no need for a counter-current in this regard – especially as practitioners typically aim to be professional, making their own stand against the ineffectual currying of favour; of spoon feeding. And after all, hippies customarily purchased their LSD and much else of alternative significance besides.

In short, although spiritualities of life might appear to be part of a broadly conceived capitalist market 'system', much does not belong to the register of the monetary. Even when the money-grasping use New Age products to help line their pockets, the link – if there is one – between 'the author' and 'the recipient' is surely not of a kind to facilitate the transmission of money-grabbing intentions.

Concluding Thoughts

Writing in response to the 'naked, shameless, direct, brutal exploitation' which they largely attributed to 'Free Trade' capitalism, Marx and Engels' (1985) ten concrete 'measures' were radical (pp. 104–5). Some have more or less come to pass, including 'Free education for all children in public schools' (p. 105); some might well meet with the approval of a number of holistic participants – a 'heavy progressive or graduated income tax' (p. 104), for example; some would probably be rejected on the grounds that the centralized state generates regulative control, pressure, dependency. What Marx and Engels would think of the holistic today is best left to the reader's imagination.

In comparison with their ten measures, contemporary mind-body spirituality is modest – a gentle current, not a torrent or 'force' (as powerful flows of water are called in the Yorkshire Dales where I live). In comparison with most of the previous counter-cultural manifestations of the expressivistic-cum-humanistic trajectory of modernity, it is also fairly modest. The mainstream of modernity is not criticized as it was by the Romantics ('dark Satanic Mills'); alternatives like the communes of the 1960s are not sought. However, as I have previously indicated, the very modesty of what is taking place today could be a great virtue. No doubt writing with an eye on the counter-culture of the time, Roland Robertson (1972) refers to 'the affairs of the empirical being subordinated to the non-empirical' (p. 47). The prioritization of 'non-empirical' states of liberated, individual consciousness by so many counter-culturalists largely explains why 'empirical' ways of life, such as all those communes which became routinized, did not last long. And it also helps explain why counter-culturalists did little to attempt to change or improve 'the system' from within itself. Even if they were old enough to do so, few counter-culturalists were attracted by the possibility of exercising authority by working within mainstream schools, hospitals or businesses. Things are different today. There is *real* engagement within the mainstream, often involving people like educationalists, management trainers or HRD personnel with real influence. Furthermore, although the accusation of 'hyper-individualism' (Ward, 2006, p. 185) which is so often levelled at New Age spiritualities of life today could apply to those counter-culturalists who sacrificed relationality, communalism or tribalism in favour of exploring their own altered states of consciousness, the accusation is much less relevant today. For the emphasis now lies with exploring or developing 'consciousness', that is subjective-life, through relationships: in holistic groups and one-to-one encounters; with the dying person in the hospice; within the workplace.

'All you need is love' still rings in the minds of those who came of age during the sixties. The utopianism of '*All* you need is love' has become a memory. Typically, subjective-life 'utopianism' has gone inside out. In *The New Age Movement* (1996a), I asked the question, 'Given that New Agers tend to be highly critical of mainstream education, why are there not more alternative educational practices?' (p. 80). Since the time I researched that volume, 'alternative' educational practices have flourished: not just the alternative 'mainstreamed' (Waldorf, Montessori, etc.), but also in the hands of agencies like Ofsted. Not the life of the hippie, rather the life of the teacher, the nurse, the manager. Bruce's claim, cited earlier, that 'There is little or no impact on the world at large', would seem to ignore the extent to which the impact is now clearly visible: embedded in many institutions, where holistic 'teachings' and activities are surely making a degree of difference; and albeit less clearly in sight, with regard to the wellbeing of personal relations. The 'institutionalization' of holistic activities provides pretty hard evidence against the 'little or no impact' claim.

I have indicated that the available evidence is unlikely to convince the critic. Inward bound, outward bound: the critic will presumably agree that the former trajectory is operative, especially when in consumptive mode – but not the latter. More research is needed to evaluate the argument that spiritualities of life serve the self *and* what lies beyond the individual *qua* individual. As things stand, though, it is probably *more* difficult to argue the 'no impact' case than the 'making a difference' one. Whatever, the challenge lies with doing this research, in particular paying heed to the old adage, that 'actions speak louder than words'. 'Micro-activities', where change might be tracked, can be virtually inaccessible to the academic: one-to-one holistic healing or counselling sessions, for example. It is far from easy to shadow people who regularly practice spiritual reflexology to see how it might enter into their intimate relationships. Taking place during the spiritually informed management trainings of 'zenployment', 'micro-politics' might well escape the attention of the academic. So might the consequences of the experiential teaching of university management schools. As I know only too well, trying to ascertain the significance of after-school yoga for an eight-year-old is far from easy. Neither is it easy to ascertain the significance of inclusivistic, inner-life, humanistic spirituality in schools where racism is a problem (and where Christianity is rejected more or less *in toto* by the pupils). Neither is it at all easy to track the contribution which holistic spirituality might be making to 'happy-being', then tracking how this might contribute to economic productivity. (See *The Economist* of 23 December–5 January, 2007, on 'hedonimetrists', the turn of economics to 'feelings', and the implications for work and the productivity of the nation.)

Some research will be easy to do, for example establishing the percentage of retired people (who it will be recalled approach a quarter of the Kendal Project questionnaire sample) who devote time to charitable works in their local communities; arriving at a better picture of the role played by inner-life spirituality within some new social movements; or determining more accurately the number of holistic practitioners and participants who link up with each other in interactive communities of value. Other research will most definitely not be easy. How many find that holistic activities help keep their spirits high? How many find that they can 're-experience' their nagging back pains, becoming friendlier, more invigorated husbands in the process? Questions are legion. How do we test the idea that among other things meditation serves as a mental training, developing capacities such as attentiveness and concentration which are beneficial *for* life more generally? That the sense of union generated by a 'good' yoga group is extended into everyday life? That mind-body-spirituality publications can make a difference?[7]

Governmental support certainly points to efficacy 'without'.[8] So does capitalist investment. (The objection that market research simply allows spa companies (etc.) to capitalize on preferences is met by arguing that unless customers felt better 'about themselves', spas (etc.) would go out of business.) So do available ethnographic accounts, including film footage of people at work. Then there is the simple but powerful consideration that highly practical forms of holistic activities have long been deployed in eastern settings. There is absolutely no reason to suppose that what helps alleviate ill-being or enhance wellbeing in the east (laughing yoga before going to the office in Chennai) cannot work just as well in the west: that is when there is little to differentiate activities at the practical level. The dream of pioneers like Vivekananda and Sivananda – to get things 'back on track' – is coming to some fruition (Strauss, 2005, p. 138).

The critic might now argue: 'Yes, all well and good. But people like Vivekananda and Sivananda are long dead. Haven't you forgotten about those half a million or so people in Britain who are participating in holistic groups or one-to-one activities, provided by spiritual practitioners during any given week, who do not report anything of spiritual significance?' Together with the consideration that there is nothing to show that *this* means they are consumeristic, the answer is simple enough. They too encounter humanistic, expressivistic assumptions, values, modes of expression, all serving to contextualize and inform what counts as wellbeing. Nothing unfamiliar to them – but quite possibly serving to remind, enhance or inspire, with their activities quite possibly helping them to clear out some of the 'junk' in their lives; quite possibly providing them with a time for reflecting on priorities; quite possibly opening up 'new' avenues – 'new' ways of relating with others, or appreciating the environment and shopping accordingly; perhaps galvanizing those who are in the position to influence mainstream policies. Whether or not the spiritual dimension of the growing number of holistic activities is experienced during practice, the activities can nevertheless serve as an aid to living up to what are taken to be the 'higher' things of everyday life – especially as the great majority of participants are in any case 'believers' in spirituality and probably are holistically orientated.[9] Furthermore, although the development of New Age spiritualities of life within settings like spas, hotels, beauty salons or health and fitness centres might be associated with 'secularization', it is very unlikely that the same can be said for developments in the hands of primary school teachers, nurses and so on. There is nothing to suggest that these developments are accommodating to 'cultural norms' (Bruce, 2002, p. 102), most especially secular consumer culture.

Summation

Reflecting thus far, to reduce the values, assumptions and expressions of the ethic of humanity and the ethic of authenticity to consumption is of course ridiculous. But in effect this is what many critics do. At the very heart of the language of consumption lies the idea that intake is for the self itself; more exactly, for the self content with being itself via capitalistic provisions and expectations; content with *being* in terms of what consumer culture has to promise. In contrast, although holistic activities involve experiential 'intake', the primary concern of practitioners and many participants is to inform their lives by what they 'take' to be spiritual experiences. Whatever other contributions inner-life spirituality might make to life, the importance of the values, assumptions and expressions of expressive humanism means that they are sacralized. What is good enough for middle aged, discerning, people-centred, postmaterialistic, professional women might not be good enough for the likes of Bauman (with his 'orgasmic experience') or Ward (with his 'hyper-individualism'). (These are women like my mother, with her Quaker, inner-life, educationalist, feminist outlook!) For those who seek to make a modest contribution to the life around them, though... And for those like teachers, nurses and activists among the retired, who are 'person-influential'... The ethicality of humanity-cum-expressivism in sacred operation. And even if 'the sacred' could be shown to be some kind of false consciousness, the values of expressivistic humanism are surely considerably less open to this criticism, if at all.

Hindu Magazine provides a graphic example of the permissive, self-indulgent message. Discussing the theme of 'For her own good', Kalpana Sharma (1993) writes that an advertisement

> showed an attractive young woman sitting on a living room floor, wearing a scuba diving mask and flippers on her feet. She had ski poles in one hand, a tennis racquet in the other. The caption reads: 'I love me.' It went on to say, 'I'm just a good friend to myself and I like to do what makes me feel good. Me, myself and I used to sit around putting things off until tomorrow... But now I make my dreams come true today, not tomorrow.' The message from this and similar advertisements is clear: what you want is what you should have. There is no concept of either need or greed.

Neither is there a concept of being a friend with others. The accusation of selfishness – putting oneself first and last by not contributing to others – probably applies to this young woman. But it *hardly* applies to many holistic participants – possibly the least likely of all sectors of the population to deserve this accusation.

To think in terms of John Donne's famous lines, 'No man is an island, entire of itself', neither is 'inner' wellbeing. Wellbeing is *not* easily hidden.

Activities devoted to the nurturing of spirituality typically bring much in their wake: the expression of wellbeing in the workplace, with one's children, for instance. Self-fulfilment, making the best of oneself, living life to the full, can be selfish, as when one fills oneself up with consumptive experiences (Gabriel and Lang, 2006, p. 8). However, a life enriched by quality experiences (including what can be learnt from 'negative' experiences) most emphatically need not involve selfishness. To 'fill up' with experiences of this variety is quite probably to be a better person for others. The accomplishment of making the best of oneself normally requires recognition by others; what one's life expresses normally is for others. To experience the sacred in nature, in the spirit of the Romantics, can make a difference to the wellbeing of the natural realm. What is good for one's own life is good *for* life more generally. Colin Sedgwick's (2004) blanket dismissal – 'feelgood', 'selfish religion' – is incorrect. Basically, we are talking about the non-theistic (as transcendent), holistic aspect of what Gordon Lynch (2007) calls 'progressive spirituality'. To develop capacities through expressive practices with others, through the self-work ethic at work, with the 'right' values in evidence, is not to be selfish. Neither is being enthusiastic about life in general.

Progressive: now with an eye on those with influence, not least policy makers, the importance of academic research can *really* be emphasized: research on the experiential outcomes of UK government initiatives to provide CAM (including spiritual CAM) for the elderly; on the existential efficacy of the holistic for palliative care; on the introduction of holistic spirituality to citizenship studies in schools (helping 'form' the citizen with sensibilities?); on whether it is a good idea to devote resources to teaching spirituality to students studying nursing at university; on whether holistic networks can help address that homelessness at home experienced by some of the retired, taking them out of the memories of their hearts; on what the holistic 'wise woman' might be contributing to rural communities; on what holistic activities might contribute to stress and happiness in primary schools; on whether companies are justified in investing in holistic management trainings; on whether there is a connection between experiencing the sacred in nature and shopping selections; and so on. Drawing from a key finding from the Burnley Project (details on Google), which I have helped run, let me provide a concrete example. One of the schools we have looked at is virtually entirely 'white'. The great majority of the socioeconomically disadvantaged 15-year-old students of this school most emphatically reject or ignore Christianity; and around half are racist. If holistic spirituality were taught to them (I hesitate to suggest practised), it would be wonderful to see if the universalism of this spirituality could mitigate in-group, out-group racism: not implausible, for students might be more engaged by the 'exotic' (perhaps Sufi), meaning that the perennialist message of inner-life spirituality could be appreciated.

One thing is certain. 'Simply' self-indulgent or the (waning) forms of prosperity spirituality activities aside, the evidence does *not* support the idea that inner-life spirituality encourages the poisoned fruits of (relatively) free-market capitalism – the increasing equality gap, the erosion of some communities, the excesses of individualism, the vaunting of ambition, the 'I-pride'. As for the sapping of the political will, my answer is: at the micro-level, almost certainly no; at the macro-level of national politics, probably not. As things currently stand, although New Age spiritualities of life are not winning the cultural war against the repressive, they are contributing to the quality of life. In praise of wellbeing! Caring for the wellbeing of others, and oneself, is rather important – the quality of the 'well'-led life to die with.

The romantic or expressivist trajectory of modernity has for long served as a counter-balance or antidote to the sins of capitalistic modernity. Relative to where utilitarian individualism – or corporate anality – can lead, I cannot but conclude that informed as it is by expressivist, humanistic values, the inner world of the politics of life serves as a *real* life for a politics of wellbeing. The *life* paths of this form of 'inside out' can make valuable contributions to life as we know it in the contemporary west. *Inner values for inside out.* Government initiatives are surely worthy of support. And we surely have to agree with the Dalai Lama's (1998) enthusiasm for corporate enterprises which cultivate spiritual humanism; which endeavour to combat disharmonious inequality.

Looking to the future, if expressivistic and humanistic values continue to become more important, and if the former – in particular – become ever-more squashed by the ever-increasing monitoring, regulation and erosion of life-freedoms which is so clearly taking place, the expectation is that New Age spiritualities of life will become more important: both in the numerical sense, and in the ways in which they will contribute to people resisting or otherwise engaging with regulatory imperialism. Inner-directed resistance is significant as a counter-current. There are a lot of jobs to be done. And given that approaching a third of the UK adult population apparently 'believe' in the 'God within', there are already plenty of people (including teachers) who so-to-speak form a pool of potential recruits, including those who could become inner-life activists, working to implement or stimulate inner-life values in the mainstream. Not the 'State' centralism of Marx and Engels (1985) to bring about a situation 'in which the free development of each is the condition for the free development of all' (pp. 104–5), but a more modest contribution to developing the personalized, expressivistic-humanistic strand of modernity; working to turn Ronald Inglehart's (1977) 'silent revolution' into something more vocal.

As for the objection that practitioners of mind-body-spirit activities are 'preaching to the converted', a parallel can be drawn with the oft-repeated point that Nonconformism bred generations of people of sterling worth and transparent honesty. The objection that Nonconformist Christianity was in fact largely preaching to people who had already been raised with concordant values is the same objection as that which can be levelled against mind-body-spirituality practitioners. And no doubt there is some truth to this concern. The fact remains, however, that just as the Nonconformist Christian leader encouraged, inspired, reaffirmed, reinforced, validated, magnified certain values, so does the holistic practitioner – only more gently. Both serve to provide the opportunity for learning more about how to live out a better life – the journey through the everyday world.[10] And like traditional Nonconformist activities, the holistic is increasingly entering territories where there are real challenges: including schools with a significant number of prejudiced, blinkered pupils, inner-city healthy living centres or corporate enterprises.

Secularization theorists have countered the claim that New Age spiritualities of life are growing by arguing that they are in fact declining and/or are numerically insignificant. They have also argued the case for insignificant salience. I do not agree. When life is taken to be an adventure in self-development and expression, over and above money as the major or sole measure of success, the sacred serves as a locus and focus for what cannot be measured. As a state of affairs which is incompatible with the sins of consumption. As a state of affairs which has to do with acting out of values, not acting out of measurable choices. Or so it can be experienced.

In *Der Deutsche Mensch als Symptom*, Robert Musil writes:

> The enormous cruelty of our political and economic social structures, which do violence to the feelings of individuals, is so unescapable because these very social structures at the same time give the individual a shape and the possibility of an expression. Thus, one might say that man becomes man only through expression that is formed in the context of social structures.

True – to an extent. For we must not forget that alongside the narcissistic personality – the self-love, the lack of empathy, the compulsion to instrumentalize and exploit others – which tends to be 'shaped' by the political-economic orders of capitalistic modernity, there exists the romantic trajectory. One where the sacred is pivotal. Even if the sacred does not exist as an ontological *sui generis*, it serves as a meaningful reality, affirming (some might say 'symbolizing') what the positivistic aspects of our times treats as the fluff of the intangible. Not having had *the* experience myself, for me this affirmation is what the sacred of inner-life spirituality is all about.

Consumption is not the measure of success for holistic practitioners (and I don't know of any who promote disciplines for self-interest in quite the spirit of Ayn Rand); neither is it for a considerable number of participants. By carrying the beacon of sacralized values, holistic participants enter the struggle which lies at the heart of western modernity: the qualitative versus the quantitative, the expansive versus the restrictive, the expressive versus the channelled, the priceless versus the philistine, the bloom versus the cage. Nothing new about this. And nothing new about the way the struggle keeps modernity itself *alive*. But there is a great deal to be said of that libaratarian moralism which spiritualities of life are basically about – that creativity which lies at the heart of relational human flourishing; that humanism which devalues the ultimately exploitative nature of consumer culture expectations when they are put into (fully-fledged) practice.

One of Goethe's characters, Werner, advises his brother-in-law, Wilhelm Meister, 'This then is my merry confession of faith: to do business, make money, amuse yourself with your own people and have no further care for the rest of the world, except in so far as you can make use of it' (Goethe, 1795–6, p. 77). Today, with the talk of 'brain training', 'mental toughness', 'the Prozac nation', even 'natural' pleasures are under threat. In complicated ways, 'life-as' formations are developing – not least by way of the culture of the economic (or economically significant) target, with targets dictating the nature of those human resources ('mental toughness', etc.) which are required for target performance. No longer of a significantly religious nature in Britain (and elsewhere), life-as formations nevertheless disrupt the 'rounded life'. Aristotelian *eudaimonia*, namely the focus on personal development and character that enables people to live rich, aspectual and intrinsically rewarding lives, does not flourish. One in two Britons want a second, more compassionate career for the last two decades of their working life, alternative therapy being one of the top ten second-career options.

This is the context for reflecting on the modest contributions of New Age spiritualities of life (modest, although every little bit helps.) Sometimes mopping up some of the sins of capitalism; sometimes healing fissures, such as the conflicts between work and life at work; sometimes restoring trust; more or less always aiming to replace alienation and division with connection, the 'rounded life' of the holistic. Returning to the beginning of this book, where I wrote of 'the expressive self undergoing the suffocating squeeze', it can readily be argued that consumer culture provides the context for exercising freedom to compensate for the 'pressure shop' of much of the mainstream. I think it is fair to conclude that for many holistic participants the more vamped-up aspects of consumer culture are themselves a component of the squeeze. Not a form of submersion for the 'whole life'.

In the spirit of Aldous Huxley's 'Experience is not what happens to a man. It is what a man *does* with what happens to him' (1949; my emphasis), I hope I have made some progress in making the case that the 'doing' is well in evidence, and generally is a force for good. And as I now extend the argument, this evaluation is even more pertinent in impoverished countries, where spiritualities of life have vastly more important roles to play that serving the consumptive self-interests of the wealthy.

Epilogue: Birthright Spirituality Beyond the West

> *If religion is a delusion, it is a delusion with a future, which it may be hazardous for us to deny. A shared conception of the soul, the sacred and transcendental values may be a prerequisite for any viable society.* (Richard Shweder, 2006)

> *...the most significant institutional revolution of the twentieth century – the growth of universal human rights.* (Bryan Turner, 2006, p. 6)

> *We need to adopt Sufism in our lives to end oppression and suppression.* (Chaudhry Shujaat Hussain, Pakistan Muslim League president, Dawn, 13 October, 2006, p. 3)

> *Religion can in principle offer a great deal to the public culture of a pluralistic democracy [specifically India].* (Martha Nussbaum, 2007, p. xi)

Although attention is increasingly being turned to the matter, the study of the role played by inner-life spiritualities in developing countries is relatively embryonic. Since the inner-life spiritualities of many of these countries are functioning within different circumstances than those prevailing in the west, consideration is first paid to two of the most significant differences: those to do with religion and poverty. This paves the way for saying something about the jobs which inner-life spirituality can perform in more impoverished lands.

Religion and Poverty

Generally speaking, the population of the world is religious. Adherents.com provides the most reliable and up-to-date information. As of 2005, 33 per cent of 'adherents' belong to the category Christianity, 21 per cent to Islam, and 14 per cent to Hinduism. Just 16 per cent belong to the category 'non-religious' – a percentage which includes atheists, agnostics and secular humanists, together with people who report 'none' or who have no religious preference. Atheists constitute a small subset of this grouping. Many of the non-religious are European. Elsewhere, the situation tends to be very different. Beliefnet.com – which draws on Pearson Education's database – provides the most reliable and up-to-date information on developing countries (as well as those which are in economic decline). As of 2007, 100 per cent of the population of Nigeria is religious (50 per cent Islam, 40 per cent Christianity, 10 per cent indigenous beliefs). The same total percentage applies to Uganda (33 per cent Roman Catholic, 33 per cent Protestant, 16 per cent Islamic, 18 per cent indigenous beliefs), as it does to Pakistan (97 per cent Sunni and Shiite, 3 per cent Christian, Hindu and other).

Most adherents or believers in developing countries are theistic, with a considerable number belonging to what can be thought of as 'hard' forms of tradition. They belong to forms of tradition which emphasize 'The Truth' – forms of tradition which correspondingly regard traditions other than themselves as inferior, false or blasphemous; whose adherents are judged sinful, less than human, inhuman, even non-human.

Under particular sociocultural conditions, tendencies already present within 'hard', exclusivistic forms of theistic religion are likely to become more pronounced. That is to say, their inherent tendencies to disparage, demean and discredit forms of life which deviate from 'The Truth' are exacerbated. Of these conditions, arguably the most important concern poverty and the unequal distribution of resources. According to a December 2006 UN report, the world's richest 2 per cent of adults owns more than half the global household wealth (measured by criteria like land ownership), with half the world's population owning just 1 per cent. More significantly for present purposes, within virtually all developing countries discrepancies between the affluent and the poor are growing. Exploitation is clearly in evidence. Water shortages and population pressures serve to intensify competition for resources among the impoverished themselves. Under these circumstances, hard forms of exclusivistic religion – such as Ten Commandment Christianity in sub-Saharan Africa – serve as vehicles for remedial action, empowering, legitimating and otherwise facilitating poverty alleviation and resource acquisition in ways which target others.

The hardening of theistic traditions widely seen in developing (and regressing) countries today means that liberal forms of religion are under threat. Their very inclusivity, the value attached to respecting the other, helps explain why they do not find it easy to cope with the powers of the exclusivistic. So does the perception among many of the poor that liberal forms of religion are associated with the better educated, the wealthier, an exploitative elite. Furthermore, those foundational values of the ethic of humanity emphasized by liberal theism – in particular the basic equality of all humans – are often seen as 'secular', western-contaminated attacks: attacks on the foundational values of that exclusivistic tradition which alone will lead to a better world.

Birthright Spirituality

Before arguing that 'birthright spirituality' has a great deal to contribute to the lives of the impoverished-cum-religious, the term needs to be introduced. One contrast is with secular renderings of the ethic of humanity, renderings which legitimate the ethic by referring to 'the people' rather than (explicitly) referring to the nature of people at birth. Thus the Preamble of the Constitution of India begins, 'We, the people of India, having solemnly resolved to constitute India into a sovereign social secular democratic republic and to secure all its citizens: Justice . . . Liberty. . . Equality. . . and to promote among them all Fraternity.' In other secular renderings of the ethic of humanity, however, birth is in evidence. Consider, for example, Article 1 of the Universal Declaration of Human Rights, adopted and proclaimed by the UN General Assembly on 10 December 1948: 'All human beings are born free and equal in dignity and rights. They are endowed with reason and conscience and should act towards one another in a spirit of brotherhood.' On one reading of this Article, what can be called 'naked-life' – namely, that which all humans have in common before they are differentiated by society and culture – provides the ontological foundation of the ethic. This is the life humans are born with (hence, 'naked'); the 'life-itself' which is universal; the life which is equally dignified in and of itself; the life with provides the capacities to exercise reason, conscience, freedom and the 'spirit of brotherhood' as maturation takes place. This is the life-in-common which justifies the right to be treated equally before the law, for example. More generally, by virtue of birth, people are entitled to the rights of the UN's Universal Declaration.

Other formulations of the ethicality of naked-life are sacralized. When the sacred is incorporated, values, rights, obligations and moral sentiments grounded in human nature at birth take two broad forms. One is provided by liberal versions of theistic traditionalism. A good illustration is provided by Pope John Paul II. During an Address to the UN General Assembly, he spoke of 'a moral logic which is built into human life'; a moral logic grounded in the fact that 'Each and every human person has been created in the "image and likeness" of the One who is the origin of all that is' (1995, pp. 295, 299). The other is provided by the sacrality of life of and in itself; the spirituality we are all born with; the inheritance of what it is to *be* human. Recall the Dalai Lama's 'basic spirituality'. Good illustrations are also found in the work of Gandhi: 'I know that God is neither in heaven, nor below, but in every one'; 'God is not a Power residing in the clouds. God is an unseen Power residing within us and nearer to us than finger-nails in the flesh'; writing of God as 'the essence of life' (cited by Hay, 1988, pp. 270–1). Gandhi often expressed himself in terms of what we are calling inner-life spirituality. Although he did not greatly favour the legalistic language of human rights, there is absolutely no doubt that he emphasized the underpinning values as forcefully as he could. The values of the God-life embedded in birth-nature.

Some Virtues of Birthright Spirituality

Whether liberal theistic, inner-life non-theistic, or some interrelationship between the two, human rights are grounded, informed and legitimated by a sacred ontology of humanity-itself. In developing countries, where the sacred is widely in evidence, this means that the authority and power of the sacred can be brought to bear to propagate the values and codifications of human rights. To illustrate, although the Constitution of India took a secular form from the moment of its inception, and although Gandhi was not a member of the Drafting Committee, the universalistic spiritual humanism which he did so much to advance helped establish that climate of values – transcending sociocultural differentiations – which facilitated the implementation of the Constitution. Other factors undoubtedly had a role to play (Sarbani Sen, 2007). However, the influence of Gandhian inclusivism, together with the contribution of leaders like Tagore (1961) with his 'religion *of* man' (my emphasis), played a crucial role in paving the way for the greatest of democratic revolutions to date.

The virtues of inner-life spirituality are not limited to the sphere of human rights; are not limited to helping generate that recognition of equality which is required for all adults to be seen as worthy of the right to vote, for instance. The phrase 'ethic of humanity' refers to more than legalistic human rights, especially when they emphasize 'negative freedom' (Berlin, 1969) – that is, freedom from unjustified interference or assault. For it also refers to positive agency: the freedom to develop and express one's capacities; the motivations, moral sentiments, responses to suffering, ethically significant aspects of understanding oneself and others regarding what it is to be truly human. Spirituality present from birth 'as of right' contributes accordingly, Gandhi, for example, writing of 'the transformed conduct and character of those who have felt the real presence of God within'; of his own goal to 'identify myself with life, with everything that lives'; of the fact that since 'God is in every one of us … we have to identify ourselves with [and 'love'] every human without exception'; of his own endeavour 'to see God through service to humanity' (cited in Hay, 1988, p. 271).

To emphasize the role which inclusivistic inner-life orientated birthright spirituality can play in responding to conflictual difference, and its advantages over liberal religion, consider contemporary Pakistan. Here, the main, ostensive point of conflict is between liberal and conservative forms of Islam.

No doubt with leaders of conservative factions having in mind the second sentence of the Preamble of the Constitution of the Islamic Republic of Pakistan, where reference is made to 'the will of the people', as well as articles to do with gender equality (etc.), conservatives criticize or reject the Constitution as 'secular' or worse (c.f. Sachedina, 2007). Since the ruling factions are (currently) committed to the Constitution, they too are tarred by the same brush and are seen as using liberal Islam – which they generally favour – to counter the aspirations of 'true' Muslims: to establish an Islamic theocracy. Accordingly, liberal Islam is not an especially effective vehicle for propagating the ethic of humanity among the more conservative of the population.

This is where inner-life spirituality enters the picture. Increasingly, the attempt by those running the country is to reduce conflict by finding common ground between liberal and conservative forms of Islam – as well as, for that matter, between the Sunni and the Shiite versions of Islam – by appealing to universalistic, humanistic and widely respected Sufi spirituality. A 'third way', found *within* virtually all the numerically significant forms of Islam in Pakistan, including the highly conservative Islams of the 'tribal' areas where the so-called Taliban are active. By virtue of not being associated with any particular form of Islam, the idea is that the Sufi emphasis on what is shared by virtue of the creation of human life can help undermine the clash of localized traditions. And Sufi teachings and practices are peculiarly suited for the task. On the one hand, timeless and placeless; on the other, highly context-specific: meaning that Sufism can so-to-speak shift between the theistic and the non-theistic – thereby appealing to the conservative as well as the liberal. Furthermore, unlike liberal Islam, Sufism in Pakistan is not tarred by the brush of secularity.

Utopian?

Remaining with Pakistan, it is all too easy to dismiss the idea that spiritualities of life – in the form of aspects of Sufism (and other inner-life teachings) – have anything much to offer. Talking with the previous Foreign Minister, Riaz H. Khokhar, now the Prime Minister's Special Envoy for Inter-Civilizational Relations, I was told that 'religion continually gets in the way' of what universalistic spirituality has to offer. 'A great idea', he said, but 'hopeless'.

I begged to disagree. For one thing, I had the President on my side of the argument – the Patron-in-Chief of the National Council of Sufism, working to combat hard forms of exclusivistic, anti-democratic Islam. I also had the leaders of the powerful Pakistan Muslim League on board. The National Council is chaired by the head of the League. As Secretary General of the League, Senator Mushahid Hussain made his case in a recent speech: 'the 500 million Muslims of South Asia owe gratitude to Sufi saints like Syed Ali Hamdani and it was their contribution which projected the true essence of Islam based on love, tolerance and peaceful coexistence'. The

Senator said that his party 'would support all... initiatives for projecting the philosophy of such great Sufi saints since they are rooted in Islam and they are also the antidote of extremism' (reported in *Dawn Islamabad*, 19 October 2006, p. 18).

And it is not as though there is not already a great deal to encourage. According to Jurgen Frembgen (2006), a leading authority on Sufism in contemporary Pakistan, 'the local cultures of Punjab and Sindh in particular are deeply permeated and shaped by Islamic mysticism' (p. 1). 'These lowland regions of the Indus valley are virtually dotted with innumerable shrines', he goes on to write, 'the "abodes of bliss and peace"' (p. 1). Typically emphasizing peace and unity, teaching through practice the importance of helping, caring, and healing those in need, these 'abodes' (including one located behind the centre of government in Islamabad, where Lala Ji Sarkar is a central figure attracting large numbers from diverse walks of life) might not announce the ethic of humanity in formal terms. But the sacralized values and sentiments of the ethic are there.

Another strand of my argument with Riaz Khokhar focused on what can be called 'the influential elite factor'. Whereas popular Sufism in Pakistan revolves around the *murshid* or *pir*, combining (or contextually oscillating between) inner-life spirituality – where the aim is to 'refine the divine qualities hidden in the human soul' (Frembgen, 2006, p. 5) – with a 'theistic orientation' (p.1), among the elite of cosmopolitan cities like Islamabad and Lahore (or cities like Tehran for that matter) 'God-within' aspects tend to come to the fore. Here we find immanentist Sufism taking its place alongside the voluminous mind-body-spirituality literature found in all the major bookshops. Here we find the wife of the Foreign Minister running the largest private school system in Pakistan (and, so it is claimed, the world), Beacon House: inspired by the truth-within 'philosophy' of Maria Montessori – the author of the lines, 'From birth the child has a power in him. We must not just see the child, but God in him. We must respect the laws of creation in him' (1989, p. 98). Here we find the heartlands of inner-life humanistic – and, to an appropriately modest degree, expressivistic – spirituality among the professionals.

In *Modernization, Cultural Change, and Democracy* (2005), Ronald Inglehart and Christian Welzel draw on survey data collected between 1981 and 2001 from 81 countries containing 85 per cent of the world's population, to arrive at the following, interrelated conclusions:

> Socioeconomic development brings cultural changes that make individual autonomy, gender equality, and democracy increasingly likely, giving rise to a new type of society that promotes human emancipation on many fronts. (p. 2)
>
> Socioeconomic modernization involves 'a cultural shift toward a rising emphasis on self-expression values'. (p. 2).
>
> With socioeconomic modernization, 'There is a shift from institutionally fixed forms of dogmatic religion to... spiritual religion'. (p. 31)

Without going into the 'causal' dynamics of the interrelationships involved, the message provided by the survey data is clear. Socioeconomic development, especially evident in the cosmopolitan cities of countries like Pakistan, results in increasing interest in inner-life spirituality. So long as socioeconomic development continues, the opposition to exclusivistic traditionalism is surely going to gain in strength among those who influence national affairs, in particular educationalists (cf. Hefner and Zaman, 2007).

Back to the Poor

Whether it be inner-life or inner-life-cum-theistic forms of Sufism (or equivalents within other traditions elsewhere in the developing world), their significance cannot be emphasized enough. Assuming they grow, that is. For by providing a sacralized basis for the ethic of humanity, more is at stake than contributing to the struggle against radicalized religious exclusivism *per se*.

In Pakistan, the average time spent by girls attending primary school is 1.3 years. In some of the rural areas of the North West Frontier Province which I have visited the veil is rarely worn – the reason being that women have no need of it because they virtually never leave their homesteads during daylight hours. Inequality and oppression is rife. Conservative mullahs work with 'feudal' landowners and their money lenders to exploit the poor of the Punjab. Thinking of healthcare, human life is not equally respected, in particular with regard to budget allocations to provision for the poor, more especially with regard to poor women, and even more especially with regard to that religiously sensitive issue, natal care. In these and many other instances, versions of the ethic of humanity which draw on the authority of the sacred can do a great deal to alleviate poverty and suffering.

Referring to Martha Nussbaum's *Women and Human Development: The Capabilities Approach* (2000), Bryan Turner (2006) writes, 'Economic development cannot take place without the development of social and political rights, and social development cannot take place without women's equality, especially through the provision of education' (p. 80). In Pakistan, as elsewhere, most INGOs, many NGOs and other agencies would concur emphatically. Individual rights, together with the 'right' of communities to have their say, are taken to be a, if not *the*, key to development: by increasing the possibility of income-generating work by enabling girls and younger women to go to school, college or university, for example. And education matters. Accordingly to Inglehart and Welzel's (2005) scale which can be used to measure conformity, Pakistan is currently the most conformist country of all (p. 220). As well as stifling the entrepreneurial spirit, conservative 'replication of the past' teaching methods in Pakistan tend to go together with the exclusivistic, quite possibly the divisive and disruptive – hardly a recipe for the kinds of cooperation required for 'enlightened modernization', as the government calls it. The ethic of humanity in the classroom is called for. Sufi spirituality is just the job: hence Mushahid Hussain of the National Council of Sufism recently announcing, 'a Ph.D. degree programme on teaching Sufism will be initiated in all universities of the country' (*Dawn*, 13 October 2006, p. 3). (See Sachedina, 2007, pp. 52, 60.)

Then there is the matter of 'good work' after formal education. Founded by Sufi mystic and Pakistani financier Aghan Hasan Abedi in 1972, the Bank of Credit and Commerce International grew to be the fifth largest in the world. Ideally, it was run by way of inner-life Sufism. Very much Sufism in engaged, progressive mode, it can be emphasized – a bank whose founder saw as serving the 'under-privileged'; a bank which Abedi wanted to become 'the largest possible organization performing a service to humanity' (cited in Heelas, 1992c, p. 2). Given the fate of the bank, drowned in criminality by 1991, it is easy to be cynical about this attempt to alleviate the lot of the poor via the fulfilment of birthright spirituality via Sufism in practice. However, credence is lent to Abedi's highly expressivistic spiritual humanism by virtue of the consideration that in 1982 BCCI, the United Nations Centre for Human Settlements, and the Government of Pakistan signed an agreement to help develop the Orangi Pilot Project (Hasan, 2005, pp. xxiii–xxiv). Itself under the guidance of inner-life spiritual humanist Akhtar Hameed Khan, the Orangi Pilot Project has since 'helped transform the lives of people in the biggest hatchi abadi of Asia' (Ali, 2006). Poverty alleviation not quite on the scale of Nobel Peace Prize recipient, Muhammad Yunus, and the Grameen Bank of Bangladesh, but certainly a world-famous example, in development circles, of what can be done when grassroots, 'only connect' community-centred activity is inspired by someone committed to birthright spirituality: committed to the motivational, value-laden, sentiment-laden value of spirituality as birthright, a spirituality serving to emphasize the importance of recognizing and including others as equally human, fully deserving good will and assistance when called for; and serving as the critical foundation for human rights in a religious country.

Conclusion

Richard Shweder's (2006) suggestion – that 'A shared conception of the soul, the sacred and transcendental values may be a prerequisite for any viable society' – might be unrealistic and unnecessary (see also Shweder et al., 2004). But it serves to draw attention to the fact that nations are hardly likely to be 'viable' when the sacred forces of the exclusivistic are deployed to overrule those of the inclusivistic. What remains to be ascertained is the extent to which birthright spirituality – the sacralization of human rights, obligations and moral sentiments from within 'naked' human nature – is already at work in developing countries, especially those where the sacred is pervasive, drawing on faith in the sacred to serve values which counter inhuman forms of exclusivistic, repressive or exploitative difference. A vital topic for research, replete with policy implications, addressed by a growing body of literature which I very much hope to contribute to: not least to arrive at a more comprehensive and accurate picture than the one I have been able to provide here. Hesitantly, though, a conclusion about what is developing in Pakistan. The signs are that Sufism has the sacred authority, capacity and appeal to serve as a way of countering at least some of the consequences of capitalist exploitation, whilst also countering that other response to the inequality found in impoverished regions – namely Islam, empowered the 'hard' way. The Orangi Pilot Project has demonstrated what humanistic, inner-life inspiration can contribute; so does the welfare work of the local *murshid* or *pir*. And, it can be added, Sufism has a stature within the Islamic culture of a 'seriously' religious, generally conservative, country which probably explains why there is little evidence of it being used as a hedonistic plaything among the elite. The 'real' sanctity of life itself is too much at stake. Sufism in action. Sufi pantheism or panentheism, not dissimilar from what is found in the works of the revolutionary Thomas Paine – albeit 'beyond' reason; or Shaftesbury's innate endowment (Taylor, 1989, p. 255).

'Life is calling', says a Smirnoff advertisement. In the developing world, the 'calls' of life are rather a more serious matter than calls for alcohol to consume. Vulnerability requires the cultivation of humanity, not consumption. When the sacred is widely abroad, engaged spirituality of an inclusivist nature has a huge amount to commend it. The rights of human life. The wellbeing of the spiritually suffused, grounded, ethic of humanity.

To counter the objection that the cultivation of transhumanistic birthright spirituality in countries like Pakistan is somehow bound up with the colonization of western human rights, the obvious point to make is that indigenous 'traditions' are at work. To counter the objection that the ethic of humanity takes away the unique, the theme is that 'we're all the same and yet different': the same at the basic level of spirituality *per se*; different by virtue of the exercise of autonomy and the particularities of the life circumstances of any given individual. And to counter the objection that birthright spirituality readily comes to be associated with repressive, restrictive ways of life, we can think of Kant's (1959) point that, 'Out of such crooked material as man is made of, nothing can be hammered quite straight' (p. 27). Unless spirituality *per se* is actually at work, the clashes between the values of the sacralized (or not) ethic of humanity can never be resolved, leaving ample scope for choice, debate, even conflict (cf. Hunter, 1999). *The Crooked Timber of Humanity* (Berlin, 1991) does not lend itself to *the* system, *the* world order. Then there is Edward Shils' (1968) related point:

> The proposition that life is sacred is no more than a guiding principle. The forms of human life that are sacred, however, are so variegated, so often in

tension with each other, and so resistant to being placed on a clear-cut scale of degrees of sacredness, that infinitely difficult problems remain in deciding what is permissible or intolerable. (p. 2)

So long as the sacralized values of human life coexist – typically in unresolved tension – rather than being ranked hierarchically, the particularities of self-expression are assured – albeit *within* the values of the ethic as a whole (see Sen, 2006, pp. 16–17). Freedom to consume, for instance, albeit with an eye on the implications for others. Or so it should or could work in practice.

Comparison

In western cultures, I have argued that New Age spiritualities of life are called upon to contribute to the task of sustaining or developing the 'expressive life'. They contribute to 'the resistance': the resistance against the erosion of the expressive, that crucial aspect of the 'fully human', by those powerful forces bent on hierarchical control; bent on focusing ever more on what it is to be human in terms of that supreme target, wealth creation; bent on implementing the maximal 'squeeze' to 'construct' the self in terms of this ultimate goal. The languages and experiences of spirituality, it might be said, serve as a vehicle for critical reflection, with humanistic 'secular' usage also entering the picture by affirming non-materialist experiences or values of much the same order.

Rather than contributing to the perpetuation of the Romantic trajectory of western modernity, enhancing the subjective quality of life, or attending to the 'prosperous discontent' of the better-off, in South Asian cultures spiritualities of life are called upon to do considerably more serious work: ultimately to do with life-itself. Specifically discussing the 'clash of civilizations' *within* India, Martha Nussbaum (2007) writes, 'One civilization delights in its diversity and has no fear of people who come from different backgrounds; the other feels safe only when homogeneity reigns and the different are at the margins' (p. 332). Infused with the love of humanity, of *affinity*, spiritualities of life enter into the resistance which Nussbaum explores in her volume to help combat those who are unable to *live* with others of different persuasions.

Whether west or east, whether in Christian countries like Brazil where theistic aspects are more in evidence (Boff, 1997), spiritualities of life and how they work as ethically laden, universalistic sources of significance, have much in common. Namely, the cultivation of those values of the spirit of life which are disrupted, perhaps eradicated, by the operation of 'systems' which serve to dictate from beyond the person; which maintain that they are 'The Truth'. In this regard, long *live* the spirit of the sixties! Long *live* efforts to erode or bypass 'the encumbering', the 'target-conditioning' of life, the mutilation of the Wordsworthian 'spirit of life'!

232 Epilogue

To end with the birthplace of our son, India. The world's largest democracy; now with the world's largest middle class; and now with a large and rapidly growing mind-body-spiritual-wellbeing sector rooted in both the indigenous and the western (Warrier, 2005; cf. Hatcher, 2007). It will be interesting in the extreme to track how this sector might contribute to the humanistic liberality of so many of the middle class as they experience 'the clash within': Nussbaum's clash within Indian society *and* within themselves as they encounter 'dangerous' difference. Perhaps Tagore's 'classic' expressivistic humanism will thrive yet more as the beacon of life with (a) difference.

> Your children are not your children.
> They are the sons and daughters of Life's longing
> for itself.
> They come through you but not from you,
> And though they are with you yet they belong
> not to you.
> You may give them your love but not your thoughts,
> For they have their own thoughts.
> You may house their bodies but not their souls,
> For their souls dwell in the house of tomorrow,
> which you cannot visit, not even in your dreams.
> You may strive to be like them, but seek not
> to make them like you.
> (Kahlil Gibran, 1976, p. 20)

An extract from *The Prophet*, written by a 'Christian' Arab of a humanistic anarchist persuasion, serving to illustrate birthright spirituality (in effect operating hermaphroditically at the most basic of levels), with the emphasis on life, love and autonomy. Widely read by counter-culturalists during the 1960s, and very considerably more popular today, Gibran's 'way' does not value 'Know yourself' in an intellectual or self-identity sense. What matters is to 'Expand your horizons' – the Romantic theme of moving beyond the mediocrity of life through experience, creation, expression with others (see Waterfield, 1998).

My work is my love. (Sufi dental hygienist, Islamabad)

Appendix: Evidence Indicative of Inner Life 'Beliefs'

First, according to Robin Gill, C. Kirk Hadaway and Penny Long Marler's (1998) review of almost one hundred surveys carried out in Britain, during the 1940s and 1950s, 38 per cent believed in 'God as Spirit or Life Force' – a figure which can be compared with 43 per cent who believed in 'God as Personal'. During the 1990s, however, the respective figures became 40 per cent and 31 per cent (p. 509).

Second, in answer to the question, 'Which of these statements comes closest to your beliefs?', 21 per cent of respondents to the 'Soul of Britain' 2000 survey selected the 'There is some sort of spirit or life force' option, 23 per cent 'There is something there' – a total of 44 per cent, compared with the 26 per cent 'There is a personal God' response. In addition, in answer to the question, 'Independently of whether you go to church or not, which of these would you say you are?', 31 per cent reported 'A spiritual person', 27 per cent a 'religious person' (Heald, 2000).

Third, and turning to Denmark, Lars Ahlin (2006) reports a European Value Systems Study Group finding of a 2000 survey, namely that 'belief in a personal God' rests at 25 per cent. This compares with surveys which show that 21 per cent believe in 'an impersonal higher power or energy' and the 35 per cent that hold the 'god is something that is inside man rather than outside' belief (pp. 1–2).

Fourth, and turning now to Sweden, Eva Hamberg (2003) draws on the 1981 European Values Study to report that 37 per cent affirmed belief in 'some kind of spirit or life force' – another survey showing that this figure had risen to 44 per cent by 1990, with the figures for belief in a personal God dropping from 20 per cent in 1981 to 15 per cent in 1990 (p. 48). (See also Frisk, 2003, p. 244, on percentages from the EVSSG survey of 1990 – and how they compare with her questionnaire study of some New Age groups in Sweden.)

Fifth, to look more closely at the situation in Sweden by drawing on findings from the Enkopingstudien questionnaire (2004; $N = 958$) and comparing them with RAMP figures for the country as a whole (1998; N = 1007), in response to the question, 'Which of the following statements most correctly reflects your view?', 14.6 per cent of the 1,000 or so respondents from Enkoping selected 'I believe in a God with whom I can have a personal relationship' (RAMP Sweden 18 per cent), 16.4 per cent 'I believe in an impersonal spirit or life force' (RAMP Sweden 19.7 per cent), 24.4 per cent 'I believe that God is something within each person, rather than something out there' (RAMP Sweden 36 per cent), 15.3 per cent 'I don't believe there is any sort of God, spirit or life force' (RAMP Sweden 11.6 per cent), and 29.2 per cent 'I really don't know what to believe' (RAMP Sweden 14.7 per cent) (Palmer and Willander, forthcoming, for the Enkopingstudien data; Pettersson and Gustafsson, 2000 for Swedish/Nordic RAMP data). It can be added that according to Harri Heino's (2006) summary of the 1995/6 World Values survey, in Sweden (and Denmark) 'more than half the population (56 per cent) believe in God in a different way from that taught by the church'.

Sixth, now moving west to Norway, Pal Botvar (2006) writes, 'One way to separate the "New Age sympathizers" is to put in one category those who believe in the majority of such New Age ideas as astrology, reincarnation, Karma, fortune tellers and spiritism. By doing this we end up by calling approximately 15 per cent of the population "New Agers." One way to operationalize church orientated religiosity is by making a category out of those who believe in a personal god and regard Jesus Christ to be their saviour (about 20 per cent of the population)' (p. 2).

Seventh, a 2004 survey of the 'religious identity' of urban young adults in the Helsinki metropolitan area, reported by Kati Niemela (2006), finds that 34 per cent identity themselves as 'spiritual but non-religious', a percentage which can be compared with the 8 per cent who are 'religious but non-spiritual' (p. 157).

Eighth, and briefly moving beyond northern Europe, Ralph Hood (2005) reports 'The persistent finding that about 25–30 per cent of individuals in US culture identify themselves as spiritual but not religious' (p. 350).

Ninth, to return to Britain, data provided by Lynda Barley (2006) shows that 26 per cent 'believe in a personal God' and 67 per cent 'believe in God' – which means that 41 per cent believe in a non-conventional or detraditionalized God (p. 2).

Tenth, to think of Scotland and the 2001 Scottish Social Attitudes Survey, Tony Glendinning and Steve Bruce (2006) write, 'The Scottish sample was more or less equally split between respondents who believed in a personal God, those who believed in a "spirit or life-force," those who held a more diffuse belief in "something there," and secular respondents who believed none of these things' (p. 402).

And eleventh, to conclude with an overview of countries, Dick Houtman and Stef Aupers' analysis of 1981, 1990 and 2000 World Values Survey data from a number of European nations shows that 'mean affinity with spirituality' is highest in the Netherlands, followed by Great Britain, Sweden, France, Belgium, and West Germany, southern (Mediterranean) countries, Spain and Italy, being lower (Houtman and Aupers, 2007). The sequence of those not attending church (indicated by 'post-traditionalism') runs along broadly similar lines (Houtman and Aupers, 2007).

Notes

Introduction

1. To say that this is *the* great issue is not to deny that there are other important matters crying out for more attention, However, a considerable amount of progress has recently been made in Europe (in particular) in connection with two other main issues: exploring the question of growth (including current numerical significance) and explaining growth when it is in evidence (including the role played by the fact that at least until very recently significantly more women than men have participated in holistic, mind-body-spirituality activities).
2. The term 'familiar' is used in a similar way to that developed by Kim Knibbe (2007). In her highly illuminating *Faith in the Familiar. Continuity and Change in Religious Practices and Moral Orientations in the South of Limburg, the Netherlands*, she argues that the Spiritual Association of the Hills (and the humanistic Christian Pastoral Centre) serve to '"familiarize" and domesticate authority' (p. 194) – thereby infusing aspects of local, familiar life with religious/spiritual significance.
3. Significantly enough – for it indicates the 'seriousness' with which holistic activities and themes are taken within the mass media, and there is little need to 'take on' those contributing to mass media provisions – contributions are generally favourable; arguably, too favourable. There is not even much joking of the 'Spa Special. The world's best places to get thin, get fit, get spiritual and, erm, get a colonic' variety (front cover, *The Sunday Times Style*, 31 December, 2006).
4. See Herdt (1981), for example, on the efficacy of rites of passage.
5. Inverted commas are placed around the term 'reduction' to signal the fact that fully-fledged reduction is only in evidence when analysis moves beyond participant understanding to another (in this case consumptive) frame of reference, with the latter transgressing the former.
6. The argument was first presented at the Engelsberg Seminar 2001 (published in Almqvist and Wallrup, 2006 – see Heelas, 2006d), later developed as a major theme of the *Spiritual Revolution* volume (Heelas and Woodhead, 2005, pp. 82–94).
7. The 'sixties' is taken to mean the time span between approximately 1965 and 1975, during which period the counter-cultural impetus waxed and waned.

8 In his foreword to Inglehart and Welzel (2005), Klingemann (2005) reports that in 1971 'materialists outnumbered postmaterialists heavily – by about four to one – in...six Western societies...Today, postmaterialists have become as numerous as materialists in all six of these societies' (pp. ix–x). The category 'postmaterialists' is much the same as what others call 'expressive individualism' (Bellah et al. 1985), the cultural terrain of selfhood where one is most likely find explicit use of the language of 'self-fulfilment'.

9 Thus, for Bruce (2002), the New Age has 'little social impact' (p. 91). Putting it rhetorically, he asks, 'where are the New Age schools, nurseries, communes, colleges, ecological housing associations, subsistence farming centres, criminal resettlement houses, women's refuges, practical anti-racism projects and urban renewal programmes?' (p. 97). Comparing the New Age with Methodism, he writes, 'Methodism profoundly changed those people who adopted it and it profoundly changed their society. The New Age has changed very little' (p. 98).

Chapter 1 From the Romantics: The Repertoire

1 Whilst the basic generic terms I use are (the interchangeable) 'inner-life spirituality' and 'spiritualities of life', I am also using affiliated expressions like 'expressive spirituality', 'subjective-life spirituality', 'life-itself spirituality', 'mind-body-spirituality', 'holistic spirituality', 'seminar spirituality', 'wellbeing spirituality', 'birthright spirituality', and 'New Age spiritualities of life'. (I refrain from using the term 'New Age Movement'; given its popularity, the expression 'New Age' is of some value, although it should not be taken to infer that matters astral are especially significant today in holistic circles.) These spirituality are used to draw attention to the differences which exist between – say – the Romantic Movement (expressive spirituality being a useful term here) and the countercultural spirituality of the sixties (subjective-life spirituality now being a useful term). Thinking of the term 'Self', it remains appropriate for those periods when the word 'Self' was used much more frequently than 'life' among participants and in publications, but it is considerably less appropriate today: even with a capital 'S' to signal the universal, the term has too many individualistic connotations.

2 I try to avoid the term 'monism'. It emphasizes the unitary at the expense of the unique; it does not encompass beliefs of the 'God within the individual self, not without' variety, it does not handle criticism of the negative (M.C. Taylor, 2007, p. 298). Neither, do I greatly favour the term 'immanent' in connection with inner-life spirituality. It tends to imply a progression from the transcendent to that which lies within. As for the term 'transcendent', although it is often used in connection with inner-life spirituality to refer to going beyond the lower self to deeper realms, it is best reserved for the kind of transcendence found in traditional Christianity. Thinking of the term 'the new spirituality', the problem is that there is little that is 'new' – other than popularity, that is. Overall, it is best to use other expressions to characterize (aspects of) spiritualities of life, such as 'indwelling', 'life-itself', 'subjective-life spirituality', 'pantheism' (although this term implies that God is everything, which is by no means always the case), and so on.

3 For information on the Kendal Project, see www.kendalproject.org.uk. With the Kendal Project informing much of *The Spiritual Revolution* (Heelas and

Woodhead, 2005), further information is found there. Given that later an essay written in 1999, called 'The Spiritual Revolution' (2002), laid out the main ideas of the Kendal Project and linked volume, and given that I was the Principal Applicant, with 'prime and direct responsibility for the research and its writing up', I should perhaps mention that criticisms of the Project and its main outcomes are best directed at me – in particular the study of the holistic milieu (Heelas and Woodhead, 2005, p. 152). On the topic of holism, it can be noted that there is a spectrum from 'dissolution holism' (where the self dissolves into the whole) to 'individuated holism' (where everything is the expression of the person).

4 The characterizations which follow are based on a very considerable amount of research. It goes without saying that the Romantic Movement, in particular, is of very great complexity and elusiveness (for what is involved in portrayal, see Berlin, 2000; Honour, 1979). It also goes without saying that my focus on several 'waves' of inner-life spirituality does not mean that I am unaware of what has taken place in between the waves. Far from it.

5 It can be noted that a number of popular versions of CAM, to use contemporary parlance, are rooted in nineteenth-century popular romanticism – especially in Germany, where CAM is probably more popular than anywhere else.

6 Interviewing avant-garde artists, James Davidson Hunter and associates (1994) show that the Romantic emphasis on art remains of at least some importance: 'Expression, for these artists, is the measure of our being existence. To express oneself is to participate in the creation of reality, a process coterminous with life itself. Conversely, not to express oneself is not to exist'. 'Life is sacred' is a continual refrain (p. 88).

7 One 'resolution' of this tension lies in seeing the exercise of autonomy as vital for progressing along the path to unity; another lies in the idea of 'a grain of sand in an ocean'. Michel Le Bris (1981) follows this formulation with the lines, 'What the Romantics discovered, or came to believe, following the footsteps of William Blake and Caspar David Friedrich, is that while each grain is unique and irreplaceable, it also contains within it the whole ocean and the whole world' (p. 9). As the title of Gerald Izenberg's (1992) volume, *Impossible Individuality*, indicates, the tension was fundamental – as in Coleridge's 'distinction without division'. On 'the Sun', see Carter (2007).

8 Gordon Kennedy's *Children of the Sun* (1998) tracks the emigration of nineteenth-century German counter-culturalists to the USA, and their contribution, then their descendents', to counter-cultural aspects of life in their new homeland, then later in the 1960s.

9 Written during the early 1990s, *The New Age Movement* (Heelas, 1996a) drew on research largely carried out during the 1980s – the period when dualistic seminar spirituality and prosperity spirituality reached their apogee in western settings. The fact that wellbeing mind-body-spirituality was of relatively little significance during the 1980s explains why it is not emphasized, this also explaining why *The New Age Movement* only serves to provide the background to certain specific aspects of the present work. For more on (arguably) strongly instrumentalized, materialistic prosperity spirituality (of the kind seen in the Successories chain today), see for example Harris (1981, pp. 141–65) and Heelas (1996a); see also chapter 7, below. Douglas Ezzy (2006) draws attention to the rather exceptional: that contemporary 'purveyors of white Witchcraft do not challenge or question the goals of consumer capitalism, but explicitly celebrate them' (p. 15; c.f. 2003).

10 Previously, I have sometimes used the expression 'theistic spiritualities *of* life (see, for example, Heelas, 2002, pp. 366–9). I now think that this is a misnomer, a self-contradiction.
11 This term does not imply that other forms of Christian spirituality are not 'transcendent': the term is used in order to emphasize a particular 'kind' of spirituality. The same point applies to other terms introduced here.
12 Attempts to make the distinction between spiritualities of life and spiritualities/religions for life based on how feelings or emotions are expressed or are otherwise 'toned' are doomed to failure. Matters are too variegated and there is little difference in this kind of regard between a meditation group at Dent and a Friends meeting, for example.
13 During the Kendal Project our resources, together with our theoretical frame of reference, meant that we were not able to devote adequate attention to this 'middle ground', especially among congregants, and those who have been active within – or still retain some links with – congregations. As a consequence, *The Spiritual Revolution* provides an unrealistically polarized picture of the sacred, overemphasizing the 'gulf' between the holistic milieu and the congregational domain to effectively ignore what can be thought of as a middle territory: a middle ground where languages of inner-life and theistic spiritualities are used (Heelas, 2007a). In retrospect, I think we were wrong to agonize about whether certain activities belong to the congregational *or* the holistic camps, finally allocating them to one or the other. The misgivings that I, for one, felt at the time would have been avoided if we had adopted the strategy of drawing up a third category to add to the congregational and the holistic: activities which work with the logically incompatible, namely external *and* internal equally *primary* whilst *different* sources of significance and authority. Not either-or, but both-and (Heelas, 2007a; forthcoming). This said, however, it is often possible to 'allocate' to the holistic milieu or the congregational domain. For example, the former when 'Christian' Richard Schacht (in Phillips and Tessin, 1997) claims that the divine *is* a quality of human experience, nothing more; something *we* should celebrate. It can be noted that the terms 'pantheism' and 'panenthesim', or what Gordon Lynch (2007) calls 'pan(en)theism' (p. 11), do not apply to the middle ground. For these forms of spirituality revolve around one God, thereby not operating with two different and absolute sources of authority. Quakers, for instance, often use inner-life language. But the fact that many retain theism in panen*theistic* mode, typically with a moralistic emphasis, means that these Quakers are probably best thought of as belonging to traditional theistic Christianity. Conversely, pantheistic paths, where immanence is 'total', are probably best considered to belong to the realm of inner-life spiritualities. This said, it is terribly difficult, if not impossible, to draw a boundary line between more egalitarian forms of pantheism (egalitarian by virtue of universal immanence, 'the "One" *as* the all') and more hierarchical forms of panentheism (hierarchical by virtue of the Godhead incorporating human life, 'the all *in* the "One"' ').
14 For a brilliant analysis of the interplay between 'other side' paranormality and spiritualities of inner-life, see Kim Esther Knibbe (2007) – an analysis which includes discussion of consumption. Some of the best statistical (etc.) research on the paranormal has been carried out by Ulf Sjodin (see, for example, Sjodin, 2003). Although 60.5 per cent of respondents to the questionnaire distributed to holistic participants during the Kendal Project agree that there is 'a spirit

world', this is related to in an egalitarian manner – which means that the 'spirit world' enters into New Age spiritualities of life. However, there is almost certainly a spectrum from egalitarian relationships to those where spirits serve as externally powerful agencies. With a spectrum in evidence, it is almost certainly impossible to say 'this is where inner-life spirituality ends; external authority has become too influential' (Heelas, 1996a, p. 35). It is clear, though, that with Christians, atheists and agnostics holding paranormal 'beliefs', the orbit of the paranormal extends well beyond the orbit of inner-life spirituality.

Chapter 2   Wellbeing Spirituality Today

1 In contemporary parlance, the terms 'wellbeing' and 'wellness' overlap considerably in meaning. However, although one can say 'I am worried about my daughter's wellbeing as a voluntary worker in the Sudan', one would probably not use the term 'wellness' in this context. In general, I prefer the more encompassing term, wellbeing. See Baer (2004) on the roots of 'wellness' (p. 91).
2 This figure – to be exact 193,677 as of 2001 – is extrapolated from data provided in Heelas and Woodhead (2005, p. 40). '*Separate* activities' means any activity (say a form of yoga) which is provided by a practitioner for a group/s or for a client/s. A practitioner running four similar yoga groups during a particular week is counted as providing four activities; a practitioner providing the same kind of spiritual aromatherapy for a number of clients during one week is counted as one providing one activity. Many practitioners, it can be noted, run more than one kind of activity. It can also be noted that for reasons discussed in Heelas (2007b), I am now pretty convinced that we underestimated the percentage of the population of Kendal and environs who were participating in the holistic milieu during the week of our 'census'. The figure is more likely to be 2.2 than 1.6 per cent: a figure which is hardly 'minute' (Bruce, 1996, p. 273) (a term which Bruce applies to those 'who have shown any interest', not just to participants); a percentage which, *contra* Bruce (2002), more than serves to 'fill the space left by the decline of just one denomination' (p. 81); and a percentage which is not all that much less than that for all the regular churchgoers of Sweden.
3 Useful information on the topics which are now addressed, and other topics, can be found in Partridge's two volumes (2004, 2005) and in Campbell (2007). Heelas and Woodhead (2005) provide a certain amount of information, including evidence concerning the growth of subjective wellbeing culture and specific activities like yoga. I have box files of relevant material, which unfortunately cannot be drawn on for present purposes. Lambert (1999) presents an overall picture of change.
4 Containing as it does the term 'medicine', CAM is something of a misnomer. Meredith McGuire's (1997) 'non-medical healing' (p. 1) is much more suitable. More data on CAM and its growth can be found in Heelas (2006b); see also Heelas and Woodhead (2005), especially pp. 52–53 and p. 72. It can be noted that an estimated 15 million Americans are involved in some form of 12-step programme, many of which have affinities with CAM. Sharma (2002) provides a useful discussion, with data on 'integrated medicine'.
5 Earle-Levine (2004) and O'Dell (2005) provide data on spas; the latter also providing an illuminating account.

6 Addition of the figures for New Age and Evangelical Christianity provides a figure which is very close to the total – which suggests these are the two major forms of 'spirituality' within the world of business.
7 Albeit only touching on spirituality (see p. 115), Madeleine Bunting's *Willing Slaves* (2004a) provides a first-rate analysis of the dynamics which move companies into the 'soul' and the 'soul' into companies. Good ethnographic material can be found in Salamon and Ramstedt (forthcoming) and Lofgren and Willim (2005). For more general considerations, see Casey (2002) and Giacalone et al. (2005). Ramstedt's portrayal and analysis, 'New Age and Business' (2007), is of considerable value. See also Gockel (2004); Zohar and Marshall (2005).
8 The study *of* religion and/or spirituality in schools is clearly another matter. Here, teachers are not trying to facilitate 'spiritual' experiences, or encourage the adaptation, or intensification, of particular beliefs or truths.
9 See Lau (2000) on New Age suppliers, especially in the USA. More data on provisions is supplied by Redden (2002), including information on market research, trade organizations and trade magazines.
10 The experiential empiricism of inner-life spirituality means that the word 'belief' (or 'faith': Bruce, 2002, p. 79) is not very appropriate. What matters is 'knowing' at first hand, carrying out experiments to find out what is true in experience; what matters is going beyond the beliefs of traditions to experiences of them. The veracity of 'what I *know* to be *true*'. As New Age shaman Leo Rutherford says on a TV documentary, 'Not beliefs but knowledge from within'. On the fragility of 'belief' as a category within our own culture, let alone cross-culturally, see Rodney Needham's brilliant *Belief, Language, Experience* (1972). Galina Lindquist (1997), in her excellent account of neo-shamanism in Sweden, notes the advantages of 'commitment' over 'belief' (p. 258). One can argue that commitment and doubt interplay, sometimes with the former taking precedence, sometimes the latter. As for the term 'faith', many participants are happy to use it in connection with trust ('I have faith in myself'; 'I have faith in you'), but would not be happy with using it as in 'act of faith'. There is no need for such an act when experiential veridicality is in evidence.
11 As for the number of 'believers' who practise alone, although detailed research has yet to be done, indications are that numbers are considerable.

Chapter 3 The Debate

1 Extensiveness of use, and evidence (apparently) supporting Ekstrom and Brembeck's 'trickling into all areas of human life' point, is indicated by Richard Wilk (2004), who includes 'putting a painting on the wall' and 'lying on the beach in the sun' – together with 'flushing the toilet' – as 'acceptable examples of consumption' (p. 16), also writing that 'we consume music' (p. 17). Robert Bocock (1992) includes 'novel reading' and 'ideas of romantic love...in songs and poetry' among the 'patterns of consumption' he discusses (p. 123). Christopher Lasch (1980) states that 'education is itself a commodity, the consumption of which promises to "fulfil...creative potential"' (p. 151), with Howard Newby claiming that 'students are consumers and should be treated as such' (cited by Whybrow, 2006, p. 17). Raymond Tallis (2004) notes how National Health Service patients have come to be called 'consumers'

(p. 89). Colin Campbell (2004) writes of 'goods and services which are consumed by the community (such as defence or law and order)' (p. 28). John Urry has written *The Tourist Gaze* (1990) and *Consuming Place* (1995), the former 'about consuming goods and services which are in some sense unnecessary' (p. 1).

2 See also Sampson (1994), arguing that 'Once established [the] culture of consumption is quite undiscriminating and everything becomes a consumer item, including meaning, truth and knowledge' (p. 31); Lyon (2000), that 'consumerism leaves no area of life untouched' (p. 80); and the editorial of the 2003 Introduction to the *Hedgehog Review*'s issue on *The Commodification of Everything* (p. 5): 'We now live not only in a market *economy*, but also in a market *society*, where the market and its categories of thought have come to dominate ever more areas of our lives'. Smith (2005) provides an excellent formulation of the operation of capitalism in general vis-à-vis the culture: 'Capitalism is not merely a system for the efficient production and distribution of goods and services; it also incarnates and promotes a particular *moral order*, an institutionalized normative worldview comprising and fostering particular assumptions, narratives, commitments, beliefs, values and goals' (p. 176).

3 The Latin *consumere* is defined by the *OED* as 'to take up completely, make away with, eat up, devour, waste, destroy, spend' – largely negative meanings which remain potent today.

4 If intensity of experience is at issue, then this might have to be qualified – that is, if high-risk experience sports, which 'take it to the limit', are counted as belonging to the register of consumption. One might also want to think of drug addicts. However, holistic spirituality (supposedly) enables *everyday* consumer culture to arrive at its 'perfect ending', taking it to its 'cultural extremity' (Heelas, 2001).

5 For more on the meaning of the term 'spiritual revolution', see Heelas (2002) and Heelas and Woodhead (2005); for use of the term in the plural, see Heelas (2006c).

6 I am indebted here to an essay being prepared by Deborah Sawyer for publication.

7 An excellent illustration of strongly traditionalized Christianity is provided by Christopher Hill: 'It [the Church 'down to the seventeenth century'] guided all the movements of men from baptism to the burial service, and was the gateway to that life to come in which all men fervently believed. The church educated children; in the village parishes – where the mass of the people was illiterate – the parson's sermon was the main source of information on current events and problems, of guidance on economic conduct...The church controlled men's feelings and told them what to believe...That is why men took notes at sermons; it is also why the government often told preachers exactly what to preach' (Hill 1955, pp. 10–11). Another excellent illustration, written from first-hand experience, is recounted in Malachi O'Doherty's *I Was a Teenage Catholic* (2003). At the other end of the spectrum under consideration, where the realm of the post-traditional is apparently entered, we find books (for example) with titles like *If You Meet the Buddha on the Road, Kill Him!* (Kopp, 1974) and *On Having No Head* (Harding, 1971). (You can hardly follow a tradition with no head!) In intermediary territory we find, for example, less formal forms of Christianity, where consumeristic trends would appear to be in evidence: see Robert Wuthnow's (1994) study of small groups in the USA for concrete illustrations of (relatively) detraditionalized Christianity, Wuthnow arguing that

many participants are looking for a God who is 'now less of an external authority and more of an internal presence' (p. 3), the sacred becoming more 'serviceable' in meeting individual needs and 'more a feature of group processes' (p. 4). See Heelas et al. (1996) for more on the concept of detraditionalization.

8   A record has been kept of primary material (booklets, leaflets, etc.) of this kind, care having been paid to retaining copies of material which are probably difficult to obtain by readers in the west. Copies are available for research purposes. More generally, given the widespread use of Google and similar search engines, web material which appears in quotation marks, and which is not referenced in this volume, can readily be accessed. One advantage of this is that one can also look at the citations in their broader, webpage contexts. To ensure that a record is kept in case web material gets removed (or changed), a copy of everything has been filed.

9   An excellent, albeit somewhat exaggerated formulation of what is involved in the 'massive subjective turn', is provided by Simmel: 'The essence of the modern is psychologism, the experience and interpretation of the world according to the reactions of our inner selves, as if in an inner world; it is the *dissolving* of all stability in subjectivity' (cited by Rider, 1993, p. 29). Advertisers (etc.) attempt to 'play' with 'the reactions' to satisfy subjectivities accordingly.

10 Without going into details here, together with continually fuelling utopian expectations by the 'what can be achieved if you purchase suitable commodities to make your perfect home perfect with its perfect experiences' kind of message, consumer culture also contributes to the appeal of mind-body-spiritualities by propagating mind-body-spirituality language or themes.

11 Thinking of the quotation from David Tacey with which I began this chapter, it is reasonably clear that Tacey 'believes' in the 'deep primal source'. I should perhaps emphasize that I am not advocating this strategy in the present context. Among those who are *not* afraid to make non-academic judgements of the *reverse* kind, that is, denying the existence of spirituality, it is fair to count Bauman: people might talk about their authentic and true selves, but they are really just striving to become 'perfect *consumers*' (1998, p. 71; my emphasis), with 'fickle and plastic dreams of authenticity and an "inner self" waiting to be expressed' (2001, p. 14).

12 The matter is complicated. If someone were to say, for example, that their spirituality was in their body, a body which *is* physical, research to date indicates that the person would nevertheless probably be referring to spirituality as an 'invisible' or 'mysterious' dimension *of* their body. After all, that is what being holistic is about. (Mysterious) metaphysical physicality.

Chapter 4   The Language of Consumption and Consumeristic Aspects of Mind-Body-Spiritualities of Life

1   An example in connection with Christianity is provided by Grace Davie (2001). She writes, 'those congregations which derive their strength from consumption – i.e. this is something that I choose to do . . . display close similarities to the leisure pursuits of the secular world' (pp. 105–6). A suggestive observation – but without the detailed analysis of the 'close similarities' which it deserves.

2. A *Which?* guide to yoga is only a matter of time.
3. Many schools in Pakistan, including the madrassa-akin establishment facing me across the road from where I am writing (whose motto is 'Learning with Faith'), are populated by 'consumers' according to Stark's definition.
4. As should be apparent from the section of the last chapter on the limitations of academic inquiry, it suffices to make the point that I do not think that it is possible for academics to study whether 'spiritual purists' like Chogyam Trungpa (1973) are correct when they claim that the task of moving beyond the blocks set up by 'ego' or 'lower self', in anything like a successful manner, takes a considerable amount of time.
5. 'Do you believe in horoscopes and things like that?', journalist Jose Olivar asks Sophia Loren. 'I do when they say nice things, otherwise I forget about them', comes the response (Olivar, 1996, p. 7). As long ago as 1970, Benita Luckmann wrote of the private sphere where 'man is free to choose and decide on his own what to do with his time, his home, his body, and his gods' (1970, p. 581)
6. 'Western' religion-cum-popular spirituality is also seen as undergoing the same process, journalist Jonathan Freedland (1998), for example, writing that '*The Little Book of Calm* works by offering the comforts of religion, with none of the aggregation'.
7. Fortunately, for the purposes of this volume there is no need for us to enter the tricky ethical territory of the rights and wrongs of 'expropriation', 'appropriation', 'cultural rights' and the claim of 'cultural theft' (see Brown, 2004, for an excellent discussion). The empirical, ethnographic matter of whether 'ransacking' other cultures for spirituality, as it is sometimes put, leaves little or nothing for the recipient is returned to in chapter 6.
8. As it has been said, clothes have more to do with identity than the weather.
9. On 'counter-cultural' articulations of individuality and uniqueness, see Heath and Potter (2006); and see Thomas Frank's *The Conquest of Cool. Business Culture, Counterculture and the Rise of Hip Consumerism* (1998).
10. The matter of materialistic prosperity spirituality was introduced in chapter 1 and is returned to in chapter 7.
11. Critics have a field-day with this kind of material: spirituality put to use as a component of the '25 Steps to Happy, Healthy Partying', as a magazine article by Jacqui Ripley (2002, p. 311) is called; the 'God is unlimited. Shopping can be unlimited' claim of Ray (1990, p. 135), with spirituality helping 'attract more prosperity and fun to yourself' (p. 130).
12. In their eminently useful volume, which argues that 'the consumer has become a totem pole around which a multitude of actions and ideologies are dancing', Gabriel and Lang (2006) work with the following 'faces of the consumer': the consumer as 'chooser', 'communicator', 'explorer', 'identity-seeker', 'hedonist', 'artist', 'victim', 'rebel', 'activist' and 'citizen' (p. 8). Those senses which bear on creativity, activity and self-fulfilment are discussed later in the present volume. Alan Aldridge (2003), in another extremely useful book on consumption, provides a discussion and elaboration of Gabriel and Lang's map of senses (pp. 10–22). Additional works addressing themes we have been looking at include Caru and Cova's edited collection, *Consuming Experience* (2006), and Lash and Lury's *Global Culture Industry. The Mediation of Things* (2007).

Chapter 5 The Sacred and the Profane: Spiritual Direction or Consumer Preference?

1. Carrette and King (2005) tend to use a somewhat different strategy, one which is less frequently encountered among scholars, although common among New Age activists – mainstream-critiquing, engaged forms of spirituality-cum-religion are used as the touchstone to identify the consumeristic.
2. Together with the evidence of skill provided by participant observation (including from my own research), skills are demonstrably required in order to cater for discerning, predominantly professional mid-life women who provide the main clientele, whose jobs (or previous jobs) in person-centred careers have provided them with the (relatively) sophisticated ability to spot the less-than-skilful, let alone rubbish. Indeed, numbers have (or have had) careers which require psychological expertise. Regarding the matter of 'judgement', Michael Brown (1997) provides a sophisticated analysis. If judgements are too harsh, it can be added, the harmony of the 'learning environment' of holistic activities is likely to be disrupted. In general, the aim is to ensure that person-person judgements are made on the basis of 'experience' which includes others. Given that everyone is equally spiritual, ultimate judgements are ruled out of court.
3. Evidence for this kind of liberation, including reference to those who have taken early retirement from careers in the heartland of capitalism, is provided by Houtman and Aupers (forthcoming).
4. 'Emotional tone' should not be taken to imply that the same kind of emotional tone is found across all activities. Far from it: some, like 'stilling' meditations, are predominantly quietist; others include 'spells' of cathartic release.
5. The relationality of holistic activities is one of the major themes explored in *The Spiritual Revolution*: see, for example, Heelas and Woodhead (2005, pp. 27–9, 96–105). The importance attached to relationality obviously goes together with the value attached to the theme of holistic integration. Relationality incontestably facilitates recognition, validation, legitimation. Obviously, the relationality is encouraged by the relatively non-judgemental or tolerant tone of most activities today, this in turn being bound up with the value ascribed to each and every life.
6. Discussing Colin Campbell's (1987) analysis of 'imaginative hedonism' (pp. 88–95), John Urry (1990) writes, 'If Campbell is right in arguing that contemporary consumerism involves imaginative pleasure-seeking, then tourism is surely the paradigm case. Tourism necessarily involves daydreaming and anticipation of new or different experiences from those normally involved in everyday life' (p. 13). However, for Urry, 'such daydreams are not autonomous; they involve working over advertising and other media-generated signs, many of which relate very clearly to complex processes of social emulation' (p. 13). Although the imagination is clearly influenced by cultural provisions, the participant testimonies which we will look at in chapter 6 surely provide evidence that consciousness, awareness, senses of significance, can be expanded in experience.
7. The (Romantic) theme of growing with and through others, of the self-in-relation, is central to the analysis of holistic activities carried out in Heelas and Woodhead (2005, e.g. pp. 27–9). Aikedo provides an excellent example of a

holistic practice in which relationality is strongly emphasized: to work, it is imperative that participants pay the closest of attention to each other – not just by way of their movements, and their movement-integrated discussions, but also by way of discerning what lies behind talk (and other noises) and movement (a theme explored by Dia Miller whose Ph.D. I am supervising). As Amitai Etzioni (1990) formulates the general point, 'The I's need a We to be' (p. 9).

8   Hasselle-Newcombe's (2005) case study of Iyengar yoga arrives at a similar percentage. Although not enough systematic research has been carried out to be entirely sure, it is highly likely that the 80 or so per cent figure is typical of the situation in Britain (and probably elsewhere, in countries like Holland and Sweden). For more data, and discussion, see Heelas (2007a, 2007b; Heelas and Houtman, forthcoming). On the representativeness of data from research in Kendal, see Heelas and Woodhead (2005, esp. pp. 52–3).

9   For further discussion of the ethic of humanity, in more secular and in more sacred modes, see Heelas (1996c, 1996d, 2001). The evidence demonstrating the significance of the ethic of humanity within holistic circles is incontestable: elements of the ethic, if not the ethic more or less as a whole (Bloom, 2004), appear time and time again, not just in activities but also in the literature, films, etc. Furthermore, given the backgrounds of the people participating in activities, it can hardly be doubted that the great majority adhere to the ethic. Thinking of what might be called 'motivational monism', together with the motivations associated with the values which are experienced as 'flowing' from the universal, there is the basic sense that 'you *are* me and I *am* you' – to be valued accordingly. See Tipton (1982, 1983); for more on the 'emotional' current of humanistic sentiments, see below, chapter 9; and Taylor (1989, pp. 248–65).

10 Reflecting on a course on Buddhist spirituality which he had taken, Lin Fang-ju (1995) writes: 'The emphasis was on life and living, and the Professor made an observation that we should not slavishly follow the views of others, but with freshness and vigour, act according to our own personal views in judging people, the material world, and various other issues' (p. 46). I mention this because even if it were the case that practitioners expected participants to 'slavishly' follow their views, participants might well not require it: as we shall see, many are already of a postmaterialist orientation – and so require little if any encouragement, let alone strict leadership, to lighten the load of whatever issues they might have with the material world.

11 Evidence for moral individualism/the expressive ethic within holistic activities is summarized in Heelas and Woodhead (2005). See also Heelas (1996a) for evidence concerning this ethic during earlier periods of the development of the New Age.

12 As the foremost sociology of religion critic of rational choice theory, with the importance that theorists of this persuasion attach to preferences and needs, it is interesting to note that Bruce also emphasizes preferences.

13 During the two years he spent preparing for death, my father frequently spoke of his burnt-out shell – as opposed to his *lively* spirit. It will be interesting to see how widely this kind of language will be adopted as those who came of age during the sixties enter the dying zone.

14 A very considerable amount of evidence, going back to studies of the sixties, shows that there is a strong connection between holistic participation or inner-life 'beliefs' and those who already hold humanistic, expressivistic or

postmaterialistic values. As well as Heelas and Woodhead (2005), see for example Inglehart and Welzel (2005), Houtman and Mascini (2002), Grant et al. (2004) and Heelas (1996a). The significant matter of the *intentions* or *motivations* of those participating in mind-body spiritualities is looked at in the next chapter – where we will see that the thrust is towards the non-materialistic rather than using spirituality as a means for materialistic ends. Even in the heartlands of capitalism, where one might expect utilitarian spirituality to flourish, it appears that those attracted are of an expressivistic/humanistic persuasion. Rather than being converted to this persuasion, the evidence quite clearly shows that in the great majority of instances this is already their outlook on life.

15 See Heelas and Woodhead (2005) for information on downsizing.
16 See chapter 1. It can be added that we found virtually no signs of money-making, instrumentalized prosperity spirituality in Kendal and environs when we carried out the Kendal Project (Heelas and Woodhead, 2005, p. 30).
17 See also Partridge (1999) on modernist conceptions of truth.
18 Prior 'experience' or 'knowledge' derived from mind-body-spirituality literature or other sources of information is indicated by responses to question 20 of the holistic questionnaire used during the Kendal Project (www.kendalproject.org.uk). Among other findings, 60 per cent of respondents say they have read 'spiritual or religious' (not specifically Christian) books or magazines. It is unlikely that many started reading once they had come to participate. Thinking of how the literature can contribute to the 'solidity' of holistic activities (and 'beliefs'), *contra* all those such as Bruce who maintain that the literature, activities, etc., are too fragmented, with too many different messages, 'to create a cultural movement with momentum' (Bruce, 2000, p. 234; see also Hunt, 2005, p. 169), there is very considerable consistency of message, which can thus help 'solidify' (reinforce, lend plausibility to) reception. Andrew Ross (1991) even goes so far as to argue: 'In the absence of any central institutional forum, its networking communities and the internal debates about the direction of the New Age movement (quite explicit in the pages of prominent magazines like *New Age*) take on the function of *regulating codes* that hold the disparate range of practices and disciplines together' (p. 72; my emphasis). See also Partridge (1999) on 'some common themes running through New Age thinking' (p. 78); Redden (2005) on 'recurrent motif[s] in teachings' (p. 232), the 'New Age lingua franca' (p. 238) and the presence of 'established themes' (p. 240); Aupers and Houtman (2006); and compare Lewis (2007). Specifically thinking of practices, these commonalities have a great deal to do with the fact that activities almost always show internal coherence – not rag-bag, cobbled-together *bricolage*: an integrative quality which also owes a great deal to the skill of practitioners in interfusing, say, tennis and Zen to arrive at Zennis; and to the theme of the universal. See Hervieu-Leger (2006); Heelas (2006a, 2007a). On the role of 'cultural language' as a 'cultural resource' which helps 'guide' what is called 'reflexive spirituality', see Besecke (2001, 2005). Regarding the feedback process, Stark (2006) makes the general point that 'An individual's confidence in religion is strengthened to the extent that *others express* their confidence in it' (pp. 55–6). Wood (2007), it can be noted, emphasizes the role of social authority and spirit possession (the latter replicating and enhancing the former). I would prefer to emphasize the ways in which spirit guides (etc.) contribute to cohesiveness by serving as 'additional' practitioners.

19 A great deal could be said about how *action*-based learning environments operate ethically. From the practitioner's perspective, the publications of the most influential of all yoga teachers – B. K. S. Iyengar – are recommended (e.g. Iyengar 2005). Strauss (2005) is illuminating on yoga from an academic viewpoint; more generally, see also Heelas (2006a), and below, chapter 8. Anthropologist Roy Rappaport (1999) argues that ritual is the basic *social* act.
20 It should be emphasized, though, that if those participating in one-to-one activities (where there is no danger of upsetting the progress of the group) request the pleasures of the comfort zone, practitioners might acquiesce.
21 Thinking of the fact that just 7.6 per cent of holistic respondents to the questionnaire of the Kendal Project stated that they had been attracted by reasons to do with pleasure, enjoyment or a treat, few exercise the authority of the payment to ask for 'mere' pampering, perhaps trumping the authority of the practitioner in the process.

Chapter 6 The Matter of Personal Significance: Profaned Superficiality?

1 I am not for one moment implying that superficiality reigns supreme in everyday purchasing culture. For robust arguments demonstrating the significance, the *value* of shopping, arguments which draw attention to the importance of purchasing for others and the exercise of thrift, see Daniel Miller (1998).
2 Only a handful of the 252 people who responded to the questionnaire answered with a 'none'.
3 The greater the seriousness of intentions, the less the likelihood of 'mere' preferences ruling the roost – a point which can be added to those made in the last chapter. Lyon (1994b) argues that in postmodern culture religion and spirituality have 'become a neatly packaged consumer item – taking its place among other commodities that can be found or bypassed according to one's *consumption whims*' (p. 62; my emphasis); as he also writes, New Age 'clearly has little to do with the conventional monotheism of Christianity and much to do with the market place ... of religion and quasi-religious elements focused *on self and choice*' (1994a, p. 117; my emphasis). In similar vein, Bibby (1987) writes of religion and spirituality as 'commodities that can be bought or bypassed according to one's consumption *whims*' (p. 2; my emphasis). The presence of significant intentions is clearly incompatible with 'I feel like a spot of . . .' whims.
4 Like Muir, Catherine Garrett (1998) provides an illuminating, academically informed account of participant understanding and experience. CAM research is becoming increasingly sophisticated: see, for example, the House of Lords report (2000), Lake and Spiegel (2007) and the many articles in the journal *Complementary Therapies in Medicine* on therapeutic benefits (or not). For first rate research on the efficacy of spirituality, see King et al. (2006) and Walsh et al. (2002). For an exploration of the significance of spirituality for 'midlife transition', see Geertsma and Cummings (2004). Barraclough's edited volume, *Integrated Cancer Care* (2001), is most helpful; so are the growing number of volumes on nursing and mental health care, including Koenig (2007), Lake and Spiegel (2007), O'Brian (2002), Taylor (2007) and White (2006). For a review,

see Heelas (2006b, pp. 70–1). Although it does not focus specifically on inner-life spirituality, Robert Wuthnow's *All in Sync* (2005) contains a judicious appraisal of the 'spirituality is shallow' claim (pp. 21–55). On CAM in general, whilst that arch-critic Dawkins rejects participant testimonies of efficacy as 'anecdotal', he rather contradicts himself by saying, 'The belief, I'm sure, is therapeutic' ('The Enemies of Reason', Channel 4, 20 August 2007).

5 Kendal Project questionnaire results show a certain *intensification* of spirituality. With active involvement, 'looking for spiritual growth' overtakes 'health and fitness' as the most important reason for participation. According to Voas and Bruce's (2007) analysis of the Kendal Project data, 33 per cent were originally 'looking for spiritual growth', a percentage which rises to 41 with participation. Also on the subject of 'arriving with' spirituality, see Hasselle-Newcombe's (2005) discussion of a 'pre-existing orientation towards spirituality' (p. 24). See also Heelas (2007b). 'I used to be an atheist until I realized I *was* God', it says on a card I received recently: a rare event in connection with any form of the sacred.

6 Thinking back to the last chapter, a major reason for coherence of practice is that practitioners have a common stock of themes to draw upon, not least provided by the mind-body-spirituality literature and that experiential, perennialistic interpretation of 'different' religious traditions which is characteristic of the genre.

7 Although it cannot be gone into here, much supports the contention that New Age spiritualities are not primarily about meanings as explanations, let alone serving to provide 'identity'. Rather than talking about 'meanings', it is frequently more appropriate to refer to 'meaning*ful* experiences'. Regarding identity provision, the ongoing *process* of healing, say, is not best described in terms of the language of identity, including, in many instances, those to do with gender (Heelas, 2008b). The processual, the potential, the possible, the unfolding, the interruption, the dynamic, and, it can be added, the mysterious, are much more useful terms than 'identity'. So are expressions like 'restoring faith in ourselves' after having experienced 'low self-esteem' (expressions frequently deployed by Oprah Winfrey) (Harris and Watson, 2007). Obviously, meanings enter into experiences, feelings, sentiments and so on; and as we shall observe later, meanings-*as*-purposes are also important. Purposes, the purposes of life (perhaps sharing what one has to offer with others) are not properly reducible to matters of identity. The language of identity, of identity politics, primarily belongs to the rhetorics of collective, essentialized, quantifiable formations – not the conflictual, creative diversity so characteristic of human life (Berlin, 1991). Indeed, there is much to be said of the contention that the thrust of New Age spiritualities of life, with their 'open' horizons, is to enable participants to liberate themselves from the restrictive horizons of socially 'laid down' role, national, ethnic, etc. identity formations to experience the less determinate (see, for example, Heelas, 1996a). In measure, to 'de-identify'.

Chapter 7   Work: Consumptive or Productive?

1 Thinking of myself, the (hopefully creative) effort put into writing this book has seemed to depend on the consumption of nicotine.
2 The same is not so true of provisions, some of which promise more or less automatic, passive intake, change (see chapter 4).

3 A 'half-alive' to 'near-alive' to 'fully alive' route facilitated by confrontation is brought brilliantly to life by the film and novel, *Fightclub*.
4 The texts drawn upon by Elster include those where Marx-the-Romantic is clearly in evidence. The 'utopian' (Elster, 1986, p. 101); the 'essential nature' of the human (p. 120); the value of expressivity.
5 Campbell's approach, developed in his seminal *The Romantic Ethic and the Spirit of Modern Consumerism* (1987), has certain affinities with Jackson Lears' (1983) work. For the latter, products are idealized by advertising. 'Therapeutic promotion' aims to 'arouse consumer demand by associating products with imaginary states of wellbeing' (p. 19), as vehicles for self-realization. They provide therapeutic outcomes for the consumer for whom selfhood has 'grown fragmented, diffuse and somehow unreal' (p. 4): an idea which first became pervasive in the marketing cultures of the late nineteenth and earlier twentieth centuries when the shift of emphasis from informational advertising to therapeutic 'imaginary' states of wellbeing took place. Freud's nephew came to play a major role in this development.
6 Use of the term 'productive' should not be taken to imply 'production' as in 'mass production', for example. In many ways, New Age activities are best thought of as a 'craft', a term which has come to belong to the realm of individualistic expressivism. Were it not for the fact that it is too individuated, too much smacking of cobbled 'together' *bricolage*, the expression 'do-it-yourself spirituality' has much to be said for it, alluding as it does to the theme of 'making'.
7 I write 'generally speaking' because there are examples which flow against the tide. In several departments at Lancaster University, including my own, recent moves have meant that administrative jobs are now 'measured' before they are done (from a sociological point of view, an ideal case study...). Writing of 'targets, targets everywhere', Briscoe (2005) provides a useful discussion of 'target setting terms' (p. 41) (he lists 25), 'the measurement culture' (p. 40), and the pros and cons of working with targets.
8 Issues about paid work and inner-life spirituality which fully deserve further attention are legion. Are we witnessing a capitalist trick – the velvet glove in an iron cage? Is it best to speak of the employee in terms of 'make up' (du Gay, 1996, p. 53), even 'making it up', *or* 'making out'? Then there is the matter of the self-employed, setting their own targets, having greater freedom to link means with ends, and engaging in their own self-monitoring. There is also the matter of spiritual humanism entering into ethical businesses, a development which the Dalai Lama is especially interested in advocating: see, for example, his introduction to Wedemeyer and Jue's *The Inner Edge. Effective Spirituality in Your Life and Work* (2002), an exploration of 'inner values'. A great deal more could be said about how inner-life spirituality is advocated as a way of 'transforming' workplace ethicalities for the better; see, for example, Heelas, 2008b; for a more general discussion, see Carrette and King (2005, pp. 169–82). In addition, there is the issue of the relationship between horizons and targets. Can it be argued that targets can serve to 'stretch' the self within existing horizons, thereby opening up new horizons?

Chapter 8   A 'Fag Ending' of the Sacred or Fit for the Future?

1 I should emphasize that the image of the 'fag' only refers to cigarettes. Briefly mentioning the 'fag ending' argument in connection with Christianity, Davie

(1994) argues that those who stop going to church or chapel on anything like a regular basis 'drift' away from whatever orthodox Christian beliefs they might have held in the first place (p. 76). Having ceased to be immersed in congregational life, and with the culture no longer doing much to transmit Christian teachings, people's beliefs become increasingly attenuated, inconsequential, vague or 'nominal' (p. 43). A considerable amount of belief, in other words, amounts to something approaching the last flicker of Christianity – perhaps set to fade away altogether in the near/ish future. At the same time, however, Davie states that 'Nominal (as opposed to organized) Christianity...provides a rich seedbed for alternative [New Age, etc.] versions of the *sacred*' (p. 43; my emphasis). Without going into the issue of whether an important 'seedbed' lies here, Davie's use of the term 'sacred', together with her statement that 'the New Age provides yet further evidence that the British are far from being – or becoming – a secular society in any strict sense of the term, "particularly if by that omnibus adjective we mean an increasing approximation of average thinking to the norms of natural and social science" (Martin, 1969, p. 107)' (pp. 83–4), shows that she belongs to the ranks of those who see much of Christianity entering the fag-ending zone, with the New Age being on a different trajectory with regard to secularity.

2 Hanegraaff's (1998) account is qualified by the consideration that he also writes of a 'qualitatively new syncretism of esoteric and secular elements' (p. 521).

3 'Get spiritual', writes Wilde (2005) in her 'Vanessa Wilde's Secret Diary' on 'extreme beauty', in the 'Style' section of the *Sunday Times*, continuing: 'I've always known that thinking beautiful thoughts makes you beautiful – very good for stress and toxins and your skin tone – and kabbalah is still very now, obviously' (p. 30).

4 Recall what has already been said, most noticeably in chapter 1, concerning the relative unimportance of prosperity teachings today. There are not even that many of the 'best of both worlds' (wealth within and without) people around in most western settings.

5 Of the many volumes on this-worldly orientations found in *all* the 'major' religions, I just refer to Lise McKean's *Divine Enterprise. Gurus and the Hindu Nationalist Movement* (1996).

6 Fierce attacks from within the medical establishment are also no doubt due to prestige, turf-war factors.

7 During the autumn of 2001, 30 per cent of the acts of weekly participation involved respondents to the holistic milieu questionnaire of the Kendal Project who were *currently* practising more than one activity; on average, *all* respondents had previously been involved with six of the activities comprising the milieu in 2001, a figure which rises if one included their current activities; 55 per cent meditate at home, 46 practise yoga (also at home) and 60 per cent read relevant literature (www.kendalproject.org.uk; Heelas, 2006a, p. 235; as well as the website, the list of current activities can also be found in Heelas and Woodhead, 2005, pp. 156–7).

8 Writing of 'employees consumed or used', Paul du Gay (1996, p. 174) illustrates how the language of consumption readily gravitates to 'use' contexts.

9 Although it smacks of market promotion, I am happier with the term 'do-it-yourself religion' (used by Cor Baerveldt, 1996, for example) – more of the 'making', less of the consuming, is clearly implied.

10 'Beliefs' enter the market in that they are associated with particular products. It is highly unlikely that they are sold *per se*, with people purchasing 'belief' *in* holistic spirituality. See chapters 2 and 4.

11 Providing a powerful index of the extent to which spiritualities of life have entered the mainstream, journalists and newspaper editors – who are in the best position to do any influential 'dirty work' – do not often rubbish New Age mind-body-spirituality as consumer dross. Far from it. Generally speaking, the message is one of positive benefits or significance. This cultural input serves as a massive counter-weight to whatever negative messages nurses, teachers and so on might receive from more academic quarters. Regarding the (apparent) role of opiates in connection with the placebo effect, 'hippies' would surely applaud.

12 The figure for Great Britain was probably more than that in 2001 (Heelas, 2007b); it is almost certainly higher today.

13 See Nussbaum and Sen (1993) for useful discussions of the meaning of 'substantive', namely those 'elements that make human life valuable' (p. 5). See also Taylor (1994) on the distinction between 'procedural' forms of moral commitment and those of a substantive nature, the later 'concerning the ends of life' (p. 92).

14 See Taylor (1994) on the clash which can occur between 'the ideal of authenticity' and universal human values (p. 82). It can be borne in mind that clashes are also minimized by virtue of the fact that 'the unique' derives from the sum of one's life-experiences. Although the 'voice' coming from within might be experienced as the ultimate values of one's true-cum-'universal' self, expressive ethicality flows through one's own socialized, 'experience-full' self. Since no one else has had the experiences, the education, the socialization that one has had oneself, since spirituality is experienced as flowing through, or expressed through, one's own 'blocks', 'barriers' or 'divisions', the unique is firmly in evidence (cf. Tipton, 1982, p. 284). 'Big truths' (Partridge, 1999, p. 80) are relativized in the sense of being experienced in the context of one's unique life. This is neither 'unmediated universalism' nor 'unmediated individualism'.

15 Significantly, the language of 'needs' – widely deployed within the NHS, for example – often explicitly frames the teleological in terms of the deontological. NHS Forth Valley (2004), for example, refers to 'A need to give and receive lov...A need to be valued as a human being...A need to express feelings honestly' (p. 1).

16 Although there is no hard and fast line to be drawn, activities, teachings and beliefs which emphasize structure, dictation, external authority or hierarchy to the extent of generating what is taken to be conformism or dependency – rather than experiences of the liberation, freedom or expressivity of the unique – should not be included within the camp of New Age spiritualities of life (Heelas, 1996a, 2007a; forthcoming).

17 And if there is a Freudian 'I know better than you, I've seen it all before' operative on occasion – which, human nature being what it is, there surely must be – it is unlikely to interfere with a key point of good practice – to acknowledge and nurture the true self of the participant/s. For to interfere would encourage participants to leave.

18 Issues under consideration here intersect with major debates in related fields of inquiry. Thinking of the controversy over the nature and exercise of authority

within more secular forms of therapy, there are those such as Giddens (1991) who emphasize 'the reflexive project of the self' (p. 180); then there are those such as Furedi (2004) who emphasize the substantive and therefore the imposition of conformity. There is also, of course, the debate within consumer culture studies – between the passive, 'taken in by', victim approach and the activist, meaning-making consumer. The literature on self-help is relevant as well.

19 Only interested in religious-cultural traditions of 'lasting and visible societal importance', Weber adopted a 'scathing attitude towards [the] individualistic, diffuse religious tendencies [found in] industrial societies' (Robertson, 1978, p. 55). I wonder what he would make of the fact that spiritualities of life of much the same kind that he saw around him are very much alive and well today.

20 Enough is known from a range of sources to be reasonably sure that the 'balancing act' account is along the right lines and worthy of further examination: to explore the ways in which 'non-directive directions' operate, for example. Further research is also required to try to arrive at a better idea of the numbers who experience a basically similar 'Durkheimian' sacred of expressivistic-cum-humanistic values and sentiments. Conversely, more research is required to arrive at an overall determination of the extent to which 'marks' of consumption are in evidence with regard to those engaging with activities, services or products. As for the future vitality of New Age spiritualities of life, the reader is referred to the closing chapter of Heelas and Woodhead (2005). Inglehart and Welzel (2005) provide a valuable account of the cultural trends – most significantly involving 'self-expression values' (p. 3) – which will surely sustain momentum in the future, especially if those holding these values feel suffocated by increasing restrictions within the workplace, the restrictions encouraging them to seek 'alternative' contexts for 'growth'. At a time when belief and externally imposed duties are progressively being replaced by experiential, New Age versions of the biblical 'O taste and see that the Lord is good' (Psalm 34: 8) within the sphere of the sacred, humanistic expressivists seeking deeper growth or 'richer' lives will almost certainly be attracted in increasing numbers. Especially as there is the 'pool' of around a third of the adult population who appear to 'believe' in 'the God within and not without' to serve as a basis for the future. And especially with so many seeking to downsize; to find 'Zenployment' (*Daily Telegraph*, 11 May 2007, p. 15).

Chapter 9 Inside Out

1 It can readily be argued that the psycho-ethical tyranny of the ethic of comfort, seen for example in the ways in which harassment legislation is formulated, owes a considerable amount to the value which 'feeling comfortable' has been accorded by that major comfort-promising feature of western society: consumer culture.

2 Hunt (2005) attaches considerable significance to the privatization of alternative spiritualities (pp. 150, 173).

3 Hugh Honour (1979) is among all those who have drawn attention to the emotionally charged aspects of that primary source of the expressivist strand of modernity, Romanticism: the artist as 'a passionate individualist'; the importance

of the '*way* of feeling' (p. 14; my emphasis); the 'inner truth' of 'emotional "authenticity"' (p. 20). Although many of the Romantics certainly expressed the sentiments of the ethic of humanity, it is of course true that their art far transcended the compass of what is expressed today by holistic participants.

4 Since virtually nothing is known about the behavioural consequences of the inner-life 'beliefs' held by the large numbers of Britons who 'believe' but (apparently) do not practise, the matter is not pursued any further for now.

5 Arguably, the focus on subjective-life *per se* is most likely to be found among those who feel homeless at home: the lonely, the retired who live alone; the elderly who have lost many of their friends and longstanding neighbours; the ill, where the 'home' has become the hospital or hospice; those who have just retired and experience the loss, perhaps shock, of losing their 'outside' life. The focus on subjective-life *per se* could very well be in evidence among those who are intent on 'finding life again' after having had to leave what they have experienced as the 'iron cage' of the workplace.

6 Discussed in volumes edited by Lynne Hume and Kathleen McPhillips (2006) and Jeffrey Kaplan and Helene Loow (2002), more radical oppositional, often inner-life, organizations or networks function today. Typically, though, they are small in size.

7 It is wonderful that research is now underway, such as Knibbe (2007) and in my own department, research students looking at the significance of holistic activities, and 'sacred texts', for people's self-understanding and daily lives. It could be argued that Victor Turner's (1974) account of how 'communitas' operates is helpful. Perhaps it is in general, context-setting terms – but is marred by being unduly speculative. Naturally, the most formidable problem facing research is that the significance of subjective realities, like 'loving others', is terribly difficult to gauge, precisely because so many aspects are beyond the measure of the quantitative. Deploying ingenious research strategies, Siobhan Chandler (2008, forthcoming) paves the way for the future. An outstanding essay, helping to confirm the 'socially engaged' thesis.

8 The administration of the Third Reich led the way by allocating large sums to develop health and fitness; general wellbeing of a holistic order for the nation (Baronowski, 2004).

9 A key finding from the Kendal Project is that 82 per cent of holistic questionnaire respondents 'believe' in humanistic spirituality. Even in relatively secular forms of CAM, it can be added, the search for wellbeing typically takes place within the context of humanistic-expressivistic values. To feel better *about* oneself, together with these values, makes it likely that one will have a happy heart for others as well as oneself.

10 My concern with the term 'spiritual seekership', it can be added, derives from the fact that it tends to imply that spirituality is quested as an end in itself – thereby downplaying the significance of the spiritual journey *through* everyday life *with* spirituality.

References

Abrams, M. H. 1973: *Natural Supernaturalism*. London: W. W. Norton.
Adatto, Kiku 2003: Selling Out Childhood. *Hedgehog Review* (2&3), pp. 24–40.
Adorno, Theodore W. 1967: *Prisms*. London: Neville Spearman.
Adorno, Theodor W. 1973: *The Jargon of Authenticity*. London: Routledge and Kegan Paul.
Adorno, Theodore W. 1982: On the Fetish Character of Music. In Andrew Arato and Eike Gebhardt (eds), *The Frankfurt School Reader*. New York: Continuum, pp. 48–69.
Adorno, Theodore W. 1994: *Adorno. The Stars Down to Earth and Other Essays on the Irrational in Culture*. London: Routledge.
Agamben, Giorgio 1998: *Homo Sacer. Sovereign Power and Bare Life*. Stanford: Stanford University Press.
Ahlin, Lars 2006: A Spiritual Revolution in Denmark? Paper delivered to the 18th Nordic Conference in Sociology of Religion, University of Aarhus, August.
Aldridge, Alan 2003: *Consumption*. Cambridge: Polity Press.
Ali, F. 2006: Messiah of the Poor. *Dawn Islamabad Metropolitan*, 27 November, p. 13.
Almqvist, Kurt and Erik Wallrup (eds) 2006: *The Future of Religion. Perspectives from the Engelsberg Seminar 2001*. Stockholm: Axel and Margaret Ax:son Johnson Foundation.
Aphonen, Pirkkoliisa 1990: Signifying the Signs. Simulating Cultural Political Subjectivity in Postmodernity. *Acta Sociologica*, 33 (4), pp. 341–57.
Arato, Andrew and Eike Gebhardt (eds) 1982: *The Frankfurt School Reader*. New York: Continuum.
Archer, Margaret S. 1990: Theory, Culture and Post-Industrial Society. In Mike Featherstone (ed.), *Global Culture. Nationalism, Globalization and Modernity*. London: Sage, pp. 97–119.
Ashley, Tim 2000: Angel at My Table. *Guardian*, 8 September, p. 10.
Aupers, Stef 2005: *In de Ban van Moderniteit*. Amsterdam: Het Spinhuis.
Aupers, Stef and Dick Houtman 2006: Beyond the Spiritual Supermarket. The Social and Public Significance of New Age Spirituality. *Journal of Contemporary Religion*, 21 (2), pp. 201–22.

Baerveldt, Cor 1996: New Age Religiosity as a Process of Individual Construction. In Miranda Moerland (ed.), *The Fence, the Hare, and the Hounds in the New Age*. Utrecht: Jan van Arkel, pp. 33–48.
Barber, Benjamin 2007: *Consumed. How Markets Corrupt Children, Infantilize Adults, and Swallow Citizens Whole*. New York: W. W. Norton.
Barker, Eileen 2004: The Church Without and the God Within: Religiosity and/or Spirituality? In Dinka Marinovic Jerolimov, Sinisa Zrinscak and Irena Borowik (eds), *Religion and Patterns of Social Transformation*. Zagreb: Institute for Social Research, pp. 23–47.
Barley, Lynda 2006: *Christian Roots, Contemporary Spirituality*. London: Church House Publishing.
Baronowski, Shelly 2004: *Strength Through Joy. Consumerism and Mass Tourism in the Third Reich*. Cambridge: Cambridge University Press.
Barraclough, Jennifer (ed.) 2001: *Integrated Cancer Care. Holistic, Complementary and Creative Approaches*. Oxford: Oxford University Press.
Bartley, William 1978: *Werner Erhard*. New York: Clarkson N. Potter.
Bateson, Gregory and Catherine Bateson 1987: *Angels Fear. An Investigation into the Nature and Meaning of the Sacred*. London: Rider.
Baty, Phil 2007: Psychic Offers Career Advice. *The Times Higher Educational Supplement*, 27 April, p. 2.
Baudrillard, Jean 1988: *Selected Writings*. Cambridge: Cambridge University Press.
Baudrillard, Jean 1995: *The Gulf War Did Not Take Place*. Sydney: Power Publications.
Bauman, Zygmunt 1991: *Modernity and Ambivalence*. Cambridge: Polity Press.
Bauman, Zygmunt 1992: *Intimations of Postmodernity*. London: Routledge.
Bauman, Zygmunt 1998: Postmodern Religion? In Paul Heelas, Scott Lash and Paul Morris (eds), *Religion, Modernity and Postmodernity*. Oxford: Blackwell, pp. 55–78.
Bauman, Zygmunt 2001: Consuming Life. *Journal of Consumer Culture*, 1 (1), pp. 9–29.
Bauman, Zygmunt 2007: *Consuming Life*. Cambridge: Polity Press.
Bechtel, William and Robert C. Richardson 1998: Vitalism. *Routledge Encyclopaedia of Philosophy*, Vol. 9. London: Routledge, pp. 639–43.
Beck, Clive 1986: Education of Spirituality. *Interchange*, 17, pp. 148–56.
Beckford, James A. 1984: Holistic Imagery and Ethics in New Religions and Healing Movements. *Social Compass*, 32 (2–3), pp. 259–72.
Bell, Daniel 1976: *The Cultural Contradictions of Capitalism*. London: Heinemann.
Bellah, Robert N. 1999: Max Weber and World-Denying Love. A Look at the Historical Sociology of Religion. *Journal of the American Academy of Religion*, 67 (2), pp. 277–304.
Bellah, Robert N., forthcoming: *Religion in Human Evolution. From the Paleolithic to the Axial Age*.
Bellah, Robert N., Richard Madsen, William M. Sullivan, Ann Swidler and Steven Tipton 1985: *Habits of the Heart*. Berkeley: University of California Press.
Benhabib, Seyla 1992: *Situating the Self*. Cambridge: Polity Press.
Berg, Michael 2004: *The Secret*. San Francisco: Kabbalah Publishing.
Berger, Peter L. and Richard John Neuhaus 1970: *Movement and Revolution*. New York: Doubleday.
Berger, Peter L., Brigitte Berger and Hansfried Kellner 1974: *The Homeless Mind*. London: Penguin.
Berlin, Isaiah 1969: *Four Essays on Liberty*. Oxford: Oxford University Press.

Berlin, Isaiah 1991: *The Crooked Timber of Humanity.* London: Fontana.
Berlin, Isaiah 2000: *The Roots of Romanticism.* London: Pimlico.
Berlin, Isaiah 2001: *Against the Current.* Princeton: Princeton University Press.
Besecke, Kelly 2001: Speaking of Meaning in Modernity. Reflexive Spirituality as a Cultural Resource. *Sociology of Religion*, 62 (3), pp. 365–81.
Besecke, Kelly 2005: Seeing Invisible Religion. Religion as a Societal Conversation about Transcendent Meaning. *Sociological Theory*, 23 (2), pp. 179–196.
Bibby, Reginald W. 1987: *Fragmented Gods. The Poverty and Potential of Religion in Canada.* Toronto: Stoddart.
Black, Paula 2004: *The Beauty Industry.* London: Routledge.
Blackman, Shane J. 2004: *Chilling Out. The Cultural Politics of Substance Consumption, Youth and Drug Policy.* Milton Keynes: Open University Press.
Blackmore, Susan 2006: Take a Trip to Ease Your Final Journey. *The Times Higher Educational Supplement*, 10 February, p. 23.
Bloch, J. P. 1998: *New Spirituality, Self, and Belonging. How New Agers and Neo-Pagans Talk about Themselves.* Westport: Praeger.
Bloom, Adi 2007: Spirituality Isn't Instant Soup. *The Times Educational Supplement*, January 26, p. 14.
Bloom, William (ed.) 1991: *The New Age. An Anthology of Essential Writings.* London: Rider.
Bloom, William 2004: *Soulution. The Holistic Manifesto.* London: Hay House.
Bloom, William 2006: Spiritual Companions Statement version 2. www.williambloom.com.
Bocock, Robert 1992: Consumption and Lifestyles. In Robert Bocock and Kenneth Thompson (eds), *Social and Cultural Forms of Modernity.* Cambridge: Polity Press, pp. 119–67.
Bocock, Robert 1993: *Consumption.* London: Routledge.
Boff, Leonardo 1997: *Cry of the Earth, Cry of the Poor.* New York: Orbis.
Bollier, David 1991: *Citizen Action and Other Big Ideas. A History of Ralph Nadir and the Modern Consumer Movement.* www.nader.org/history_bollier.html.
Botvar, Pal Ketil 2006: The 'Spiritual Revolution' in Norway. Why New Age Spirituality Will Not Oust Christianity. Paper delivered to the 18th Nordic Conference in Sociology of Religion, University of Aarhus, August.
Bowman, Marion 1999: Healing in the Spiritual Marketplace. Consumers, Courses and Credentialism. *Social Compass*, 46 (2), pp. 181–9.
Boyd-MacMillan, Eolene M. 2006: *Transformation.* Oxford: Peter Lang.
Boyle, David 2000: *The Tyranny of Numbers.* London: Harper Collins.
Branigan, Tania 2007: Happy Land. Some Reasons to be Cheerful in England. *Guardian*, 10 August, p. 8.
Brierley, Peter 2003: *UK Christian Handbook. Religious Trends 4.* London: Christian Research.
Brierley, Peter 2006: *UK Christian Handbook. Religious Trends 6.* London: Christian Research.
Briscoe, Simon 2005: *Britain in Numbers.* London: Politico's.
Brodin, Jenny-Ann 2003: A Matter of Choice. A Micro-Level Study on how Swedish New Agers Choose their Religious Beliefs and Practices. *Rationality and Society*, 15 (3), pp. 381–405.
Brown, Michael F. 1997: *The Channeling Zone. American Spirituality in an Anxious Age.* Cambridge, MA: Harvard University Press.

Brown, Michael F. 2004: *Who Owns Native Culture?* Cambridge, MA: Harvard University Press.
Brown, Mick 1998: The Buddha of Suburbia. *Telegraph Magazine*, 12 December, p. 22.
Bruce, Steve 1993: All Wrapped Up in a Pick and Mix Religion. *Herald*, 10 April, pp. 2–3.
Bruce, Steve 1995: *Religion in Modern Britain*. Oxford: Oxford University Press.
Bruce, Steve 1996: Religion in Britain at the Close of the 20th Century. A Challenge to the Silver Lining Perspective. *Journal of Contemporary Religion*, 11 (3), pp. 261–75.
Bruce, Steve 2000: The New Age and Secularization. In Steven Sutcliffe and Marion Bowman (eds), *Beyond New Age. Exploring Alternative Spirituality*. Edinburgh: Edinburgh University Press, pp. 220–36.
Bruce, Steve 2002: *God is Dead*. Oxford: Blackwell.
Bruce, Steve 2006: Secularization and the Impotence of Individualized Religion. *Hedgehog Review*, 8 (2), pp. 35–45.
Bruni, Luigino and Pier Luigi Porta (eds) 2007: *Handbook on the Economics of Happiness*. Abingdon: Edward Elgar.
Buber, Matin 2004: *I and Thou*. New York: Continuum.
Bullard, Maria 1988: Yoga for People with a Mental Handicap. *Mencap News*, November, pp. 4–5.
Bunting, Madeleine 2000: The Sacred in Life. In Jonathan Rutherford (ed.), *The Art of Life*. London: Lawrence and Wishart, pp. 19–34.
Bunting, Madeleine 2004a: *Willing Slaves. How the Overwork Culture is Ruling Our Lives*. London: Harper Collins.
Bunting, Madeleine 2004b: I Work, Therefore I Am. *Guardian*, 14 June, pp. 2–3.
Byrne, Rhonda 2006: *The Secret*. New York: Atria.
Byron, Lord Alfred 1974: *Byron's Letters and Journals*, vol. 3, ed. Leslie A. Marchand. Cambridge, MA: Harvard University Press, Belknap.
Calhoun, Craig 1996: *Habermas and the Public Sphere*. Cambridge, MA: MIT Press.
Campbell, Colin 1987: *The Romantic Ethic and the Spirit of Modern Consumerism*. Oxford: Blackwell.
Campbell, Colin 2004: I Shop Therefore I Know That I Am: The Metaphysical Basis of Modern Consumerism. In Karin M. Ekstrom and Helene Brembeck (eds), *Elusive Consumption*. Oxford: Berg, pp. 27–44.
Campbell, Colin 2007: *The Easternization of the West. A Thematic Account of Cultural Change in the Modern Era*. London: Paradigm Publishers.
Campbell, Colin (in preparation): The Craft Consumer: Culture, Craft and Consumption in a Postmodern Society.
Carrette, Jeremy and Richard King 2005: $elling Spirituality. *The Silent Takeover of Religion*. London: Routledge.
Carter, Simon 2007: *Rise and Shine*. Oxford: Berg.
Cartner-Morley, Jess. 2001: Spirit of Beauty. *Guardian*, 16 November, p. 1.
Caru, Antonella and Bernard Cova (eds) 2006: *Consuming Experience*. London: Routledge.
Casey, Catherine 2002: *Critical Analysis of Organizations*. London: Sage.
Chandler, Siobhan 2008: The Social Ethic of Religiously Unaffiliated Spirituality. *Religion Compass*.
Cheshire, Andrea 2001: What Provisions are Available for the New Age Individual on Kendal High Street? Unpublished Dissertation, Lancaster University.

Chesterton, G. K. 1909: *Orthodoxy*. London: Bodley Head.
Chidvilasananda, Swami and David Katz 2006: *Yoga of Discipline*. New York: SYDA Foundation.
Clark, David B., Marcus A. Doel and Kate M. L. Housiaux (eds) 2003: *The Consumption Reader*. London: Routledge.
Clough, Patricia Ticineto (ed.) 2007: *The Affective Turn*. Durham, NC: Duke University Press.
Cohen, David 2000: Oprah Understood. *Guardian Education*, 2 May, p. 9.
Combe, Victoria 1998: Rome Takes Hard Line on Sharing Eucharist with Other Churches. *Daily Telegraph*, 1 October, p. 6.
Connell, Camilla 2001: Beyond the Image: Art Therapy and a Note on Poetry. In Jennifer Barraclough (ed.), *Integrated Cancer Care. Holistic, Complementary and Creative Approaches*. Oxford: Oxford University Press, pp. 94–107.
Corrywright, Dominic 2003: *Theoretical and Empirical Investigations into New Age Spiritualities*. Oxford: Peter Lang.
Coser, Lewis A. and Bernard Rosenberg 1964: *Sociological Theory. A Book of Readings*. New York; Macmillan.
Coulter, Ian 2004: Integration and Paradigm Clash. The Practical Difficulties of Integrative Medicine. In P. Tovey, G. Easthope and J. Adams (eds), *The Mainstreaming of Complementary and Alternative Medicine*. London: Routledge, pp. 103–22.
Crook, Stephen, Jan Pakulski and Malcolm Water 1992: *Postmodernization*. London: Sage.
Crossley, Nick 2004: The Circuit Trainer's Habitus: Reflexive Body Techniques and the Sociality of the Workout. *Body and Society*, 10 (1), pp. 37–69.
Cupitt, Don 1999: *The New Religion of Life in Everyday Speech*. London: SCM.
Cupitt, Don 2001: *Taking Leave of God*. London: SCM.
Dart, Tom and Jonathan Keane 2002: Modern Life Makes Us Ill. *The Times Magazine*, 19 October, pp. 31–4.
Davie, Grace 1994: *Religion in Britain since 1945*. Oxford: Blackwell.
Davie, Grace 2001: The Persistence of Institutional Religion in Modern Europe. In Linda Woodhead et al. (eds), *Peter Berger and the Study of Religion*. London: Routledge, pp. 101–11.
Davie, Grace 2004: New Approaches in the Sociology of Religion. A Western Perspective. *Social Compass*, 51 (1), pp. 73–84.
Davie, Grace 2006: Is Europe an Exceptional Case? *Hedgehog Review*, 8 (1&2), pp. 23–34.
Davis, Joseph E. 2003: The Commodification of the Self. *Hedgehog Review* (2&3), pp. 41–9.
de Ras, Marion E. P. 2008: *Body, Femininity and Nationalism. Girls in the German Youth Movement 1900–1934*. New York: Routledge.
Debord, Guy 1995: *The Society of the Spectacle*. New York: Zone Books.
Demerath, N. J. 2000: The Varieties of Sacred Experience. Finding the Sacred in a Secular Grove. *Journal for the Scientific Study of Religion*, 39, pp. 1–11.
Devlin, Hannah 2007: How Power of the Mind Can Help Patients Feel Better. *The Times*, 18 June, p. 22.
Dobson, R. 2003: Half of General Practices Offer Patients Complementary Medicine. *British Medical Journal*, 327, p. 1250.
Dormann, Christian and Fred R. H. Zijlstra (eds) 2003: Call Centre Work. Smile by Wire. *European Journal of Work and Organizational Psychology*, 12 (4), pp. 305–430.

Droogers, Andre 2007: Beyond Secularization versus Sacralization. Lessons from a Study of the Dutch Case. In Kieran Flanagan and Peter C. Jupp (eds), *A Sociology of Spirituality*. Aldhershot: Ashgate, pp. 81–99.
du Gay, Paul 1996: *Consumption and Identity at Work*. London: Sage.
Duffy, Eamon 1998: The Pagan Millennium? *Daily Telegraph*, 31 December, p. 30.
Dunning, David 2005: *Self-Insight. Roadblocks and Detours on the Path to Knowing Thyself*. London: Psy Press.
Durkheim, Emile 1971 [1912]: *The Elementary Forms of the Religious Life*. London: George Allen and Unwin.
Durkheim, Emile 1984 [1893]: *The Division of Labour in Society*. Basingstoke: Macmillan.
Durman, Paul 2006: Simple Idea for Soap Spas Chain. *The Sunday Times, Business*, 20 August, pp. 1, 3.
Eagleton, Terry 2007: *The Meaning of Life*. Oxford: Oxford University Press.
Earle-Levine, J. 2004: Glorious, Luxurious Mud. *Financial Times*, 22–3 May, p. W10.
Economist 2007: The Wellness Boom. 6–12 January, pp. 51–2.
Edwards, Gill 1993: *Stepping Into the Magic. A New Approach to Everyday Life*. London: Piatkus.
Ekstrom, Karin M. and Helene Brembeck 2004: Introduction. In Karin M. Ekstrom and Helene Brembeck (eds), *Elusive Consumption*. Oxford: Berg, pp. 1–7.
Elliott, John 2007: Happiness is a Chat over the Fence. *The Sunday Times*, 7 January, p. 4.
Elliott, John and Claire Newell 2006: Coming Soon. The Viking Guide to Happiness. *The Sunday Times*, 30 July, p. 19.
Elliot, Richard and Kritsadarat Wattanasuawan 1998: Brands as Symbolic Resources for the Construction of Identity. *International Journal of Advertising*, 17 (2), pp. 131–44.
Elster, John 1986: Self-Realization in Work and Politics. The Marxist Conception of the Good Life. *Social Philosophy and Policy*, 3 (2), pp. 97–126.
ESRC 2006: *The Edge*, Issue 23, edge@esrc.ac.uk.
Etzioni, Amitai 1990: *The Moral Dimension. Towards a New Economics*. New York: Free Press.
Etzioni, Amitai 1998: *The New Golden Rule. The Community and Morality in a Democratic Society*. New York: Basic Books.
Evans-Pritchard, E. E. 1937: *Witchcraft, Oracles, and Magic among the Azande*. Oxford: Clarendon Press.
Ewen, Stuart and Elizabeth Ewen 1982: *Channels of Desire*. New York: McGraw-Hill.
Ezzy, Douglas 2003: New Age Witchcraft? Popular Spell Books and the Re-enchantment of Everyday Life. *Culture and Religion*, 4 (1), pp. 47–65.
Ezzy, Douglas 2006: White Witches and Black Magic: Ethics and Consumerism in Contemporary Witchcraft. *Journal of Contemporary Religion*, 21 (1), pp. 15–31.
Falk, Pasi and Colin Campbell (eds) 1997: *The Shopping Experience*. London: Sage.
Fang-ju, Lin 1995: Dialogue with Life. *Inter-Religio*, Winter (38), pp. 36–48.
Featherstone, Mike 1987. Lifestyle and Consumer Culture. *Theory, Culture and Society*, 4, pp. 55–70.
Featherstone, Mike 1991a: *Consumer Culture and Postmodernism*. London: Sage.

Featherstone, Mike 1991b: Consumer Culture, Postmodernism, and Global Disorder. In Roland Robertson and William R. Garrett (eds), *Religion and Global Order*. New York: Paragon House, pp. 133–59.
Ferguson, Marilyn 1982: *The Aquarian Conspiracy. Personal and Social Transformation in the 1980s*. London: Granada.
Ferguson, Tim W. and Josephine Lee 1996: Coin of the New Age. *Forbes*, 9 September, pp. 86–7.
Fest, Joachim C. 1974: *Hitler*. New York: Harcourt Brace Jovanovich.
Fevre, R. W. 2000: *The Demoralization of Western Culture*. New York: Continuum.
Fidler, Kel 2006: Accusations of Bullying Tactics are Annoying. *Times Higher Educational Supplement*, 15 October, p. 5.
Fiske, John 1989: *Understanding Popular Culture*. London: Routledge.
Flanagan, Kieran 2007: Introduction. In Kieran Flanagan and Peter C. Jupp (eds), *A Sociology of Spirituality*. Aldershot: Ashgate, pp. 1–21.
Fodor, John and Eliza Fodor 1995: *The Light Within. A Celebration of the Spiritual Path*. Dent: Usha Publications.
Foucault, Michel 1991: *Discipline and Punish*. London: Penguin.
Foucault, Michel 1988: Technologies of the Self. In Luther H. Martin, Huck Gutman and Patrick H. Hutton (eds), *Technologies of the Self*. London: Tavistock, pp. 16–49.
Frank, Thomas 1998: *The Conquest of Cool. Business Culture, Counterculture and the Rise of Hip Consumerism*. Chicago: University of Chicago Press.
Freedland, Jonathan 1998: It's the New Religion – Putting the Me back into Meaning. *Guardian*, 15 April, p. 9.
Frembgen, Jurgen Wasim 2006: *The Friends of God. Sufi Saints in Islam*. Karachi: Oxford University Press.
Freud, Anna 1968: *The Ego and the Mechanisms of Defence*. London: Hogarth Press.
Freud, Sigmund 1938 [1919]: *Totem and Taboo*. London: Penguin.
Friedan, Betty 1965: *The Feminine Mystique*. London: Penguin.
Friedman, Jonathan (ed.) 1994: *Consumption and Identity*. London: Routledge.
Frisby, David 1985: *Fragments of Modernity*. Cambridge: Polity Press.
Frisk, Liselotte 2003: New Age Participations in Sweden. Background, Beliefs, Engagement and Conversion. In Mikael Rothstein and Reender Kranenborg (eds), *New Religions in a Postmodern World*. Aarhus: Aarhus University Press, pp. 241–55.
Froebel, Friedrich 2007 [1903]: *Autobiography of Friedrich Froebel*. London: Kessinger.
Furedi, Frank 2004: *Therapy Culture*. London: Routledge.
Gabriel, Yiannis and Tim Lang 2006: *The Unmanageable Consumer*. London: Sage.
Gallup, George, Jr. and Timothy Jones 2000: *The Next American Spirituality*. Colorado Springs: Chariot Victor.
Garnoussi, Nadia 2005: Le Developpement de nouvelles ressources de sens 'psycho-philo-spirituelles'. Deregulation des savoirs et nouvelle offre ideologique. *Social Compass*, 52 (2), pp. 197–210.
Garrett, Catherine 1998: *Beyond Anorexia. Narrative, Spirituality and Recovery*. Cambridge: Cambridge University Press.
Gawain, Shakti 1993: *The Path of Transformation. How Healing Ourselves Can Change the World*. Mill Valley: Natarji.

Geertsma, Elisabeth J. and Anne L. Cummings 2004: Midlife Transition and Women's Spirituality Groups. A Preliminary Investigation. *Counseling and Values*, October, 49, pp. 27–36.
Gergen, Kenneth J. 2000: *The Saturated Self*. New York: Basic Books.
Gerth, H. H. and C. Wright Mills 1997: *From Max Weber*. London: Routledge.
Giacalone, Robert A. and Carole L. Jurkiewicz (eds) 2004: *Handbook of Workplace Spirituality and Organizational Performance*. Gurgaon: Spring Books.
Giacalone, Robert A., Carole L. Jurkiewicz and Louis W. Fry 2005: From Advocacy to Science. The Next Steps in Workplace Spirituality Research. In Raymond F. Paloutzian and Crystal L. Park (eds), *The Handbook of the Psychology of Religion and Spirituality*. New York: Guilford Press, pp. 515–28.
Gibran, Kahlil 1976: *The Prophet*. London: Heinemann.
Giddens, Anthony 1991: *Modernity and Self-Identity*. Stanford: Stanford University Press.
Gill, Robin, C. Kirk Hadaway and Penny Long Marler 1998: Is Religious Belief Declining in Britain? *Journal for the Scientific Study of Religion*, 37, pp. 507–16.
Gimlin, Debra L. 2002: *Body Work*. Berkeley, CA: University of California Press.
Glendinning, Tony and Steve Bruce 2006: New Ways of Believing or Belonging. Is Religion Giving Way to Spirituality? *British Journal of Sociology*, 57 (3), pp. 399–414.
Gockel, Annemarie 2004: The Trend Toward Spirituality in the Workplace. Overview and Implications for Career Counseling. *Journal of Employment Counseling*, 41, pp. 156–67.
Goethe, Johann Wolfgang von 1795–6: *Wilhelm Meister's Years of Apprenticeship*. London: John Calder.
Goodman, Martin 1998: *In Search of the Divine Mother. The Mysteries of Mother Meera*. London: Thorsons.
Goodman, Matthew 2006: A Thing of Beauty. *The Sunday Times (Business)*, 20 August, p. 1.
Grant, Don, Kathleen O'Neil and Laura Stephens 2004: Spirituality in the Workplace. New Empirical Directions in the Study of the Sacred. *Sociology of Religion*, 65 (3), pp. 265–83.
Gratton, Lynda 2007: *Hot Spots. Why Some Teams, Workplaces, and Organizations Buzz with Energy – And Others Don't*. London: Berrett-Koehler.
Griffith, Nanci 2001: A Life in the Day. *The Sunday Times*, Magazine section, 21 October, p. 90.
Hahnemann, Samuel 1982 [1842]: *Organon of Medicine*. Washington, DC: Cooper Publishing.
Hale, Christopher 2004: *Himmler's Crusade*. London: Bantam.
Hall, Peter A. 1999: Social Capital in Britain. *British Journal of Politics*, 29, pp. 417–61.
Halpin, Tony 2006: Universities Must Make Students an Offer They Can't Refuse. *The Times 2*, 6 June, p. 9.
Hamberg, Eva 2003: Christendom in Decline. The Swedish Case. In Hugh McLeod and Werner Ustorf (eds), *The Decline of Christendom in Western Europe, 1750–2000*. Cambridge: Cambridge University Press, pp. 47–62.
Hamilton, Malcolm 2000: An Analysis of the Festival for Mind-Body-Spirit, London. In Steven Sutcliffe and Marion Bowman (eds), *Beyond New Age*. Edinburgh: Edinburgh University Press, pp. 188–200.
Hanegraaff, Wouter J. 1998: *New Age Religion and Western Culture. Esotericism in the Mirror of Secularism*. New York: State University of New York Press.

Hanegraaff, Wouter J. 1999: New Age Spiritualities as Secular Religion. A Historian's Perspective. *Social Compass*, 46 (2), pp. 145–60.
Harding, Douglas 1971: *On Having No Head. Zen and the Re-discovery of the Obvious*. London: Arkana.
Hardman, Robert 1998: Palace Focuses on Public Opinion. *The Times*, 1 May, p. 1.
Harrington, Anne 1999: *Reenchanted Science. Holism in German Culture from Wilhelm II to Hitler*. Princeton: Princeton University Press.
Harris, Marvin 1981: *America Now*. New York: Simon and Schuster.
Harris, Jennifer and Elwood Watson 2007: *The Oprah Phenomenon*. Lexington: University Press of Kentucky.
Harris, Sarah 2006: Stressed-out Pupils will get Lessons in Happiness. *Daily Mail*, 10 July, p. 32.
Hartshorne, Charles 1987: Transcendence and Immanence. In Mircea Eliade (ed.), *The Encyclopedia of Religion*, Vol. 15. London: Collier Macmillan, pp. 16–20.
Harvey, David 1989: *The Condition of Postmodernity*. Oxford: Blackwell.
Hasan, Arif 2005: Introduction. In Akhtar Hameed Khan, *Orangi Pilot Project*. Karachi: Oxford University Press Pakistan, pp. xi–xli.
Hasselle-Newcombe, Suzanne 2005: Spirituality and 'Mystical Religion' in Contemporary Society. A Case Study of British Practitioners of the Iyengar Method of Yoga. *Journal of Contemporary Religion*, 20 (3), pp. 305–21.
Hatcher, Brian A. 2007: Bourgeois Vedanta. The Colonial Roots of Middle-Class Hinduism. *Journal of the American Academy of Religion*, June, 75 (2), pp. 298–323.
Hay, Stephen (ed.) 1988: *Sources of Indian Tradition*, Vol. 2. New Delhi: Penguin Books India.
Heald, Gordon 2000: *Soul of Britain*. London: Opinion Research Business.
Heath, Joseph and Andrew Potter 2006: *The Rebel Sell. How the Counter Culture Became Consumer Culture*. New York: Capstone.
Hedgehog Review 2003: *The Commodification of Everything*, 5 (2), pp. 1–121.
Hedges, Ellie and James A. Beckford 2000: Holism, Healing and the New Age. In Steven Sutcliffe and Marion Bowman (eds), *Beyond New Age*. Edinburgh: Edinburgh University Press, pp. 169–87.
Heelas, Paul 1987: Exegesis: Methods and Aims. In Peter Clarke (ed.), *The New Evangelists. Recruitment, Methods and Aims of New Religious Movements*. London: Ethnographica, pp. 17–41.
Heelas, Paul 1989: Identifying Peaceful Societies. In Signe Howell and Roy Wallis (eds), *Societies at Peace. Anthropological Perspectives*. London: Routledge, pp. 225–43.
Heelas, Paul 1991: Reforming the Self. Enterprise and the Characters of Thatcherism. In Russell Keat and Nicholas Abercrombie (eds), *Enterprise Culture*. London: Routledge, pp. 72–90.
Heelas, Paul 1992a: Enterprise Culture. Its Values and Value. In Paul Heelas and Paul Morris (eds), *The Values of the Enterprise Culture – the Moral Debate*. London: Routledge, pp. 1–15.
Heelas, Paul 1992b: The Sacralization of the Self and New Age Capitalism. In Nicholas Abercrombie and Alan Warde (eds), *Social Change in Contemporary Britain*. Cambridge: Polity Press, pp. 139–66.
Heelas, Paul 1992c: God's Company. New Age Ethics and the Bank of Credit and Commerce International. *Religion Today*, 8 (1), pp. 1–4.

Heelas, Paul 1994: The Limits of Consumption and the Post-modern 'Religion' of the New Age. In Russell Keat, Nigel Whiteley and Nicholas Abercrombie (eds), *The Authority of the Consumer*. London: Routledge, pp. 102–15.

Heelas, Paul 1996a: *The New Age Movement. The Celebration of the Self and the Sacralization of Modernity*. Oxford: Blackwell.

Heelas, Paul 1996b: Introduction: Detraditionalization and its Rivals. In Paul Heelas, Scott Lash and Paul Morris (eds), *Detraditionalization. Critical Reflections on Authority and Identity*. Oxford: Blackwell, pp. 1–20.

Heelas, Paul 1996c: Detraditionalization of Religion and Self. The New Age and Postmodernity. In Kieran Flanagan and Peter Jupp (eds), *Postmodernity, Sociology and Religion*. London: Macmillan, pp. 64–82.

Heelas, Paul 1996d: On Things Not Being Worse, and the Ethic of Humanity. In Paul Heelas, Scott Lash and Paul Morris (eds), *Detraditionalization. Critical Reflections on Authority and Identity*. Oxford: Blackwell, pp. 200–22.

Heelas, Paul 1999: Diana's Self and the Quest Within. In Jeffrey Richards, Scott Wilson and Linda Woodhead (eds), *Diana. The Making of a Media Saint*. London: I. B. Tauris, pp. 98–118.

Heelas, Paul 2000: Expressive Spirituality and Humanistic Expressivism. Sources of Significance Beyond Church and Chapel. In Steven Sutcliffe and Marion Bowman (eds), *Beyond New Age*. Edinburgh: Edinburgh University Press, pp. 237–54.

Heelas, Paul 2001: New Age Utopianism, Cultural Extremities and Modernity. In Kieran Flanagan and Peter Jupp (eds), *Virtue Ethics and Sociology*. London: Macmillan, pp. 155–69.

Heelas, Paul 2002: The Spiritual Revolution. From 'Religion' to 'Spirituality'. In Linda Woodhead, Paul Fletcher, Hiroko Kawanami and David Smith (eds), *Religions in the Modern World*. London: Routledge, pp. 357–77.

Heelas, Paul 2005: Postmodernism. In John R. Hinnells (ed.), *The Routledge Companion to the Study of Religion*. London: Routledge, pp. 259–74.

Heelas, Paul 2006a: The Infirmity Debate: On the Viability of New Age Spiritualities of Life. *Journal of Contemporary Religion*, 21 (2), pp. 223–40.

Heelas, Paul 2006b: Nursing Spirituality. *Spirituality and Health International*, 7, pp. 8–23.

Heelas, Paul 2006c: Challenging Secularization Theory: The Growth of 'New Age' Spiritualities of Life. *Hedgehog Review, Critical Reflections on Contemporary Culture*, 8 (1&2), pp. 46–58.

Heelas, Paul 2006d: The Sacralization of Life and the Future of Wellbeing Spirituality. In Kurt Almqvist and Erik Wallrup (eds), *The Future of Religion. Perspectives from the Engelsberg Seminar 2001*. Stockholm: Axel and Margaret Ax:son Johnson Foundation, pp. 37–42.

Heelas, Paul 2007a: The Spiritual Revolution of Northern Europe: Personal Beliefs. *Nordic Journal of Religion and Society*, 1, pp. 1–28.

Heelas, Paul 2007b: The Holistic Milieu and Spirituality: Reflections on Voas and Bruce. In Kieran Flanagan and Peter C. Jupp (eds), *A Sociology of Spirituality*. Aldershot: Ashgate, pp. 63–80.

Heelas, Paul 2008a (forthcoming): *Expressive Life*.

Heelas, Paul 2008b: Spiritualities of Life. In Peter Clarke (ed.), *The Oxford Handbook of the Sociology of Religion*. Oxford: Oxford University Press.

Heelas, Paul (forthcoming): Research Note: Conceptualizing the Relationship between Inner-Life and Transcendent Spiritualities – An Interface, or Interactive?

Heelas, Paul and Dick Houtman (forthcoming): Research Note. RAMP Findings and the Question of the 'God Within'.

Heelas, Paul, Scott Lash and Paul Morris (eds) 1996: *Detraditionalization. Critical Reflections on Authority and Identity*. Oxford: Blackwell.

Heelas, Paul and Benjamin Seel 2003: An Ageing New Age? In Grace Davie, Paul Heelas and Linda Woodhead (eds), *Predicting Religion*. Aldershot: Ashgate, pp. 229–47.

Heelas, Paul and Linda Woodhead 2005: *The Spiritual Revolution. Why Religion is Giving Way to Spirituality*. Oxford: Blackwell.

Hefner, Robert W. and Muhammad Qasim Zaman (eds) 2007: *Schooling Islam. The Culture and Politics of Modern Muslim Education*. Princeton: Princeton University Press.

Hegel, G. W. F. 1988: *Early Theological Writings*. Philadelphia: University of Pennsylvania Press.

Heino, Harri 2006: The Status of Traditional Religiosity in the Nordic Countries. www.evl.fi/kkh/ktk/english/norden.htm.

Henderson, Sara and Alan Petersen 2001: *Consuming Health*. London: Routledge.

Hendin, Herbert 1975: *The Age of Sensation*. New York: W. W. Norton.

Henriksen, Jan-Olav 2005: Spirituality and Religion – Worlds Apart? *Tidsskrift for Kirke Religion Samfunn*, 1 (18), pp. 73–88.

Herdt, Gilbert H. 1981: *Guardians of the Flutes*. New York: McGraw-Hill.

Herrick, James 2003: *The Making of the New Spirituality. The Eclipse of the Western Religious Tradition*. Downers Grove: Intervarsity Press.

Herrigel, Eugen, 1953: *Zen in the Art of Archery*. London: Routledge and Kegan Paul.

Hervieu-Leger, Daniele 1998: The Figure of the Converted as Descriptive Figure of Religious Modernity. A Reflection Based on the File of Conversions to Catholicism in France. In Rudi Laermans, Bryan Wilson and Jaak Billiet (eds), *Secularization and Social Integration*. Leuven: Leuven University Press, pp. 277–85.

Hervieu-Leger, Daniele 2006: In Search of Certainties. The Paradox of Religiosity in Societies of High Modernity. *Hedgehog Review*, 8 (1&2), pp. 59–68.

Hickman, Leo 2006: Health and Fitness. *Guardian* (G2), 9 January, pp. 4–5.

Hicks, Douglas 2003: *Religion Within the Workplace. Pluralism, Spirituality, Leadership*. Cambridge: Cambridge University Press.

Hill, Christopher 1955: *The English Revolution 1640*. London: Lawrence and Wishart.

Hinderer, Walter and Daniel O. Dahlstrom (eds) 1998: *Friedrich Schiller. Essays*. New York: Continuum.

Hochschild, Arlie Russell 2003: *The Commercialization of Intimate Life*. Berkeley: University of California Press.

Honour, Hugh 1979: *Romanticism*. London: Allen Lane.

Hood, Ralph 2005: Mystical, Spiritual, and Religious Experiences. In Raymond F. Paloutzian and Crystal L. Park (eds), *Handbook of the Psychology of Religion and Spirituality*. London: Guilford Press, pp. 348–64.

House of Lords 2000: *Science and Technology – Sixth Report*.

Houtman, Dick and Stef Aupers 2007: The Spiritual Turn and the Decline of Tradition: The Spread of Post-Christian Spirituality in 14 Western Countries, 1981–2000. *Journal for the Scientific Study of Religion*, 46 (3), pp. 305–20.

Houtman, Dick and Stef Aupers (forthcoming): The Spiritual Revolution and the New Age Gender Puzzle. The Sacralization of the Self in Late Modernity

(1980–2000). In Giselle Vincett, Sonya Sharma and Kristin Aune (eds), *Women and Religion in the West. Challenging Secularization*. Aldershot: Ashgate.

Houtman, Dick and Peter Mascini 2002: Why Do Churches Become Empty, While New Age Grows? Secularization and Religious Change in the Netherlands. *Journal for the Scientific Study of Religion*, 41 (3), pp. 455–73.

Hume, Lynne and Kathleen McPhillips 2006: *Popular Spiritualities. The Politics of Contemporary Enchantment*. Aldershot: Ashgate.

Hunt, Stephen J. 2002: *Religion in Western Society*. Basingstoke: Palgrave.

Hunt, Stephen J. 2005: *Religion and Everyday Life*. London: Routledge.

Hunter, James Davidson 1999: *Culture Wars*. New York: Basic Books.

Hunter, James Davidson, James L. Nolan and Beth A. Eck 1994: Is "Nothing" Sacred? "Sacred" Cosmology among the Avant-Garde. In Arthus L. Greil and Thomas Robbins (eds), *Religion and the Social Order*, Vol. 4. London: JAI Press, pp. 79–94.

Huxley, Aldous 1949: *Texts and Pretexts*. London: Chatto and Windus.

Huxley, Julian 1941: *Religion Without Revelation*. London: Watt.

Huysmans, J.-K. 1959: *Against Nature*. London: Penguin.

Hyde, Jeannette 1997: When in Rio Head for the Slums. *Weekend Telegraph*, 11 January, p. 21.

Inglehart, Ronald 1977: *The Silent Revolution*. Princeton: Princeton University Press.

Inglehart, Ronald 1990: *Culture Shift in Advanced Industrial Society*. Princeton: Princeton University Press.

Inglehart, Ronald and Christian Welzel 2005: *Modernization, Cultural Change, and Democracy*. Cambridge: Cambridge University Press.

Ives, Laurel 2007: Beyond Belief. *The Sunday Times, Style*, 21 January, pp. 10–12.

Iyengar, B. K. S. 2005: *Light on Life. The Journey to Wholeness, Inner Peace and Ultimate Freedom*. London: Rodale.

Izenberg, Gerald N. 1992: *Impossible Individuality. Romanticism, Revolution and the Origins of Modern Selfhood, 1787–1802*. Princeton: Princeton University Press.

James, William 1960: *The Varieties of Religious Experience*. London: Collins.

Jameson, Frederic 1991: *Postmodernism, or the Cultural Logic of Late Capitalism*. Durham, NC: Duke University Press.

Jammer, Max 1999: *Einstein and Religion*. Princeton: Princeton University Press.

Jarvis, Simon 1998: *Adorno. A Critical Introduction*. Cambridge: Polity Press.

Kampion, Drew and Phil Catalfo 1992: All in the Family. *New Age Journal*, July/August, Vol. 2, pp. 54–9, 127–9.

Kant, Immanuel 1959 [1784]: Idea of a Universal History from a Cosmopolitan Point of View. In Patrick Gardiner (ed.), *Theories of History*. New York: Free Press, pp. 22–34.

Kant, Immanuel 1978: *Anthropology from a Pragmatic Point of View*. Carbondale: Southern Illinois University Press.

Kaplan, Jeffrey and Helene Loow (eds) 2002: *The Cultic Milieu. Oppositional Subcultures in an Age of Globalization*. Walnut Creek: AltaMira Press.

Keat, Russell 1992. The Authority of the Consumer. Unpublished document, Lancaster University.

Keat, Russell, Nigel Whiteley and Nicholas Abercrombie (eds) 1994: *The Authority of the Consumer*. London: Routledge.

Kennedy, Gordon 1998: *Children of the Sun*. Ojai: Nivaria Press.

Ketola, Kimmo 2005: Review of Paul Heelas and Linda Woodhead *The Spiritual Revolution* and Jeremy Carrette and Richard King *Selling Spirituality*. *Temenos, Nordic Journal of Comparative Religion*, 41 (2), pp. 287–92.
Keyserling, Hermann, Graf von 1937: *The Art of Life*. London: Selwyn and Blount.
King, Michael, Louise Jones et al. 2006: Measuring Spiritual Belief. Development and Standardization of a Beliefs and Values Scale. *Psychological Medicine*, 36, pp. 417–25.
Klingemann, Hans-Dieter 2005: Foreword. In Ronald Inglehart and Christian Welzel, *Modernization, Cultural Change, and Democracy*. Cambridge: Cambridge University Press, pp. ix–x.
Knibbe, Kim E. 2007: *Faith in the Familiar. Continuity and Change in Religious Practices and Moral Orientations in the South of Limburg, the Netherlands*. Amsterdam: De Vrije Universiteit Amsterdam.
Koenig, Harold G. 2007: *Spirituality in Patient Care*. Pennsylvania: Templeton Foundation Press.
Kopp, Sheldon 1974: *If You Meet the Buddha on the Road, Kill Him!* London: Sheldon Press.
Kovel, Joel 1999: *History and Spirit. An Inquiry into the Philosophy of Liberation*. Warner, NH: Essential Book.
Kraut, Richard 2007: *What is Good and Why. The Ethics of Well-Being*. Cambridge, MA: Harvard University Press.
Krishna, Gopi 1997: *Kundalini. The Evolutionary Energy in Man*. San Francisco: Shambhala.
Kynaston, David 2007: *Austerity Britain 1945–51*. London: Bloomsbury.
LaChette, Aleisha 2006: Protest or Community? Unpublished research, Lancaster University.
Laing, R. D. 1967: *The Politics of Experience*. London: Penguin.
Lake, James H. and David Spiegel (eds) 2007: *Complementary and Alternative Treatments in Mental Health Care*. London: Eurospan.
Lama, Dalai, and Howard C. Cutler 1998: *The Art of Happiness. A Handbook for Living*. London: Hodder and Stoughton.
Lama, Dalai, and Daniel Goleman 2003: *Destructive Emotions*. London: Bloomsbury.
Lambert, Yves 1999: Religion in Modernity as a New Axial Age. Secularization or New Religious Forms? *Sociology of Religion*, 60 (3), pp. 303–33.
Lane, Robert E. 2000: *The Loss of Happiness in Market Democracies*. New Haven: Yale University Press.
Lasch, Christopher 1980: *The Culture of Narcissism*. London: Picador.
Lasch, Christopher 1987: Soul of a New Age. *Omni*, October, pp. 78–80, 82, 84–5.
Lash, Scott and Celia Lury 2007: *Global Culture Industry. The Mediation of Things*. Cambridge: Polity Press.
Lau, Kimberly J. 2000: *New Age Capitalism*. Philadelphia: University of Pennsylvania Press.
Le Bris, Michel 1981: *Romantics and Romanticism*. London: Macmillan.
Leach, Edmund 1982: *Social Anthropology*. London: Fontana.
Lears, T. J. Jackson 1983: From Salvation to Self-Realization. Advertising and the Therapeutic Roots of the Consumer Culture, 1880–1930. In Richard Wightman and T. J. Jackson Lears (eds), *The Culture of Consumption. Critical Essays in American History, 1880–1980*. New York: Pantheon, pp. 1–38.

Leake, Jonathan 2006: It's a Sin to Fly, Says Church. *The Sunday Times*, 23 July, pp. 1–2.
Leary, Timothy 1970: *The Politics of Ecstasy.* London: Paladin.
Leder, Drew 1990: *The Absent Body.* Chicago: University of Chicago Press.
Levenda, Peter 2003: *Unholy Alliance. A History of Nazi Involvement with the Occult.* New York: Continuum.
Lewis, C. S. 1967: *Studies in Words.* Cambridge: Cambridge University Press.
Lewis, Sarah 2007: *The New Age.* London: I. B. Tauris.
Lindquist, Galina 1997: *Shamanic Performances on the Urban Scene.* Stockholm: Stockholm University Press.
Lofgren, Orvar and Robert Willim (eds) 2005: *Magic, Culture and the New Economy.* Oxford: Berg.
Long, Barry 1983: *Knowing Yourself.* London: Barry Long Centre.
Lorimer, David 2003: *Radical Prince. The Practical Vision of the Prince of Wales.* Edinburgh: Floris Books.
Lucas, Catherine 2005: My Grief Poured Out. *The Times* (T2), 15 June, pp. 6–7.
Luckmann, Benita 1970: The Small Life-Worlds of Modern Man. *Social Research*, 37 (4), pp. 580–96.
Luckmann, Thomas 1967: *The Invisible Religion.* London: Collier-Macmillan.
Luckmann, Thomas 1990: Shrinking Transcendence, Expanding Religion? *Sociological Analysis*, 50 (20), pp. 127–38.
Lury, Celia 1996: *Consumer Culture.* London: Routledge.
Lynch, Gordon 2007: *The New Spirituality. An Introduction to Progressive Belief in the Twenty-first Century.* London: I. B. Tauris.
Lyon, David 1994a: A Bit of a Circus. Notes on Postmodernity and New Age. *Religion*, 23, pp. 117–26.
Lyon, David 1994b: *Postmodernity.* Buckingham: Open University Press.
Lyon, David 2000: *Jesus in Disneyland.* Cambridge: Polity Press.
McCarthy, Thomas 1979: Translator's Introduction. *Jürgen Habermas. Communication and the Evolution of Society.* London: Heinemann, pp. vii–xxiv.
McConaghy, Cathryn 2000: *Rethinking Indigenous Education. Culturalism, Colonialism and the Politics of Knowing.* London: Post Pressed.
McDannell, Colleen 1996: *Material Christianity.* New Haven: Yale University Press.
McGrath, Alister E. 1999: *Christian Spirituality.* Oxford: Blackwell.
McGuire, Meredith 1997: Mapping Contemporary American Spirituality. A Sociological Perspective. *Journal for the Society for the Study of Christian Spirituality*, 5 (1), pp. 1–8
MacIntyre, Alasdair 1971: *Against the Self-Images of the Age.* London: Duckworth.
MacIntyre, Alasdair 1985: *After Virtue.* London: Duckworth.
McKean, Lise 1996: *Divine Enterprise. Gurus and the Hindu Nationalist Movement.* Chicago: University of Chicago Press.
MacLaine, Shirley 1988: *It's All in the Playing.* London: Bantam.
McLeod, Hugh 2007: *The Religious Crisis of the 1960s.* Oxford: Oxford University Press.
Macpherson, C. B. 1964: *The Political Theory of Possessive Individualism.* Oxford: Oxford University Press.
Mansell, Warwick 2007: *Education by Numbers. The Tyranny of Testing.* London: Politico.

Marcus, Jon 2006: Students Who Pay the Piper May Call the Tune. *The Times Higher Educational Supplement*, 18 August, p. 9.
Marler, Penny Long and C. Kirk Hadaway 2002: 'Being Religious' or 'Being Spiritual' in America: A Zero-Sum Proposition? *Journal for the Scientific Study of Religion*, 41 (2), pp. 289–300.
Martin, Bernice 1983: *A Sociology of Contemporary Cultural Change*. Oxford: Blackwell.
Martin, David A. 1969: *The Religious and the Secular*. London: Routledge.
Martin, Luther H., Huck Gutman and Patrick H. Hutton 1988: *Technologies of the Self. A Seminar with Michel Foucault*. London: Tavistock.
Marty, Martin 1983: Religion in America since Mid-Century. In Mary Douglas and Steven Tipton (eds), *Religion and America*. Boston: Beacon Press, pp. 273–87.
Marx, Karl and Friedrich Engels 1985: *The Communist Manifesto*. London: Penguin.
Matrisciana, Caryl 1985: *Gods of the New Age*. Eugene: Harvest House.
Mears, D. P. and C. G. Ellison 2000: 'Who Buys New Age Materials?' Exploring Sociodemographic, Religious, Network, and Contextual Correlates of New Age Consumption. *Sociology of Religion*, 61 (3), pp. 289–313.
Melville, Kenneth 1972: *Communes in the Counter Culture*. New York: William Morrow.
Miles, Steven, Kevin Meethan and Alison Anderson 2002: Introduction. The Meaning of Consumption; the Meaning of Change? In Steven Miles, Alison Anderson and Kevin Meethan (eds), *The Changing Consumer*. London: Routledge, pp. 1–9.
Miller, Barbara Stoler 1998: *Yoga. The Discipline of Freedom*. London: Bantam.
Miller, Daniel 1998: *A Theory of Shopping*. Cambridge: Polity Press.
Miller, Lucy 2003: Yourself. *Daily Express* (Express Woman), 6 January pp. 34, 39.
Mitroff, Ian and Elizabeth Denton 1999: *A Spiritual Audit of Corporate America*. San Francisco: Jossey-Bass.
Montessori, Maria 1989 [1935]: *The Child, Society and the World*. Oxford: Clio Press.
Mosse, George L. 2003: *Nazi Culture. Institutional, Cultural and Social Life in the Third Reich*. Madison: University of Wisconsin Press.
Muir, Stewart 2005: *Healing and Redemption. New Age and Alternative Spiritualities and Aboriginality in Southeast Australia*. La Trobe.
Murcott, Toby 2005: *Alternative Medicine on Trial?* Basingstoke: Macmillan.
Musil, Robert 1961: *Der Deutsche Mensch als Symptom*. Hamburg Rowohlt.
Needham, Rodney 1972: *Belief, Language, Experience*. Oxford: Blackwell.
NHS Forth Valley 2004: Spiritual Care Policy. Caring for the Whole Person. March. Edinburgh: Health Planning and Quality Division, pp. 1–11.
Niemela, Kati 2006: Does Religious Upbringing Matter? In Kirsi Tirri (ed.), *Religion, Spirituality and Identity*. Oxford: Peter Lang, pp. 153–69.
Nipperdey, Thomas 1988: *Religion in Umbruch. Deutschland 1870–1914*. Berlin: C. H. Beck.
Norman, Edward 1994: Church's Net Loss. *Sunday Telegraph*, 6 March, p. 29.
Nussbaum, Martha C. 1997: *Cultivating Humanity. A Classic Defense of Reform in Liberal Education*. Cambridge, MA: Harvard University Press.
Nussbaum, Martha C. 2000: *Women and Human Development. The Capabilities Approach*. Cambridge: Cambridge University Press.
Nussbaum, Martha C. 2007: *The Clash Within. Democracy, Religious Violence, and India's Future*. Cambridge, MA: Harvard University Press.

Nussbaum, Martha C. and Amartya Sen (eds) 1993: *The Quality of Life*. Oxford: Clarendon Press.

O'Brian, Mary Elizabeth 2002: *Spirituality in Nursing*. London: Jones and Bartlett.

O'Dell, Tom 2005: Meditation, Magic and Spiritual Regeneration. Spas and the Mass Production of Serenity. In Orvar Lofgren and Robert Willim (eds), *Magic, Culture and the New Economy*. Oxford: Berg, pp. 19–36.

O'Doherty, Malachi 2003: *I Was a Teenage Catholic*. Dublin: Marino.

Ofsted, 1994: *Handbook for the Inspection of Schools. Part 4. Inspection Schedule Guidance. Consolidated Edition*. London: HMSO.

Ofsted, 2004: Promoting and Evaluating Pupils' Spiritual, Moral, Social and Cultural Development. www.ofsted.gov.uk.

Olivar, Jose 1996: Sophia Loren Opens Her Heart. *Hello!*, 405, 4 May, pp. 4–12, 22.

Oxley, Robin 2001: *Insight. Journeys to Happiness*. Kendal: Lakeland Health.

Packard, Vance 1957: *The Hidden Persuaders*. London: Longmans Green.

Palmer, Brian and Erika Willander (forthcoming): Is Sweden Leading the Spiritual Revolution?

Palmisano, Stefania (forthcoming): Spirituality in Italy.

Parkins, Geoffry 1994: *I Ching* Theme Park Opens Soon. *The Times Higher Educational Supplement*, 17 June, p. 14.

Parsons, Talcott 1968: *The Structure of Social Action*, Vol.1. London: Collier-Macmillan.

Parsons, Talcott 1978: *Action Theory and the Human Condition*. New York: Free Press.

Partridge, Christopher H. 1999: Truth, Authority and Epistemological Individualism in New Age Thought. *Journal of Contemporary Religion*, 14 (1), pp. 77–95.

Partridge, Christopher H. 2004: *The Re-Enchantment of the West*, Vol. 1. London: T. & T. Clark.

Partridge, Christopher H. 2005: *The Re-Enchantment of the West*, Vol. 2. London: T. & T. Clark.

Passmore, John 1970: *The Perfectibility of Man*. London: Duckworth.

Pasternak, Anna 1999: Mind and Body. *The Sunday Times, Style*, 23 May, pp. 34–5.

Paterson, Mark 2006: *Consumption and Everyday Life*. London: Routledge.

Paton, Graeme 2007: Universities 'Cash in by Running Soft Courses'. *Daily Telegraph*, 27 July, p. 14.

Penman, Ian 2006: Quality Time. *The Sunday Times, Style*, 5 March, pp. 48–9.

Pettersson, Thorleif and Goran Gustafsson 2000: *Folkkyrkor och Religios Pluralism. Den Nordiska Religiosa Modellen* [*Folk Churches and Religious Pluralism. The Nordic Religious Model*]. Stockholm: Verbum.

Phillips, D. Z. and Timothy Tessin (eds) 1997: *Religion Without Transcendence?* London: St. Martin's Press.

Pickering, William 1968: Religion – a Leisure-time Pursuit? In David Martin (ed.), *A Sociological Yearbook of Religion in Britain*. London: SCM, pp. 77–93.

Pilzer, Paul 2003: *The Wellness Revolution. How to Make a Fortune in the Next Trillion Dollar Industry.* London: John Wiley.

Pope John Paul II 1995: The Fabric of Relations among Peoples. *Origins*, 25 (18), pp. 293, 295–9.

Possamai, Adam 2000: A Profile of New Agers. Social and Spiritual Aspects. *Journal of Sociology*, 36, pp. 364–77.

Possamai, Adam 2003: Alternative Spiritualities and the Cultural Logic of Late Capitalism. *Culture and Religion*, 4 (1), pp. 31–45.
Possamai, Adam 2005: *Religion and Popular Culture. A Hyper-Real Testament.* Oxford: P.I.E.-Peter Lang.
Pye, Michael 1978: *Skilful Means. A Concept in Mahayana Buddhism.* London: Duckworth.
Ramstedt, Martin 2002: Empowering the Self. The Authority of Transformative Experience and New Forms of Religiosity in Secularized Dutch Society. Paper delivered to the 2002 CESNUR International Conference.
Ramstedt, Martin 2007: New Age and Business. In Daren Kemp and James R. Lewis (eds), *Handbook of New Age*. Leiden: Brill, pp. 185–205.
Rappaport, Roy A. 1999: *Ritual and Religion in the Making of Humanity.* Cambridge: Cambridge University Press.
Ray, Paul H. and Sherry Ruth Anderson 2000: *The Cultural Creatives.* New York: Three Rivers Press.
Ray, Sondra 1990: *How to be Chic, Fabulous and Live Forever.* Berkeley: Celestial Arts.
Redden, Guy 2002: The New Agents. Personal Transfiguration and Radical Privatization in New Age Self-Help. *Journal of Consumer Culture*, 2 (1), pp. 33–52.
Redden, Guy 2003. The New Agents. New Age Ideology and the Fashioning of the Self. Ph.D. dissertation, University of Queensland, Media and Cultural Studies Centre.
Redden, Guy 2005: The New Age. Towards a Market Model. *Journal of Contemporary Religion*, 20 (2), pp. 231–46.
Rhinehart, Luke 1976: *The Book of est.* New York: Holt, Rinehart and Winston.
Rider, Jacques Le 1993: *Modernity and Crises of Identity.* Cambridge: Polity Press.
Ripley, Jacqui 2002: 25 Steps to Happy, Healthy Partying. *Cosmopolitan*, December, pp. 311–2.
Roberts, Robert C. 2007: *Spiritual Emotions.* London: Eerdmans.
Robertson, Roland 1972: *The Sociological Interpretation of Religion.* Oxford: Blackwell.
Robertson, Roland 1978: *Meaning and Change. Explorations in the Cultural Sociology of Modern Societies.* Oxford: Blackwell.
Roof, Wade Clark 1999a: *Spiritual Marketplace. Baby Boomers and the Remaking of American Religion.* Princeton: Princeton University Press.
Roof, Wade Clark 1999b: American Spirituality. *Religion and American Culture*, 9, pp. 131–9.
Rose, Nikolas 1990: *Governing the Soul. The Shaping of the Private Self.* London: Routledge.
Rosenberg, Larry 2000: *Living in the Light of Death. On the Art of Being Truly Alive.* London: Shambhala.
Ross, Andrew 1991: *Strange Weather.* London: Verso.
Rousseau, Jean-Jacques 1954 [1781]: *The Confessions of Jean-Jacques Rousseau.* London: Penguin.
Rowling, J. K. 1997: *Harry Potter and the Philosopher's Stone.* London: Bloomsbury.
Ryle, Gilbert 1963: *The Concept of Mind.* London: Penguin.
Sachedina, Abdulaziz 2007: The Clash of Universalisms: Religious and Secular in Human Rights. *Hedgehog Review*, 9 (3), pp. 49–62.
Sacks, Jonathan 1990: The Persistence of Faith. The Reith Lectures, Radio 4.

Sagoff, Mark 1990: *The Economy of the Earth*. Cambridge: Cambridge University Press.
Salamon, Karen Lisa G. and Martin Ramstedt (eds) Forthcoming: *Spiritual Capitalism. Alternative Spirituality in the Corporate World.*
Salkeld, Audrey 1996: *A Portrait of Leni Riefenstahl*. London: Jonathan Cape.
Sampson, Philip 1994: The Rise of Postmodernity. In Philip Sampson, Vinay Samuel and Chris Sugden (eds), *Faith and Modernity*. Oxford: Regnum, pp. 29–57.
Sandel, Michael J. 2003: What Money Shouldn't Buy. *Hedgehog Review*, 5 (2), pp. 77–97.
Savage, Mike, James Barlow, Peter Dickens and Tony Fielding 1992: *Property, Bureaucracy and Culture*. London: Routledge.
Schleiermacher, Friedrich 1958 [1799]: *On Religion. Speeches to Its Cultured Despisers*. London: Harper and Row.
Schmidt, Leigh 2006: *Restless Souls. The Making of American Spirituality*. San Francisco: Harper San Francisco.
Schor, Juliet B. 2003: The Commodification of Childhood. Tales from the Advertising Front Lines. *Hedgehog Review*, Summer (2&3), pp. 7–23.
Schweitzer, Albert 1996: *The Spiritual Life. Selected Writings of Albert Schweitzer* (Charles R. Joy, ed.). Hopewell, NJ: Ecco Press.
Sedgwick, Colin 2004: Gimme that Organized Religion. *Guardian*, 12 June, p. 17.
Sen, Amartya 1993: Capability and Well-Being. In Martha Nussbaum and Amartya Sen (eds), *The Quality of Life*. Oxford: Clarendon Press, pp. 31–53.
Sen, Amartya 2005: *The Argumentative Indian*. London: Penguin.
Sen, Amartya 2006: *Identity and Violence. The Illusion of Destiny*. London: Allen Lane.
Sen, Sarbani 2007: *The Constitution of India. Popular Sovereignty and Democratic Transformations*. New Delhi: Oxford University Press India.
Senge, Peter M. 1999: *The Fifth Discipline. The Art and Practice of the Learning Organization*. London: Random House.
Sennett, Richard 1977: *The Fall of Public Man*. Cambridge: Cambridge University Press.
Sennett, Richard 2008: *The Craftsman*. Forthcoming.
Sharma, Kalpana 1993: Metaphors for Consumer Culture. *Hindu Magazine*, 28 November, p. 1.
Sharma, Ursula 2002: Integrated Medicine. In Gillian Bendelow, Mick Carpenter, Caroline Vautier and Simon Williams (eds), *Gender, Health and Healing*. London: Routledge.
Sharma, Ursula and Paula Black 1999: *The Sociology of Pampering. Beauty Therapy as a Form of Work*. Working paper. University of Derby, Centre for Social Research.
Shepherd, Jessica 2006: Top-Up Teens Want More for Their Money. *The Times Higher Education Supplement*, 30 June, p. 8.
Shweder, Richard A. 2006: Atheists Agonistes. *New York Times*, 27 November.
Shweder, Richard, Martha Minow and Hazel Rose Markus (eds) 2004: *Engaging Cultural Differences*. New York: Russell Sage Foundation.
Shils, Edward 1968: The Sanctity of Life. In Edward Shils et al. (eds) *Life or Death*. Seattle: University of Washington Press, pp. 1–23.
Shils, Edward 1981: *Tradition*. London: Faber and Faber.
Silber, K. 1965: *Pestalozzi: The Man and His Work*. London: Routledge and Kegan Paul.

Simmel, Georg 1976 [1917]: The Crisis of Culture. In P. A. Lawrence, *Georg Simmel, Sociologist and European*. Sunbury-on-Thames: Thomas Nelson, pp. 253–66.
Simmel, Georg 1978 [1900]: *The Philosophy of Money*. London: Routledge and Kegan Paul.
Simmel, Georg 1997 [1918]: *Essays on Religion*. New Haven: Yale University Press.
Sjodin, Ulf 2003: The Paranormal in Swedish Religiosity. In Grace Davie, Paul Heelas and Linda Woodhead (eds), *Predicting Religion*. Aldershot: Ashgate, pp. 203–13.
Smith, Christian, with Melinda Lundquist Denton 2005: *Soul Searching. The Religious and Spiritual Lives of American Teenagers*. Oxford: Oxford University Press.
Smith, David and Dipesh Gadher 2006: Britons Happier, but Not with Britain. *The Sunday Times*, 31 December, p. 7.
Smith, Michael 1993: Buddhists March Back to the Present Day. *Daily Telegraph*, 8 March, p. 34.
Smithers, Rebecca 2004: Ofsted Chief says Scrap Law on Worship. *Guardian*, 22 April, p. 6.
Solomon, Robert C. 2002: *Spirituality for the Skeptic. The Thoughtful Love of Life*. Oxford: Oxford University Press.
Spangler, David 1989: *Defining the New Age*. London: World Goodwill Occasional Papers.
Spangler, David 1993: The New Age. The Movement Toward the Divine. In D. S. Ferguson (ed.), *New Age Spirituality. An Assessment*. Louisville: Westminster/John Knox Press, pp. 77–105.
Stark, Rodney 1992: *Sociology*. Belmont: Wadsworth.
Stark, Rodney 2006: Economics of Religion. In Robert Segal (ed.), *The Blackwell Companion to the Study of Religion*. Oxford: Blackwell, pp. 38–60.
Stark, Rodney and L. Iannaccone 1993: Rational Choice Propositions about Religious Movements. In David Bromley and Jeff Hadden (eds), *Handbook on Cults and Sects*. Greenwich, CT: JAI Press, pp. 19–31.
Strauss, Sarah 2005: *Positioning Yoga*. Oxford: Berg.
Sutcliffe, Steven J. 2006: Rethinking 'New Age' as a Popular Religious *Habitus*. A Review Essay on *The Spiritual Revolution. Method and Theory in the Study of Religion*, 18 (3), pp. 294–314.
Tacey, David 2004: *The Spirituality Revolution. The Emergence of Contemporary Spirituality*. New York: Brunner-Routledge.
Tagore, Rabindranath 1961 [1931]: *The Religion of Man*. London: Unwin.
Tallis, Raymond 2004: *Hippocratic Oaths. Medicine and Its Discontents*. London: Atlantic Books.
Taylor, Charles 1989: *Sources of the Self. The Making of the Modern Identity*. Cambridge: Cambridge University Press.
Taylor, Charles 1991: *The Ethics of Authenticity*. Cambridge, MA: Harvard University Press.
Taylor, Charles 1994: The Politics of Recognition. In David Theo Goldberg (ed.), *Multiculturalism. A Critical Reader*. Oxford: Blackwell, pp. 75–106.
Taylor, Charles 2002: *Varieties of Religion Today*. Cambridge, MA: Harvard University Press.
Taylor, Charles 2007: *A Secular Age*. Cambridge, MA: Harvard University Press.
Taylor, Elizabeth Johnston 2007: *What Do I Say? Talking with Patients about Spirituality*. West Conshohocken, PA: Templeton Foundation Press.

References

Taylor, Mark C. 1992: *Disfiguring. Art, Architecture, Religion*. Chicago: University of Chicago Press.
Taylor, Mark C. 2007: *After God*. Chicago: University of Chicago Press.
Thompson, E. P. 1997: *The Romantics*. Woodbridge, Suffolk: Merlin Press.
Thompson, Judith and Paul Heelas 1986: *The Way of the Heart. The Rajneesh Movement*. Wellingborough: Aquarian Press.
Thrift, Nigel 2005: *Knowing Capitalism*. London: Sage.
Tipton, Steven 1982: *Getting Saved from the Sixties*. Berkeley: University of California Press.
Tipton, Steven 1983: Making the World Work. Ideas of Social Responsibility in the Human Potential Movement. In Eileen Barker (ed.), *Of Gods and Men. New Religious Movements in the West*. Macon, GA: Mercer Press, pp. 265–82.
Tovey, Philip, John Chatwin and Alex Broom 2007: *Traditional, Complementary and Alternative Medicine and Cancer Care*. London: Routledge.
Troeltsch, Ernst 1960 [1911]: *The Social Teaching of the Christian Churches*, Vol. 2. New York: Harper and Brothers.
Trungpa, Chogyam 1973: *Cutting Through Spiritual Materialism*. London: Watkins.
Turner, Bryan 2006: *Vulnerability and Human Rights*. Philadelphia: Pennsylvania State University Press.
Turner, Victor W. 1974: *The Ritual Process*. London: Penguin.
Urry, John 1990: *The Tourist Gaze*. London: Sage.
Urry, John 1995: *Consuming Place*. London: Routledge.
Vallentine, Antonina 1954: *Einstein. A Biography*. London: Weidenfeld and Nicolson.
Van Hove, Hildegard 1999: L'Emergence d'un marche spirituel. *Social Compass*, 46 (2), pp. 161–72.
Versteeg, Peter 2007: Spirituality on the Margin of the Church. Christian Spiritual Centres in The Netherlands. In Kieran Flanagan and Peter C. Jupp (eds), *A Sociology of Spirituality*. Aldhershot: Ashgate, pp. 101–14.
Voas, David and Steve Bruce 2007: The Spiritual Revolution. Another False Dawn for the Sacred. In Kieran Flanagan and Peter Jupp (eds), *A Sociology of Spirituality*. Aldershot: Ashgate, pp. 43–61.
Walsh, Val, Michael King, Louise Jones, Adrian Tookman and Robert Blizard 2002: Spiritual Beliefs May Affect Outcome of Bereavement. A Prospective Study. *British Medical Journal*, 324, pp. 1551–4.
Walter, Tony 1985: *Need. The New Religion. Unmasking Today's Secular Morality*. Downers-Grove: Intervarsity Press.
Ward, Graham 2006: The Future of Religion. *Journal of the American Academy of Religion*, 74 (1), pp.179–86.
Warrier, Maya 2005: *Hindu Selves in a Modern World. Guru Faith in the Mata Amritanandamayi Mission*. London: Routledge Curzon.
Waterfield, Robin 1998: *Prophet. The Life and Times of Kahlil Gibran*. London: Penguin.
Weaver, Maurice 1992: The World's Top Tourist Attraction. *Daily Telegraph*, 14 May, p. 18.
Weber, Max 1985 [1904–5]: *The Protestant Ethic and the Spirit of Capitalism*. London: Unwin.
Webster, Phillip and Angela Jameson 2005: Policy on Choice Opens Leadership Campaign for Reid. *The Times*, 28 January, p. 2.

Wedemeyer, Richard A. and Ronald W. Jue 2002: *The Inner Edge. Effective Spirituality in Your Life and Work.* London; McGraw-Hill.
Wetzel, M. S., D. M. Eisenberg and T. J. Kaptchuk 1998: Courses Involving Complementary and Alternative Medicine at US Medical Schools. *Journal of the American Medical Association*, 280, pp. 784–7.
Wexler, Philip 2000: *Mystical Society. An Emerging Social Vision.* Boulder: Westview Press.
Wheen, Francis 2004: *How Mumbo-Jumbo Conquered the World.* London: Fourth Estate.
Whibley, Charles 1920: *Literary Portraits.* London: Macmillan.
White, Curtis 2004: *The Middle Mind.* London: Penguin.
White, Gillian 2006: *Talking about Spirituality in Health Care Practice.* London: Jessica Kingsley.
Whybrow, Peter 2006: My, My, Haven't We Grown? *The Times Higher Educational Supplement*, 6 January, pp. 16–17.
Wigmore, Nigel 1985: Eavesdropping on Another World. *Guardian*, 15 May p. 8.
Wilde, Vanessa 2005: Extreme Beauty. *Sunday Times Style*, 2 January, p. 30.
Wilk, Richard 2004: Morals and Metaphors. The Meaning of Consumption. In Karin M. Ekstrom and Helene Brembeck (eds), *Elusive Consumption.* Oxford: Berg, pp. 11–26.
Williams, Raymond 1976: *Keywords. A Vocabulary of Culture and Society.* Glasgow: Fontana.
Winch, Peter 1963: *The Idea of a Social Science and Its Relation to Philosophy.* London: Routledge and Kegan Paul.
Wolff, Isabel 1997: Henry's Spiritual Home. *Weekend Telegraph*, 31 May, p. 3.
Wood, Matthew 2007: *Possession, Power and the New Age. Ambiguities of Authority in Neoliberal Societies.* Aldershot: Ashgate.
Wuthnow, Robert 1976: *The Consciousness Reformation.* Berkeley: University of California Press.
Wuthnow, Robert 1994: *Sharing the Journey.* London: Free Press.
Wuthnow, Robert 1998: *After Heaven. Spirituality in America Since the 1950s.* Berkeley: University of California Press.
Wuthnow, Robert 2005: *All in Sync.* Berkeley: University of California Press.
Yankelovich, Daniel 1974: *The New Morality. A Profile of American Youth in the 70s.* New York: McGraw-Hill.
York, Michael 2001: New Age Commodification and Appropriation of Spirituality. *Journal of Contemporary Religion*, 16 (3), pp. 361–72.
Zaidman, Nurit 2007: The New Age Shop – Church or Marketplace? *Journal of Contemporary Religion*, 22 (3), pp. 361–74.
Zinnbauer, Brian J. et al. 1997: Religion and Spirituality. Unfuzzying the Fuzzy. *Journal for the Scientific Study of Religion*, 36 (4), pp. 549–64.
Zohar, Danah and Ian Marshall 2005: *Spiritual Capital. Wealth We Can Live By.* London: Bloomsbury.

Name Index

Abedi, Aghan Hasan 229
Abercrombie, Nicholas x
Abrams, M. H. 25, 26–7, 29–30, 41, 42, 52, 54
Adatto, Kiku 198
Adorno, Theodore W. 101, 109, 191, 201
Agamben, Giorgio 3
Ahlin, Lars 233
Aldridge, Alan 84, 101, 107, 108, 109, 154, 184, 204, 244
Ali, F. 206
Almqvist, Kurt 236
Aphonen, Pirkkoliisa 107
Aranold, Matthew 39
Arato, Andrew 101
Archer, Margaret S. 197, 200, 208
Ashley, Tim 155
Aupers, Stef 108, 132, 143, 208, 234, 235, 245, 247

Baer, Hans 68, 240
Baerveldt, Cor 251
Bailey, Alice 32
Bailey, Fay 38, 39
Barber, Benjamin 82
Barker, Eileen 22, 63, 73, 184
Barley, Lynda 234
Baronowski, Shelly 46, 254
Barraclough, Jennifer 20, 140, 248
Bartley, William 51
Bateson, Gregory and Catherine 204

Batey, Jan Ford 34, 38
Baty, Phil 52
Baudrillard, Jean 82, 102, 109, 115, 180
Bauman, Zygmunt 3, 82, 83, 91, 109, 115, 129, 147, 169, 170, 200, 217, 243
Bechtel, William 174
Beck, Clive 35
Beckford, James A. 21, 68
Beethoven, Ludwig van 35
Bell, Daniel 109, 190, 208
Bell, David 35, 71, 197
Bellah, Robert N. 21, 109, 129, 130, 173, 202, 237
Benhabib, Seyla 181
Berg, Michael 52, 195
Berger, Peter L. 50, 191, 206
Berlin, Isaiah 225, 230, 238, 249
Besecke, Kelly 247
Bibby, Reginald W. 111, 115, 182, 184, 248
Black, James 12, 103
Black, Paula 103, 178
Blackman, Shane J. 152
Blackmore, Susan 12
Blair, Tony 12
Blake, William 41, 51, 238
Bloch, J. P. 208
Bloom, Adi 137
Bloom, William 1, 4, 25, 26, 92, 117, 125, 151, 246

Name Index

Bocock, Robert   101, 102, 107, 155, 177, 241
Boff, Leonardo   231
Bollier, David   81, 100
Botvar, Pal Ketil   234
Bowman, Marion   172, 184
Boyd-MacMillan, Eolene M.   55
Boyle, David   2
Brand, Stewart   49
Branigan, Tania   179
Brembeck, Helen   82, 97–8, 241
Brierley, Peter   65
Briscoe, Simon   250
Brodin, Jenny-Ann   100, 144
Brown, Michael F.   20, 244, 245
Brown, Mick   77
Bruce, Steve   x, 10, 20, 22, 50, 60, 76, 81, 85, 86, 91, 93, 100, 103, 104, 105, 106, 113, 118, 126, 128–9, 132, 133, 137, 147, 156, 167–8, 169, 170, 172–5, 184, 187, 191, 193, 195, 204–5, 212, 215, 216, 234, 237, 240, 241, 246, 247, 249
Bruni, Luigino   179
Buber, Martin   120, 123
Bullard, Maria   140
Bunting, Madeleine   32, 69, 198, 241
Byrne, Rhonda   52
Byron, Lord Alfred   36, 45

Cadbury, George   44
Calhoun, Craig   82
Cameron, David   179
Campbell, Colin   x, 20, 22, 45, 60, 76, 81, 82, 90, 91, 95, 103, 117, 158–9, 178, 186, 189, 194, 199, 240, 242, 245, 250
Carpenter, Edward   37
Carrette, Jeremy   20, 83, 106, 109, 169, 188, 199, 200, 245, 250
Carter, Simon   238
Cartner-Morley, Jess   85
Caru, Antonella   82, 244
Casey, Catherine   241
Chandler, Siobhan   254
Charles, Prince   208
Chartre, Richard   3
Cheshire, Andrea   73

Chesterton, G. K.   1, 4, 6, 18, 29, 39, 44, 83, 123, 202
Chidvilasananda, Swami   155
Chopra, Deepak   35
Christensen, Helena   68
Clark, David B.   152, 160
Clough, Patricia   62
Cohen, David   10
Coleridge, Samuel Taylor   36, 37, 42, 238
Combe, Victoria   133
Comte, Auguste   18
Connell, Camilla   1
Corrywright, Dominic   184
Coulter, Ian   174
Crook, Stephen   134, 197
Crossley, Nick   124, 133, 192
Cupitt, Don   22, 32
Cutler, Howard   32

Darre, Walther   46
Dart, Tom   69
Dass, Ram   39
Davie, Grace   22, 115, 182, 243, 250–1
Davis, Joseph E.   198, 213
Dawkins, Richard   93, 249
de Ras, Marion E. P.   43
Debord, Guy   3
Demerath, N. J.   173, 182
Dent-Brocklehurst, Henry   142
Devlin, Hannah   185
Diana, Princess   110
Dobson, R.   68
Donne, John   217
Dormann, Christian   161
Droogers, Andre   20
du Gay, Paul   160, 211, 250, 251
Duffy, Eamon   184
Dunning, David   155
Durken, Bernhard   46
Durkheim, Emile   21, 28–9, 44, 54, 94, 114–16, 118, 120, 126–7, 134, 163, 173

Eagleton, Terry   137
Earle-Levine, J.   240
Eccles, Janet   131
Edwards, Gill   31, 32, 202

Name Index

Einstein, Albert 92, 160
Ekstrom, Karin M. 82, 97–8, 241
Eliot, T. S. 40
Elliot, Richard 152
Elliott, John 179
Elster, Jon 157–9, 161, 163, 186, 250
Engels, Friedrich 157, 197, 198–9, 205, 210, 212, 213–14, 219
Erhard, Werner 51
Esseintes, Duc Jean des 151, 152, 163
Etzioni, Amitai 21, 129–30, 192–3, 246
Evans-Pritchard, E. E. 93
Ewen, Stuart and Elizabeth 117
Ezzy, Douglas 238

Fang-ju, Lin 156, 246
Featherstone, Mike 85, 104, 108, 109
Ferguson, Marilyn 37
Ferguson, Tim W. 68
Fest, Joachim C. 47
Fevre, R. W. 197
Fidler, Kel 198
Fiske, John 177, 178, 194
Flanagan, Kieran 2
Fodor, Eliza and John 34, 35, 53, 121
Forestal, Celia 39
Foucault, Michel 33, 94, 191, 195
Frank, Thomas 244
Frazer, James 114
Freedland, Jonathan 244
Frembgen, Jürgen Wasim 227
Freud, Anna 154
Freud, Sigmund 114, 250
Friedan, Betty 177
Friedman, Jonathan 152
Friedrich, Casper David 121, 238
Frisby, David 108
Frisk, Liselotte 233
Froebel, Friedrich 44, 63
Furedi, Frank 253

Gabriel, Yiannis 218, 244
Gallup, George Jr. 74
Gandhi 224–5
Garnoussi, Nadia 18
Garrett, Catherine 248
Gawain, Shakti 205
Geertsma, Elisabeth J. 248

Gehlen, Arnold 190
Gergen, Kenneth J. xii
Giacalone, Robert A. 71, 241
Gibran, Kahlil xii, 232
Giddens, Anthony 253
Gill, Robin 233
Gimlin, Debra L. 178
Glendinning, Tony 234
Gockel, Annemarie 241
Goethe, Johann Wolfgang 43, 221
Goodman, Martin 26, 33
Goodman, Matthew 69
Gorbachev, Mikhail 66
Grant, Dan 163, 247
Gratton, Lynda 163
Green, Gill 34
Griffith, Nanci 35
Gurdjieff, G. I. 176
Gustafsson, Goran 234

Habermas, Jürgen 82
Haglund Heelas, Mia x, 19
Hahnemann, Samuel 43–4
Hale, Christopher 47
Halpin, Tony 104
Hamberg, Eva 233
Hamdani, Syed Ali 226–7
Hamilton, Malcolm 184
Hanegraaff, Wouter J. 5, 20, 125–6, 147, 167, 170, 251
Harding, Douglas 49, 242
Hardman, Robert 105
Harrington, Anne 46–7
Harris, Jennifer 249
Harris, Marvin 238
Harris, Sarah 179, 249
Hartshorne, Charles 27
Harvey, David 103–4, 152
Hasan, Arif 229
Hasselle-Newcombe, Suzanne 246, 249
Hatcher, Brian A. 232
Hay, Stephen 225
Heald, Gordon 138, 144, 200, 233
Heath, Joseph 108, 125, 181, 244
Hedges, Ellie 21, 68
Heelas, Paul ix, 20, 21, 36, 41, 49, 55, 56, 57, 65, 68, 75, 76, 91, 92, 94, 100, 101, 107, 108, 109, 110, 127,

130, 131, 137, 138, 140, 141, 142, 144, 146, 148, 154, 161, 162, 171, 175, 178, 179, 181, 184, 187, 192, 197, 204, 208, 209, 229, 236, 237–8, 239, 240, 242, 243, 245, 246, 247, 248, 249, 250, 251, 252, 253
Heelas, Sebastian xi, 232
Hefner, Robert W. 228
Hegel, G. W. F. 27, 39, 43, 46
Heino, Harri 234
Henderson, Sara 82
Hendin, Herbert 197
Henriksen, Jan-Olav 56
Herder, Johann Gottfried 42, 43
Herdt, Gilbert H. 236
Herrick, James 20, 61–2
Herrigel, Eugen 161
Hervieu-Leger, Daniele 247
Hesse, Herman 43
Hickman, Leo 69
Hicks, Douglas 70
Hill, Christopher 242
Himmler, Heinrich 46, 47
Hinderer, Walter 34, 35
Hitler, Adolf 47
Hochschild, Arlie Russell 198, 210, 211
Holderlin, Friedrich 42
Honour, Hugh 42, 43, 238, 253–4
Hood, Ralph 234
Houtman, Dick xi, 20, 22, 75, 108, 118, 143, 208, 234–5, 245, 246, 247
Hufeland, Charles 43
Hume, Lynne 254
Hunt, Stephen J. 7, 11, 91, 107, 115, 116, 118, 173, 191, 199, 247, 253
Hunter, James Davison 230, 238
Hunter-Wetenhall, Celia 34
Hussain, Chaudhry Shujaat 222
Hussain, Mushahid 226, 229
Huxley, Aldous and Laura ix, 1, 4, 12, 14, 111, 221
Huxley, Julian 17
Huysmans, J.-K. 151, 152
Hyde, Jeannette 110
Hyman, Gavin xi

Inglehart, Ronald 109, 146, 179, 180, 219, 227, 228, 237, 247, 253
Ives, Laurel 12
Iyengar, B. K. S. 154, 248
Izenberg, Gerald N. 238

James, William 36
Jameson, Frederic 102
Jammer, Max 92
Jarvis, Simon 191
John Paul II, Pope 224
Jones, Louise 248
Julie 1, 4, 18, 139–41, 142, 145, 147, 150, 153, 154, 155, 194, 203

Kant, Immanuel 17, 43, 111, 202, 230
Kaplan, Jeffrey 254
Keat, Russell x, 118
Kennedy, Gordon 238
Ketola, Kimmo 56
Keyserling, Hermann, Graf von 26, 33
Khan, Akhtar Hameed 229
Khokhar, Riaz H. 226, 227
King, Michael 248
King, Richard 20, 83, 106, 109, 169, 188, 199, 200, 245, 250
Klingemann, Hans-Dieter 237
Klint, Hilma af 25, 33, 35
Knibbe, Kim E. 20, 203, 236, 239, 254
Koenig, Harold G. 248
Kopp, Sheldon 242
Kovel, Joel 20
Kraut, Richard 31
Krishna, Gopi 32
Kynaston, David 48

LaChette, Aleisha 200–1
Laing, R. D. 8, 9, 205
Lake, James H. 248
Lama, Dalai 9, 10, 32, 102, 180, 182, 219, 224, 250
Lambert, Yves 240
Lane, Robert 20, 179, 213
Lasch, Christopher 1, 4, 7, 8, 18, 83, 101, 102, 105, 109, 113, 126, 134, 137, 146, 149, 151, 163, 170, 184, 187–8, 190, 192, 195, 196, 197, 241

Name Index

Lash, Scott x, 244
Lau, Kimberly J. 83, 102, 105, 107, 108, 168–9, 185, 241
Lawrence, D. H. 32
Le Bris, Michel 238
Leach, Edmund 37
Leake, Jonathan 3
Lears, T. J. Jackson 250
Leary, Timothy 14, 152
Leder, Drew 36
Levenda, Peter 47
Lévi-Strauss, Claude 94
Lewis, C. S. 32
Lewis, Sarah 247
Lindquist, Galina 241
Lofgren, Orvar 241
London, Jack 122
Long, Barry 40, 120
Loren, Sophia 244
Lorimer, David 208
Lucas, Catherine 143
Luckmann, Benita 244
Luckmann, Thomas 60, 111
Lury, Celia x, 152, 177, 244
Lynch, Gordon 20, 22, 218, 239
Lyon, David 81, 184, 242, 248

McCarthy, Thomas 94
McConaghy, Cathryn 210–11
McDannell, Colleen 178
McEwan, Ian 16
McGrath, Alister E. 55
McGuire, Meredith 240
MacIntyre, Alasdair 82, 94, 123–4, 196
McKean, Lise 251
MacLaine, Shirley 4, 201
McLeod, Hugh 48
Maistre, Joseph de 37
Mansell, Warwick 160
Marco 143
Marcus, Jon 211
Marler, Penny Long 167
Martin, Bernice 22, 50, 206
Martin, David A. 22, 251
Marty, Martin 61
Marx, Karl 152, 157, 158, 160, 187, 197, 198–9, 205, 210, 212, 213–14, 219, 250

Mascini, Peter 20, 118, 247
Matrisciana, Caryl 28
Mauss, Marcel 111–12
Mears, Daniel P. 72–3, 77, 101
Meera, Mother 26, 107
Melville, Kenneth 50
Miles, Steven 102, 103, 182, 191
Mill, John Stuart xii
Miller, Arthur 120
Miller, Barbara Stoler 192
Miller, Daniel 152, 248
Miller, Dia 246
Mitford, Nancy 11
Mitroff, Ian 70
Montessori, Maria 44, 227
Morris, Paul x
Mosse, George L. 46
Muir, Stewart 137, 144, 146, 248
Murcott, Toby 68
Musharraf, Pervez 6, 226
Musil, Robert 220

Nader, Ralph 81, 100
Needham, Rodney 241
Newby, Howard 241
Niemela, Kati 234
Nipperdey, Thomas 43
Norman, Edward 194
Novalis, Friedrich 42
Nussbaum, Martha 5, 13, 63, 67, 182, 222, 228, 231, 232, 252

O'Brian, Mary Elizabeth 248
O'Dell, Tom 240
O'Doherty, Malachi 242
Olivar, Jose 244
Oxley, Robin 32

Packard, Vance 81, 100
Paine, Thomas 230
Palmer, Brian 234
Palmisano, Stefania xi, 75
Parkins, Geoffry 110
Parsons, Talcott 31, 35, 48, 50, 114
Partridge, Christopher H. 20, 68, 140, 240, 247, 252
Passmore, John 33
Pasternak, Anna 107, 143, 147, 180
Paterson, Mark 109, 194

Paton, Graeme 68
Penman, Ian 171
Perry, Foster 143, 147, 180
Pestalozzi, Johann 44
Pettersson, Thorleif 234
Phillips, D. Z. 239
Pickering, William 115
Pilzer, Paul 60
Pirsig, Robert 18
Possamai, Adam 83, 97, 98, 133, 184, 190
Pratchett, Terry 85
Pye, Michael 191

Rajneesh, Bhagwan Shree ix, 49, 144, 184
Ramstedt, Martin 32, 241
Rand, Ayn 220
Rappaport, Roy A. 248
Rasmussen, Steve and Zeba xi
Ray, Paul H. 158
Ray, Sondra 52, 244
Redden, Guy 81, 103, 169, 184, 210, 241, 247
Regan, Ronald and Nancy 62
Reid, John 152
Rhinehart, Luke 51
Rider, Jacques Le 243
Riefenstahl, Leni 47
Rilke, Rainer Maria 43
Ripley, Jacqui 12, 244
Roberts, Robert C. 202
Robertson, Roland 5, 44, 202, 214, 253
Rolle, Richard 35
Roof, Wade Clark 20, 21, 33, 74, 87, 137, 139, 147, 149
Rose, Nikolas 94
Rosenberg, Larry 32
Ross, Andrew 247
Rousseau, Jean-Jacques 35, 38, 43, 44, 63
Rowling, J. K. 151, 163
Rubin, Gerry 184
Rutherford, Leo 241
Ryle, Gilbert 76, 175

Sachedina, Abdulaziz 226, 229
Sacks, Jonathan 211
Sagoff, Mark 117, 196
Salamon, Karen Lisa G. 241
Salkeld, Audrey 47
Sampson, Philip 242
Sandel, Michael J. 211
Savage, Mike 76
Sawyer, Deborah xi, 242
Schacht, Richard 239
Schelling, Friedrich Wilhelm Joseph 43
Schiller, Friedrich 34, 35, 149
Schlegel, Friedrich 43
Schleiermacher, Friedrich 41
Schmidt, Leigh 20
Scholl, Andreas 155
Schor, Juliet B. 198
Schweitzer, Albert xi
Sedgwick, Colin 102, 153, 218
Seel, Benjamin 144, 178
Sen, Amartya 13, 63, 67, 182, 231, 252
Sen, Sarbani 13, 225
Seneca 136
Senge, Peter M. 67, 70
Sennett, Richard 3, 204
Shaftesbury, Anthony 230
Sharma, Kalpana 217
Sharma, Ursula 178, 240
Shepherd, Jessica 198
Shils, Edward 76, 230–1
Shweder, Richard A. 222, 229
Silber, K. 44
Simmel, Georg 21, 25, 29, 44, 58, 108, 197–8, 211, 243
Sivananda 216
Sjodin, Ulf 239
Smith, Christian 88, 90, 148, 242
Smith, David 179
Smith, Michael 153
Smithers, Rebecca 35
Smuts, Jan Christian 45
Snow White 151, 163, 170
Solomon, Robert C. 20
Spangler, David 184, 195
Spinoza, Benedict 92
Standen, Elissa xi
Stark, Rodney 102, 106
Steiner, Rudolf 44
Strauss, Sarah 216, 248
Strong, Maurice 66
Sutcliffe, Steven J. 57

Tacey, David 20, 81, 167, 195, 243
Tagore, Rabindranath 225, 232
Taji-Farouki, Suha 22
Tallis, Raymond 68, 241
Taylor, Charles ix, 20, 21, 29, 31, 33, 37, 38–9, 41, 42, 43, 45, 47–8, 119–20, 120, 121, 124–5, 126, 131, 135, 155–6, 157, 187, 194, 195, 230, 246, 252
Taylor, Elizabeth Johnston 248
Taylor, Glenda 12
Taylor, Mark C. 20, 21, 42, 237
Taylor, Scott xi
Tennyson, Alfred 37
Thatcher, Margaret 100
Thompson, E. P. 33, 36, 37
Thompson, Judith ix, 49
Thrift, Nigel 69
Tipton, Steven 20, 21, 37, 76, 124, 189, 192, 246, 252
Tocqueville, Alexis de 187, 204
Tolstoy, Leo 32
Tovey, Philip 20
Troeltsch, Ernst 44
Trungpa, Chogyam 49, 52, 105, 172, 244
Tumelty, Gemma 198
Turner, Bryan 222, 228
Turner, Victor W. 50, 193, 202, 254
Tyers, Beth 117

Urry, John x, 108, 242, 245

Vallentine, Antonina 92
Van Hove, Hildegard 184
Versteeg, Peter 20
Vivekananda 216
Voas, David 93, 167–8, 174–5, 249

Walsh, Val, 248
Walter, Tony 197
Walton, Elizabeth xi

Ward, Graham 8, 11, 84, 133, 147, 152, 214, 217
Warne, Jenny 117
Warrier, Maya 232
Waterfield, Robin 232
Weaver, Maurice 110
Weber, Max 3, 11, 21, 43, 44, 149, 163, 204, 253
Webster, Phillip 152
Wedemeyer, Richard A. 250
Wetzel, M. S. 68
Wexler, Philip 3, 20
Wheen, Francis 178
Whibley, Charles 43
White, Curtis 104–5, 154
White, Gillian 248
Whiteley, Nigel x
Whybrow, Peter 241
Wigmore, Nigel 143
Wilde, Vanessa 102, 251
Wilk, Richard 97, 98, 99, 184, 241
Willander, Erika 234
Williams, Helen 34
Williams, Raymond 184
Willim, Robert 241
Wilson, Bryan 22
Winch, Peter 94
Winfrey, Oprah 10, 105, 249
Wolff, Isabel 142
Wood, Matthew 247
Woolf, Virginia 32
Wordsworth, William 25, 26, 36, 37, 42, 43, 176
Wuthnow, Robert 20, 21, 27–8, 151, 192, 242–3, 248–9

Yankelovich, Daniel 48
York, Michael 190
Yunus, Muhammad 229

Zaidman, Nurit 186
Zohar, Danah 184, 241

Subject Index: Some Main Themes and Arguments

'beliefs' 73–5, 233–5
birthright spirituality 224–32
capitalism, absorbed by 6–7, 199–201
commodification 210–13
conclusions 133–6, 186–9, 193–4, 213–20, 229–32
consumeristic aspects 97–112
consumption, language of 83–4, 97–112, 181–6
consumption, religion 87–8
consumption and growth 79–96
controversies 10–13
counter-currents and the counter-cultural 2–4, 47–50, 201–10
ethicalities, expressive/humanistic, 30–2, 189–90
functionality 132–3, 190–3
happiness 179–81
holistic spiritualities of life 5
horizons 120–3
humanity, religion of 126–8
introducing the argument 8–9
modernity, sins of 196–9
modernity and the consumer 81–3
Nazi spirituality 46–7
participant understanding 92–6
practices and authority 123–6
preferences 128–32

prosperity spirituality 52
reductionism 8, 168–70
sacred-profane 114–18
secularity 170–7
seminar spirituality 51–2
significance, personal 137–50
spiritualities of life, business 69–71, 160–3
spiritualities of life, central themes 1–2, 25–32
spiritualities of life, critical reflections 56–8
spiritualities of life, differences within the recurrent 40–54
spiritualities of life, education 71–2
spiritualities of life, indeterminacies 58–9
spiritualities of life, key words 32–40
spiritualities of life, provisions 72–3
spiritualities of life, the Romantic Movement 41–6
spiritualities of life and health 67–9
spiritualities of traditions of transcendent theism 54–6
subjective wellbeing culture 62–7, 177–9
targeting spirituality 160–2
wellbeing spirituality 52–4, 60–78
work 118–20, 151–63